Beginning CSS
Web Development

From Novice to Professional

Simon Collison

Beginning CSS Web Development: From Novice to Professional

Copyright © 2006 by Simon Collison

ISBN-13 (pbk): 978-1-59059-689-0

ISBN-10 (pbk): 1-59059-689-7

Printed and bound in the United States of America 9 8 7 6 5 4 3 2

Lead Editor: Chris Mills
Technical Reviewers: Richard Rutter and Dan Rubin
Editorial Board: Steve Anglin, Ewan Buckingham, Gary Cornell, Jason Gilmore, Jonathan Gennick,
    Jonathan Hassell, James Huddleston, Chris Mills, Matthew Moodie, Dominic Shakeshaft, Jim Sumser,
    Keir Thomas, Matt Wade
Project Manager: Beth Christmas
Copy Edit Manager: Nicole LeClerc
Copy Editor: Ami Knox
Assistant Production Director: Kari Brooks-Copony
Production Editor: Laura Esterman
Compositor: Susan Glinert
Proofreader: Nancy Riddiough
Indexer: John Collin
Artist: Susan Glinert
Cover Designer: Kurt Krames
Manufacturing Director: Tom Debolski

Distributed to the book trade worldwide by Springer-Verlag New York, Inc., 233 Spring Street, 6th Floor, New York, NY 10013. Phone 1-800-SPRINGER, fax 201-348-4505, e-mail orders-ny@springer-sbm.com, or visit http://www.springeronline.com.

For information on translations, please contact Apress directly at 2560 Ninth Street, Suite 219, Berkeley, CA 94710. Phone 510-549-5930, fax 510-549-5939, e-mail info@apress.com, or visit http://www.apress.com.

The source code for this book is available to readers at http://www.apress.com in the Source Code section.

For Mam and Dad.
Sorry about the lack of plot . . .

Contents at a Glance

PART 1 ■■■ Get to Know CSS

PART 2 ■■■ Logical Layouts

Contents

PART 1 ▪▪▪ Get to Know CSS

Foreword

As a bloke of that "certain age," I can remember the television series that were shown in the 1970s and early 1980s. My brother and I would stay glued to the telly each Saturday teatime. From Roddy McDowell's unconvincing ape suit in the TV spin-off from the *Planet of the Apes* movies, to *Logan's Run*; from "Grasshopper" David Carradine in *Kung Fu*, to my own personal favorite, Bill Bixby and Lou Ferrigno in the pre-CGI *Incredible Hulk*; we couldn't get enough.

These shows and many more just like them shared a common 1970s theme. While the Hulk of the original comic books just got angry, the television Banner, unexpectedly dosed by gamma radiation before he could slap on the sun block, lived outside of society. Sure, he got angry and ripped his trousers, but as he traveled across the country from place to place, along the way he met new people and helped to solve their problems—problems that no one had been able to solve before.

Like the rag-tag band of ships that followed Battlestar Gallactica on its quest for a faraway Earth, each of the characters in these series knew where they wanted to go, they just didn't know how to get there. The map to Earth or Logan's Sanctuary, or for the Hulk a course on anger management, just hadn't been written.

By now you might be wondering, "What on Earth is Malarkey rambling on about? This book is about web design, not television trivia from the decade that time best forgot." But as a web designer who came late to the world of meaningful markup and CSS, I can identify with the Hulk.

Solving problems is what web designers do, and not just for half an hour every Saturday teatime. We solve problems every day for our clients and for their visitors; we also solve the problem of how to implement our designs with web standards.

When I started my own journey toward web standards, I knew very little about CSS floats and positioning, and I got angry when my design layouts fell apart in a browser. While my trousers (almost) always stayed intact, I was filled with an inner rage when my columns dropped, my margins collapsed, or my font sizing misbehaved. I knew the results that I wanted to achieve and where I wanted to go, but I didn't know how to get there. At that time there was no clear map for people like me who understood design but needed a book to show the way between my design visuals and the standards-based web pages that I wanted to deliver to my clients.

If you are starting out on a similar journey, you're in luck. Simon Collison has written that roadmap, a book that clearly explains how to make your designs a reality using XHTML and CSS. Simon knows what it's like to design at the sharp end of the web design business. He comes to web standards not from an academic interest but from a real need to get stuff done. I have long admired his design skills and his uncanny ability to explain complex subjects in clear language.

I know that beginning to work with web standards will sometimes make you angry; that's unavoidable. I also know that this book will help you to keep any outbursts free from shirt button popping, trouser ripping, or maybe even car throwing. Thanks to Simon Collison, the world is a safer place for us to live.

Andy Clarke
June 2006

About the Author

SIMON COLLISON has been working with web sites for almost six years. In 1999, he didn't even have a computer and was a bit web-phobic. How times change.

Simon runs Ersckine Design (www.erskinedesign.com), a full-service web agency established in late 2006. As the lead web developer at Agenzia (www.agenzia.co.uk) from 2002 to 2006, he worked on numerous web projects for record labels (Universal, Vertigo, and Poptones), high-profile recording artists (the Libertines, Dirty Pretty Things, and the Beta Band), and leading visual artists and illustrators (Jon Burgerman, Black Convoy, and Paddy Hartley). Simon also oversaw a production line of business, community, and voluntary secor web sites, passionately ensuring that everything was accessible and complied with current web standards.

Away from the office, Simon runs the popular blog Colly Logic (www.collylogic.com), and he is an active member of the so-called Britpack—a collective of laid-back designers and developers who all share a passion for responsible web design. When prised away from the laptop, Simon can most likely be found in the pub or at a gig, waffling incessantly about good music, football, or biscuits.

Simon has lived in many cities, including London and Reykjavik, but has now settled back in his beloved Nottingham, where the grass is green and the girls are pretty.

About the Technical Reviewers

Music, design, typography, web standards, South Florida beaches—what could these things possibly have in common? **DAN RUBIN**, that's what . . . er, who. From vocal coaching and performing to graphic design and (almost literally) everything in between, Dan does his best to spread his talent as thin and as far as he possibly can while still leaving time for a good cup of tea and the occasional nap.

His passion for all things creative and artistic isn't a solely selfish endeavor either—you don't have to hang around too long before you'll find him waxing educational about a cappella jazz and barbershop harmony (his design of the Rounders web site [http://roundersquartet.com] is just one example of these two worlds colliding), interface design, usability, web standards, graphic design in general, and which typeface was on the bus ad that just whizzed by at 60 mph.

In addition to his work on sites including Blogger, the CSS Zen Garden, and Microsoft's ASP.net portal, Dan has been known to write the occasional entry on his blog, SuperfluousBanter (http://superfluousbanter.org—you might even find a podcast or two if you poke around enough), and his professional work can be found at his agency's site, http://webgraph.com.

RICHARD RUTTER is cofounder and production director of Clearleft (http://clearleft.com), a web design consultancy based in Brighton, UK. Richard has been designing and building web sites for over ten years, and is a practitioner and evangelist of the web standards approach to developing web sites. He is coauthor of *Web Accessibility: Web Standards and Regulatory Compliance* (friends of ED, 2006) and *Blog Design Solutions* (friends of ED, 2006).

A more personal side of Richard can be found at Clagnut (http://clagnut.com), a popular weblog where he writes about accessibility and web standards issues, as well as his passions for music and mountain biking.

About the Foreword Writer

ANDY CLARKE is a sought-after designer, writer, and speaker who is passionate about design, web standards, and accessibility. He specializes in the design of user experiences for web applications and e-commerce stores, and bridges the gap between design and code. Andy writes about aspects of design and popular culture on his personal web site, And All That Malarkey (www.stuffandnonsense.co.uk) and is the author of *Transcending CSS: The Fine Art of Web Design* (New Riders Press, 2006).

Acknowledgments

The Icelanders have a word called *trúnó*, which they use when somebody explodes with embarrassing love for their friends, family, and colleagues. I am about to hit you with some serious *trúnó*.

My eternal gratitude to my friends and colleagues at Agenzia: Lee Hickman, Simon Rudkin, Maxwell Harrison, and Alun Edwards. Without my years at Agenzia, I wouldn't be anywhere near qualified to write this book. You've pushed me hard, and I thank you for it.

Love, hugs, and gushing praise to my unbelievably tolerant and close friends Oliver Wood, Emma Crosby, Michael Armstrong, Jamie Craven, Jon Burgerman, Lee Walker, Si, Cass, Ben, Sally, Sarah, Rick, Josh, and Rob—I'm gonna come out to play again soon!

Unparalleled thanks to my very patient Mam and Dad, and also the Granddads (who don't realize how much I admire them). Thanks too to my Auntie Christine for inspiring me to be creative when I was a nipper. I should probably thank the cats, too—Ziggy, Bear-Face, and Mute-Puss.

I can't thank the Apress team enough. I am indebted to Chris Mills (you, Sir, are a true legend), Beth Christmas, Ami Knox, and Laura Esterman (and all the behind-the-scenes folks, too). It has been a pleasure to have Richard Rutter and Dan Rubin doing the tech reviewing, and I'm over the moon that the incomparable Andy Clarke agreed to write the foreword. Collectively, you all made it so much easier.

A big thanks to my pant-wearing BritPack friends, and to the foreigners who keep me inspired (or give me free stuff), particularly Roger Johansson, Cameron Moll, Veerle Pieters, Shaun Inman, Jason Santa Maria, Ryan Carson—and anyone anywhere who has adopted or advanced web standards.

Geeky love to the ExpressionEngine team, and hat doffs to the creators of the other tools I used while writing this book: MAMP, DropSend, Basecamp, TextMate, Transmit, good browsers, my trusty Powerbook, iTunes, and the person who invented tea.

Finally, I must thank all Colly Logic readers for keeping my ego waxed, and last but not least, you, the reader, for buying the book. You've made my day!

Introduction

How excited are *you* then? Is the prospect of becoming a professional CSS genius getting you tingling in all the right places? Once you have read this book, you're going to be a full-fledged web wizard, using CSS to save you and your clients time, money, and stress.

Before you board the bus to CSS enlightenment, it is worth acquainting yourself with some of the terms bandied about by web designers and developers, and this author in particular.

Web Standards and Accessibility

This demands a brief history lesson. In 1994, as dinosaurs lay gasping their final breaths, the World Wide Web Consortium (www.w3.org) was formed to promote common approaches and interoperability for the Internet. Part of their work was to create web standards specifications such as (X)HTML and CSS, evolving these specifications in line with the requirements of web developers and web users to make the Web a better place for all of us.

For years, web standards didn't carry much weight with browser manufacturers, who were often slow to realize their importance. Web sites built using standards would render inconsistently across user agents, making the whole thing very frustrating for designers and users alike. If you weren't around in these bad old days of web design, then you are very lucky indeed.

Helping to fight the corner since 1998 has been the Web Standards Project (WaSP), which fights for standards that reduce the cost and complexity of development while increasing the accessibility and long-term viability of any site published on the Web. The WaSP team works with browser manufacturers, authoring tool makers, and web designers to push for greater web standards. Fueled by the blood, sweat, and tears of passionate, responsible web evangelists, the Web Standards Project is a grassroots coalition fighting for standards that ensure simple, affordable access to web technologies for all. Visit http://webstandards.org, the opening page of which you see in Figure 1, for more of the "buzz."

In 2003, a very nice man with a woolly hat wrote a book called *Designing with Web Standards* (New Riders). That man was Jeffrey Zeldman (www.zeldman.com), and his book revolutionized the way many approached web design. A core text cited by many as the beginning of the true revolution, Jeffrey's book made many think twice about how they built web sites, and uncompromisingly made the case for using CSS, while also increasing awareness of accessibility and usability.

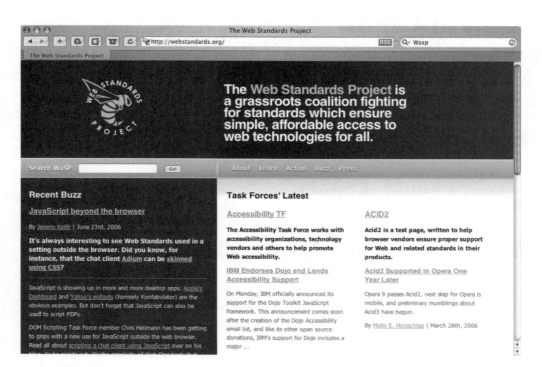

Figure 1. *The Web Standards Project (WaSP) web site at http://webstandards.org*

The Benefits

Web standards bring many benefits. Web pages are reduced in size, making download times faster, in turn using much less bandwidth. Compatibility with user agents (browsers, cell phones, PDAs, assistive software) is increased, making sites more accessible. Importantly, sites built with web standards are future-proof—primed and ready for whatever path the Web takes next. In addition, standards also are great because they allow for the separation of content from presentation and do wonders for site accessibility. Let's have a little look at what these terms mean.

Separating Content and Presentation

Perhaps the most fundamental rule of web standards is that content should be separated from presentation—by applying all decorative presentational richness using an external style sheet, the core content (the (X)HTML) remains pure and focused. With all presentational material kept separate from the markup, sitewide style changes can be made with little or no fuss by amending a single CSS file, rather than having to update every page in the site, making whole-sale redesigns a veritable breeze. Equally important is the facility for users to take control of your content themselves by applying their own style sheet to your web site should they need to.

Accessibility

This is the great thing about designing with web standards—accessibility comes as default. Sure, there are further methods and approaches that can enhance accessibility and provide greater benefits to the user, but by keeping presentation separate from content, and by using the right markup for the right job, you increase the chances that any visitor, regardless of ability, can access your content unhindered.

The golden rule of accessibility is simple. Anyone, anywhere, regardless of platform, technology, experience, or ability, should be able to access your core content. By adhering to web standards with your content, you are free to apply outrageous presentation using CSS, safe in the knowledge that under the hood, none of your content is compromised, so a person with visual impairments using a screenreader will be able to use your web site just fine. Of course, web accessibility isn't just about visual impairments—there are also cognitive disabilities to consider, and many more. For more information about web accessibility, check out the book *Web Accessibility: Web Standards and Regulatory Compliance* (friends of ED, 2006) and look at the great online resources available, such as www.accessify.com and http://diveintoaccessibility.org.

This book specifically looks at CSS for accessibility in Chapter 14.

Making the Move Toward Standards

So, I think that by now you can see the arguments for moving to web standards–based web design . . . you probably knew before you picked up the book in fact! But why hasn't everyone adopted CSS for styling and layout? Many argue that CSS is difficult to implement; that it only works for certain browsers; that the learning curve is too steep. The big problem is that a large quantity of old-school designers are slow to adopt web standards. Many still make a living creating appallingly weighty web sites using outdated markup, often reliant on tables for layout, and littering the code with font tags and other extraneous, deprecated methods. They can still make their money doing what they do, and they don't see the need to change. These people are dangerous and should not be approached.

Still, the Internet community is chock-full of good, responsible people, and the benefits of web standards have not gone unnoticed. Since Zeldman wrote that book, thousands have made the move to CSS-based design, and very few would ever go back. The myth that an accessible site is an unattractive site has long since gone away, and some of the most accessible, usable web sites out there are also the most attractive, stylish designs thanks to smart and experimental use of CSS (see the examples in Figure 2).

I hope that after reading this book, you too will be producing designs that challenge, excite, and inspire. It's in *your* hands.

Figure 2. *Stunning web sites produced using 100% web standards. From top: Veerle's Blog (http://veerle.duoh.com); BearSkin Rug (www.bearskinrug.co.uk); And All That Malarkey (www.stuffandnonsense.co.uk).*

About This Book

This is the book I needed when I began experimenting with CSS. If I'd had this book, I'd have saved myself an immeasurable amount of wasted time. It assumes a fairly comfortable knowledge of (X)HTML markup, but little or no knowledge of CSS. For the latter, we start from scratch.

Some books wrap you in cotton wool, gently easing you in. Not this book. The first three chapters attempt to explore the core concepts of CSS, giving you a firm foundation for the chapters that follow. CSS is a simple technology, but its magic stems from the complex approaches and quirks at the heart of the specification. Therefore, the first three chapters establish grounding for everything that follows. It is not essential to read these first, but it is important to become familiar with their subject matter so that you can quickly refer back when a technique mentioned in a later chapter gets a bit involved. For example, if I mention "the cascade" in Chapter 14 and you are not sure what I mean, you know you can flick back to an early chapter to work out what this is.

After this deep-end, lung-filling beginning, each following chapter of Part 1 focuses on styling a particular markup group, such as tables, links, lists, or text, providing a sensibly structured reference of common approaches to element styling.

For Part 2 of the book, the focus shifts to layout and real-world issues. Here, you begin thinking like a professional web designer, looking at methods for pulling everything you have learned into accessible, lightweight, and stylish templates. Part 2 also sprinkles a few extras into the mix, detailing useful hacks, filters, and accessibility techniques that give you even greater power.

Finally, many of the techniques used in the book are pulled together for the *Dead Goods* case study, which details the ins and outs of styling a living, breathing web site with pure, honest-to-goodness CSS. It's a revelation!

I have also provided a CSS syntax reference at the back of the book detailing all the properties and values covered, allowing you to look up those troublesome properties, etc., quickly and easily.

You can read this book from cover to cover if you wish, as it has a logical narrative. Likewise, it works as a dip-in reference guide for the astute designer who simply wants to get on with the job. Either way, I think you'll enjoy it.

Conventions Used in This Book

For the most part, any strange references in this book will have been explained in earlier chapters. That said, there are a few conventions worthy of your attention before we begin:

- (X)HTML refers to both the HTML and XHTML languages.

- Unless otherwise stated, all CSS is compliant with the CSS 2.1 specification.

- It is assumed that all (X)HTML examples in this book are placed within the `<body>` of a valid document, while the CSS is placed in an external style sheet linked from the `<head>` of the (X)HTML document, unless stated otherwise.

- In most cases, when an (X)HTML tag appears followed by the word *element* in the text, this refers to the whole element. For example, **`<strong>` element** refers to the whole element, from the opening `<strong>` tag to the closing `</strong>` tag and everything contained within.

- Tea and biscuits are recommended throughout. For the sake of clarity, the tea is traditional English tea, and the biscuits are typically chocolate digestives.

I think that's it, so put the kettle on, kick off your slippers, and get set for enlightenment!

PART 1

■ ■ ■

Get to Know CSS

And so our journey begins, logically at Part 1. The first three chapters explore the major whys and wherefores of CSS, getting as much of the technical theory out of the way as quickly as possible.

From then on, Part 1 deals with the common elements of any design and how to transform them with CSS, and for the most part, these elements—headings, forms, tables, paragraphs, and so on—will be familiar to you. Each chapter builds a little on the preceding chapters, gradually increasing your CSS aptitude before throwing you into Part 2, where you'll get to grips with layout and more advanced approaches.

Chapter 1, "Getting Started," sets you on your way by analyzing first the methods of applying style sheets to your (X)HTML. Within a few minutes, you will be ready to pick and choose from several possible methods, and be aware of when to use each approach. This chapter also looks at correct CSS syntax and ideas for making everything more manageable.

Chapter 2, "Core Concepts of CSS," looks into IDs and classes—two core methods of calling styles within your documents. This chapter also helps to explain the intricacies of style sheets by examining the cascade itself, and some of the more complicated magic within. The chapter concludes with an overview of CSS measurements—when to use them, and why.

Chapter 3, "CSS Building Blocks," examines the tools used to extend the capabilities of both your markup and your CSS, with particular attention to things called divs and common CSS properties such as margins, padding, borders, and dimensions.

Chapter 4, "Text," lets you loose with your existing (X)HTML elements, by discussing the numerous methods available for controlling text, and making it more legible, more accessible, and more attractive. There is also an overview of font use and responsibility regarding the Web.

Chapter 5, "Color, Backgrounds, and Images," fills the gap left by many CSS books by exploring issues relating to color and image use. Which image type should you use, and when? What methods are available for applying color for cross-browser support? How can background images be used to decorate the (X)HTML document? All of these questions and more are answered in this chapter.

Chapter 6, "Lists," looks at the humble list, and how to magically transform it using pure CSS and occasional additions to the markup. Ordered and unordered lists are examined in detail, including how to use a list for site navigation and how to use custom bullets.

Chapter 7, "Links," takes umbrage with the boring old blue and purple hyperlinks, and gives them a complete makeover. From simple changes of color, to smart links with background images, this chapter gets you thinking about links in a completely new way and also extends the list-based navigation you created in Chapter 6.

Chapter 8, "Tables and Definition Lists," details ways of organizing related data using web standards. The case for tables is made, and some cunning CSS tablecloths are added to spice things up. The second half deals with the unsung definition list, a very flexible method of ordering related items that can also be magically manipulated using good old style sheets.

Chapter 9, "Forms," knows that you don't like dealing with these frighteningly nightmarish beasts. To counter your fright, the markup is stripped down to a bare minimum and reinvented using three different techniques, each making use of some simple yet effective CSS to aid usability and accessibility. You'll also learn how to develop a reusable set of styles that can be employed to dress up all of your forms to save on time and stress.

CHAPTER 1

Getting Started

As you've already seen from the introduction, Cascading Style Sheets (CSS) are the saviors of responsible web design. The impact of CSS upon the way developers build web sites has been immense, and the possibilities they bring are endless. Removing most or all of the presentational information from an (X)HTML file and placing it in a style sheet has numerous advantages, including reduced file sizes, huge bandwidth savings, and easier maintenance. What's more, by keeping all presentational information separate from the core content of a site, the web designer is able to make small or large changes to a whole web site in a matter of seconds. These are just a few advantages that style sheets give us, and as you progress through this book, you'll begin to realize just why CSS is so important, and why web designers cannot stop talking about it.

However, no matter how beautifully crafted your CSS, it is pretty useless on its own. Applying styles to well-formed (X)HTML is the first step that may seem arbitrary to you, but this vital procedure is very often the first stumbling block for newcomers. Many seasoned developers still fail to exploit the true flexibility of CSS at this stage, and never fully embrace the glory of the cascade.

In this initial chapter, you'll explore the variety of methods available for applying CSS to (X)HTML, and discover the benefits and pitfalls of each. In every facet of web design, there are numerous methods available to us, and it's important to identify the right method for the right task. Applying CSS falls comfortably into this description, and while one particular method will be strongly suggested above all others, the ability to call on others when required will see you armed for any eventuality.

The chapter closes with several productivity recommendations that explore good organizational practice, essential for keeping your style sheets legible and well organized. Let's dig in.

Applying CSS to (X)HTML

Working through this chapter from start to finish will have you fully prepared for anything this book will throw at you. The result will be a set of (X)HTML files, each taking their basic styling from CSS served using all the available methods. It's then up to you which method you choose to work with through the following chapters. It's time to learn the methods one by one.

Preparing a Base (X)HTML Template

For each example in this chapter, you'll need a fresh copy of the **base template** provided in this section. This is a very simple (X)HTML page consisting of some standard document sections

(<head> and <body>) and familiar elements (headings, paragraphs, and links to further templates in an unordered list) thrown in, all of which you'd expect to see in a typical web page. We won't deal with tables or images just yet.

To appreciate the effects of the applied CSS, it is worth copying this template verbatim at this stage, as that'll help you understand the examples discussed. Note that the list of links will tie together further templates in this section, giving you a cut-out-and-keep mini-site for reference.

The (X)HTML is also available to download from www.apress.com if you're one of those who doesn't like typing very much. For reference, it's also printed here:

```
<!DOCTYPE html PUBLIC "-//W3C//DTD XHTML 1.0 Strict//EN"➡
"http://www.w3.org/TR/xhtml1/DTD/xhtml1-strict.dtd">
<html>
  <head>
    <title>Applying CSS Mini-site</title>
  </head>
  <body>
    <h1>Applying CSS Templates</h1>
    <p>A mini-site containing several (X)HTML templates, each being➡
       styled using a different method of CSS application.</p>
  <p>Click an example below.</p>
  <h2>Examples</h2>
    <ul>
      <li><a href="base.html">Base template</a></li>
      <li><a href="inline.html">Inline CSS template</a></li>
      <li><a href="embedded.html">Embedded CSS template</a></li>
      <li><a href="external.html">External CSS template</a></li>
      <li><a href="imported.html">Imported CSS template</a></li>
    </ul>
  </body>
</html>
```

Note that there has as yet been no CSS in this chapter whatsoever. So to create a base template file, go through the following steps:

1. Create a new file called base.html.

2. Add the (X)HTML.

3. Save the file to a new folder on your computer.

4. Drag the file onto an empty browser window to see the basic web page as it stands.

Now you are ready to build a set of templates, each influenced by CSS in a different way. This mini-site can then be used to revisit and play with the methods discussed in this book, applying the CSS however you see fit.

5. Next make four copies of base.html, and name them inline.html, embedded.html, external.html, and imported.html.

6. Ensure you save these new files to the same folder as base.html.

7. The four new files should now be available from your base.html file in your web browser.

Great! Now for each following method, you will have a corresponding (X)HTML file with which to work. Let's work through the main methods of applying CSS to XHTML one by one. Later you'll learn how the numerous methods can be combined for a more powerful effect.

Inline Styles

Inline styles make use of the style attribute applied to specific tags within the document, where the actual style value is declared using the form *name:value*, or *property:value*, if you want to use the correct terminology. There is a more detailed explanation of correct CSS syntax later in the "Effective CSS Syntax" section.

1. Open inline.html in your text editor.

2. Find the first opening paragraph tag <p>.

3. Replace the <p> with <p style="color: #F00"> and save the template. This very simple declaration will ensure that the paragraph text will be red.

Notice now that the text contained within that paragraph will be red. Only that paragraph is affected, and the second paragraph defaults to black. This method can be applied to any (X)HTML element within the <body> of the page.

Pros of Inline Styles

There are times when this method is useful, but these times are few and far between. You've just learned how to make a paragraph red using CSS—that was useful, right? This method might also be useful for testing out simple CSS examples within this book. However, I think it best to skip to the "Cons of Inline Styles" paragraph rather than seek poor justification for inline CSS—as you'll soon find out when you have a bit more experience, it's not a good idea generally.

Cons of Inline Styles

Your (X)HTML should always be as presentation-free as possible. Peppering your code with inline styles is going to weigh the page down significantly. As if that were not reason enough, imagine having to declare the styles for every paragraph, every link, every header, and so on. To further scare you off, consider redesigning a site containing hundreds of pages where inline styles litter the markup. You'd have to go into *every* page and change each CSS property individually—not good.

Embedded Styles

Embedded styles still have you working exclusively within the (X)HTML template, but this time all styles are grouped together in the head of the document, as part of one element.

1. Open `embedded.html` in your text editor.

2. Within the `<head>` section of the template, just after the `<title>` element, paste the following: `<style type="text/css">p {color: #F00;}</style>`. Again, you are using a simple CSS declaration to render the text red.

3. Save the template, and open it in the web browser.

Notice now that the text contained within both paragraphs is red. This time around, all paragraphs in the document are affected by the declaration, as the style is applied without exception to all `<p>` tags within the page.

Pros of Embedded Styles

There are times when this method is useful, but again they are rare. Admittedly, this approach is much better than inline CSS, as it allows you to make blanket changes to all instances of an element rather than using duplicated inline styles. The idea of grouping all styles in one place is much more sensible too, although as before, the actual (X)HTML document isn't the best place for this. Many seasoned developers will tell you that this method can be ideal during initial testing.

Cons of Embedded Styles

Embedded styles are again loading presentational bloat into the document. Also, the styles need to be downloaded again and again with every page load. Every page of your web site will need its own embedded styles, and making sitewide style changes is going to be very labor intensive (unless perhaps you pull the styles in as an include). Hey, that's a good idea actually. Let's move on.

External Styles

I don't want to influence you too much here, but please *use this method* for your day-to-day CSS sites! Forget all the pros and cons of inline and embedded styles, and rejoice over **external style sheets**. In this example, your external style sheet will only contain one rule, but this sheet will grow to be the most influential file of the whole web site.

1. Open `external.html` in your text editor.

2. Within the `<head>` section, and after the `<title>` element, paste the element `<link rel="stylesheet" type="text/css" href="external.css" />` and save the file. This line tells the browser to look for an external file called `external.css`, which is a CSS file, and that it is stored in the same directory.

3. Create a new file called `external.css`.

4. Into external.css paste the following: p {color: #F00;}.

5. Save external.css to the same folder as the .html files, and again open it in your web browser.

See that the paragraphs are again red, but note that there is not a single CSS rule or style element anywhere in your (X)HTML file. Your (X)HTML is free of presentational bloat, and the color is being controlled via the external style sheet.

The big take-home message here is that you can now use the link element as seen earlier to apply the style sheet to any number of other (X)HTML pages, resulting in the paragraphs on those pages also being turned red! So you can now change styles on 10 or 100 web pages, just by altering one style sheet—now that's control!

Pros of External Styles

How long have we got here? First, when you think about CSS for your site, you think only about one external style sheet, and not the markup, which means sitewide style changes are a one-sheet job. Second, once the browser accesses the style sheet, it is cached and need not be downloaded again. The result of this is that not only are pages rendered faster, but also the saving on bandwidth is considerable, with just one CSS file replacing the same or similar code that would be needed in each and every (X)HTML page if working with embedded CSS. Third, your markup can be devoid of any presentational information, keeping it lean and content-only.

Cons of External Styles

Not much to report here really. Maybe if the external CSS was for some reason unavailable, none of the (X)HTML pages would be styled, but this is a rare occurrence.

So, you should now understand and have examples of the three basic methods of applying CSS to a (X)HTML document. At such a stage, many developers will stick with linking to an external file and live happily ever after. There's nothing wrong with that, and they will feel that they have for themselves a very comfortable methodology; but this is CSS, and the possibilities for improvement are endless.

There's another method of applying styles to a web page called **importing**, and we'll look at that next.

Importing and Combining Styles

Serving presentational information with the @import rule is a key part of web standards flexibility. The site structure—the actual content—is uncompromised, and you are free to make separate choices about the presentational styling. The @import rule was not designed to be used in the (X)HTML document, and is meant as a method for importing one or more style sheets via the main external style sheet. However, by importing an external style sheet via the (X)HTML, you can ensure that old browsers such as Netscape 4.x and IE4 ignore specific styles. You would then provide a standard link to an external style sheet for those browsers. We'll look at further uses of @import in Chapter 2, but first it is worthwhile to gain a basic understanding of how this method works.

The following example assumes you created the style sheet `external.css` in the previous section:

1. Open `imported.html` in your text editor.

2. Within the `<head>` section, and after the `<title>` element, paste the element `<style type="text/css">@import url(external.css);</style>` and save the file.

3. Save `imported.html` and view it in the browser.

Nothing looks any different, and the paragraphs are still red, but you've just taken a very important step toward sensible and productive style sheet management, which you'll find out more about in the "Maintaining and Organizing Style Sheets" section that follows shortly.

The `@import` rule is particularly useful for hiding your style sheet from old and infirm browsers with poor CSS support, such as Netscape 4.*x*, which don't support `@import`. Rather than attempt to do something half-useful with your CSS, that browser will just completely ignore your style sheet and leave the (X)HTML unstyled. If you served the CSS as usual, and poor old Netscape tried to follow its rules, it would more than likely balk at many of them and produce an unhinged mess, which is best avoided.

Print Style Sheets

At some point in the (hopefully near) future, your sites will be wonderful works of art full of color, graphics, and interesting column separation. Good for you, and good for the screen, but that's not so good for printing. Nobody wants to print an article written in white text on a solid black or extravagant rainbow background. That uses way too much ink, and is thankfully avoidable.

All modern browsers support the most common `media` attributes, which are applied within the `<link>` element to target specific style sheets in a specific situation. For example, to ensure only visitors viewing the web site on a monitor see your glamorous design, you add `media="screen"` to the `<link>` element to call your default style sheet. Underneath that, a second `<link>` element can be used with `media="print"` added to call a print style sheet with only basic styling, such as black text on a plain white background, and all graphics removed:

```
<link rel="stylesheet" media="screen" type="text/css" href="screen.css" />
<link rel="stylesheet" media="print" type="text/css" href="print.css" />
```

If a style sheet has a media type of `screen`, it will not be used when the page is printed. If no media type were specified, the style sheet would influence the printed result. Note also that any style sheet intended only for printing purposes must be given the `print` media type to prevent it from being implemented on screen. It is therefore very important to specify media type correctly. The finer aspects of print style sheet management are covered in Chapter 14 much later in this book, but it's very useful to understand the possibilities of the media attribute at this stage.

Other Style Sheets

Why stop with print style sheets? The next most popular media attribute is `media="handheld"`, which, while not supported by all mobile devices, is still in common use as browsers will ignore its content, allowing many cell phone or PDA users to access a stripped-down version of your styling depending upon support. Again, all that is required is another `<link>` element with `media="handheld"` specified, calling a specific style sheet such as `handheld.css` or `mobile.css`.

■Note The only `media` declarations currently supported by IE are `all`, `screen`, and `print`, so many of the other declarations, such as `projection` (for projectors, funnily enough), `aural` (for speech synthesizers), and `braille` should only be used when you are targeting a specific device for a specific end audience.

Maintaining and Organizing Style Sheets

Ask developers proficient in CSS about its virtues and they'll wax lyrical until the cows come home. Ask those same developers how they organize their style sheets, and you may get a less informed response. Like it or not, your external style sheet will invariably start small, and end up ballooning out of control. The more rules you add, the longer the style sheet. Consider this for a large organization such as the BBC (`www.bbc.co.uk`), which has an almost unique design for each of its many sections, and style sheets can soon become unmanageable. What was that rule you wrote to define the style for sublists only in the third column and only when the page is defined as an "article" page? Where was that rule put again? You need a system of organization, and this is a principle you will do well to employ very early on.

Multiple Directories

You might be thinking about serving a default style sheet, a print style sheet, and maybe one for mobile devices in the future. That's superb, but remember that it's really important to keep things well organized. Soon we'll look at multiple style sheets for one platform—if that method is combined with style sheets for other platforms, things can get a bit unmanageable.

The best approach here is to use folders. This might seem obvious, but you'd be amazed how few people do this, and it can be a challenge to work with someone else's design if such methods haven't been implemented. When you are ready to make use of alternate style sheets, the following example can be employed. Here a new folder is created for each potential platform or action (such as `handheld` for mobile devices and `print` for the printable, stripped-down version of the page):

1. Create a high-level folder called `css`.

2. Inside that, create a folder for each platform you'll be catering to, such as `handheld`, `print`, `screen`, and so on.

3. Inside each subfolder, you then place the actual CSS files for that platform.

So, you end up with a sensible folder structure that can be reflected in your `<link>` elements, as these examples show:

```
<link rel="stylesheet" media="screen" type="text/css" ➥
href="css/screen/default.css" />
<link rel="stylesheet" media="print" type="text/css" href="css/print/default.css" />
<link rel="stylesheet" media="handheld" type="text/css" ➥
href="css/handheld/default.css" />
```

This might not seem important, or even worthwhile at the moment, but when you start using multiple style sheets for a particular platform, it's useful to be able to keep them inside a specific folder.

Keep this approach in mind should you need to serve different style sheets for different sections on a larger site. For example, if your main pages use your default screen styles, they'll live in the css/screen folder, yet your member pages are styled differently and so would live in css/screen/members. This is a simple approach, but more useful than might seem apparent right now.

Multiple Style Sheets

Consider a style sheet that contains all of the rules you've created for an entire site. Let's say that site is equivalent in size to the BBC web site, which is very, very big indeed. All the styles required would result in one long, unmanageable style sheet, so splitting the style sheet into manageable chunks is a much better option here.

Modular CSS

It pays here to think of your CSS as modules. For example, many rules will apply directly to layout—a number of key rules (font control, color, headings) will apply to every page and can be considered as your default rules. On the other hand, some rules will be applied to <form> elements, so will only be used on a few pages.

So how about creating a specific style sheet for each module, such as the default module, forms module, navigation module, and so on? By combining each module, you end up with the CSS for a complete site, yet everything remains separated, and you can be pretty sure that you placed your submit button styles in the forms style sheet.

This is where our friend @import again comes in very handy. First, you link to a basic style sheet that in turn imports all the modular sheets using @import. Such a method has other benefits such as easier debugging and problem solving.

In the following example, the basic style sheet (external.css) is used to import two modular ones (default.css and layout.css) to have a combined effect on the (X)HTML:

1. Create a new style sheet called default.css.

2. Place the CSS p {color: #F00;} in it and save the file.

3. Create another new style sheet called layout.css.

4. Place the following CSS into layout.css: #header {height: 100px; width: 100%; border: 1px solid #999;}; save the file.

5. Open external.css and replace the existing CSS with the following:

```
@import url("default.css");

@import url("layout.css");
```

6. Save the file.

The CSS is now prepared and still hidden from Netscape 4.*x* by @import. What you now have is three style sheets. The first (external.css) is used to import the two modular style sheets default.css (your basic styling for the body, paragraphs, color, etc.) and layout.css (for layout elements such as the header you just created styles for).

7. Open external.html and ensure the link to external.css is still in place.

8. Find `<h1>Applying CSS Templates</h1>` and wrap this with the hooks for the header, so you end up with `<div id="header"><h1>Applying CSS Templates</h1></div>`.

9. Save external.html and view it in your browser.

Notice that the CSS from default.css is still giving you a red paragraph, but also that the header rule from layout.css is placing a box 100 pixels high by 100% width around the heading text. The external.css file is successfully combining the two style sheets it imports for a complete effect upon the (X)HTML.

From that point on, you would then think about adding the most common rules to default.css and anything to do with layout to layout.css. Already this means that you are thinking about well-organized CSS that remains manageable from the earliest design stage.

Utilizing Screen Style Sheets for Other Devices

Earlier I mentioned how modular CSS can help you manage style sheets aimed specifically at other platforms. Take for example a style sheet aimed specifically at print media. It's fairly likely that this style sheet will be devoid of any layout or form styling, and all you really need is some well-formed type to be printed on a clean white background.

Instead of creating a whole new style sheet for printing, why not just serve up your default.css styles using the media="print" attribute in the `<link>` element? Because default.css contains no layout styles, and does not itself import any other style sheets, the resulting printout will ignore all other styles assigned to your design. If you are following the modular approach with a certain amount of discipline, it makes sense to simply knock out the other modular sheets and just leave the font, paragraph, and other common rules available for the printed version. By adding the `<link>` for print media below your main style sheets, you bypass any further importing controlled by the external.css file. Note also that if no print-specific style sheet is specified, then the printer will do its best to print your design as it appears on the computer screen, potentially costing your users a fortune in ink.

1. In external.html, add the media declaration for screen to the existing <link> element: <link rel="stylesheet" **media="screen"** type="text/css" href="css/screen/external.css" />.

2. Next, add the <link> element and media declaration for print devices: <link rel="stylesheet" media="print" type="text/css" href="css/screen/default.css" />.

3. Save external.html and refresh or load it in your browser.

The first thing to note is that this method goes against the sensible folder structure discussed earlier, in that the print style sheet is now coming from the css/screen folder. To get around this, either don't use the folder structure method, and just keep all your CSS files in one folder, or retain the folder structure, and put your default.css file in the css root folder as it is no longer media specific, seeing as it is being used for both screen and print.

The benefits far outweigh the problems anyway, as now your site is using one less style sheet, and any changes you make to the default CSS styles in default.css will impact upon any printed pages also. Again, if you are disciplined about what you place in the default.css style sheet, this can only be a bonus.

As default.css only contains basic style rules, it seems sensible to use it for handheld devices, thereby removing all layout information for them also, although if you're a control freak, you'll appreciate the much more specific approaches to handhelds in Chapter 15.

Effective CSS Syntax

Sensibly organizing your style sheets is vital, but of equal importance is how you structure the actual CSS within those sheets.

None of the methods in this section actually affect functionality, but they do aid navigation and debugging, and certainly make it easier for you or a colleague to revisit the CSS to make tweaks later on.

Defining a Style

At this stage, all CSS rules you create will follow a very simple formula. CSS syntax is made up of a **selector** (the element or tag you wish to control), followed by at least one **declaration** comprising a **property** and its **value**, as Figure 1-1 illustrates.

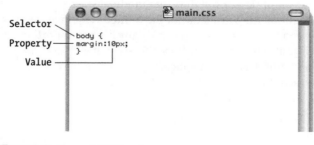

Figure 1-1. *Correct CSS syntax*

The selector defines the exact element(s) that will be affected by the rule you create. The following example uses the paragraph tag as the selector, and the `color` property set with the hexadecimal reference for red as the value:

```
p {
  color: #F00;
  }
```

Note that after the selector, the property and value are contained within curly braces. Almost without exception, this syntax will define all your CSS rules. See that a colon follows the property (`color:`) and a semicolon follows the value (`#F00;`). To omit either the colon or a curly brace will result in the style sheet failing to various degrees, so it is vital to watch for syntax errors that occur easily while busily defining new rules. Failing to include the semicolon after each value when adding more properties will also screw things up. If there is only one property and value, or it is the last of several, the semicolon can be omitted.

Any further properties and values for that selector are added within the curly braces. You do not have to place them on a new line so long as each is separated with a semicolon, but for clarity it is recommended that each does fall on a new line:

```
p {
  color: #F00;
  font-size: 12px;
  }
```

Now all paragraphs will not only be red, but will also have a set font size of 12 pixels. The selector (in this case the p) acts as the link between the CSS and the (X)HTML, and as a result all paragraphs will be styled accordingly. Note that the selector is defined in lowercase, as required by XHTML only, as HTML is case insensitive

It's then a case of adding new rules to the style sheet using the same syntax. Here, a rule to make all top-level headings (`<h1>`) dark gray and 16 pixels high is added to the style sheet:

```
p {
  color: #F00;
  font-size: 12px;
  }
h1 {
  color: #333;
  font-size: 16px;
  }
```

Very simple properties are used in this example, and property syntax will be explored in much more detail in the following chapters. For now though, we'll concentrate on how a style sheet is structured.

Commenting

Defining rules is one thing, but consider how unmanageable a style sheet can become once it holds 20 or 30 rules. This is where commenting becomes invaluable. The following example includes simple comments that remind us what the rules are there for:

```
/* Default styling for paragraphs */
p {
  color: #F00;
  font-size: 12px;
  }

/* Make all top-level headings gray and 16px high */
h1 {
  color: #333;
  font-size: 16px;
  }
```

Introducing some plain English into the style sheet makes things much more friendly immediately. All comments begin with a forward slash and asterisk (/*), and end with the asterisk followed by the forward slash (*/). This is a very simple and easy to remember method that you may prefer to use in more complicated or important styles, so you can work out what does what when you return to your style sheets at a later date. Also bear in mind that adding comments will increase file sizes, but this shouldn't have a significant impact, especially as browsers only have to load the style sheet file once.

A method preferred by many designers further highlights the rule by adding a dashed line with the comment—a great way of carving up the style sheet and making it more visually manageable:

```
/* Default styling for paragraphs
------------------------------------------------------- */
p {
  color: #F00;
  font-size: 12px;
  }
```

Again this is very easy to add on the fly, and is arguably the best approach to commenting. Without question, commenting makes troubleshooting and revisits to old designs much more bearable, and is a huge timesaver.

Flagging Rules

Basic comments are of great benefit when scrolling through a style sheet, but there is a quicker way to track down a rule—vital with large style sheets. Douglas Bowman (www.stopdesign.com) introduced the idea of **flags**, where a character not typically found in style sheets is used at the beginning of a comment to aid retrieval in conjunction with your text editor's Find tool. It should also be noted at this point that some CSS-specific software such as TopStyle and CSSEdit have selector searches built into their feature sets.

Doug suggests adding an equals sign at the beginning of the comment, immediately followed by the selector to act as a flag. Doing a search in the style sheet for p would typically find all instances of p, either alone or within other words, and would be pretty useless. However, searching for =p would bring the rule into focus immediately, as that character combination is unlikely to appear anywhere else.

```
/* =p Default styling for paragraphs
-------------------------------------------------------- */
p {
  color: #F00;
  font-size: 12px;
  }
```

This technique requires discipline, and is something to either adopt completely or leave well alone. You could end up searching for something you think you've flagged, but haven't. Therefore I recommend that you flag all rules in this way if you intend to make use of this method.

Indenting for Clarity

Further to sensible commenting and flags, responsible CSS developers can make their style sheets even more legible. The following example makes use of comments and flags, but also aims to make the layout even more legible using white space:

```
/* =p Default styling for paragraphs
-------------------------------------------------------- */
  p {
    color: #F00;
    font-size: 12px;
    }

/* =h1 Make all top-level headings gray and 16px high
------------------------------------------------------------*/
  h1 {
    color: #333;
    font-size: 16px;
    }
```

For the purposes of this book, I'm using two-space indents for the selector and four-space indents for the declarations. Indenting is used to provide clarity. In the real world (or your favorite text editor, to be precise), many developers use one tab click to indent the selector, and two tab clicks to indent the declarations and closing curly brace. This might seem arbitrary, but such a layout makes regular searching for rules a whole lot easier. The eye can scan immediate left for comments, next right for the selectors, and farthest right for the rules.

Embracing such methods at this stage is not essential, but doing so will certainly help you stay focused and avoid confusion as your style sheets begin to grow. Very few developers consider these methods as they begin to learn CSS, but thinking and coding logically from day one are two of the things that separate a great CSS designer from an average one.

You're Ready to Proceed

If you have followed this chapter from start to finish, you are now armed to proceed with all the organizational skills of any renowned CSS developer. Sticking to these recommendations should help you avoid any confusion as you progress and learn to write your own CSS rules.

The basic templates you have created in this chapter can form the starting point for other examples in this book. As for your method of applying the CSS, that is up to you. Whether you choose to work with an embedded style sheet as in embedded.html, or prefer to use the combination of external.html and external.css is your choice. Perhaps you'll want to stick with modules and may therefore decide to place your additional rules in the existing style sheets (default.css and layout.css) and also add new ones later for other modules, importing them through external.css. The important thing is that you are aware of the methods of applying CSS and have a choice.

So, what's next? Well, we've covered the organizational groundwork you'll need to take on board before starting your CSS development, so next we'll dive into the core CSS basics—all that juicy syntax stuff!

CHAPTER 2

■■■

Core Concepts of CSS

Or "Why didn't anyone explain all of this madness to me when I began?"

Use CSS sparingly to control a few page elements, and you'd be right to call it a simple methodology. Start pushing the envelope and begin working across multiple style sheets with all sorts of conflicting selectors, and all hell can break loose.

The thing is, this "hell" is intentional. Well, not intended to be hell as such, but it is a system designed to flex its muscles and produce results more powerful than anyone could imagine when they begin to toy with CSS.

CSS cascades, it inherits, it can be grouped and contextualized. As if that were not enough, there are numerous units of measurement to be considered before diving in, each relevant to a particular scenario. I'm not trying to alarm you here, but I am suggesting that a basic knowledge of these quirky goings on can give you a much greater awareness of what is possible with CSS, and allow you to make informed decisions throughout the following chapters. Be brave, and don't be afraid to reread this section. Understanding these core concepts will turn you into a pro overnight!

Specifically, I'll cover

- ID vs. class

- Using the cascade

- Grouping

- Inheritance

- Contextual selectors

- CSS measurements

ID vs. Class

So far you've only looked at **base selectors** to perform styling. A base selector takes an existing (X)HTML tag and redefines some or all of its default properties to style the whole element, such as the following rule which sets all paragraphs to red:

```
p {color: #F00;}
```

Thankfully, CSS allows you to define your own custom selectors, known as **ID** and **class** selectors. IDs and classes are applied to (X)HTML elements as simple attributes that provide much tighter control and more hooks for your design.

Throughout the history of time, many developers have confused IDs with classes, either failing to utilize the real purpose of each or simply using one instead of the other.

■Note Let's begin with a very simple definition. Think of ID as identification. Your ID is unique to you and is not shared with anyone else. A class is different, in that there can be many people in a class, be it at school, in society, or wherever. This translates to CSS where an ID can only be used once per page, whereas classes can be used an unlimited number of times.

IDs

An ID can only be used once per page, and is a **unique identifier** to an element. Typically, an ID is used for any unique page element such as the header, main navigation, footer, or other key part of the user interface.

Applying an ID

The most common way to apply an ID is to reference it in the (X)HTML using the `id="name"` attribute immediately after the opening tag within an element. In this case, our two IDs are named `highlight` and `default`, respectively, and are applied to two paragraphs:

```
<p id="highlight">This paragraph has red text.</p>
<p id="default">This paragraph has dark gray text.</p>
```

The corresponding CSS uses the hash (#) character to denote the rule is a unique ID. The hash is combined with the ID name to start the rule, followed by the property declarations:

```
/* Define highlighted text */
 #highlight {
    color:#F00;
    }
/* Define default text */
 #default {
    color:#333;
    }
```

Combining IDs with Selectors

Existing or new IDs can be combined with selectors in the style sheet to add further control. In the following example, the base CSS defines all h2 headings as dark gray and 16 pixels in size:

```
/* Basic heading style */
  h2 {
    color:#333;
    font-size:16px;
    }
```

That is fine for most uses of <h2>, but let's say the main <h2> on your page (the title of an article) needs to be emphasized with a different color. This calls for a new rule where the selector is defined in the form *element#name*:

```
/* Adjust the color of h2 when used as a title */
  h2#title {
    color:#F00;
    }
```

Here the new rule will override the default <h2> color (color: #333;) with red (color: #F00;) whenever an <h2> is identified with id="title" in the (X)HTML. The new rule does not redefine font-size, so that will be carried over and unchanged. Simply add the unique identifier to the page:

```
<h2 id="title">Title Of My Article</h2>
```

Remember that title is a unique identifier, so it cannot be used again within that template. Any other instances of <h2> on the page will be rendered with the default styling.

When to Use an ID

Only one element on each page can be styled by each unique ID, and therefore IDs should be reserved for unique, single-use elements such as a header or sidebar, or the main navigation or page footer. This makes scanning your markup easier, as all ID attributes will denote unique content areas or special regions of the page, while also providing greater flexibility for more complex CSS application. Later in this chapter, further uses for IDs will be discussed in the "Contextual Selectors" selection.

When to Avoid an ID

IDs must be avoided when there is more than one requirement for the CSS rule. Do not use an ID for anything you are likely to multiply in the future, such as multiple images, link styles, or paragraphs where more than one will need to be styled a particular way.

Class

A class can be used an infinite number of times per page, making it a very flexible method of applying CSS. A class defines an element as belonging to a group, or as a reusable object or style. Classes solve problems in the short term, but can provide less flexibility for more complicated CSS designs.

Applying Classes

The most common way to apply a class is to reference it in the (X)HTML using a class="*name*" attribute of an element. As with our ID example, the two classes are named highlight (for red text) and default (for dark gray text):

```
<p class="highlight">This paragraph has red text.</p>
<p class="default">This paragraph has dark gray text.</p>
<p class="default">This paragraph also has dark gray text.</p>
```

Note that as the identifiers are classes, they can be used more than once, hence in the example two paragraphs have been identified as default, so will be styled the same way. That would not be acceptable if using IDs.

The corresponding CSS uses a full stop (.) character to denote the rule is a reusable class. The full stop is combined with the class name to start the rule, followed by the property declarations:

```
/* Define highlight class */
 .highlight {
    color:#F00;
    }
/* Define default class */
 .default {
    color:#333;
  }
```

Combining IDs with Multiple Classes

Classes are especially useful when you wish to have control over a number of elements. Consider the following drinks list, the source code for which is available in the drinks.html file:

```
<ul id="drinks">
 <li class="alcohol">Beer</li>
 <li class="alcohol">Spirits</li>
 <li class="mixer">Cola</li>
 <li class="mixer">Lemonade</li>
 <li class="hot">Tea</li>
 <li class="hot">Coffee</li>
</ul>
```

Note first that the unordered list (<ul>) is given a unique ID. Thus, id="drinks" will not be used again on the page at any time, allowing that particular list to be styled uniquely. Note also that Beer and Spirits are within list elements defined with class="alcohol", Cola and Lemonade are within list elements defined with class="mixer", and finally Tea and Coffee are defined in list elements with class="hot". This allows each drinks group to be treated individually.

The CSS declares that the default text for that list will be red, so any list items without a class attribute will default to red text:

```
/* Drinks list styling */
  ul#drinks {
    color:#F00;
    }
```

Next, the classes for each drink type are defined with unique shades of gray for font color:

```
/* Define alcohol color */
  .alcohol {
    color:#333;
    }
/* Define mixer color */
```

```
.mixer {
  color:#999;
  }
/* Define hot drinks color */
.hot {
  color:#CCC;
  }
```

The result sees the list of items move through shades of gray (defined by the classes). Any further drinks added to the list can be assigned to a particular drinks group, such as `<li class="alcohol">Wine</li>`. Thus a logical color key is established using simple CSS classes.

■**Tip** Before adding a class to an element, be sure that the element needs it. Too often web designers overuse classes when the (X)HTML is already providing more than enough hooks for the CSS. Make sure that the element cannot be targeted using a descendant selector or other method before opting for a class. This will help keep your code lean and make future redesigning much easier.

Overriding Base Styling with Classes

Later in the book you will learn much better methods for controlling repeated elements within a page, and in reality there are far easier ways of defining paragraph styles and other elements that do not require identifiers to be added to the (X)HTML. In fact, you have already been doing this to a degree.

In Chapter 1, an example base CSS rule was used to turn all paragraphs red. Let's use that base rule again, declaring all instances of paragraphs red, but this time add a class rule to the CSS that will bleach out any element it is identified with by turning text light gray:

```
/* Default styling for paragraphs */
p {
  color:#F00;
  font-size:12px;
  }
/* Use this style to turn anything light gray */
.bleached {
  color:#CCC;
  }
```

All paragraphs will still be red by default, but this can still be overridden when necessary by identifying an element with the bleached class, as in this (X)HTML:

```
<p>This paragraph has red text.</p>
<p class="bleached">This paragraph has light gray text.</p>
```

The second paragraph will now be light gray, as the color declaration in bleached overrides the red. Note that the paragraph is still rendered 12 pixels high, as bleached does not redefine font-size. Add a font-size declaration in bleached, and that value will override the original size for all paragraphs identified with class="bleached".

Linking a Class Directly to an Element

In this example, the CSS is constructed with the class attached directly to the element in the form *element.classname*, and like before, it is referenced using the class="*classname*" format within the (X)HTML.

```
/* Use this style to turn anything light gray */
  .bleached {
    color:#CCC;
    }
/* Override the color of bleached when it identifies a paragraph */
 p.bleached {
  color:#000;
  }
```

This method would be used when the standard declaration for the bleached class needs to be overruled. For example, any element given a class of bleached will remain light gray (color: #CCC;), but any instances of paragraph elements with a class of bleached will be rendered black (color: #000;). This method is useful when numerous instances of a class are littering your (X)HTML, and it would be too difficult to remove them all manually. Instead, simply target that class when it identifies the element you need to change using the form *element.classname*.

When to Use a Class

As described previously, classes are a very flexible method for applying your CSS rules, and can be used again and again within a page. Use classes to control elements that belong to a group, for temporary items, and also to enhance the behavior of an ID.

When Not to Use a Class

It is not recommended that classes be used for main structural elements within a page, such as headers and main navigation, although they will work. Doing so would decrease the flexibility of your design and make further customization difficult without overhaul or extra markup. Also, be sure a class is needed, and make sure the element cannot be targeted by defining a rule for the existing (X)HTML before getting class-happy. Remember that a class is used for exceptions to normal styling, and not to define the standard.

Using the Cascade

CSS. Cascading Style Sheets. *Cascading.* Lovely word. Hmm. Many never stop to think about that first word, and we are all guilty of just referring to CSS as style sheets. It is a shame that many ignore the first part of the acronym, when it is the cascade that gives CSS developers the most power.

Remember that a class value will override that of a base CSS rule. Well, there is also a hierarchy to be embraced with multiple style sheets dependent on the order and method by which they are applied to the (X)HTML. That is the cascade.

If you are applying CSS only from one external style sheet, then there is no cascade, as nothing is applied before or after that style sheet. Things get interesting when you begin to combine style sheets or methods of application. Let's look at three examples.

The Cascade Through Varying Methods of Application

In Chapter 1, you learned of the various methods for applying CSS—inline, embedded, external, and importing. It is possible to combine these methods to have an effect on the cascade.

Let's say that you are storing all of your CSS rules in an external style sheet that is dictating the presentation across your vast web site. For whatever reason, you need to overrule some of the external styles for just one web page.

Time to embrace the cascade. For that one web page, you could use embedded CSS in the <head> of the page, redefining the appropriate rules right there. When that web page is loaded, the browser will apply the CSS it first encounters—the embedded CSS—before looking at your external CSS to apply the remaining rules. Any identical selectors in the external style sheet will be ignored.

Need further control? No problem. At the top of the hierarchy are inline styles—the CSS added directly to the (X)HTML elements. Whatever styles you apply inline will overrule any declarations in the <head> of the page or in an external style sheet.

Example

To see this in action, you can run through the following simple example:

1. Open external.css and define the default paragraph color (as in Chapter 1) with p {color#F00;} and save the file.

2. View external.html in your browser. Assuming you are still applying CSS using external.css, any default paragraphs should be red.

3. Now open external.html and apply the embedded style <style type="text/css">p {color: #333;}</style> in the head of the template and save the file.

4. Reload external.html in your browser. Now any default paragraphs should be dark gray, as the embedded CSS is overriding the linked style sheet.

5. Finally, find a default paragraph in external.html and define it with an inline style, such as <p style="color: #CCC">, and save the template.

6. Reload external.html in your browser. Now the paragraph to which you applied the inline style should be light gray, as the inline CSS is overriding the embedded CSS and the linked style sheet. Any other default paragraphs should still be dark gray based on the embedded style.

Thus the hierarchy is in place. The browser performs the inline rule first, and then looks to perform any other rules embedded in the <head>, and finally looks to any external files to complete its understanding of the CSS you created.

The Cascade Through Multiple External Style Sheets

Another method of exploiting the cascade uses multiple external style sheets. You already know how to link to one or more external style sheets for various platforms (such as printers and mobile devices), and this approach is similar, except all the external files here are specifically for the screen:

```
<link rel="stylesheet" media="screen" type="text/css" href="css/screen/one.css" />
<link rel="stylesheet" media="screen" type="text/css" href="css/screen/two.css" />
<link rel="stylesheet" media="screen" type="text/css" href="css/screen/three.css" />
```

Imagine that each of the three style sheets features a rule called #header. The declaration for #header in each style sheet features the same properties (say height, width, and color), although the value of each is different in some way.

In this instance, the browser will consider the last linked style sheet (three.css) as most important and perform any rules it contains first of all. Any rules not defined in three.css will be performed from the second style sheet (two.css). Any duplicate selectors in two.css will be ignored, overridden by the selectors in three.css. Finally, the browser will perform any remaining styles from one.css, assuming they are not also defined in the preceding style sheets.

So the rule for #header that was declared in three.css is performed, while any other instances of it are ignored. Always remember that the later a rule is specified, the more weight it is given.

The Cascade Through Imported Style Sheets

The hierarchy is also present with imported style sheets. As with the previous examples, it's all about the order in which the style sheets are specified. In Chapter 1, we looked at modular CSS, where the CSS for a site is organized into relevant style sheets, such as default styles, layout styles, navigation styles, and so on. Here's a similar example where four modules are imported via a master external style sheet called external.css. external.css contains the following lines:

```
@import url("default.css");
@import url("layout.css");
@import url("navigation.css");
@import url("forms.css");
```

As you'd expect from the order, forms.css is highest in the hierarchy, whereas default.css is apparently lowest. Let's assume that in navigation.css (second in the hierarchy) there is a class called highlight, used to render text red. Let's also assume that highlight appears in default.css, but is used to render text orange. As navigation.css has more weight due to its place in the hierarchy, the rendered text will be red.

Yet still, forms.css isn't necessarily top of the tree. Remember that these style sheets are being imported via a master external style sheet. In Chapter 1, you used external.css to call in two modular sheets. Here external.css can be used again to import the modular sheets. If you define highlight in external.css, the declared color will override either the red or the orange specified in the imported style sheets.

Even then, the rule in external.css can still be overridden using embedded or inline CSS in the (X)HTML template. It's up to you when you stop the cascade, but be careful not to get washed away by the cascade and tie yourself in knots.

■**Note** If another style sheet were to be imported through one of the modular style sheets using @import, it would automatically be lower in the hierarchy. In a nutshell, a style sheet always has less weight than the one calling it.

Bottom of the Ladder

Always at the bottom of the cascade hierarchy is the browser's own default style sheet. Typically, the browser style sheet will have default settings for headings, paragraphs, lists, and all common (X)HTML elements. It is the browser style sheet that makes links blue and visited links purple. View any page in your browser that isn't styled with CSS, and you will see the default browser styles.

So long as you define all the elements you wish to control, the default browser CSS will be overridden. Remember that the default styling was designed for numerous reasons, specifically legibility, accessibility, and common understanding. It is up to you to integrate these accepted conventions into your designs, and seek to improve them, not disregard them.

Careful with the Cascade

It can sometimes be hard to track the cascade across several style sheets. For example, if two selectors have matching properties but varying values, e.g., each instance of a selector was made up of font-family, color, and background, but with different values for each, the selector in the style sheet with the highest hierarchy would win out and be rendered. Things get even more interesting when each selector has unique properties.

Let's clarify this with an example. Imagine that in a modular style sheet such as forms.css you have defined a class called highlight as follows:

```
/* Highlight important form information */
  .highlight {
    color:#F00;
    font-style:italic;
    text-decoration:underline;
    }
```

Should there be no other instance of that selector in any style sheets higher up the hierarchy, highlight will indeed be rendered in red italicized text with a neat underline. However, imagine that a few weeks later in external.css, a style sheet of more hierarchical importance, you've forgotten about the original class and decide to reuse highlight as follows:

```
/* Highlight author's name underneath articles */
  .highlight {
    color:#F00;
    font-style:normal;
    }
```

First, the cascade dictates that the font-style value for highlight in external.css (font-style: normal;) is of greater importance than the value in forms.css (font-style: italic;). Therefore, all instances of highlight sitewide will be normal red text, not italicized. Without realizing it, you have just turned all your lovely italicized form text into boring normal text, and you probably won't notice until you revisit your forms in your browser.

And to further illustrate this pitfall, the new highlight class in external.css does not define a value for text-decoration, so the normal red text you wished to create will be underlined, taking that value from forms.css. Sure, your new highlight class takes precedence in the hierarchy, but unless you turn off the underline in external.css, the cascade will still find its way to the original rule and look for anything not being overruled.

Grouping

Another key principle for creating well-organized CSS is **grouping**. Consider the following CSS, used to apply styles to the first three (X)HTML headings:

```
/* Heading styles */
 h1 {
   font-family:Helvetica,Arial,sans-serif;
   line-height:140%;
   color:#333;
   }
 h2 {
   font-family:Helvetica,Arial,sans-serif;
   line-height:140%;
   color:#333;
   }
 h3 {
   font-family:Helvetica,Arial,sans-serif;
   line-height:140%;
   color:#333;
   }
```

Note that aside from the selector, every rule is the same. The rules are using 13 lines and are bloating the style sheet unnecessarily. Thankfully, the three rules can be grouped to save space and keep things manageable:

```
/* Heading styles */
 h1, h2, h3 {
   font-family:Helvetica,Arial,sans-serif;
   line-height:140%;
   color:#333;
   }
```

That's now just five lines! The three selectors (h1, h2, and h3) are grouped in a comma-separated list, and this technique can be used to group any selectors with common values. If later you should decide to treat h3 differently, simply remove it from the list and isolate the h3 style.

Group Exceptions

What if you still wish to treat one of those headings slightly differently? Let's say you're happy with the font, line-height, and color, but wish to render the <h1> heading in italicized text. Luckily, there is a way to do that while still grouping h1 with the other selectors.

To create the italicized text, none of the existing declarations need to be altered. A new declaration, font-style: italic, is required, however. If that were to be added to the group, all headings would be italicized. Instead, a new style is added to the existing group:

```
/* Heading styles */
  h1, h2, h3 {
    font-family:Helvetica,Arial,sans-serif;
    line-height:140%;
    color:#333;
    }
/* Additionally, render all h1 headings in italics */
  h1 {
    font-style:italic;
    }
```

Now the browser will collate both h1 selectors (one from the grouping and the stand-alone selector) to render top-level headings as specified in the grouping and also in italics. Again, this method can be applied to any selectors.

Inheritance

Inheritance describes situations where (X)HTML elements inherit stylistic properties from a parent element. By not declaring a particular CSS value for the child element, that child element may in some circumstances inherit the CSS value given to the parent element. Where CSS cascades, so (X)HTML inherits.

Inheritance is both a blessing and a curse, and is another very powerful methodology that is often misunderstood. It can cause confusion across multiple style sheets—especially when debugging your CSS, and is something to be aware of from the start. On the plus side, it can be embraced to minimize the size of style sheets and markup, and enable wholesale changes to many CSS rules with minimal work. Generally, inheritance is always happening to your (X)HTML elements, and in most cases intervention is only necessary to control the inherited values for a specific reason.

Parents and Children

To understand inheritance, it pays to think of some (X)HTML elements as **parents**, and the elements they contain as **children**. A parent owns a child, and passes what he or she knows down to the child. In CSS, inheritance works in a similar way, except that it hands down style values, and not advice about education or the opposite sex.

Moving through (X)HTML markup, it is clear that some child elements act as parents to other child elements and so on, and thus a containment hierarchy develops. This containment hierarchy is also referred to as the **tree**.

So How Does Inheritance Work?

To illustrate inheritance, let's stay with headings. The <h1> heading in this example is styled with the following very simple rule:

```
/* Top-level heading */
  h1 {
    color:#333;
    }
```

The rule is pretty simple, and you are right to assume that the heading will be rendered dark gray. Now let's assume that in the (X)HTML the markup dictates that a few of the words should be emphasized using `<em>`:

```
<h1>This is the greatest heading <em>in the world</em></h1>
```

At this stage, no CSS rule exists to manipulate the `<em>` element. Therefore, the text within the `<em>` element will inherit the color from the h1 rule (its parent element) and will therefore also be dark gray. To overrule this inherited color, simply define `<em>` in the style sheet:

```
/* Make emphasized text shine brightly */
  em {
    color:#F00;
    }
```

Now all emphasized text sitewide will be rendered in red, and the element is no longer inheriting its color from any parent element. Note that unless otherwise defined in your em selector, other declarations will still be inherited. Thus, if you want just your emphasized text to be twice the font-size it currently is, declare that specific font-size in your em rule. If you defined this rule in the p rule, *all* the text would grow to twice the size.

Inheriting the Body

It is strongly recommended that all serious CSS designs begin with a `<body>` element declaration in the main style sheet. The `<body>` element is more than just a requirement of a well-formatted (X)HTML page, it is also the parent of every visible element in your template (i.e., not those within the `<head>`, which concern meta information and other items not displayed by the browser), and every element can inherit from it.

```
<body>
  <h1>Absolutely everything else!</h1>
  <p>Yep, every visible element is contained within the body.</p>
  <p>And so on.</p>
</body>
```

Therefore it makes sense to define all default CSS using body as the first selector in the first style sheet. Later in the book, the body selector will be used to define key elements such as a margin for the page, the background color or tiled image, the default font and font color, and so on, as in this example:

```
/* Define all main values for the web site */
  body {
    margin:10px;
    font-family:Helvetica,Arial,sans-serif;
    background:#CCC;
    color:#000;
    }
```

As a result of these declarations, every other rule in the CSS will inherit the values unless specified otherwise. So all headers, paragraphs, lists, and other elements will be rendered with black text (color: #000) using the first available font from the suggested options on the end user's machine (font-family: Helvetica, Arial, sans-serif;) unless the selector for each child element specifies otherwise, or that child element is housed inside a more immediate parent (such as a column or container) that contradicts the inherited values from body.

Note that some style properties are not inherited from the parent element—the background property being the main example. The child element does not actually inherit the light gray background (background: #CCC;), but rather the parent element's background appears by default. In other words, the child element can be thought of as having the inherited font color, but it should not be assumed that it has the same background color.

Note It is worth remembering that all elements have a transparent background unless you specify otherwise.

A Word of Warning

Much like the cascade through multiple style sheets, inheritance can cause severe headaches if you do not keep track of what is going on. Often, CSS is as much about what you don't do as what you do. The following is a classic example of how inheritance can cause confusion.

Let's say you are using nested lists (that's at least one list within another list). The markup might be something like this three-level list:

```
<ul>
<li>Top level one</li>
<li>Top level two
 <ul>
 <li>Second level one</li>
 <li>Second level two
  <ul>
  <li>Third level one</li>
  <li>Third level two</li>
  </ul>
 </li>
 <li>Second level three</li>
 </ul>
</li>
<li>Top level three</li>
</ul>
```

You might then apply some basic CSS to that list to control font-size, as follows:

```
/* Font size for list elements */
  li {
    font-size:2em;
    }
```

Your first thought might be that this selector would ensure that all text will be 2em in size, but this is not the case. Each nested list will inherit the font-size value from the one above, and as the em is a relative measurement (more on that later in the "Ems" section), this will result in the text size being doubled with every nested list. So, a list item within another list will inherit the font-size rule and become twice as big as its parent.

In Chapter 6, you will learn all about lists and how to apply CSS correctly to avoid such a hazard, but this is a fine example of how inheritance can cause problems. The flip side of this is that there will be many times where such powerful inheritance can also be used to do the work of several targeted selectors, and it's all about knowing when it's happening and when it needs to be tamed.

■Caution "Where on earth did that underline come from?" Inheritance can confuse anyone working across multiple style sheets. Be very careful not to duplicate an existing selector unwittingly. If in doubt, search your style sheets and ensure there won't be a conflict. It pays to develop your own system of control here, perhaps noting all ID/class names you've used in a separate text file or notepad.

Contextual Selectors

Now there's a horribly scary term. In the previous section, a heading containing emphasized text was used to illustrate basic inheritance. Remember that the em selector was added to ensure the <em> element in the (X)HTML would be rendered with red text. Here's the CSS again:

```
/* Top-level heading */
  h1 {
    color:#333;
    }
/* Make emphasized text shine brightly */
  em {
    color:#F00;
    }
```

The downside of this is that all emphasized text across the whole web site would also become red, regardless of its parent element. Assuming the rule is only meant to target the <em> element when a child of <h1> headings, a simple adjustment can be made to put the emphasized text into context:

```
/* Make emphasized text shine brightly ONLY when it's the child of an h1 heading */
  h1 em {
    color:#F00;
    }
```

Contextual selectors consist of two or more simple selectors separated by whitespace. Here the contextual selector is constructed to show that the rule will only have an effect when the last selector (em) is a direct descendent (be it a child, grandchild, great grandchild, or so on) of the first selector (h1). If the browser does not find an exact match (i.e., it only finds <em> elements outside of <h1> elements), it will not apply the styles dictated by the contextual selector to them.

Here's similar markup to the original example, but with a paragraph acting as the parent to a second <em> element:

```
<h1>This is the greatest heading <em>in the world</em></h1>
<p>I'm sorry but it simply is <em>not</em>, you fool.</p>
```

The `<em>` element owned by the `<h1>` element will be red, whereas the one owned by the paragraph will not—it will inherit the default font color. To control the style of any emphasized text that is out of context, simply define a new selector for em with the values you desire, or maybe create a new contextual selector with p as the parent to your em.

In Chapter 6, contextual selectors will be used to gain tight control of nested elements such as hierarchical lists and other problematic situations.

CSS Measurements

CSS rules can be declared to control text height, text spacing, border widths, spacing between any element and its neighbor—pretty much any necessary measurement you need.

One of the strengths of a CSS-based design is its ability to remain flexible. As a designer, you want your finely crafted masterpieces to look the same for every end user, and the desire to pin elements down with exact measurements can be very tempting. On the flip side, most web designers are aware of the inherent flexibility of the Web as a viewing platform, and are keen to explore methods of customization and ensure their creations are viewed in the best context for the end user.

Two options of measurement are available—**absolute** and **relative**. The former seeks to freeze a design, ensuring widths, heights, and so on are not adjusted no matter how the site is viewed. The latter enables web pages to be manipulated by the user or viewing device. So long as web designers apply a measure of control in their style sheets, relative measurements can actually do a much better job of tightening the design while also making it bulletproof in display terms.

Absolute Measurements

Absolute values have a fixed, specific measurement. They let you be exact in your measurements and control the display of your web pages. Absolute values are inches (in), centimeters (cm), millimeters (mm), points (pt), and picas (pc) as Table 2-1 describes.

Table 2-1. *Absolute CSS Measurements*

Unit	Description
in	Absolute measurement in inches.
cm	Absolute measurement in centimeters.
mm	Absolute measurement in millimeters.
pt	Absolute measurement in points. A point is $1/72$ of an inch.
pc	Absolute measurement in picas. A pica is equivalent to 12 points, or ⅙ of an inch.

Absolute measurements will only give the desired results if the browser knows how many pixels are on the screen and how big the screen is. Often, this is not the case. Not all computers know how big the screen is, as not all screens tell the computer how big they are. In these cases, the browser must make a guess.

It is my pleasure to inform you that for almost all day-to-day CSS design, no absolute measurements are needed, and to keep things on course, we can skip straight to the much more interesting relative measurements.

Relative Measurements

Relative measurements have no fixed, specific value. Instead, they are calculated in comparison to an inherited value. Relative values are percentage (%), x-height (ex), ems (em), and pixels (px), as Table 2-2 describes.

Table 2-2. *Relative CSS Measurements*

Unit	Description
%	Measurement as a percentage relative to another value
ex	Measurement relative to a font's x-height, determined by the height of the font's lowercase letter x
em	Relative measurement for the height of a font in em spaces
px	Relative measurement in screen pixels

Why Use Only Relative Measurements?

Your web sites will be viewed primarily on computer screens, but at what screen resolution and on which browser? Some end users will view your site on PDAs, cell phones, projectors, or even televisions.

Each end device has its own quirks and unique methods of display. Consider also that many users manually configure their devices to suit their own preferences (think screen resolutions), so it's imperative that your design is not compromised in such situations.

A very important issue in web design is accessibility—ensuring all visitors can access all of your content. Relative measurements are proven to provide the best solution for text resizing and the knock-on effect this has on other page elements, and can therefore be considered best practice.

While relative values give the designer less absolute control, they do create a better experience for the end user. Let's look at the primary relative measurements one by one, and consider how they apply to text size.

Pixels

Pixel measurements give designers the most control over their layouts. By far the most consistent unit of measurement, pixels are most commonly used for declaring the margin, padding, borders, height, and width of custom elements such as containers, columns, and buttons, and can be successfully combined with other relative measurements for all kinds of layout requirements.

Pixels are not, however, the best option for sizing text—text sized with pixels will ignore user preferences, so if a low-vision user has set his or her browser to always show text at 20 pixels, this will often be overridden by your pixel-based declarations.

Pixel-sized text offers consistency across most end devices. However your pages are viewed, and at whatever resolution, 11px text should always scale appropriately with text set at other pixel sizes. Thus in an ideal world, we could all use pixels without worry, safe in the knowledge that our designs will retain their integrity on any platform and in any situation. Sadly, it isn't an ideal world, as there is a rather popular browser called Internet Explorer to consider.

Consider IE/Win Users

It is very important to consider the fact that an IE/Win user cannot use the browser's text resizing tools to resize pixel-sized text. An option is to use a style switcher, which gives users an on-page option of adjusting viewing preferences. It is preferable to do this with PHP or similar languages. JavaScript-based style switcher scripts are available and make switching seem seamless, but it is always important to consider users who have JavaScript switched off. A brilliant example can be found in Chris Clark's "Build a PHP Switcher" article at the super-useful A List Apart web site (www.alistapart.com/articles/phpswitch). Another important factor with style switchers is that many users might miss the option, or fail to understand the point of it.

To ensure all end users can enforce their own viewing preferences upon your design, it is strongly suggested that you declare font size using the em measurement (examples of which follow throughout the "Ems" section).

Percentage

Providing incredible flexibility and often the solution to adventurous layouts is the percentage measurement. Percentage values are always relative to another value, such as a width or height declared in the parent element. In other words, a percentage can only be declared in relation to a defined size earlier in that rule, within a parent element, or based on the width of the browser window.

Percentage is particularly powerful for layout, and is an integral ingredient of liquid designs where pages and their elements stretch to fit the browser window. You can learn more about that aspect of percentage in Part 2 of this book.

Caution must be applied with percentage values, where inheritance can cause chaos. While pixels and ems retain a modicum of control, the results of percentage values can end up somewhat different than what you might expect when calculated by the browser, and as a result layouts can be chewed and elements misplaced or shunted underneath each other.

Example

Here the percentage value is given for line-height, used to control the distance between the lines of text, and relates directly to the font-size value within the rule.

```
/* Define default paragraph values */
  p {
    font-size:10px;
    line-height:120%;
    }
```

In this case, line-height will be applied to the text as a pixel value that is 120% of 10px, which gives a line height of 12px.

Ems

It is a great shame that the humble em is the most misunderstood unit of relative measurement in CSS, as it is by far the most flexible, and is ideally suited to a design principle where the end user's viewing device and text preferences are unpredictable.

The origin of the word itself is useful, for it stems from the idea of an em roughly equaling the size of an uppercase letter *M*, hence it is pronounced "emm." However, in reality an em is actually larger than that. The em is a traditional typographic measurement, though because some fonts don't even have an *M* in them, the term has come to mean the height of the given font.

The thing about ems is that they make your style sheets scalable. Unlike the traditional, typographic em, the CSS measurement can be employed to define the lengths (and by "length" I mean both horizontal and vertical) of almost any CSS property. This makes it especially powerful when applied to fonts and their containing elements. Resize the text with the browser tools, and the containing element (be it a column, header, or more immediate container) can scale with it. Reduce that text, and the scaling works the other way too. Remember that IE/Win will not allow users to resize text that has been sized in pixels.

So How Do Ems Scale?

Well, an em is a measurement equal to the size of the type. Therefore, if within a given element the font-size is set to 11 pixels, one em is equal to 11 pixels. If the font-size in another element is 30 pixels, one em in that element is equal to 30 pixels, and so on. Thus 1em can have many different values within one style sheet. The key to successful em usage is an understanding of a given em's relative status.

Richard Rutter (www.clagnut.com) explains this methodology with a similar example to the following. Two rules for basic containers are identical except for the font-size, which is 11px and 30px,respectively. Both rules have a width and height of 1em. A black border is added to illustrate the extent of each container.

```
/* First container for the em example */
  #firstbox {
    margin:10px;
    font-size:11px;
    width:1em;
    height:1em;
    border:1px solid black;
    }
/* Second container for the em example */
  #secondbox {
    margin:10px;
    font-size:30px;
    width:1em;
    height:1em;
    border:1px solid black;
    }
```

On the resulting web page, the two boxes will look as shown in Figure 2-1.

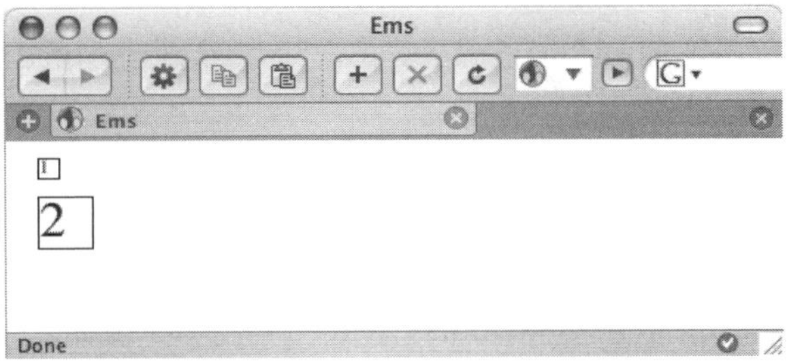

Figure 2-1. *The result of the two containers viewed in the browser*

Although both boxes have a height and width of 1em, the two different font sizes make one box larger than the other. The first box is 11px × 11px, and 1em × 1em. The second box is 30px × 30px but is still 1em × 1em.

Thus each resulting em measurement is relative to whatever contains it. Further rules within #firstbox would be free to define measurements based on the em, knowing that it is equal to 11px. For example, paragraphs that are children of #firstbox could be defined with a value of 0.8em, making the paragraph text ⅘ the size of that container's default text.

Work outside of #firstbox and em is reset to its default, unless you are working within #secondbox, where em has been defined as 30px.

■**Tip** 1em displays at the default size for a font character as it appears within an (X)HTML element where the user agent assigns the default display. Therefore, text styled with a font-size of 1em will display as if no size declarations were assigned.

Ems and the Body

For most designers, the default font size is often way too big. The usual font-size defined by the browser style sheet is 16px (which means 1em is of course equal to 16px). That's a very accessible size indeed, but most designers (and users) seem to prefer 11px.

You now know from the containers example in the previous section that the em measurement is relative to the containing element. Earlier in the chapter, we looked at how all page elements can inherit from the <body> element, as it contains all visual page elements. Therefore <body> is the ideal place to make your em declaration in order for all child elements in the tree to inherit that value.

Defining a font-size smaller than 1em for body text is a good starting point for em-based design. Let's say that you want your default text to be 11px. The following rule would ensure your text generally renders at that size:

```
/* Define all main values for the web site */
  body {
    font-family:Helvetica,Arial,sans-serif;
   font-size:0.8em;
    color:#000;
    }
```

So if no other measurements are added to the style sheet, all default text will be 0.8em or approximately 11px. However, this also means that in Mozilla-based browsers all headings (<h1> through <h6>), paragraphs, lists, and so on will also be t their default size (other browsers will stay with the defaults). Also, IE/Win will show form and table text at t the default size. Therefore, these elements need their font size to be declared in the corresponding rules.

```
/* Define all main values for the web site */
  body {
    font-family:Helvetica,Arial,sans-serif;
    font-size:0.8em;
    color:#000;
    }
/* Define paragraph text size */
  p {
    font-size:1.1em;
    }
/* Define headings font sizes */
  h1 {
    font-size:2em;
    }
  h2 {
    font-size:1.8em;
    }
  h3 {
    font-size:1.7em;
    }
...
/* Define form and table font-size */
  input, select, th, td {
    font-size:1.1em;
    }
```

Thus all appropriate page elements have font-size defined based upon the font-size declaration in body. All page text is now scalable on any browser and will scale proportionately at any setting.

BASING EM SIZES ON AN INITIAL PERCENTAGE DECLARATION

Richard Rutter suggests another method for resizing based on an initial `font-size` using percentage in his article "How to Size Text Using Ems" (`www.clagnut.com/blog/348/`), whereby all em values can be easily related to a specific pixel size.

Richard first declares `font-size: 62.5%` in the body selector (possible because although no previous measurements are defined in the style sheet, the default value of the browser style sheet is cascading into it), which effectively takes the default `font-size` down from 16px to 10px. It is then simple to think in terms of pixels, but declare sizes in ems. Based on this setting, Richard suggests some correlating values between em and pixel sizes:

- `{font-size:2em}`   `/* Displayed at 20px */`

- `{font-size:1.5em}`   `/* Displayed at 15px */`

- `{font-size:1.25em}`   `/* Displayed at 12.5px */`

- `{font-size:1em}`   `/* Displayed at 10px */`

This example is another great starting point for designers wishing to make better use of ems. It features some excellent methods for calculating sizes and further explores the relationships between parent and child selectors with regard to ems. Essential reading.

To Conclude...

In this chapter, you've encountered a number of core CSS principles, methods, and shortcuts. You probably won't be surprised to discover that there are many, many more, the majority of which will be covered throughout the rest of the book. For now, armed with what you have already learned, you will be prepared for the techniques to follow, many of which will build upon these core concepts. It's time to have some fun.

CHAPTER 3

■■■

CSS Building Blocks

In this chapter, the focus is chiefly on common CSS building blocks. For the most part, their uses should be fairly obvious, as the terms correlate well with the real world. Margin, padding, borders, widths, heights—all familiar terms for things that do what you are probably assuming they do.

One key aspect of CSS design is the use of divisions to provide greater flexibility and mark out regions of the page. As a number of building block methods rely on divisions for targeting their impact, it seems appropriate to delve into them right away.

Divisions (Divs)

Divisions—`<div>` elements, widely referred to as **divs**—are (X)HTML elements used to define areas of an (X)HTML file. A division can, if you choose, encompass everything else within the `<body>` of the page, be it additional elements, text, graphics—anything in fact, or more typically be used for distinct areas such as headers, footers, navigation bars, and so on.

Most often, the (X)HTML in your templates does not provide enough hooks upon which to hang your styles. For example, you know how to apply basic styling to a paragraph or header, but turn paragraphs or headers into boxes, and you'll find it impossible to enclose other (X)HTML elements inside the box without compromising your code and causing extreme complications.

This is where divisions (I'll refer to them mostly as *divs* from now on) are most useful—invaluable in fact. Using divs is not unlike magically inventing your own (X)HTML tags, whenever and wherever you need them.

Adding a Div

You create a division element within the (X)HTML by placing the following in the body:

```
<div>
  <p>This is our content area.</p>
</div>
```

The result is a hook to which CSS can be applied. In Chapter 2, you learned about using IDs and classes to add identifiers to a standard (X)HTML element. The same formula is used for divs by referencing the selector in the opening tag using id="*name*" or class="*name*". In this case, we've used an ID named container to define the division:

```
<div id="container">
 <p>This is our content area.</p>
</div>
```

Let's apply some simple CSS to the container ID:

```
/* Container holds all visible page elements */
  #container {
    padding: 20px;
    border: 1px solid #000;
    background: #CCC;
    }
```

With this CSS applied to our markup, the container will have a gray background with a black border, and any elements it contains will be padded 20px from that border, as you can see in Figure 3-1.

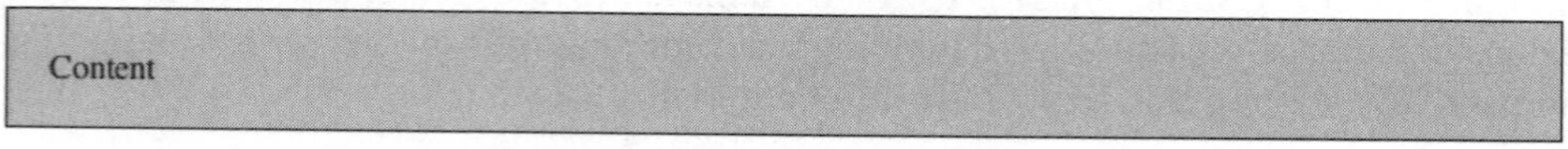

Content

Figure 3-1. *Our container div as viewed in the browser*

■Note We'll look at padding and borders in more detail in their own sections later in the chapter.

Adding Child Divs

The container div can act as parent to child divs. Here, an ID holds a reusable class called box:

```
<div id="container">
 <p>This is our content area.</p>
  <div class="box">
   <p>I'm in a box!</p>
  </div>
  <div class="box">
   <p>I'm also in a box!</p>
  </div>
</div>
```

The CSS rules for the box class are almost the same as that for the parent container, except for the background color, which will appear by default. Note that, as no set width is defined for the box, it will stretch to fit whatever contains it, be that another div or the browser window:

```
/* Define styling of our reusable box */
.box {
margin: 10px;
padding: 20px;
border: 1px solid #000;
}
```

Viewed in the browser, the containing div now holds the two boxes and their content, as Figure 3-2 demonstrates.

Figure 3-2. *Our container div now contains two equal boxes.*

Our three divisions are now clear in the design. Remember that each div can contain any elements, be they headings, paragraphs, images, more divs—the possibilities are endless.

■**Note** Like paragraphs, headings, and many other elements, divs are known as **block elements**, and unless you specify otherwise, they will always begin on a new line. Block and inline elements are revisited in more detail in Chapter 6.

Divs and Contextual Selectors

In Chapter 2, you discovered contextual selectors, which consist of two or more selectors separated by whitespace. These really come into their own when used to take control of the divisions you create.

Examples

In the previous example, each div has within it a paragraph. Let's say you want all paragraphs inside the box class to be rendered in red, but all other paragraphs must remain the default black.

There are two ways to target those particular paragraphs, the first of which will be familiar from Chapter 2. Now that divs have been introduced, however, it is no longer the best way.

The Bad Way

Knowing what you already know, it's tempting to create a new class for turning the paragraphs red, as follows:

```
/* Make text red */
 .highlight {
  color: #F00;
  }
```

Then in the (X)HTML, the identifiers for our highlight class would need to be added like so:

```
<div id="container">
 <p>This is our content area.</p>
  <div class="box">
   <p class="highlight">I'm in a box!</p>
  </div>
  <div class="box">
   <p class="highlight">I'm also in a box!</p>
  </div>
</div>
```

The paragraphs will certainly be red now, but it's taken extra markup for each opening paragraph tag to accomplish the effect. This extra markup would be required for every paragraph within the div, which is only serving to bloat the markup.

The Good Way

This time, the identifiers are not required. In fact, no changes need be made to the (X)HTML at all. Everything can be controlled within the style sheet. Time to put the paragraphs into context with the following combination:

```
/* Make text red only for paragraphs within the box class */
#container .box p {
  color: #F00;
  }
```

Using this approach, no extra markup is required. Everything needed to take complete control of the paragraphs is already in place. The contextual selector is constructed to show that the rule will only have an effect when the last selector (p) is a direct descendent (the child) of the first selector (.box). This is a strong example of how major changes to whole sections can be achieved simply by working with what you already have.

Another contextual selector could then be used to control paragraphs in the parent element (the container div).

```
/* Make text gray only for paragraphs within the container */
#container p {
  color: #333;
  }
```

Now paragraphs inside the container will be rendered dark gray, unless contained by .box, in which case they will be red.

Taking the Context Even Further

Let's now assume that you are using the box class all over the site. Sometimes the box classes are children of the container div, and sometimes they have a different parent. What if you only want the paragraph text to appear bold when the box class is inside the container? This can be achieved without extra markup also. Note that, outside of the container div, a new box div has been added, which is not parented by anything:

```
<div id="container">
 Content
  <div class="box">
   <p>I'm in a box!</p>
  </div>
  <div class="box">
   <p>I'm also in a box!</p>
  </div>
</div>
<div class="box">
 <p>I'm also in a box!</p>
</div>
```

As for the amazing CSS, the contextual selector consists of three selectors, putting the paragraphs into a more specific context.

```
/* Make text bold only for paragraphs within the box class AND within the ➥
container */
#container .box p {
  font-weight:bold;
  }
```

This contextual selector is very powerful. The first thing to note is that the markup is very clean. Yes, division elements exist to separate the content, but no identifiers are required for any base elements. The effect of the contextual selector is threefold:

- Only paragraphs (p) that are children of the box class *and* the container ID are affected.

- Paragraphs within the container but *not* within the box class are unaffected.

- Paragraphs within boxes *outside* of the container are unaffected.

Our example looks like Figure 3-3 when opened in a web browser.

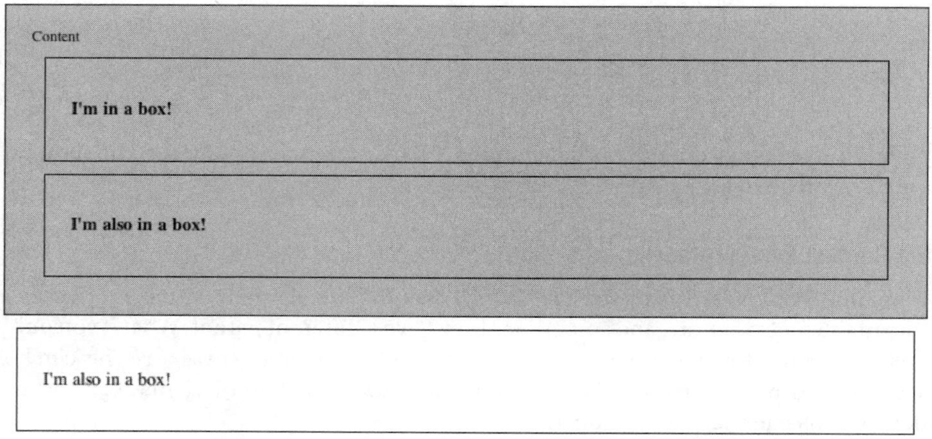

Figure 3-3. *Only paragraphs inside the box class* and *the container appear with bold text.*

Figure 3-3 shows the results in the browser window. This example has demonstrated what can be achieved based on very minimal markup. It should always be your intention to make the base (X)HTML elements work as hard as possible for you, without the need to throw lots of extraneous markup into the mix. Contextual selectors and divs add an incredible amount of flexibility to your designs, and they should be embraced wherever possible. Keep an eye open for opportunities to use them, as very often they'll already be there waiting to be harnessed.

Dimensions: Width and Height

Before moving on, it is worth mentioning two very important properties that can be declared for any element—width and height.

It might seem a little patronizing to mention them, as their uses must seem obvious. However, these two properties have already appeared in several examples, and will continue to be used throughout the book.

Both properties are essential for setting specific heights and widths of elements. Consider that an element will expand widthwise to fit its container and heightwise to encompass its content—you will start to realize before long that, in some situations, a certain amount of control is missing. By applying width and/or height rules, you can regain control.

Values can be given as a length, percentage, or auto. Note that all of these values can be influenced adversely by other rules within the style sheet, and also by the (X)HTML elements they might contain. For example, the resulting display can be affected by a number of knock-on values from margin, padding, border, or child elements.

■**Note** Most modern browsers support the declaration of minimum (min-width) and maximum (max-width) width and height values also, something you'll soon realize the need for when working with unpredictable content. We'll look at these in more detail later in Part 2 of this book, when dealing with CSS layouts.

Margin

The margin property does exactly what it says on the tin. It is used to declare the margin between an (X)HTML element and those elements outside of it. The margin can be set for the top, left, right, and bottom of the given element. Note that margin values are not inherited from parent elements. If they were, there would be chaos.

Margin Declarations

There are three choices of values for the margin property, which are length, percentage, or auto. Note that if a value is 0, you do not need to add px.

Consider the following CSS for a container div. Note that it has a fixed width of 300px and no margin properties.

```
/* Basic container */
#container {
    width:300px;
    border: 1px solid #000;
    padding: 20px;
    background: #CCC;
    }
```

Figure 3-4 shows this container in relation to the browser window. It has no declared margin properties, and so it sits to the left of the page, spaced away from the edges only by the margin and padding values declared in the <body> element.

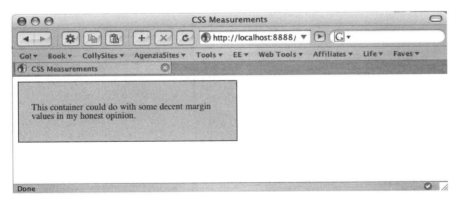

Figure 3-4. *The basic container sits in the natural flow of the document, sitting immediately left, spaced only by the <body> element's margin and padding declarations.*

By applying margin properties to each side of the container, the display can be significantly altered:

```
/* Basic container */
 #container {
    width:300px;
    margin-top: 20px;
    margin-left: auto;
    margin-right: auto;
    margin-bottom: 1em;
    border: 1px solid #000;
    padding: 20px;
    background: #CCC;
    }
```

In Figure 3-5, you can see that the container's relationship with the browser window now is completely different.

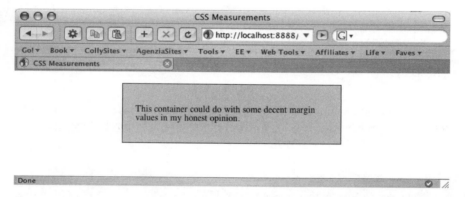

Figure 3-5. *With margins applied to each side of the container, the display is altered considerably.*

The container is now 20 pixels from the top edge of the <body> element, and is centered due to its set width combined with left and right margins set to auto (see the upcoming "Centering with margin:auto" section).

Margin Shortcuts

A couple of easy shortcuts are available to reduce up to four margin:*value* declarations into one.

```
/* Basic container */
 #container {
  margin: 20px auto 1em auto;
  }
```

The order of the values is very important here. The order is top (20px), right (auto), bottom (1em), and left (auto). It helps to get used to the order by thinking of it like a compass—north, east, south, and west, the first value always being north, or like a clock—12 o'clock, 3 o'clock, 6 o'clock, and 9 o'clock, the first value being 12 o'clock.

If all four values are the same, the declaration can be shortened even further:

```
/* Basic container */
#container {
  margin: 20px;
  }
```

These shortcuts will also work for padding and some other properties, which you'll find out more about later.

Centering with margin: auto

The best way to center an element with CSS is to use the auto value for left and right margins. For modern browsers, all this requires is a set width rule (as without it the box would naturally stretch to fit its container—in this case the browser window) and the left and right margins given the auto value. Building upon the earlier example, we have the following rule:

```
/* Container for centering all our content */
#container {
  width: 400px;
  margin: 10px auto 10px auto;
  padding: 20px;
  border: 1px solid #000;
  background: #CCC;
  }
```

Most browsers are happy with this, although IE5/Win fails miserably, usually aligning the element to the left. At the time of writing, most IE users are using IE6, and IE7 is on the way, but the percentage of IE5 users is significant enough to warrant consideration.

There is a way of making it work for IE5/Win, and it's quite simple. The trick is to make use of the text-align property in the container's parent element (in this case that is the <body>) to center the container. The downside is that all child elements within <body> will now correctly inherit that value and center all their content, which isn't good. Therefore text-align: left is applied to all main division elements to counter the centering:

```
/* Define default values for the whole site */
body {
  text-align: center;
  }
/* Container for centering all our content */
#container {
  width: 400px;
  margin: 10px auto 10px auto;
  padding: 20px; border: 1px solid #000;
  background: #CCC;
  text-align: left;
  }
```

This approach ensures that the container is centered horizontally in the browser window whatever browser is used, and acts as the perfect basis for any centered design (see Figure 3-6).

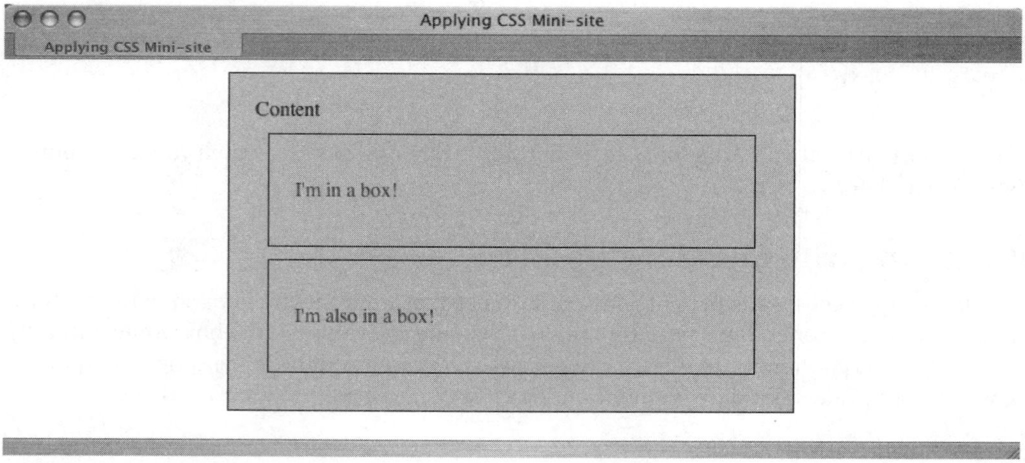

Figure 3-6. *The container is centered in the browser window.*

Padding

Padding is the distance between the edges (borders) of an (X)HTML element and the content within it, and can be applied to any element.

Padding Declarations

Both length and percentage values are available, although there is no auto value, and negative values cannot be declared for padding.

Let's take the container div again, and this time add custom padding to each side:

```
/* Basic container */
 #container {
    width:300px;
    margin-top: 20px;
    margin-left: auto;
    margin-right: auto;
    margin-bottom: 1em;
    border: 1px solid #000;
    padding-top: 20px;
    padding-left: 10%;
    padding-right: 1em;
    padding-bottom: 0;
    background: #CCC;
    }
```

Figure 3-7 shows how the paragraph within the container (highlighted by a thin border) is spaced away from each edge by the given padding value.

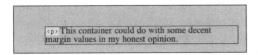

Figure 3-7. *The padding applied to each side of the shaded container informs the final position of child elements, such as this paragraph.*

Percentage in this case refers directly to the parent element's width. So if `padding-left: 10%` is declared, that equates to 10% of the parent element's given width. Using ems would also allow the padding to scale proportionately with the element. Such values come in very handy for liquid layouts, which will be discussed in Part 2 of this book.

Padding Shortcuts

The same shortcuts used for margin values are also available for padding.

```
/* Basic container */
 #container {
  padding: 20px 1em 0 10%;
  }
```

As with the `margin` property, order is top (20px), right (1em), bottom (0), and left (10px). Likewise, if all four values are the same, the padding declaration can also be shortened like so:

```
/* Basic container */
 #container {
  padding: 20px;
  }
```

Margin, Padding, and the Body

Back to good old browser default style sheets again. In order to ensure your page content sits exactly as you desire on all browsers and doesn't inherit browser defaults, it is important to consider resetting the page `margin` and `padding` in the `body` selector.

Netscape and IE place a default `margin` of 8px around the `<body>` element. The Opera browser confuses things further by applying a default `padding` of 8px. Therefore, until all browsers agree and can settle on either `margin` or `padding` to provide this default spacing, it is recommended that `margin` and `padding` be given the values you desire in the `body` selector:

```
/* Define default values for the whole site */
 body {
  margin: 0;
  padding: 0;
  }
```

Obviously values of 0 will remove the default spacing entirely, so it may be that you prefer to set the `margin` to 10px, 20px, or whatever you need.

Other methods are available that will reset all margins and padding to a defined value that is inherited throughout unless you declare otherwise. Such methods should be used with caution however, as all headings, paragraphs, lists, and so on will also inherit the value, and if the value is 0, you might end up in trouble, with all of your page elements bunched together. This would then require `margin` and/or `padding` values to be declared for all headings, paragraphs, and other elements that typically have sensible default spacing values.

Border

Borders are a simple concept with a million possibilities. Any element can have a border placed around it, and borders can be placed on all sides, or just the sides you desire. The `border` property is particularly flexible as each border can be a specific width, color, or style. As a result of the numerous values that can be applied, a greater number of shorthand declarations are available.

Border Properties

The default values are a border with a medium thickness, inheriting the text color of the parent element. Only by applying further values can this default state be influenced. The full list of border properties is

```
border-style
border-width
border-top-width
border-right-width
border-bottom-width
border-left-width
border-color
border
border-top
border-right
border-bottom
border-left
```

Controlling borders is relatively easy, but it is worth looking at each property in more detail.

border-style

The `border-style` property is used to give any element a border. The browser must first understand the style of border to be drawn before moving on to further border declarations. In other words, the style keyword is declared before the color of the border, for instance.

The property applies a defined style to one, several, or all borders. Keywords for `border-style` are `none`, `dotted`, `dashed`, `solid`, `double`, `groove`, `ridge`, `inset`, and `outset`.

■Note Some elements have default borders. The `fieldset` element (used to define a series of related form inputs) has a medium-thickness border by default. Also watch out for images used for hyperlinks, where the image will have a border matching the declared link text color for the containing element. The borders for both can be styled or removed using `border-style`. In the case of all other elements, you define your border styles from scratch.

The following CSS styles a container with a medium-thickness dashed border all around the division:

```
/* Container for centering all our content */
 #container {
    width: 400px;
    margin: 10px auto 10px auto;
    padding: 20px;
    border-style: dashed;
    }
```

When our web page is opened in a browser, the border produced is as shown in Figure 3-8.

Content

Figure 3-8. *Border applied using border-style: dashed*

Taking this further, a unique style for each side can be defined using shorthand for the border-style property; as with margin and padding, the values are ordered top, right, bottom, and left:

```
/* Container for centering all our content */
 #container {
   width: 400px;
   margin: 10px auto 10px auto;
   padding: 20px;
   border-style: dashed dotted solid ridge;
   }
```

This gives us the varied borders shown in Figure 3-9. The top border is a dashed line, the right border dotted, the bottom border a solid line, and the left border creates the illusion of a beveled ridge.

Content

Figure 3-9. *Four different borders (dashed, dotted, solid, ridge) from one declaration*

border-width

More specifically, in this section we will look at border-width, border-top-width, border-right-width, border-bottom-width, and border-left-width. These properties allow you to define the width of the element's edges one by one or all at once. Note that for a border-width value to be applied, a border-style must first be declared.

Several keyword values are available here, as well as relative lengths. The keywords are thin, medium, and thick, although caution is required as different browsers render these borders in various ways. Exactly how many pixels each browser will use does vary. Note that if you define a border-style but not a border-width, the default value is medium.

In the following example, the border-style values declared previously are combined with specific border-width keywords and relative values:

```
/* Container for centering all our content */
 #container {
  width: 400px;
  margin: 10px auto 10px auto;
  padding: 20px;
  border-style: dashed dotted solid ridge;
  border-top-width: thin;
  border-right-width: 20px;
  border-bottom-width: medium;
  border-left-width: thick;
  }
```

The result of this can be seen in Figure 3-10, where the top dashed line is thinnest, the right border is a 20-pixel dotted line, the bottom border is a medium-sized solid line, and the right border is a thick ridge.

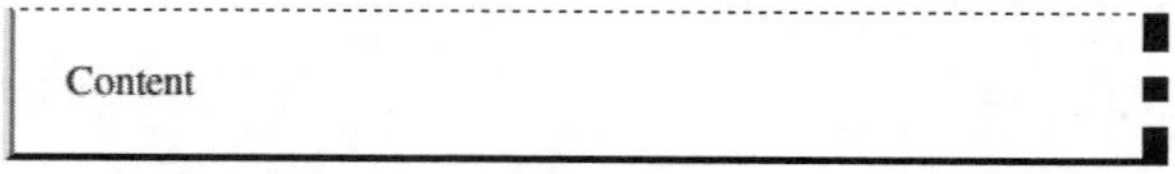

Figure 3-10. *Width values applied to style values (dashed thin, dotted thick, solid medium, ridge thick)*

border-color

Remember that, unless you declare the color for the border, it will inherit color from the element or parent element. As there is only one property for color (border-color), multiple colors must be declared using shorthand:

```
/* Container for centering all our content */
 #container {
  width: 400px;
  margin: 10px auto 10px auto;
  padding: 20px;
  border-style: dashed dotted solid ridge;
  border-top-width: thin;
  border-right-width: 20px;
  border-bottom-width: medium;
  border-left-width: thick;
  border-color: #000 #999 #333 #CCC;
  }
```

which gives us borders from black (top) to lightest gray (left) as shown in Figure 3-11.

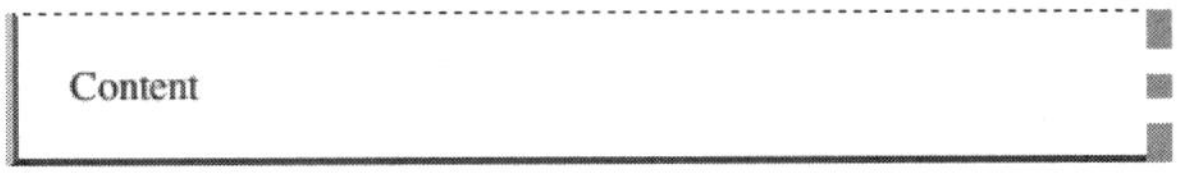

Figure 3-11. *Defining specific colors for each border*

border

Using border and the border-top, border-right, border-bottom, and border-left properties allows you to further shorten the given border-style and border-width and border-color values into one property. Let's look at an example of this shorthand.

Using the CSS from the previous example, again the same border-color, border-style, and border-width values are assigned:

```
/* Container for centering all our content */
#container {
  width: 400px;
  margin: 10px auto 10px auto;
  padding: 20px;
  border-top: #000 thin dashed;
  border-right: #999 20px dotted;
  border-bottom: #333 medium solid;
  border-left: #CCC thick ridge;
}
```

which gives us the same results, but with just four properties in the rule. If all values were to be the same, the properties can be further combined into one using border:

```
/* Container for centering all our content */
#container {
  width: 400px;
  margin: 10px auto 10px auto;
  padding: 20px;
  border: #000 thin dashed;
}
```

which gives us the version shown in Figure 3-12.

Figure 3-12. *All four borders declared in one property using border*

Bordering on the Obvious

It pays to spend some time exploring the infinite possibilities of border styles based on the preceding examples. Try applying very thick borders (say 30px or larger) to see how the corners of the division become beveled like a picture frame.

Always, always be aware of how your borders are rendered across different browsers. Remember that not all border properties are available for every browser, and that some border-style values produce very different results in IE compared with Safari, for example.

BORDERS FOR WIRE FRAMING

Applying simple borders to your divisions and other key elements is a brilliant way of creating a **wire frame**. Wire framing a design with a thin solid or dashed line around your divs can help you understand how one element relates to another, and also identify problems with alignment and juxtaposition.

You can apply a simple dashed line to all divs, for example, using a base selector for the <div> tag:

```
/* Place a thin gray border around all divisions */
  div {
    border: 1px dashed #CCC;
    }
```

This rule would be placed immediately after the body selector in the style sheet, and would ensure all divs you create inherit a thin gray border, unless you specify otherwise in that element's rule. To apply this rule to further base elements, simply group the selectors together:

```
/* Place a thin gray border around the following elements */
  div, h1, h2, h3, h4, ul {
    border: 1px dashed #CCC;
    }
```

When you are satisfied that your design is hanging together correctly, just remove the relevant selectors or the entire rule.

To Conclude...

In this chapter, yet more core CSS knowledge has been thrown at you, much of which forms the bulk of all the CSS development you'll do from now on. Grasping this basic knowledge of layout approaches will stand you in good stead for what is to follow. If you are not sure you've understood everything in the first three chapters, fear not. So long as you don't tear them out, they'll remain in place as a dip-in guide should you need to refresh your memory.

If in doubt, just keep experimenting. Your experiments may well produce unexpected results at this stage, but that's the nature of CSS. Weird things might appear to be happening, but nine times out of ten the rules are being applied correctly. The trick is to understand the reason for a particular unexpected result, and learn to use it to your advantage.

Text

Constantly overlooked when it comes to style, yet arguably the most important element of any page—that's text. Specifically, your text is your content, and your content is the key to a successful web site.

Often, all the effort will go into some incredibly beautiful masthead, logo, or background, which makes the top of the web page look great (mostly), but scroll down to the actual content, and you might find a CSS famine. Taking control of your text requires more than just specifying one of the many available web fonts (I'm joking there) or setting font size. CSS provides the conscientious designer with a multitude of tools that can be applied to boring old text, bridging the gap between print and web design, and allowing for much flexibility.

In this chapter, we'll look at methods for creative use of text, and how traditional methods of typesetting can be utilized via simple CSS rules.

Why Is Text So Important?

Well, it tells people things, for a start. Without words, your images have an awful lot of work to do. Aside from this flippant point, it should go without saying (although I'll say it anyway) that your text should be legible, to the point, and within easy reach. Visitors are rarely coming to a web site to sit back and admire your graphics—it is most often information they are seeking. Graphic embellishments are often mere decoration.

The issue of accessibility is an important one here. Responsible web developers spend a lot of time ensuring that their designs are not compromised under user-defined viewing situations. For example, if a style sheet is not available, or images are turned off, the image-based buttons in the navigation bar will need replacement text to assist navigation. Equally important is replacement text for general images, especially images that convey a particular message or act as a link to another page, and there are many circumstances where background colors can conflict with text of the same color when images are absent. We'll look at these issues in more detail later in the book in Chapter 14.

Issues such as these need consideration at every stage of the design process. Essentially, your web site should make just as much sense with or without all images, and the hierarchy of your content should remain apparent in any situation.

Convey the Mood with the Right Font

The right font for the right job communicates with the user instantly. Your text is the first ingredient to appear as the page is downloaded, and it can instantly tell the user whether the web site is serious or friendly, modern or traditional, formal or casual. Do you want the web site to give the impression of a newspaper or journal, newsletter or fact sheet? If you do not want to convey such an authoritative standpoint, then maybe something humorous or light-hearted is needed? Choosing the right font or combination of fonts is key to creating the right impression from the outset.

Later in this chapter you'll review the most common typefaces available to web designers, and look at several that can be added to this list with a sprinkling of caution. Each can suggest the tone of the web site if used carefully.

ClearType Font Smoothing

Most seasoned web designers will tell you that text renders better on Mac browsers than on their PC equivalents, because the text is **anti-aliased** (meaning jagged edges are softened by the addition of intermediately colored pixels around the characters) as shown in Figure 4-1. It is certainly fair to say that those who build mostly with Mac browsers are often disappointed when they review their work over on the office PC.

Figure 4-1. *The letter on the left is aliased, whereas the one on the right, which is anti-aliased, has softened edges with intermediately colored pixels.*

Often, however, what's actually happening is the font they specified in the CSS isn't available on the PC, and so the display defaults to the next available specified font, which can carry less clarity in some cases. However, it could also have something to do with that PC's basic settings.

The ClearType setting is a valuable asset for PC users, and is a preference local to a particular machine. In other words, it isn't something you the designer can dictate through your design. It is worth considering ClearType though, as although it makes your PC-based browsing more enjoyable, it can also give a false impression of how your PC audience will view your work.

Basically, ClearType enhances the horizontal resolution available for rendering text through software such as web browsers, resulting in a much clearer display of text on liquid crystal display (LCD) screens. The benefits of ClearType rendering are less obvious for users with CRT displays, but still worth experimenting with. The outcome is less-pixilated characters, bringing the browser display a little closer to the smooth perfection of printed text.

ClearType is regrettably turned off by default, and is only available on the Windows XP operating system or later. To enable ClearType font smoothing on your PC, right-click the desktop, choose Properties, then choose the Appearance tab and click the Effects button. In the dialog box that appears, there is a drop-down list that lets you choose between Standard and ClearType font smoothing, as you see in Figure 4-2.

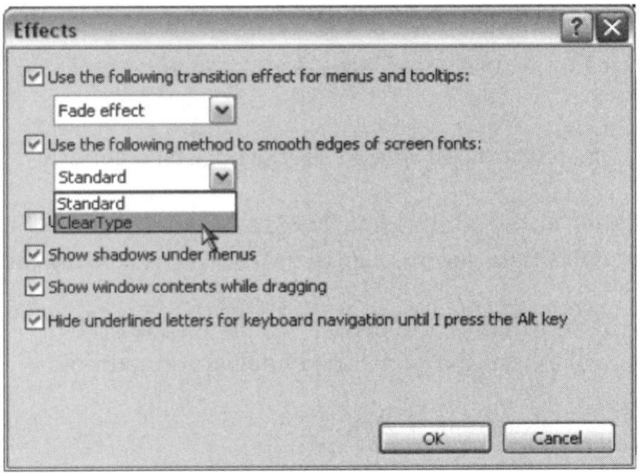

Figure 4-2. *Turn on ClearType font smoothing on your PC.*

Once you have turned on ClearType font smoothing, it is worth visiting the Microsoft help section (www.microsoft.com/typography/cleartype/tuner/Step1.aspx) to fine-tune your settings.

■**Caution** It is always important to consider users who either don't have font smoothing turned on or don't even know about it, which will be a significant number. Be sure to switch between Standard and ClearType displays when testing your design, especially prior to launch. It just might be that there is a better font for the job that can suit either preference, and other platforms, and doesn't compromise your design as a whole.

Primary Font Properties

Initially, it might seem that the manipulation of text on the Web is severely limited, but designers are constantly pushing the envelope with new and exciting methods of treating it. Later we'll delve into some more complex CSS properties, but for now it's important to understand the basic font syntax.

Specifying Fonts

First, you'll want to override some of the browser's default CSS properties, specifically the type-face and the font size. This is really straightforward, but there are a few interesting issues to be aware of. The following properties would typically be declared in the body selector, allowing all following elements to inherit the values unless you specify otherwise.

font-family

The font-family property is a list of font family names and/or generic family names for an element, specified in priority order. The browser will use the first available font on the user's machine. There are two types of font-family values:

- *Family name:* The name of a font family, like Times, Georgia, or Arial.

- *Generic family:* The name of a generic family, like serif, sans-serif, cursive, fantasy, or monospace.

Each value must be separated with a comma, and you should always suggest a generic-family name as the final option in the list.

If a family name contains whitespace, such as the family name Lucida Grande, it should be enclosed in quotes ("Lucida Grande"), although single quotes need to be used if embedding the style in HTML.

In the following example, defining the family names and generic family for the body element will ensure that all child elements will inherit the font-family declaration, unless specifically overridden.

```
/* Specify blanket rules for all elements */
 body {
  font-family:  "Lucida Grande", Arial, Sans-serif;
 }
```

Note also that Lucida Grande is specified first, and due to its whitespace character it is contained within quotes. Any machines with Lucida Grande will display text with that font, and if it isn't available, the display will default to Arial. If neither Lucida Grande nor Arial are available, the browser knows to use whatever appropriate sans serif font it can find next, as the generic family sans-serif is specified.

To overrule this blanket declaration, just specify a different font family for the appropriate element. For example, many designers like to display headings and block quotes with larger, more classic serif fonts.

font-size

In the "CSS Measurements" section of Chapter 2, you learned the various uses of the preferred measurements, namely pixels, ems, and percentage. In particular, we looked briefly at sizing text with ems, and the general consensus is that this is by far the best approach.

However, when it comes to discussing CSS and learning its ways stage by stage, I prefer to use the pixel measurement, as it is the most easily understood and ensures those who simply cannot get their head around the concept of ems can still sit at the table with everyone else. Just to recap, using ems to resize text ensures compatibility with IE6, which cannot resize text defined with pixels (jump back to Chapter 2 for a full overview of the woes and virtues of the various units of measurement).

In the following example, a new declaration is added to the body to define the size of the text in that and all child elements:

```
/* Specify blanket rules for all elements */
 body {
  font-family: "Lucida Grande", Arial, Sans-serif;
  font-size: 12px;
 }
```

By declaring font-size:12px in combination with the font-family declaration, you will ensure that all elements will be sized to 12px regardless of any inheritance (unlike ems, which can be influenced heavily through cascading rules), and will of course be rendered in the fonts you specified earlier.

There are exceptions to this blanket `font-size` declaration, however. Note that all headings (`<h1>`, `<h2>`, `<h3>`, and so on) will retain their default font sizes as declared by the browser style sheet unless you redefine them. In other words, just because you specify a size of `12px` in the body does not mean that level 2 headings will also be `12px`, as the browser style sheet has its own correctly formatted CSS rules such as `h1 {font-size:2em}`. In any case, why on earth would anyone want headings to be of equal size to their body text? This is another great example of the creators of CSS ensuring common sense is not compromised.

Font Shorthand

You probably won't be surprised to discover that there are some useful methods of shortening font declarations, pulling several into one simple statement. Later you'll combine four or five declarations into one, but for now, let's collate `font-family` and `font-size`.

As mentioned in previous chapters, the most important thing with shorthand is the order in which declarations are stated. In this case, `font-size` precedes `font-family`.

```
/* Specify blanket rules for all elements */
 body {
  font: 12px "Lucida Grande", Arial, Sans-serif;
 }
```

With this basic knowledge of the two most important CSS font properties in your arsenal, you can now begin to experiment with new and interesting font choices. To get you started, in the following section we'll plough into the vast array of available web fonts of which there is an exhaustive and unlimited choice. (I'm joking again.)

Available Fonts

Arguably the most annoying problem designers face with regard to the Web is the poor choice of fonts available. This boils down to the fact that the only fonts that can be specified are the ones certain to be installed on every computer used to view the web site. For example, just because you have *Sharktooth Italicized* installed on your computer doesn't mean everyone else has. Specify it in your style sheet, and the text on your web site, as viewed on your computer, will be rendered with it, but very few other users will have such an obscure font installed and available to their browser. The more obscure the font you specify, the more likely it is that you'll run into trouble.

Thus, it is important to think about web-safe fonts. These are few, but they can be used with confidence, as most of your visitors will have them installed.

Web-Safe Fonts

Always, always think about clarity and legibility here. Choose fonts that look good not only on your chosen platform (most look fabulous on a Mac), but also on others. How legible is your 11-pixel Times text over on a colleague's PC? What if that colleague has/hasn't enabled ClearType font smoothing? What if you need to render some information in italics? Does your chosen font cope well in such circumstances?

Certain fonts give very consistent results in a variety of situations. While some may consider the likes of Verdana and Georgia as safe bets, this is unfair. Legibility generally overrules whimsy, and certainly comes well before indulgence. Verdana, for example, is vilified in some circles as the equivalent of a Queen *Greatest Hits* album—absolutely everywhere, incredibly familiar, but not delivering anything new, i.e., boring. Take this raw source though, and give it a little remix, and who knows what could be drawn from it? My point is that the possibilities with CSS are endless, and the combination of background images, appropriate font properties, and careful spacing can give an old font new room in which to shine.

There are, in all facets of web design, rules to be followed. Web standards exist for the common good, but most rules can be treated as guidelines for good practice. Remember that nobody is forcing you to do things their way, and the web is an open playing field. Use the font you want to use, and do not be swayed by ill-considered opinion. Just make sure your visitors can actually read it.

Let's look at the web-safe fonts available at the time of writing, illustrated in Figure 4-3, and consider why some might be more useful than others, and what kind of web sites they might suit.

Verdana
Georgia
Times New Roman
Times
Arial
Helvetica
Tahoma
Comic Sans MS
Trebuchet
Courier

Figure 4-3. *Standard web fonts*

Verdana

Verdana is super-legible, and copes with smaller font sizes very well indeed. It is devoid of extraneous curly bits (technically speaking this means it is a *sans serif* font—that is, without serifs), and I'll bet my laptop that 99.9% of web users will have it installed on their machine, especially as it comes bundled with Internet Explorer. Use Verdana for a government or blue chip business web site.

Georgia

Georgia *is* a serif typeface (so it does have curly bits). It is a web designer's favorite because unlike most serif fonts, Georgia has been designed especially for the screen. Its italics, which are unusually clear and legible on screen, are a major bonus. Use Georgia for a historical information site, such as a web site about World War II.

Times New Roman

If a font has Times in the name, you can assume it will give the impression of a newspaper typeface, although this is not always a good thing on screen. Another serif font, Times New Roman is intended for PC platforms, and is hinted especially for the screen. That said, many would argue that Georgia supersedes it if you want a particularly legible serif font for your web site.

Times

Times is the Mac equivalent to Times New Roman, but is not designed specifically for screen. However, Macs being Macs, it'll still render pretty well on that platform. Use Times New Roman or Times for a financial institution's web site.

Arial

Like Verdana, Arial is another sans serif font that lends a more modern feel to web sites. It is widely used, but doesn't work very well at lower font sizes, and there isn't much default space between the characters. Use Arial for a pretentious museum's web site.

Helvetica

The closest web font to Arial for the Mac, Helvetica is another sans serif font regarded as a superstar typeface in the real world, but faring not so well on screen. Use Helvetica for a new media company's web site.

Tahoma

With so little choice for web designers, you'd think there would at least be some variety on the menu, but sadly there isn't. Tahoma resides on any computer that has Microsoft Office installed on it, and is thus available to most of your visitors, but it bears an uncanny resemblance to Verdana, and is therefore used rarely. Use Tahoma for a business web site, or alternatively just use Verdana.

Comic Sans MS

You want variety? Well, this is pretty wild. I say wild, but really Comic Sans is a bit of a joke. It's rare that you'll come across a design that demands its text be rendered in this very informal typeface. It is unfortunate that any web sites using Comic Sans tend to have that "my first web site" feel about them, and it is best reserved for unfunny jokes or printable party invitations. Use it if you wish, but steer clear if you are looking to present even a tiny amount of professionalism. Use Comic Sans for your little sister's web site about ponies.

Trebuchet

A great screen font, designed originally at a smaller size than most fonts, which usually means a font that has less unique subtleties. That said, Trebuchet manages to convey a contemporary feel in a limited space, and is a stylish choice that ships with copies of Internet Explorer. Use Trebuchet for your personal portfolio.

Courier

Courier is a monospaced font, meaning every character is the same width as you would find on a traditional typewriter, so they line up vertically as well as horizontally. Courier New is the most common monospaced font but can appear faint when anti-aliased at smaller sizes. Alternatives are Lucida Console (Windows), American Typewriter (Mac), and Monaco (Mac). Use Courier or its alternatives to display code or simulate typewriter text.

Interesting Alternatives

It's time to act like the rebellious tutor who throws course books out of the window and encourages the group to "push the envelope." In truth though, many designers are simply pursuing unsung alternatives that can sensibly be added to the accepted list of available web fonts. The gamble here is lessened thanks to the ability to suggest backup fonts should the preferred one be unavailable. Learning CSS can be challenging enough without being forced to work within difficult confines, so I encourage you to flirt with some of the following fonts, be they classic or well established, or newcomers that have shown their true worth on screen.

We'll look at the merits of each of the fonts displayed in Figure 4-4, followed by suggested family names and generic names to ensure your design isn't compromised when that font is unavailable.

Lucida Grande
Lucida Sans Unicode
Futura
Helvetica Neue
Gill Sans
Palatino

Figure 4-4. *Suggested alternative web fonts*

Lucida Grande and Lucida Sans Unicode

Lucida Grande comes preinstalled on Mac OS X, and Lucida Sans Unicode comes with Windows XP, the latter being a very close match to the former. These fonts are a brilliant Verdana alternative, being supremely legible and extremely refreshing to eyes tired of typical web fonts. Note that this author has used Lucida Grande on probably 60% of all the sites he has built!

Suggested declaration: `"Lucida Grande", "Lucida Sans Unicode", Verdana, sans-serif`

Futura

Futura is a good contemporary-looking font, comes preinstalled on Mac OS X, and is included with many Adobe applications. It is a great sans serif font that works particularly well at larger font sizes (so great for headers).

Suggested declaration: `Futura, Helvetica, Arial, sans-serif`

Helvetica Neue

A redrawn version of Helvetica that has better separation between characters across its various guises, Helvetica Neue (pronounced "noye-er") comes preinstalled with most platforms and software. It's a very stylish font that looks great in any situation.

Suggested declaration: `"Helvetica Neue", Helvetica, Arial, sans-serif`

Gill Sans

Gill Sans is classified as a humanist sans serif, making it very legible and readable in text and display work. The condensed, bold, and display versions are excellent for packaging or posters, and this description translates very well to the screen. Gill Sans exudes a modern feel due to its clear, generous, and original characters. It comes preinstalled on Mac OS X.

Suggested declaration: `"Gill Sans", "Lucida Grande", "Lucida Sans Unicode", Arial, sans-serif`

Palatino

Preinstalled on Mac OS X and many Windows machines, Palatino is a typeface based on classical Italian Renaissance forms, and is a rather nice serif font. It has become a modern classic in itself, and is popular among professional graphic designers and amateurs alike. Palatino works well for both text and display typography, and used carefully it can be a great web font.

Suggestion declaration: `Palatino, Georgia, "Times New Roman", serif`

Be Careful with Fonts

Remember that the alternative fonts suggested here need to be used with caution. Ensure sensible alternatives are listed in the `font-family` sequence, and remember that a font displayed on a Mac can look significantly different, or even be unavailable, on a PC. It is advisable to edit your font sequences at the testing stage to see how your alternative fonts work for you. For example, Georgia may be your second-choice font, but be sure it suits your design should the first choice be unavailable.

Default Browser Display

Most would agree that a browser's default style sheet does a pretty good job of making text legible. Typically, the font size will be a non-squint-inducing 16px, with black text on a white background. In the following sections, we'll start with this default styling and apply numerous CSS properties to the markup (without adding any further elements to it) in order to explore the multitude of available techniques for creating good-looking web text.

Create a new document called `text.html` and type the following (X)HTML into it. You can also grab the complete `text.html` file from the Chapter 4 folder in the code download at `www.apress.com`:

```
<html>
 <head>
  <title>Chapter 4: Text</title>
 </head>
 <body>
  <h1>Content is King</h1>
  <p>This is a paragraph. Nothing particularly special about it, but the ➥
visitor is going to read it anyway, so it may as well say something useful.</p>
  <h2>True Fact</h2>
  <p>Useful. OK. Did you know that a shrimp's heart is actually in its head? ➥
It's true.</p>
 </body>
</html>
```

A shrimp's heart is actually in its head. Bet you didn't know that, did you? This incredibly informative text (just two headings and two paragraphs) will be used throughout the rest of this chapter.

Let's get down to the serious business and forget about seafood. Firefox will display this (X)HTML as shown in Figure 4-5 using its default style sheet.

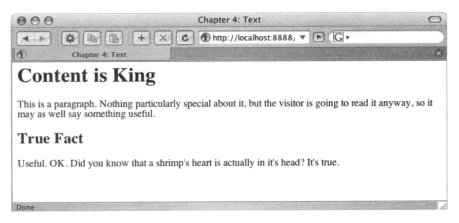

Figure 4-5. *Default browser display (Firefox)*

While this display is very legible, it isn't very stylish. It is likely that the default style sheet will specify either Arial or more likely Times New Roman for the font, giving that classic "unstyled" feel.

Apply Some Style

Through the following section, you will take that existing text in text.html and manipulate it in a number of ways that make use of some key CSS properties.

Define Your Style Sheet

The first step is to override the browser's default style sheet with one of your own. In Chapter 1, you learned how to apply an external style sheet, so repeat that process and apply a style sheet called text.css using the following link element within the head of the document:

```
<head>
  <title>Chapter 4: Text</title>
  <link rel='stylesheet' media="screen" type='text/css' href='text.css' />
</head>
```

Reload text.html in your browser. Nothing looks different, but text.css is now higher in the cascade than the browser style sheet. As there are no rules in text.css to override the browser style sheet yet, the latter's rules currently still take precedence.

Body Declarations

The first task with any new web site is to consider what blanket rules can be declared in the body selector. Remember that every element contained in the body element will inherit its values unless you specify otherwise. For example, to avoid having to declare the font-family and font-size for every element, some blanket rules can be applied from the outset.

The first selector to define in text.css is for body. Notice that margin, border, and padding properties have been declared, but more importantly so have the font-family and font-size properties using shorthand. These are specified for the whole web page, and any others that take their style from `text.css`:

```
/* Specify blanket rules for all elements */
 body {
  margin: 10px;
  border: 1px solid #000;
  padding:10px;
  font: 12px Verdana, Arial, Sans-serif;
 }
```

Save `text.css` and then reload `text.html` in your browser. The display should look something like Figure 4-6.

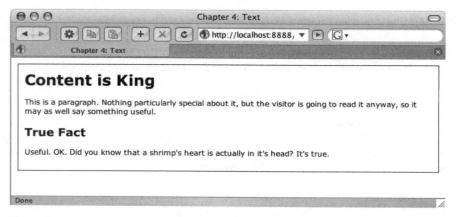

Figure 4-6. *Now text.html is taking its styling from text.css.*

With the `font-size` reduced to 12px, the display looks a little more professional, and Verdana makes the text a little easier on the eye. Notice that the declared `font-size` has no effect on the headings (`<h1>` and `<h2>`), which retain their default font sizes, as discussed earlier.

Please, Please Use line-height!

Adjusting the spacing between lines of text makes a huge difference to the look of your text, and it is almost always required to enhance legibility. Please, please use it!

The `line-height` property is easy to understand, simple to implement, but most often forgotten about. With careful `color`, `size`, and `font-family` properties set, and the text placed within a beautifully executed section of the page, it is easy to consider the job done. The revelation that something as simple as adjusting `line-height` can then bring to what is considered finished is something one never forgets, and once you see this for yourself, you will use it in every subsequent design.

Setting the line-height Using Percentage

It is worth setting line-height in the body selector, as all elements can benefit from inheriting this value. Headings that wrap to two or more lines, lists, block quotes, and so on can all use some space for clarity, but it's the paragraphs where the increased legibility will be most noticeable. The rule is simple:

```
line-height:150%;
```

In this example, the spacing between the lines of text will be the given percentage of the current font-size. So, a line-height of 100% will make no difference, whereas a line-height of 150% will create a space half the size of the font. A line-height of 200% will create a space equal to the size of the font, and so on. Here, the line-height declaration is added to the existing body selector:

```
/* Specify blanket rules for all elements */
body {
  margin: 10px;
  border: 1px solid #000;
  padding:10px;
  font: 12px Verdana, Arial, Sans-serif;
  line-height:200%;
}
```

In Figure 4-7, this line-height of 200% can be seen on the right, compared with the default on the left.

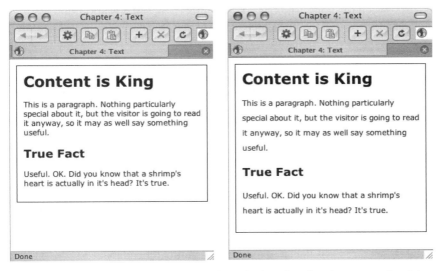

Figure 4-7. *Default line-height on the left and a line-height of 200% on the right*

The browser window on the right clearly shows that a line-height of 200% creates spacing equal in height to the size of the text characters. This is great for the example, but in the real world, a value of 150% or 160% would probably be more appropriate.

Other line-height Values

As well as the very flexible method of setting line-height using percentage, some other values can be used.

Normal

Sets what the experts call a "reasonable distance between lines." In actuality, this setting is exactly the same as specifying no line-height at all, and it is only useful if you wish to override inherited line-height for a particular element.

```
line-height:normal;
```

Number

Sets a number that will be multiplied with the current font-size to set the distance between the lines. For example, if the font-size is 12px, then specifying a line-height of 2 will result in a space of 24 pixels between lines of text.

```
line-height:2;
```

Length

Sets a fixed distance between the lines, which is great for precision, but it is important to remember that when text is resized, the line spaces will not increase or decrease at the same ratio as the text.

```
line-height:8px;
```

To ensure appropriate scaling when text is resized, use a flexible length measurement such as ems or percentage.

letter-spacing (Tracking)

In the real (print) world, the spacing of characters has the professional name of **Tracking**. Again, CSS has enabled web designers to emulate this tight text control with the letter-spacing property. Where line-height creates extra whitespace between lines of text, so letter-spacing is used to adjust the spacing between characters. Again, normal can be declared to override inherited letter-spacing, but mostly you will declare letter-spacing in pixels. In the following example, letter-spacing is declared only for the grouped headings:

```
/* Specify blanket rules for all elements */
body {
  margin: 10px;
  border: 1px solid #000;
  padding:10px
  font: 12px Verdana, Arial, Sans-serif;
  line-height:150%;
  }
h1, h2 {
  letter-spacing:3px;
  }
```

The result can be seen in Figure 4-8, where the headings have 3 pixels of whitespace between each character.

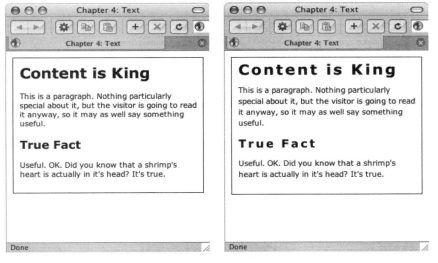

Figure 4-8. *On the right, the headings benefit from 3 pixels of letter-spacing.*

■**Note** It is worth noting that unlike line-height, here negative values are allowed, so something like letter-spacing:-0.5em can be used to bunch up the characters if required. Using the em measurement will ensure that the spacing scales if text sizes are increased. This approach is unlikely to aid legibility, however, so use negative spacing with caution. Use letter-spacing only when absolutely necessary. Increasing the whitespace between characters rarely makes text more legible, and only serves to make life more difficult for those with reading difficulties.

Many designers like to ensure many other font properties are set first, and leave `line-height` and `letter-spacing` until last. It can be that final touch that sets a design apart, and shows that the designer has a good approach to legibility and type design.

Other Key Font Properties

The following properties are often used for tighter control. Most are self-explanatory, so let's breeze through them; we'll combine them all in a sample template at the end of the chapter.

font-weight

The `font-weight` property sets how thick or thin characters in text should be displayed. Typically, the declaration will either be normal or bold, although some browsers support numeric values in increments of 100. These are 100 (lightest), 200, 300, 400 (same as `normal`), 700 (same as `bold`), 800, and 900 (even bolder!).

font-style

Again, this property is pretty obvious. The default is `normal`, but typically you would use this property to declare any text that needs to be rendered in italics. Values are `normal`, `italic`, and `oblique`. When you specify an `oblique` font style, the browser looks for any available font with "oblique" in its name or, failing that, one with "italic" in its name.

font-variant

The `font-variant` property is used to display text in a small-caps font, which means that all the lowercase letters are converted to uppercase letters, but all the letters in the small-caps font have a smaller font size compared to the rest of the text. This is useful for secondary, less-important info such as stats, figures, or footer information. Possible values are simply `normal` or `small-caps`.

Note that the browser will use a proper small-caps font if one is available; otherwise the effect is done computationally. You can see an example of small caps a little later in Figure 4-9.

text-transform

Not strictly a `font` property, but it controls the font, so it is included here. This property is a natural antidote to `font-variant`, where all characters can be rendered uppercase without reducing font size. The `text-transform:uppercase` declaration is especially useful for headings, where it is semantically incorrect to type using uppercase characters in the markup.

The other key text-transform value is capitalize, which ensures that the first character of any word is rendered as an uppercase character, which again is very useful for headings and lists.

Other possible text-transform values are none and lowercase, the latter being very useful if you need to remove all instances of uppercase characters.

Combining Several Font Properties

Applying all the preceding methods to the template will be interesting, if a little chaotic. Taking the core template, and mixing up the CSS, you'll see a myriad of declarations across the selectors. Note that shared heading declarations are grouped, whereas individual ones are defined individually:

```
/* Specify blanket rules for all elements */
body {
  margin: 10px;
  border: 1px solid #000;
  padding:10px;
  font: normal 12px Verdana, Arial, Sans-serif;
  line-height:150%;
}
p {
  font-variant:small-caps
}
h1, h2 {
  letter-spacing:1px;
}
h1 {
  font-family: Georgia, Times, serif;
  text-transform:uppercase;
}
h2 {
  font-family: "Helvetica Neue", Arial, sans-serif;
  text-transform:none;
  font-style:italic;
}
```

Throwing all of that at the template results in a real markup mash-up. Compare the basic pane on the left with the resulting pane on the right in Figure 4-9.

As a means of showing how to apply the various font values in one place, that was a good example, but in the real world it is important to make font decisions for a reason. Italicized text is considered less legible by many, so ensure you are using it because you have to.

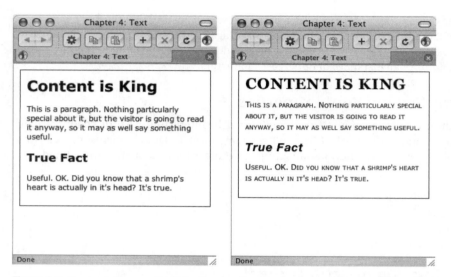

Figure 4-9. *Basic styling on the left compared with the font styling mash-up on the right*

More Font Shorthand

The previous example resulted in the CSS ballooning to 23 lines, which is avoidable with some font shorthand. While `letter-spacing` and `text-transform` cannot be included in the shorthand, all `font` properties and also `line-height` can.

Let's take all the font properties in the next example and present them in one declaration. So long as the order of values is correct, the display will be exactly the same.

First, consider the following selector for a paragraph:

```
p {
  font-style:italic;
  font-variant:small-caps;
  font-weight:bold;
  font-size:12px;
  font-family:verdana,arial,sans-serif;
line-height:150%;
}
```

Hmm, six lines are used here just to define the basic font styling for the paragraph. Building upon the basic shorthand you learned when we looked at `font-size` and `font-family`, further values can be combined to bring everything into one declaration. In the following code, note that after `font:` the value order is identified by the name of the property. The order is very important:

```
p {
  font: style variant weight size/line-height family
}
```

Now, replace each value word with an actual value from the original six lines of CSS:

```
p {
  font: italic small-caps bold 12px/150% verdana,arial,sans-serif
}
```

The result sees just one line of shorthand CSS doing the work of six longhand rules. Notice that `font-size` and `line-height` are combined as `font-size/line-height`, resulting in `12px/150%` in the example. Values can be omitted if need be, so if you wish not to declare the `font-variant`, simply leave it out. So long as the order of declared properties doesn't change, all will be fine.

Getting Clever with Text

Since dinosaurs ruled the earth, web designers have sought ways of breaking free of the restrictions forced upon them when it comes to styling text. As a result, numerous cool methods of bridging the gap between print and web design have materialized. Some of these methods incorporate existing (X)HTML elements, while others rely on nifty combinations of CSS values you've learned so far.

Quote Me on This

The (X)HTML element `<blockquote>` is a very useful tool for singling out a quote or creating a **pullquote** (a key sentence selected from a body of text and used as a draw for the reader).

Take the existing document called `text.html` and add the `<blockquote>` element into it:

```
<html>
 <head>
  <title>Chapter 4: Text</title>
 </head>
 <body>
  <h1>Content is King</h1>
  <p>This is a paragraph. Nothing particularly special about it, but the ➡
    visitor is going to read it anyway, so it may as well say something ➡
    useful.</p>
 <h2>True Fact</h2>
  <p>Useful. OK. Did you know that a shrimp's heart is actually in its➡
    head? It's true.</p>
  <blockquote><p>Collison stands by his statement that a shrimp's heart is ➡
    actually in its bottom, and doggedly refuses to believe that he is
    wrong.<p></blockquote>
 </body>
</html>
```

Save `text.html` and reload it in your browser. Now, the rendered page should look as it does in Figure 4-10. The block quote's default styling sees it indented by approximately 40 pixels while inheriting existing font styling from the body selector.

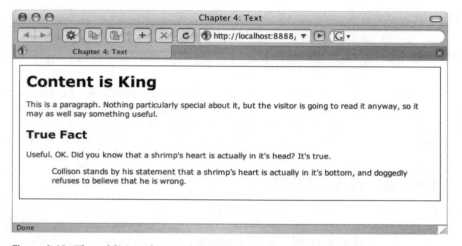

Figure 4-10. *The additional, unstyled block quote appears underneath the existing text.*

By overriding the inherited font styles, the `<blockquote>` element can be styled to stand out from the surrounding text, by declaring a different font, size, and style. Also, the default margin can be overridden to pull the text a little closer to the container's edge:

```
/* Style the blockquote */
blockquote {
  margin: 0 0 0 20px;
  line-height:150%;
  font: italic 15px Georgia,Times,serif;
}
```

The result can be seen in Figure 4-11. The quote is clearly defined to contrast heavily with the existing page text.

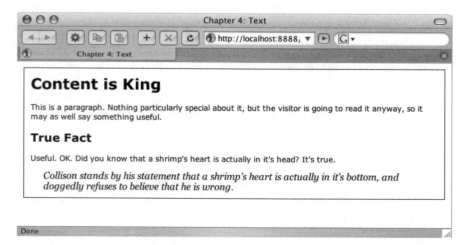

Figure 4-11. *Now the block quote is clearly defined against the surrounding text.*

Indenting Paragraphs

Another device you will be familiar with from the print world is that of indenting the first line of a paragraph. This acts as a clear hook for the reader, drawing the eye to the beginning of each paragraph, and is especially useful where line-height is quite narrow. CSS gives us the text-indent property for this.

```
/* paragraph styling */
p {
  font: 12px verdana,arial,sans-serif;
  text-indent:15px;
}
```

The result of this 15px text-indent can be seen in Figure 4-12.

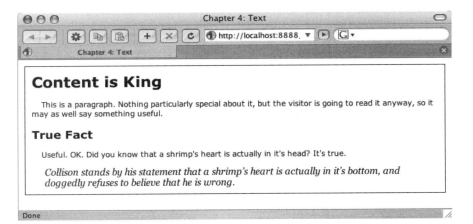

Figure 4-12. *A 15-pixel indent is added to the paragraphs.*

Ye Olde Drop Caps

Drop caps might be more familiar to you as those wonderfully illustrated opening letters of paragraphs in spell books and very olde bibles, but it is a device that has been used in probably every magazine and newspaper since mass printing began. The technique sees the very first letter of a paragraph singled out and treated differently from the rest of the text, typically many times larger than the other characters, and possibly bolder and colored differently. The drop cap may also be boxed inside its own container.

Creating a drop cap requires no extra markup in the (X)HTML, although to avoid applying this method to every paragraph, it is advisable to single out the paragraph requiring the drop cap by giving it a class.

```
<h1>Content is King</h1>
  <p class="dropcap">This is a paragraph. Nothing particularly ➥
    special about it, but the visitor is going to read it anyway, so it may as ➥
    well say something useful.</p>
```

This dropcap class ensures only this paragraph will be affected, and acts as a hook for the CSS.

Introducing the first-letter Pseudo Element

Now for a clever trick. Here, a pseudo element is introduced to the new p selector, separated by a colon. Pseudo elements are used to add special powers to selectors, and can single out the first letter of a paragraph or the first line, or be used to insert a CSS rule after an (X)HTML element. This example uses first-letter to single out the first letter of any paragraphs given the dropcap class.

```
/* Create drop cap characters */
p.dropcap:first-letter {
  float: left;
  width: 40px;
  font: 60px "Lucida Grande",Arial,sans-serif;
  line-height: 50px;
}
```

Note that float:left is declared to ensure that the remaining paragraph text "floats" around the enlarged drop cap. Floats will be discussed in more detail later in the book. The width is defined to ensure the drop cap has enough space in which to sit, and obviously the font-size is increased significantly to enlarge the character, as you see in Figure 4-13.

Content is King

This is a paragraph. Nothing particularly special about it, but the visitor is going to read it anyway, so it may as well say something useful.

Figure 4-13. *The first letter of the paragraph is turned into a drop cap.*

The font size and width need to be adjusted depending on the actual font you use. For example, a 60-pixel Georgia character demands a little more space than one rendered in Lucida Grande.

This chapter might be doubled in length if we were to fully explore such advanced tricks as these, but I urge you to investigate further, as these pseudo elements are important cross-browser problem-solving tools. For more information about pseudo elements, check out the W3 specifications (www.w3schools.com/css/css_pseudo_elements.asp).

May the Font Be with You

I expect you'll be aware that the subject of text, like any web subject, is a vast and broad landscape that is difficult to map. As new discoveries are made, and explorers find new and amazing methods of attack, the contours seem to continually shift, and the ground remains unstable.

With text being the most important content of most web sites, it is vital that the community seeks to redefine methods of approach based on usability testing and new information about how users with varying abilities use web pages. It pays to define your own constants in your designs—your own plan of attack with text. With each site you build, experiment with line height, font size, and scaling. Consider the end user at all times, and pay great attention to primary and secondary fonts, legibility, and resizing of text.

Right, where are we? Well, it's the end of Chapter 4, and a lot of ground has been covered, but surely you are itching to get a little more creative at this stage. Now that you've got your text under control, perhaps it's time to add a little flair into the mix. It's time to reward your patience and studious discipline with some playtime.

■ ■ ■

CHAPTER 5

Color, Backgrounds, and Images

The beauty of CSS is that it allows us to separate presentation from content. The entire core content such as text and key images are locked up in the (X)HTML, leaving all the actual styling kept tidily separated in the style sheet. Therefore, the style sheet is the place to specify all the creative stuff, including color and placement of decorative images.

Applying color to text and containers is pretty easy using CSS, as is the application of background images, although it is important to plan ahead and ensure the minimum number of images are used for maximum effect. That said, background images are the key to realizing the creative potential of CSS-based web design, and they literally transform your pages into works of art very quickly if used appropriately.

It should be noted that adding any images to a page, whether inline or with CSS, will increase its weight, and therefore the time it takes to be fully downloaded by the user. Many designers do more harm than good here; using CSS to apply unnecessarily large photographic backgrounds and complicated extraneous whistles and whirligigs that, when combined with (X)HTML, CSS, and other ingredients such as JavaScript, significantly increase a page's total size. The trick is to use background images sparingly, creatively—and to be aware of occasions where they can be reused and repositioned on a page.

Much advanced CSS deals specifically with incredibly ambitious background image use, and though the results can be mind-bogglingly engaging, the processes can be equally complex— even for seasoned professionals. Still, it is possible to do some very interesting things with images without straying too far from the basics.

In this chapter, you will first learn the correct ways of applying color to your web pages, and later begin to work with background images in a responsible way.

A Brief History of Color

As a human being, you understand the concept of color. It's pretty simple really. Red is red, and blue—well, that's kind of bluish, isn't it? Even those less receptive to certain colors among us (Hi, technical reviewer Rutter) and the completely colorblind can appreciate these differences through tone and gradient.

As a child, you no doubt learned the rules of the color wheel, and the results of mixing primary and secondary colors. That's great, but sadly the web is a different world, and the rules are somewhat different. Using color on the web is very easy, so long as you take the time to learn some basic application guidelines first of all.

Web Safety First?

There are just 216 colors that you may use on your web pages. Or are there? Early web settlers were bound by many rules that governed what they dare do with their designs. One of the most widely adopted was the concept of **web-safe color**. The lords of web use dictated that 216 colors were guaranteed to be displayed correctly on any platform, and that to use any others might result in the user's monitor imploding, or at least rendering the web pages with incorrect color and therefore resulting in disastrously compromised design. 216 sounds like a large enough number, but consider that most modern computers use millions of colors, and you begin to see the problem.

Web-safe palettes, or **browser-safe palettes** as they are also known, consist of 216 colors that display solidly, consistently, and without graduation on any monitor capable of displaying at least 8-bit color (256 colors). The reason why this palette doesn't contain the maximum 256 colors is that only 216 of this number will display exactly the same on all computers (the remaining 40 vary somewhat from Mac to PC, for example). Ours is not to reason why, but merely to curse at yet another line drawn in the sand.

Originally, computers were only capable of displaying a maximum of 256 colors at any time, due mainly to the amount of RAM available. These colors needed to be described in no more than 8 bits of computer information, which by no coincidence equals 256 different values (2 to the power of 8). The basic palette of 256 colors available to computers of that era contains the 216 we now call the web-safe palette.

Though most modern computers have more than enough available RAM to display infinite colors on screen at any one time, there are many old computers limited to 256-color displays, which is why the web-safe palette is still something to consider, depending on the audience.

■**Note** Your inner geek may be interested to know that web-safe colors are defined in terms of the percentages 0%, 20%, 40%, 60%, 80%, and 100%, and also the RGB values of 0, 51, 102, 153, 204, and 255—multiples of 51. Why multiples of 51? Well, 51 is 20% of 255, and as 0 is a value, we count the total colors from 0 to 255, not 1 to 256. If this fascinates you, jump to `http://en.wikipedia.org/wiki/Web_colors` for much more detail.

Specifying Color

Colors may be specified in a number of ways. Many specify color as an RGB triplet in hexadecimal format (a hex triplet). Others often use their common English names in some cases. It is also possible to use RGB percentages or decimals. The following examples are all valid for the color red:

```
#f00 /* #rgb */
#ff0000 /* #rrggbb */
red /* common English name */
rgb(255,0,0) /* integer range 0 - 255 */
rgb(100%, 0%, 0%) /* float range 0.0% - 100.0% */
```

Hexadecimal Triplets

Let's attempt to understand how the RGB declarations for red actually work. A hexadecimal triplet is a six-digit, 3-byte hexadecimal number used in (X)HTML and CSS to represent colors. The bytes represent the red, green, and blue components of the color. One byte represents a number in the range 00 to FF (in hexadecimal notation), or 0 to 255 in decimal notation. This represents the least (0) to the most (255) intensity of each of the color components. Concatenating 3 bytes in hexadecimal notation, in the following order, forms the hex triplet:

- *Byte 1*: Red value
- *Byte 2*: Green value
- *Byte 3*: Blue value

Shortening the Hex

The "web-safe" colors do not have names, but an RGB triplet can specify each. A three-digit number is used as a shorthand notation for the six-digit hexadecimal numerals. The digit 3 is equivalent to the hexadecimal numeral 33; C is equivalent to CC. For example, F63 is equivalent to #FF6633.

Using the 17 Named Colors

CSS language defines the same 16 named colors as the HTML 4 spec, plus CSS 2.1 adds the "orange" color name to the list. The 17 named colors are listed in Table 5-1 as a handy reference for your own use through this chapter and beyond.

Table 5-1. *CSS 2.1 Named Colors and Corresponding Hexadecimal Values*

Color	Hexadecimal Reference
black	#000000
navy	#000080
green	#008000
teal	#008080
silver	#c0c0c0
blue	#0000ff
lime	#00ff00
aqua	#00ffff
maroon	#800000
purple	#800080
olive	#808000
gray	#808080
red	#ff0000

Table 5-1. *CSS 2.1 Named Colors and Corresponding Hexadecimal Values (Continued)*

Color	Hexadecimal Reference
fuchsia	#ff00ff
yellow	#ffff00
orange	#ffa500
white	#ffffff

The CSS 2.1 specifications also allow web authors to use so-called **system colors**, which are color names whose values are taken from the operating system. This enables web authors to style their content in line with the operating system of the user agent.

The developing CSS3 specification will also introduce Hue, Saturation, Lightness (HSL) color space values to style sheets (see http://en.wikipedia.org/wiki/HSL_color_space for more information about this), and we can be certain that as more and more old computers fall off the end of the world, and new platforms continue to meet high specifications, the days of web-safe colors will be thankfully numbered.

Must We Be Web Safe?

For anyone without the confidence or color mastery to push their ambition over the 216 mark, be thankful that at the time of writing the web-safe palette is built into Photoshop, Paint Shop Pro, Illustrator, Freehand, Fireworks, Dreamweaver, GoLive, and numerous other applications (see Figure 5-1).

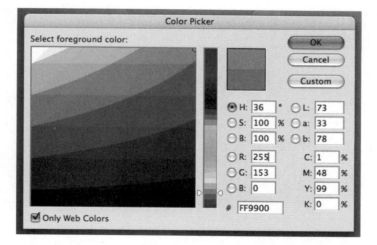

Figure 5-1. *The web-safe palette as it appears in Adobe Photoshop*

Despite all of this caution, many designers do not limit themselves to the web-safe palette. It certainly is worth considering the small percentage of web users with very old machines, custom color settings, or devices that do not support color at all, but the real world is made up of considerably more than 216 colors.

Imagine a situation where you need to extend the color of part of an image (let's assume it's a clear blue sky framing a pretty little tree) from its top to the top of its containing div. You may want to use Photoshop's eyedropper tool to find the hexadecimal reference of that blue sky, only to find the nearest web-safe match just isn't close enough. Here, a non-web-safe color is needed, and can be used with some confidence. Thus, your toolbox extends from just 216 colors to literally millions at the flick of an informed choice (see Figure 5-2).

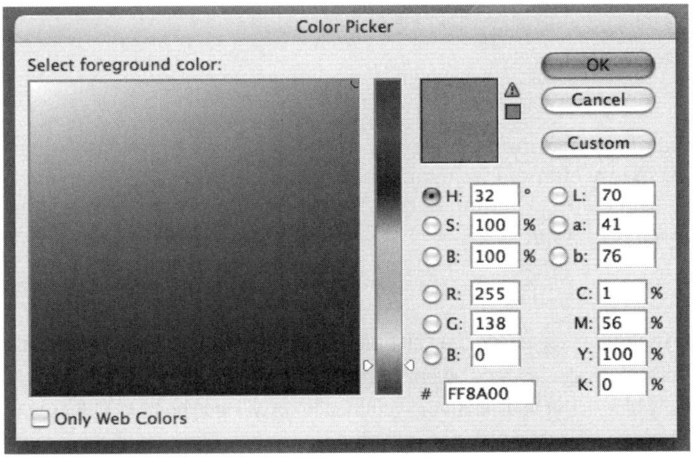

Figure 5-2. *Photoshop's main color palette*

Sampling color from images is a must for more intricate or ambitious CSS-based designs, and (I'll stick my neck out here) is recommended. Where possible, use a web-safe color, but do not feel handcuffed by this sense of responsibility. Design moves forward, as does technology, and nothing would ever have been achieved if everybody placed caution before innovation.

Selecting a Color Palette for Your Design

While it is perfectly acceptable to begin building a web site structure without giving any thought to color, to begin adding color without any sense of an overall color palette is asking for trouble.

The following web sites are excellent starting points for web palettes. ColorBlender (http://colorblender.com) allows you to export palettes in lots of formats and is very slick. It is even possible to upload an image and have a palette created from it using the Color Palette Generator (www.degraeve.com/color-palette/index.php). Finally, Colour Lovers (www.colourlovers.com) features hundreds of existing palettes submitted by visitors, and the Color Scheme Generator 2 (wellstyled.com/tools/colorscheme2/) is brilliantly intuitive.

For more in-depth analysis of color on the Web, visit www.web-colors-explained.com/ and http://en.wikipedia.org/wiki/Web_colors.

Color for Text

Way back in Chapter 1, you were already applying color to standard (X)HTML elements, turning specific paragraph text red using a shortened hexadecimal reference, as in this example:

```
p {
  color: #F00
}
```

Of course, you can also use any of the 17 named colors from Table 5-1:

```
p {
  color: red
}
```

Thus, the method of specifying color should now be perfectly obvious. The `color` declaration is all that is required to assign color to any element in any circumstance.

Use web-safe colors for text. The colors will map correctly and will not break up on color-challenged monitors, so will be easier to read.

■**Note** Color is an inherited value. Therefore, specifying the color blue on a containing div will result in all contained text (including headings, lists, block quotes, and so on) being blue, unless a specific element is given a different value. So, if you specify blue in the body element, your headings will also be blue, unless you make them green, for instance, with a dedicated value.

Background Color

The `background-color` property is used to set the background color of an (X)HTML element. It is the quickest method for transforming your site from plain black text on a white background into something much more engaging. Without doubt, this property is something you will use frequently, although it is easily abused, and more mistakes come from not using it at all.

If you decide to give your web site a solid-colored background, make it a web-safe color. That's your guarantee the color will not embarrass you when it displays on the other computer platforms. And on older computers capable of displaying but 256 colors at a time, and there are still a lot of those relics around, your background will display clean and nondithered.

With this in mind, let's move through some simple uses of the `background-color` property, looking first at how it can transform text.

Adding Background Color to Text

Everyone understands the concept of the highlighter pen, where a word or line of text is highlighted using fluorescent ink on paper. CSS can easily emulate this approach using the `background-color` property.

In the following example, a yellow `background-color` is declared alongside black text:

```
p {
  color:#000;
  background-color:#FF0;
  line-height:150%
}
```

This re-creates the effect of the highlighter pen by placing the text over a yellow strip for the whole length of the paragraph, forming a block of color, as Figure 5-3 demonstrates. Note that a line-height is declared to apply appropriate space between the wrapping lines.

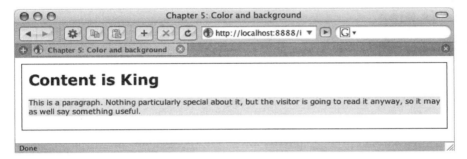

Figure 5-3. *Background color applied to the paragraph text to emulate the highlighter pen approach*

Span Text for More Specific Control

A custom <span> element can be used to control a section of the paragraph, rather than the whole chunk. Although this method demands additional markup, it really is the only way to affect a designated portion of text contained within a paragraph, unless targeting text already defined with phrase elements such as <strong> or <em>.

Rather than assign the background color to the whole paragraph, a class is created that will be used to cloak the text that needs a highlight. In the following CSS, background-color is removed from the paragraph selector, and a new class called highlight is defined:

```
/* Define basic paragraph style */
  p {
    color:#000;
    line-height:150%
  }

/* Highlight class to pick out key words or phrases */
  .highlight {
    background-color:#FF0;
  }
```

The <span> class will inherit any styles defined in the parent element, and will therefore also have a line-height of 150% and have black text. The key difference is obviously the yellow background color. The <span> class is applied to the (X)HTML as follows:

```
<p>Useful. OK. Did you know that a shrimp's <span class="highlight">heart➡
</span> is actually <span class="highlight">in its head</span>? It's true.</p>
```

As the `<span>` utilizes a class, it can be used an infinite number of times, so in this example two sections of the paragraph are emphasized, resulting in the display shown in Figure 5-4.

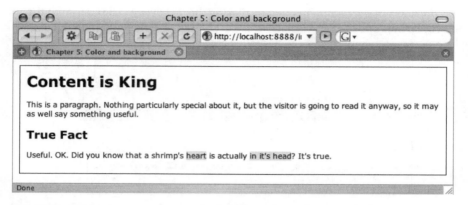

Figure 5-4. *Using a <span> class to single out portions of a paragraph*

Obviously, the text inside the `<span>` element can be treated differently from the style inherited from the paragraph element, and interesting results can be had by experimenting with underlines, `font-weight`, `font-style`, or a different font `color`.

Adding Background Color to Headings

The very nature of headings as identifiers for different sections and indications of hierarchy leads most designers to treat their display differently from other text. By default, of course, the browser will display headings in larger bold text, but a little background color can really make a difference.

To begin, start with a simple adjustment—black text on a silver background for the level 2 heading.

```
h2 {
  color:#000;
  background-color:#808080;
  padding:0.3em;
  }
```

Taking the hexadecimal reference for silver (#808080) and applying it to the `<h2>` using the `background-color` property is all that's needed. Of course, the text would push right up against the edges of the silver strip were it not for the addition of the padding.

Note The result in Figure 5-5 shows the "True Fact" heading stretching the full width of the containing div. This is because headings (<h1>, <h2>, <h3>, etc.) are **block-level** elements, meaning that if unobstructed and not limited by a specified width, they will extend for as long as they can, and will also force neighboring elements to wrap to a new line, as it were. The opposite of block level is **inline**, meaning any element that does not demand a new line or dictate its own width. CSS allows any element to be redefined as opposite of its default state, and this will be covered more in Chapter 6.

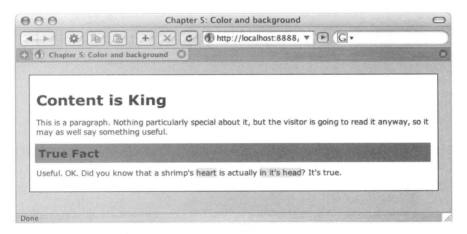

Figure 5-5. *Background color applied to the heading*

It may be wise not to specify line-height or margin in most cases, as a wrapping heading will result in whitespace between the lines of text in the header, which may not be desired.

Background for Other Elements

By now it should be obvious that you can apply a background color to any element, and it is very common for designers to apply a background color to a div, whether as part of the final design, or during the building process, in order to define the work area divisions. Adding simple background colors at the design stage is a great way of assessing whether the padding and margins you are applying are working correctly, and generally being aware of what is where and how one element relates to its neighbor.

To stick with the current example, we can set the background color of the whole page by declaring a gray background color to the <body> element, which will then be inherited by every child element unless overridden.

```
/* Specify blanket rules for all elements */
  body {
    margin:10px;
    padding:10px;
    background-color:#CCC;
    font:normal 12px Verdana, Arial, Sans-serif;
  }
```

As a result of the additional background color, the whole page is now light gray (see Figure 5-6).

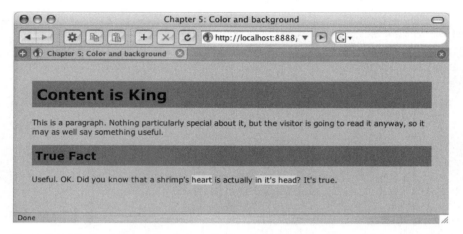

Figure 5-6. *The background-color applied to the body element produces a completely gray page.*

Fine, but obviously everything else is inheriting the gray background, except where specified. Notice that the headings still have the silver backgrounds and the spans from the previous section still produce yellow backgrounds, as a yellow background is specified in the highlight class.

It would look a lot better if the content sat on a lighter background, which we can create using a div. First, the appropriate markup for a new div with the ID container is added to the template. Here is the entire markup from the <body> of the template:

```
<body>
  <div id="container">
    <h1>Content is King</h1>
      <p>This is a paragraph. Nothing particularly special about it, but ➥
          the visitor➥
is going to read it anyway, so it may as well say something useful.</p>
    <h2>True Fact</h2>
      <p>Useful. OK. Did you know that a shrimp's <span class="highlight">heart➥
      </span> is actually <span class="highlight">in its head</span>? ➥
          It's true.</p>
  </div>
</body>
```

Next, the CSS selector for that division is added to the style sheet. Here a thin black border, a padding of 10 pixels all around every side, and most importantly, a white background are declared.

```
/* Container for all page content */
  #container {
    padding:10px;
    border:1px solid #000;
    background-color:#FFF;
  }
```

This results in a neat white container in which all page content is placed, as you see in Figure 5-7.

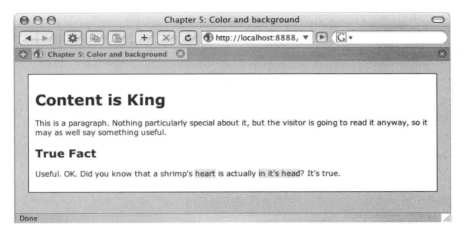

Figure 5-7. *The container div holds all page content on a white background.*

Already, with the introduction of one div and a couple of background colors, this very simple page is looking considerably different from the default browser display. As a final touch, let's bring back the silver background color for the second-level heading, and also add an identical background color to the top-level heading. No extra markup is needed, just the following selector used to group shared declarations for both headings:

```
/* Declare all shared properties for headings */
  h1, h2 {
    color:#000;
    background-color:#808080;
    padding:5px;
  }
```

Now all elements are very clearly defined using varying grays, as you can see in Figure 5-8. From a user's point of view, this design probably looks a little heavy-handed, but from a building point of view the outlined elements are very useful. If this were a color book, maybe I would have explained things with pinks and purples, so perhaps count yourselves lucky that it isn't.

There really is no limit to what you can do with background colors, so maybe experiment with applying them to lists, phrase elements, and other familiar (X)HTML elements as you work your way through the book. Some very exciting designs have been created that use pure background-color and carefully sized and spaced elements, though it's impossible to deny that when it comes to really incredible CSS design, it's the background-image property that stretches the boundaries.

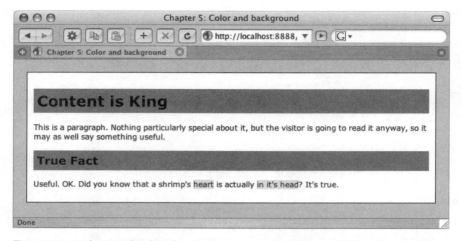

Figure 5-8. *Background colors for <body>, container, spans, and headings applied to the page*

Image Formats for Backgrounds

Before we delve into the toy box that is background images, it is worth taking a few minutes to consider which kinds of image files to use and why. Nothing compromises a great layout more than badly formatted background images, and choosing the correct format makes an incredible difference to the quality, file size, and download time. Basically, this is one of the major factors that separates a good design from a great design.

Three main formats are acceptable, namely **GIF**, **JPEG**, and **PNG** files. The latter is used considerably less than the other two, but it is still a very useful card to play when needed. In the upcoming sections, each is looked at in more detail, with suggestions for when to deploy each format and why.

GIF

Undoubtedly the ideal format for background images, the GIF (pronounced "gif" to rhyme with "whiff" by most, and "jif" by a minority of designers) format uses a proprietary compression scheme to keep the size of the file as small as possible.

The GIF was created a long time ago when color displays were limited to 256 colors and modems were slow. Instead of describing one pixel at a time in terms of its color, it describes the boundaries of an area and the single color within that area. In cases where there are large areas of certain colors, the file size is smaller. When dithering is used, the larger shapes are broken into much smaller shapes requiring more information to be stored in the file, and the file size increases.

■**Note** Dithering creates lots of new transitional pixels, which in turn creates a larger file size. You should only use dithering if the image contains a transition between colors. When you Save For Web using Photoshop, for example, you are given the option of saving the image with dithering when saving a file as a GIF.

Figure 5-9 shows a simple gradient image saved as a GIF with just eight colors to illustrate the effect of dithering. The image on the left uses no dithering, so color is broken into chunks, which makes it pretty much unusable. The image on the right is saved with dithering, which results in a smoother image that uses more colors, but has a larger file size.

Figure 5-9. *The image on the left shows how a nondithered image breaks the gradient into simple chunks of color, while the one on the right has a much smoother transition through the gradient.*

You can imagine the detrimental effect lack of dithering would have on a photograph of your cat. Poor Tiddles would end up looking like he was made out of cardboard. As a rule of thumb, use the GIF format for images that contain clean blocks of color, such as very simple logos or simple patterns.

That said, many (including this author) do use GIFs for gradients and background images that might be considered complex, but the images are often very small, and can thus be saved with more colors and dithering. Such images are created in order to tile (repeat) across a given area, which means that the files are much smaller, and the browser only needs to download one tile, not the whole pattern. Tiling background images will be discussed later in this section.

Transparent GIFs

The best thing about GIFs is that they can carry a certain amount of transparency, which can be invaluable for web design. Imagine that you wish to have a small arrow icon appear in every heading, but that headings appear on many different background colors. This is where the transparent GIF will save the day. So long as that GIF is saved with transparency, it will allow the background color to come through.

Regrettably, transparent GIFs are not perfect, and rounded or jagged edges will be saved with a few nontransparent pixels around them, floating on the transparent background (see the black pixels around my dad's head in Figure 5-10). The reason for this is when your application creates the GIF, often it will anti-alias (blend) the edge of the visible image to the background color. If you use a white background, for example, and your site has a green background, you may see speckled dots around your image.

Thankfully, Photoshop and some other image editing applications allow you to specify a matte color for these stray pixels. The goal here is to match the matte color to the background upon which the transparent image will sit. This is not as restrictive as specifying the very same color as the target background, but more a case of finding a near match for several possible backgrounds. For instance, if you specify a white matte, your transparent image will work pretty well on any very light-colored background. Equally, a dark gray matte will do the job when the image sits over a dark blue, green, gray, etc.

Figure 5-10. *Adding a black matte around my transparent Dad so that I can sit him against a dark background*

Thus in Figure 5-10, I have opted to apply a black matte around my Dad, so that he can sit comfortably upon any dark background. The black pixels around his hood will blend into the dark background and will not be visible, as Figure 5-11 illustrates.

Figure 5-11. *The black matte of the transparent GIF image is clearly visible on the white background, but blends well with the black background.*

Transparent GIFs really extend the limits of image use on the Web, but they certainly do have limitations, especially where transparent gradients are concerned. If you require a more complex solution to a transparent image, skip to the "PNG" section later in this chapter.

JPEG

The familiar image format that you will surely be used to using. JPEGs are incredibly flexible, but an image saved as a JPEG (pronounced "jay-peg") isn't analyzed for color in the same way as a GIF. This is the most commonly used standard method of lossy compression for photographic images.

■**Note** A lossy data compression method is one where compressing data and then decompressing it retrieves data that may well be different from the original, but is "close enough" to be useful in some way.

JPEG files do suffer generational degradation when repeatedly edited and saved, a bit like photocopies of photocopies. Photographic images are best stored in a lossless non-JPEG format such as Tagged Image File Format (TIFF) if they will be reedited in future, in order to avoid nasty rashes across the image.

The JPEG is not as well suited for line drawings or images containing text (that's where the GIF comes in), but the format comes into its own when saving photographs for web pages. Photoshop and most other good image manipulation applications allow you to control exactly how much of the original image you wish to retain. A key tool here is the quality controller in Photoshop, allowing you to save JPEGs as low, medium, high, or very high quality, or specify an exact percentage. In Figure 5-12, you can see the difference in quality. I wanted to save my dad as a JPEG and upload him to the Internet, where he belongs.

Figure 5-12. *In these magnified images, my Dad is first saved with a high JPEG quality, but he's a bigger file size. On the left he has a greatly reduced file size, but he's come out in a rash of squares.*

Although the images in Figure 5-12 are magnified somewhat, it is clear that the image on the left has little noticeable loss of detail or visible artifacts. However, once a certain threshold of compression is passed, compressed images show increasingly visible defects, such as the rash of squares across his face in the right image.

The moral of this tale is that more often than not, you'll want to retain as much photographic realism in your inline images as possible, and you'll forgo a little extra file size for that privilege, whereas for your background images, you'll likely need less realism and will be working with larger blocks of color or small gradient areas, and will therefore need the GIF format.

PNG

The PNG (pronounced "ping") was developed to improve upon the limitations of the humble GIF, where machines capable of displaying millions of colors were outgrowing a format limited to just 256 colors. This is the chief reason why the PNG is growing in popularity among web designers who desire greater flexibility but maximum image quality retention.

Most will resort to the PNG when a much more complex transparent image is required, perhaps one containing a very subtle gradient or shadow. The big problem there has been Internet Explorer's lack of support for the transparent PNG. Good old IE will flatten your beautiful transparent PNG and render it as a block, revealing none of the color underneath (thankfully the forthcoming IE7 does support PNG transparency). There is, however, a fairly complicated workaround for this issue, beyond the scope of this book. (See `www.alistapart.com/articles/pngopacity/` for more information about PNG use in such circumstances . . . stay there a while after you've read that article, as A List Apart is one of the greatest resources out there for web designers.)

So long as browser support for the PNG remains limited (which can be translated as "until everyone upgrades to IE7," which won't happen overnight), it is unlikely to supersede the GIF format just yet, but do take some time to consider it in preparation for the day when this superior image format is the main method of saving images for the Web. That will happen. The alpha transparency of the PNG ensures that the anti-aliasing always works against any background, and the amount of transparency can be varied across the image. This makes the PNG format ideal for drop shadows, fine gradients, and other exciting layering methods. Bet you can't wait.

Got the Picture?

So, there ends our mini-tour of the available web image formats. To conclude, remember the following. Use GIFs for images with blocks of color or text, and for images with no graduation unless it is a very small image. Use JPEGs for anything where a greater photographic quality is required, but be aware of the quality/file size compromise. Use PNGs for complex transparent images where you are designing for a specific browser that supports it, or if you are prepared to use the IE workaround.

These rules are not hard and fast, and assuming every image is different—which it most likely is—the perfect format for your image will depend on the situation. If you think it should be a GIF, but it works better as a JPEG, make it a JPEG. It's a common sense thing.

Background Image

Based on what you have already learned about image formats, I'm going to use the GIF format throughout the rest of this chapter, as the examples will use a small image that can be tiled across a given area, and even reused elsewhere, allowing the images to be saved with a little more quality.

Sensible Use

Before you start going hellbent-for-leather with background images, it is important to consider how this will affect the end user. Numerous factors mean that background image use should be carefully considered and not frivolous.

Although less important than it used to be, it is still a fact that many folks are downloading web pages using modems made of twigs and tin cans. A typical web page might contain something like 15KB of text and therefore download pretty quickly. Add 35KB of background images to that, and you are reducing the speed of their viewing experience significantly. Keep image use light, and only go overboard when it is really necessary, or you are designing for an audience you know will be using super-fast broadband.

Do not, under any circumstances, use background images to convey important information when no alternative is available should they not display, or be manually disabled by a user. There are solutions for backing up informative background images with valid (X)HTML, and you'll learn about that later. For example, don't use a background image to show the title of your web site, any navigation items, or any kind of flattened text content, unless you are providing this information with standard text should images be turned off (see Chapter 14). Background images are decorative adornments and certainly not to be considered "content"—which is why they are kept in the style sheet as separate presentation elements.

Right, that's the end of the hard-line lecturing. It's time to delve into the fascinating world of background images. Power up your image editing software, fill the teapot, and above all, concentrate.

Prepare Your Template and Style Sheet

To illustrate the flexibility of background images, it is worth your preparing a new template with which to experiment through the rest of this chapter. Create a new template called images.html, and add the following markup:

```
<html>
  <head>
    <title>Chapter 5: Background Images</title>
    <link rel='stylesheet' media="screen" type='text/css' href='images.css' />
  </head>
  <body>
    <div id="container">
    </div>
  </body>
</html>
```

Save the template. Note that the body element contains just one child element—the container div we used earlier in the chapter. That div will act as the sandbox in which just one background image will be obeying your every command as it is shunted around, duplicated, and positioned.

Note that a style sheet called images.css is linked from the head of the new template. Create that style sheet and paste the following into it:

```
/* Specify blanket rules for all elements */
  body {
    margin: 10px;
    background-color:#CCC;
  }

/* Container for all page content */
  #container {
    height:200px;
    border:1px solid #000;
    background-color:#FFF;
  }
```

Save the new style sheet. All the properties used should now be familiar to you. Notice that again the body has a gray background and a 10-pixel margin from the edges of the browser window as with the previous exercise. Again, the container is white, but this time has no padding, and has a set height of 200 pixels so that it doesn't collapse due to being empty.

Specifying a Background Image

The basic property and declaration is very similar to that of background-color. Load images.html in your browser and marvel at how plain it is. Before boredom sets in, quickly get a background image in there.

The basic GIF image is what is known as a **tile**. Just like a bathroom or floor tile, tile images can be repeated infinitely either horizontally, vertically, or sometimes both directions without causing an eye hazard, unlike my actual bathroom tiles, which are purple.

The tile you see in Figure 5-13 was created by Job Kooi and posted on über-cool design web site www.k10k.net many moons ago. It is a perfect tile because it is small, symmetrical, and will tile well in any direction.

Figure 5-13. *Job Kooi's tile image*

First, the tile can be made to appear in the container by adding the background-image property to the container selector.

```
/* Container for all page content */
  #container {
    height:200px;
    border:1px solid #000;
    background-color:#FFF;
    background-image:url(tile.gif);
  }
```

However, the result is interesting (see Figure 5-14). The image doesn't display once, it displays many, many times. By default, the background-image property will replicate the specified image as many times as necessary to fill the container.

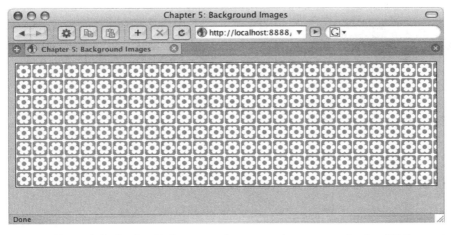

Figure 5-14. *By default, the tile is repeated as many times as required to fill the container.*

So, now you know how to use one very small image to fill a container! This default method is ideal for applying a tile to the background of the page, by specifying it in the body selector.

Repeat

So what if you need to control the way in which your image is tiled, or perhaps turn off tiling completely? Thankfully CSS has the answers, in the form of the background-repeat property.

There are four possible values—repeat, repeat-x, repeat-y, and no-repeat—all of which you will inevitably use—and often. The possible outcomes might already be apparent, but it is worth going through each in detail, skipping the repeat value, as that is already happening by default.

Turn Off Tiling

To turn off background image tiling, you will need the no-repeat value (but you'd already guessed that). Adjust the container properties as follows:

```
/* Container for all page content */
  #container {
    height:200px;
    border:1px solid #000;
    background-color:#FFF;
    background-image:url(tile.gif);
    background-repeat:no-repeat;
  }
```

This simple declaration will ensure that the image only displays once, and that it will be placed immediately inside the container, at top left, as shown in Figure 5-15.

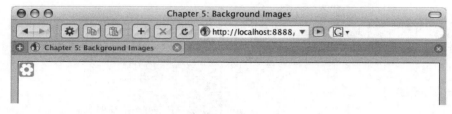

Figure 5-15. *Thanks to no-repeat, tiling is turned off.*

More fun can be had by allowing the tile to repeat either horizontally or vertically. This is an essential technique that lends itself to more adventurous CSS-based design, and allows for great flexibility. In the CSS, change the background-repeat value.

```
/* Container for all page content */
  #container {
    height:200px;
    border:1px solid #000;
    background-color:#FFF;
    background-image:url(tile.gif);
    background-repeat:repeat-y;
  }
```

What a cool result! As Figure 5-16 shows, the tile will only be displayed vertically for the full height of the container. This method is ideal for creating borders for containing elements, or for using a wide repeating strip as the main page background.

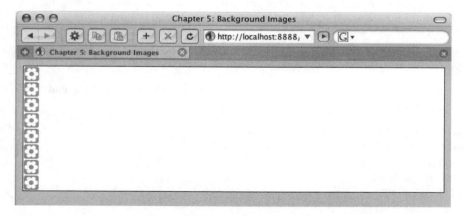

Figure 5-16. *The tile is now repeated vertically using repeat-y.*

You are probably aware from the previous example that repeat-x will force the tile to repeat horizontally. You'd be right of course (see Figure 5-17).

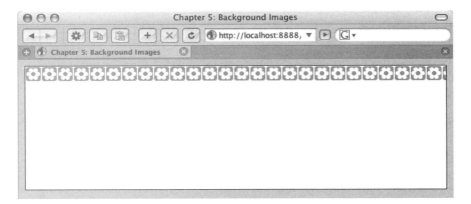

Figure 5-17. *Using repeat-x ensures that the tile repeats horizontally only.*

The repeat-x value is great for applying a tiled background image to headings, and both repeat-x and repeat-y are perfect for any situation where your image is only designed to tile in one direction (such as a heading background where a drop shadow effect is used at the base of the image). It is guaranteed that you'll be making good use of the background-repeat property not long after you've finished reading this chapter.

Position

Remember, by default the background-image property places the image (or starts the tiling process) at the top left of the container. Luckily, yet more flexibility has been provided with the background-position property, which allows you to specify exactly where the image should be placed in relation to its container.

The full list of possible values is extensive, and the basic English values can get you out of most fixes. Wish for the image to appear just once, and at the right of the container? Simply specify background-repeat:no-repeat followed by background-position:top right. If you wish the image to appear on the right, but at equal distance from the top and bottom of the container, specify background-position: center right. It sounds easy, and it is.

- top left
- top center
- top right
- center left
- center center
- center right
- bottom left
- bottom center
- bottom right

- x-% y-%

- x-pos y-pos

So what about those last two values? Well, if the general English values are too vague for your purposes, you can specify exact coordinates in pixels or as percentages instead, or combined with the English values. Look at the following examples:

```
background-position: 50px left;
background-position: 10% 50%;
background-position: 10px 20px;
background-position: 20px bottom;
```

These four values, coupled with `background-repeat:no-repeat`, will result in our tile being positioned in the four ways shown in Figure 5-18, starting from the top left and moving clockwise.

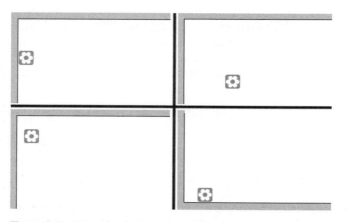

Figure 5-18. *Using background-position to reposition the image within the container*

It is advisable to not repeat the image here, as tiling would make positioning pointless in most scenarios. Again, this is a great method to experiment with, and to remember for future use. There most certainly will be a time when background positioning comes in very handy and gets you out of a situation that might have required an extra div.

Attachment

The `background-attachment` property is little used, but very effective. On the web site for top rock combo Dirty Pretty Things (www.dirtyprettythingsband.com), a fixed background image was declared in the body selector, ensuring the background image stayed stationary while the main container and everything inside it scrolled as would be expected (see Figure 5-19).

Two values are available, `scroll` (the default) and `fixed`. This method does require a certain amount of caution and careful preparation of graphics in some situations, but the results can be spectacular.

Figure 5-19. *The background image is stationary, as the rest of the content is scrolled up and down.*

Background Shorthand

Naturally, and with so many background properties available, shorthand is used to combine several background values into one line of CSS.

Combine Color with Image

In the previous example, rules for background-color and background-image are specified. These two rules can be combined by specifying the background property, and then the values in the correct order (color then image).

```
background:#FFF url(tile.gif);
```

■**Note** It is very important to specify a background color when text is to be placed over a background image. Imagine you have a very dark background image, over which you will place white text. If that background image fails to load, you could end up with white text on a white background. In this situation, specifying a black background with the background image would be sensible. Note also that for accessibility reasons a text color should always be specified for each element to which a background color or image has been applied.

Color, Image, and Position

If the image needs to be displayed to the right, and at the top of the container, the background-position value can be placed at the end of the list of values.

```
background:#FFF url(tile.gif) right top;
```

As long as the order is correct, the shorthand will work. You now have three lines of CSS combined into just one.

Color, Image, Position, and Repeat

Let's say you wish for the image to display just once, calling for no-repeat. The repeat value comes next in the list.

```
background:#FFF url(tile.gif) right top no-repeat;
```

Remember that any of the preceding values can be removed, so long as the order is the same. Obviously, if you remove the background-image value, the other image values will be worthless. Ah, the beauty of CSS shorthand. Apply this principle to as many CSS rules as you can to reduce the file size of your style sheet, and to keep it simple and manageable.

To Conclude...

Now that you have a grasp of the color and background basics, your mind is probably in over-drive thinking of possible uses for these techniques. So long as you exercise caution when using background images and consider the contrast of text against background, you'll be fine.

A great number of potentially brilliant web sites fail to be accessible due to poor color choices and irresponsible image usage. Be mindful of the end user at all times, and use the Firefox browser's Web Developer's Toolbar to turn images off and run other key tests at every stage of your site's development to emulate potential viewing scenarios. It is your responsibility to ensure that all visitors can use your web site as you intend.

In the next few chapters, you'll delve into the realm of lists, links, tables, and forms, all of which benefit greatly from the use of color and background to maximize their impact and usability. Things are going great, and they're only getting better.

CHAPTER 6

Lists

The humble list informs our everyday lives. Where would civilization be without lists? Lists for shopping, lists for chores (in my case), lists to tell us where all our lists are—almost everything is arranged into lists, and this certainly translates to the Web (think lists of bookmarks, blogrolls, link lists, site maps, file lists, and so on).

The fact is that the list is a very simple but essential tool for organizing data, and it is incredibly useful for the web designer. View the source of any web site built using web standards, and you are almost guaranteed to see a list for the navigation, a list for the external links, and probably a list for any buttons or arrays of data. Utilizing the humble list at an early stage of a web site project ensures the design will remain flexible, functional, and degrade well in any viewing scenario.

In this chapter, you'll quickly remind yourself of the basic markup and assess the different kind of lists that (X)HTML provides, particularly unordered and ordered lists. You'll apply ID and classes to lists to attain greater control, before taking things a bit further with nested lists controlled first with IDs and classes, and then manipulated with no extra markup, taking their basic hierarchies as hooks for more complex CSS control.

Why Use Lists?

A list of items can be created in numerous ways using (X)HTML, although not all are semantically correct. The lazier methods include adding a `<br />` tag after each item, or treating each item as a paragraph. The correct approach is to use an ordered or unordered list element, using simple `<li>` tags to open each item.

The major benefit of this approach is that your list will be displayed as a numbered or bulleted list without CSS, and is considerably easier to control with CSS. Using semantically correct list markup also makes it easy to single out items within a list, and also makes nested lists easier to manage.

The Unordered List

Let's begin by simplifying the drinks list used in Chapter 2. Create a new template called `lists.html` and add the following markup inside the empty body element. Notice that the unordered list is placed inside a container, which will act as a hook for more CSS later in this section.

```
<div id="container">
  <ul>
    <li>Drinks Menu</li>
    <li>Beer</li>
    <li>Spirits</li>
    <li>Cola</li>
    <li>Lemonade</li>
    <li>Tea</li>
    <li>Coffee</li>
  </ul>
</div>
```

Note This list features an initial list item "Drinks menu". Semantically speaking, this would be better as a heading (such as `<h3>Drinks menu</h3>`), but for the purposes of this chapter, it is declared as a list item so that you can see how it can be treated differently. This approach will make more sense when we look at nested lists later in the chapter.

Save the template. You now have an unordered list of the most basic kind as shown in Figure 6-1. The only styling is that inherited from the parent elements, and in this case that is none at all.

Figure 6-1. *A basic, unstyled ordered list*

Basic List CSS

Before moving on to anything particularly clever, let's first work through some of the basic CSS list properties. By default, the list will be bulleted with small discs, emulating a typical list such as you might find in Microsoft Word. Note also that even though the container has no internal padding, the list is still placed well away from the left edge—approximately 30 pixels away. This padding is actually the distance between the left edge of the unordered list and each item it contains.

list-style-type

The list-style-type property allows you to specify one of a number of possible markers instead of the default disc for each list item. There are numerous values available, many of which you won't need (Hebrew or Armenian characters, for example), but the following five values may well be useful:

- none
- disc
- circle
- square
- latin

Other possibly useful list-style-types may be required from time to time. Three useful examples include upper-alpha, lower-alpha, and upper-roman.

- upper-alpha: A, B, C, D, E, etc.
- lower-alpha: a, b, c, d, e, etc.
- upper-roman: I, II, III, IV, V, etc.

Let's try some basic list styling. Create a new style sheet called lists.css, and remember to link to it in the head of lists.html. In lists.css you can try out each of the values by first adding the following selector for the unordered list element:

```
/* Styles for all default lists */
  ul {
    list-style-type:circle;
  }
```

In Figure 6-2, the result of specifying circle can be seen. Specifying disc would have made no difference as that marker was already used by default. It goes without saying that square would produce a small squared marker.

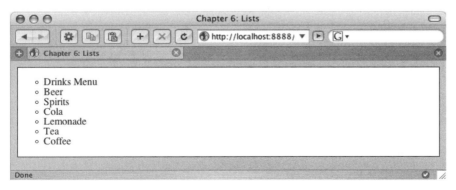

Figure 6-2. *The result of list-style-type:circle*

Of particular use if you wish to get away from any kind of basic marker is the none value, which of course removes the marker altogether (see Figure 6-3).

```
list-style-type:none;
```

You can then either stick with no bullet marker or add a custom marker of your own using an image, as you'll discover later in the chapter.

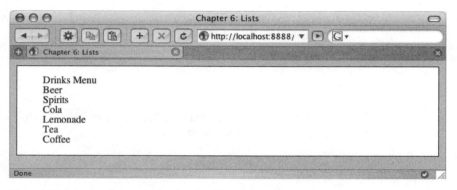

Figure 6-3. *List markers removed using list-style-type:none*

Margin and Padding

Notice, however, that the actual list items do not shunt to the left despite the lack of marker, which leaves too much whitespace in front of each item.

Therefore, the default padding applied by the browser can be reduced by specifying your preferred padding. Earlier I stated that most browsers place the list items 30 pixels away from the left edge of the unordered list (default padding) and the unordered list itself approximately 10 pixels from the top edge of the container (default margin). Figure 6-4 shows the default spacing applied to the list and its items by drawing a line around each.

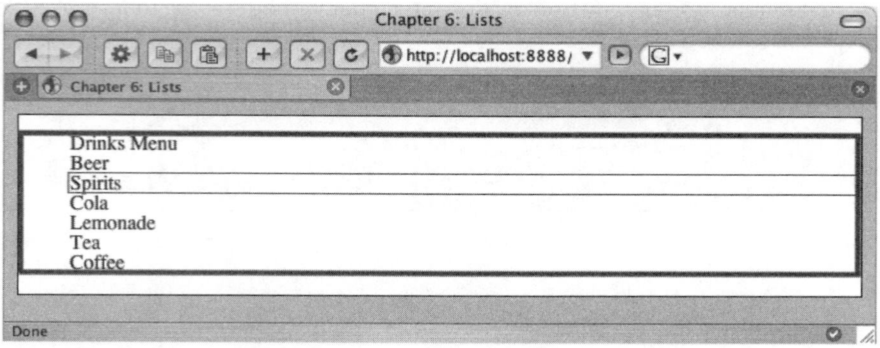

Figure 6-4. *The thick line represents the default limits of the unordered list, and the thinner line represents the default limits of the "Spirits" list item.*

Notice also that each list item is block level. Therefore it will expand to fill the width of its container, and items above and below will wrap to a new line. Each of these defaults can be overridden with simple CSS declarations.

To remove the default margin from the top and bottom of the unordered list, specify zero margins:

```
ul {
  list-style-type:none;
  margin:0;
}
```

To remove the default padding that pushes the listed items in by 30px, specify zero padding:

```
ul {
  list-style-type:none;
  margin:0;
  padding:0;
}
```

To prevent the listed items from extending the full width of the container, set a maximum width:

```
ul {
  list-style-type:none;
  margin:0;
  padding:0;
  width:200px;
}
```

Figure 6-5 shows the results of these changes.

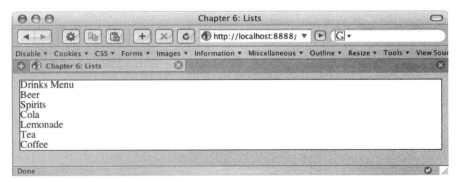

Figure 6-5. *With default margin and padding settings removed, the unordered list and its contents now sit directly against the container edges.*

The reason for all of this default padding becomes obvious if you reintroduce the list markers (see Figure 6-6). Notice that the markers appear outside of the container element.

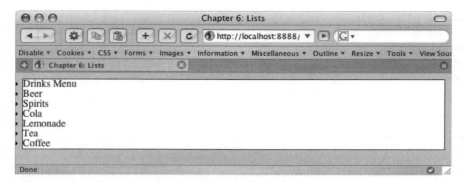

Figure 6-6. *With list markers, you'll be wishing you hadn't removed the default padding.*

Therefore, if you will be using markers, but wish to override the default 30-pixel padding, you can specify a custom left padding value. In the following example, 20 pixels are enough to ensure the markers appear just inside the container. Note that it is specified using `padding` shorthand (top, right, bottom, left).

```
ul {
  margin:0;
  padding:0 0 0 20px;
  width:200px;
}
```

Figure 6-7 shows the result of this custom padding. This example demonstrates how to place your unordered list precisely within a given container. It may be that you also wish to specify custom margins to further refine the spacing.

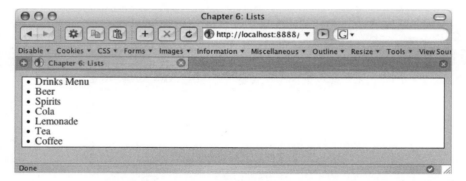

Figure 6-7. *Custom padding ensures the list markers appear exactly where required.*

list-style-position

Anyone who has created a bulleted list using a word processor will be aware that as long lines of text wrap, they line up exactly to the left, with the bullet placed further left. The bullet is not treated as a character, and simply indicates where each new list item begins. This is how (X)HTML lists also work by default.

not treated as a character, and simply indicates where each new list item begins. This is how (X)HTML lists also work by default.

However, there may be occasions when the bullet needs to be inline with the text, and this is why the list-style-position property was created. The default value is outside, and though not specified in the preceding examples, it was already in operation. To override this default, inside can be specified (note that for this example, the default padding is removed also).

```
ul {
    list-style-position:inside;
    margin:0;
    padding:0;
    width:200px;
}
```

As padding is set to zero, this will place the list marker inside the unordered list with not a pixel of padding, as shown in Figure 6-8.

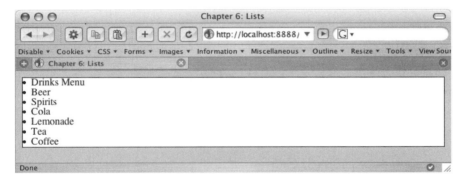

Figure 6-8. *With list-style-position:inside, the markers are placed immediately inside the unordered list.*

There may be cases where this is ideal, but in most situations, a little left padding will make things neater. Specifying padding-left:5px or padding:0 0 0 5px will be enough to shunt the markers neatly away from the edge of the unordered list. In the real world, list-style-position is little used in favor of standard list formatting, but it's worth being aware of it, just in case.

Note Remember that with a list-style-position value of inside, long lines of text will wrap and begin underneath their bullet markers, as though the marker were a normal character.

---

list-style-image

The typical bullet markers provided by CSS are fine for very simple lists, but in most cases a custom bullet marker will be more desirable.

Hooray therefore for the list-style-image property, which allows a custom image to be used in place of the boring disc, circle, square, and other basic bullets. Now that you know how to space your list items away from the left edge of the unordered list, playing with custom images of any width shouldn't be a problem.

For this example, I'm using a smaller version of the tile image from Chapter 5, reduced to 12 pixels square, which I have renamed list.gif.

```
ul {
  margin:0;
  padding:0 0 0 25px;
  width:200px;
  list-style-image:url(images/list.gif);
}
```

As list-style-image is declared, there is no need to specify list-style-type. Note also that the left padding has been increased to compensate for the width of the image. The result can be seen in Figure 6-9.

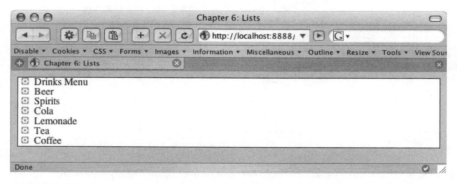

Figure 6-9. *The list now benefits from a custom bullet marker.*

The wider your custom bullet image, the more left padding you may need. The list is already looking a little more personalized, but could well benefit from some extra whitespace between the list items. It's a job for our old friend line-height.

```
ul {
  margin:0;
  padding:0 0 0 25px;
  width:200px;
  list-style-image:url(images/list.gif);
  line-height:150%;
}
```

Ah, where would we be without the line-height property? In Figure 6-10, it adds legibility to the list, making the whole thing much easier on the eye. Note that it also takes care of the spacing at the top and bottom of the list, removing the need for top or bottom unordered list margins.

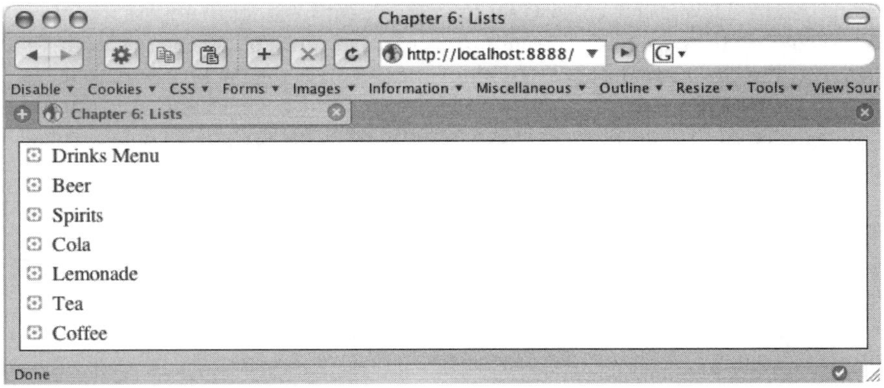

Figure 6-10. *Yet again, line-height comes in useful for legibility.*

This is only a hint of the possibilities with list styling. Later in the chapter you'll see how more properties such as border and background can be used to add more definition to unordered lists and the items they contain.

list-style for Shorthand

Yes, list properties can also be shortened into one declaration, using the list-style property.

```
list-style: none inside url(images/list.gif);
```

However, it is not often that you would need to specify all three properties. In this example, declaring a custom image with list-style-image:url(images/tile.gif) removes the need to also turn off the basic list marker, except in the shorthand. Therefore, just specifying a custom image will be all you need in most scenarios.

Using Background Images for List Bullets

Using the list-style-image property is the easiest method of assigning a custom bullet to your list items, but the results can be somewhat inconsistent. Some browsers will align the custom image directly in the middle of the list item text, while others will position it slightly higher.

To beat this problem, a custom background image can be used for each list item. Note that default bulleting is turned off in the ul selector.

```
ul {
  list-style:none;
}
li {
  background: transparent url(images/list.gif) no-repeat left center;
  padding:0 0 0 25px;
}
```

For this example, the background-color is set to transparent in order to ensure that the white background color of the container does not prevent the custom bullet images from displaying. Also, by using background-position values left center, the background image is forced to display the same distance from the top and bottom of the list element. Appropriate left padding is also declared to allow enough space in front of the list text for the image to fall into, as shown in Figure 6-11.

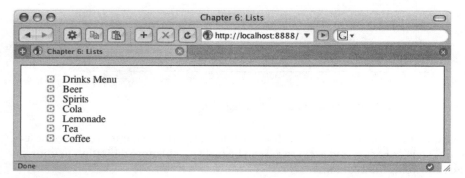

Figure 6-11. *Nothing looks different, but the list markers are actually background images.*

Later in this chapter, you'll learn how assigning classes to list items can allow for several different background bullets to be used in one unordered list.

■**Note** It is important to be aware that should the custom image fail to load or be unavailable for some reason, your list will have no visual markers. If you were to approach the same design using the list-style-image property to add your custom bullets, a normal bullet would show until the image was successfully downloaded or made available. If it's perfect bullet alignment you want, then background images are still the best bet.

The Inline List

By default, unordered list items will display vertically, with each list item on a new line. This is because the <li> element is a block-level element. There are, however, many occasions when you will need your list to display horizontally, for a main navigation bar, for example.

This calls for the default block-level value to be overridden using the display property. Let's strip back the styling from the previous examples and examine the basic behavior.

```
/* Styles for our basic list */
  ul {
    list-style-type:disc;
  }
  li {
    display:inline;
  }
```

Notice that the unordered list merely specifies the bullet marker type, and that it is the `li` selector that is now doing all the work. By giving `display` a value of `inline`, the default `block` display is overruled, forcing each list item to display on the same line, as Figure 6-12 illustrates.

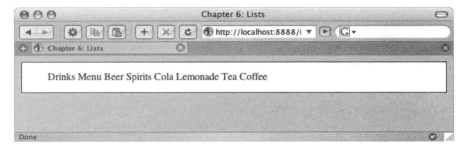

Figure 6-12. *Using display:inline to force list items to appear horizontally*

This is a great starting point for a horizontal menu, but what has happened to the bullet markers? Bizarrely, the bullet will not show when display is set to `inline`. This brings us back to using background images with list items.

Background Images and Inline Lists

Earlier you learned how to apply a custom bullet as a background image in order to get around a few cross-browser display quirks. Using this approach allows you to assign a bullet for inline lists where default bullets refuse to be displayed.

The CSS is fairly simple. Again, turn default bullets off in the `ul` selector, and ensure `display:inline` is declared in the `li` selector. Note also that the same background rules (transparent background and specific positioning) are declared.

```
ul {
  list-style:none;
}
li {
  display:inline;
  background:transparent url(images/list.gif) no-repeat left center;
  margin:0 0 0 10px;
  padding:0 0 0 15px;
}
```

As the list is now displaying horizontally, everything appears on the same line and so the definition between each item is reduced. Therefore the left padding is reduced to just 15 pixels (just enough room for the 12-pixels-wide image), and 10 pixels of left margin are applied to space out each list item, as shown in Figure 6-13.

From this starting point, it should be clear how to further control the space between each item and get this thing to display exactly as you wish. In the next section, you'll learn how to take greater control of the list elements using good old IDs and classes.

Figure 6-13. *Using background images for list items, with appropriate left margin and left padding to put space between each*

Taking Control with IDs

Remember in Chapter 2 that the drinks list was given its own unique ID? We can revisit this approach to look at methods for controlling several lists and affecting the items they contain based on this ID.

In lists.html, add the following ID to the basic list markup, acting as a vital hook for many of the styles to be added throughout this section. Also, add a second list underneath that list (but still inside the container) with different list items and the ID food.

```
<ul id="drinks">
  <li>Drinks Menu</li>
  <li>Beer</li>
  <li>Spirits</li>
  <li>Cola</li>
  <li>Lemonade</li>
  <li>Tea</li>
  <li>Coffee</li>
</ul>
<ul id="food">
  <li>Food Menu</li>
  <li>Toast</li>
  <li>Cornflakes</li>
  <li>Burgers</li>
  <li>Steak</li>
  <li>Salad</li>
  <li>Fries</li>
</ul>
```

So, each unordered list is given a unique ID. Thus, id="drinks" will not be used again on the page at any time, and allows that particular list to be styled uniquely. Likewise, the second list is the food menu, also unique. The CSS from the previous inline list example will suffice here, but if you need it again, use the following two selectors. Note that we are sticking with inline examples here, mainly to save page space, although everything is applicable to default vertical lists.

```
ul {
  list-style:none;
}
li {
  display:inline;
  background:transparent url(images/list.gif) no-repeat left center;
  margin:0 0 0 10px;
  padding:0 0 0 15px;
}
```

As things stand, the CSS will style both lists in an identical fashion, as it is not targeted to look for a particular ID (see Figure 6-14).

Figure 6-14. *Both lists are styled in the same way, as the CSS is not targeted to affect a particular ID.*

In some cases, this approach might be ideal, such as horizontal sidebar lists where all items should be rendered in the same way, but need to be separated into different unordered lists (perhaps to allow headings to be placed above each). However, the additional IDs added to each list allow you to target each with specific CSS selectors.

For example, let's assign a different background image bullet for each list. As it is only the images that need to change, the ul selector is shared across both lists, and can be left unaltered. Also, all li declarations that are shared are first grouped together, before the targeted declarations are set separately.

```
/* Unordered list for drinks and food lists */
  ul {
    list-style:none;
  }
  li {
    display:inline;
    margin:0 0 0 10px;
    padding:0 0 0 15px;
  }
```

```
/* Images for drinks list only */
  #drinks li {
    background:transparent url(images/drinks.gif) no-repeat left top;
  }
/* Images for food list only */
  #food li {
    background:transparent url(images/food.gif) no-repeat left center;
  }
```

As a result, the relevant icons are displayed for the relevant list items, as shown in Figure 6-15. Naturally, other custom values can be set for each list, such as the color of the text, borders, padding, and so on.

Figure 6-15. *The drinks list and food list have the relevant icons, thanks to targeted declarations.*

Grouping Items with Classes

Classes are especially useful when you wish to have control over a number of elements. In our two lists, there are clearly other groupings that can be defined. Back in Chapter 2, drinks were grouped into alcohol, mixer, and hot by adding a matching class to each list element.

In this example, the same approach is used to group the food, using breakfast, dinner, and side classes.

```
<ul id="drinks">
  <li>Drinks Menu</li>
  <li class="alcohol">Beer</li>
  <li class="alcohol">Spirits</li>
  <li class="mixer">Cola</li>
  <li class="mixer">Lemonade</li>
  <li class="hot">Tea</li>
  <li class="hot">Coffee</li>
</ul>
<ul id="food">
  <li>Food Menu</li>
  <li class="breakfast">Toast</li>
```

```
  <li class="breakfast">Cornflakes</li>
  <li class="dinner">Burgers</li>
  <li class="dinner">Steak</li>
  <li class="side">Salad</li>
  <li class="side">Fries</li>
</ul>
```

As before, note that the first list item has no class attribute, yet every other item is assigned a class. This allows each drinks and food group to be treated individually.

As before, the classes for each drink type are defined with unique shades of gray for font color, but this time we can also group foods using the same method, by grouping the declarations:

```
/* Define first food and drink group */
  .alcohol, .breakfast {
    color: #333;
  }
/* Define second food and drink group */
  .mixer, .dinner {
    color: #999;
  }
/* Define third food and drink group */
  .hot, .side {
    color: #CCC;
  }
```

The result sees the list of items move from black (the basic unordered list color—"drinks" and "food") through shades of gray (defined by the classes) as in Figure 6-16. Any further drinks or food added to the lists can be assigned to a particular drinks or food group, such as `<li class="side">Mashed Potato</li>`. Thus a logical color key is established using simple CSS classes.

Figure 6-16. *From black to light gray, the list items are grouped using shades of gray.*

The same approach could obviously be used to assign different icons to each food or drink group, or some other method of differentiation.

Nested Lists

There will be many instances where you need to create a hierarchy in one list, and this is where nested lists are most useful. Just to recap, (X)HTML allows you to begin an unordered list and create new lists inside that.

The following markup takes the existing food and drinks menus and nests them inside one main list. It is very important to get the markup right in such scenarios, as to forget to close a top-level list item or nested list can cause all sorts of chaos.

```
<ul>
  <li>Drinks Menu
    <ul>
      <li>Beer</li>
      <li>Spirits</li>
      <li>Cola</li>
      <li>Lemonade</li>
      <li>Tea</li>
      <li>Coffee</li>
    </ul>
  </li>
  <li>Food Menu
    <ul>
      <li>Toast</li>
      <li>Cornflakes</li>
      <li>Burgers</li>
      <li>Steak</li>
      <li>Salad</li>
      <li>Fries</li>
    </ul>
  </li>
</ul>
```

Load that in the browser window, and the default browser style sheet will use a disc bullet for the top level and a circle bullet for the second level (see Figure 6-17).

Because a hierarchy is suggested with the markup, it is possible to make significant style changes without applying IDs or classes. First, let's use CSS to change the color of the second-level list items.

```
/* Style top-level unordered list and contents */
  ul {
    color:#000;
  }
/* Style second-level unordered list and contents */
  ul li ul {
    color:#666;
  }
```

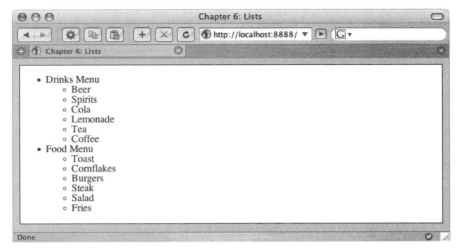

Figure 6-17. *Unstyled nested lists*

Here the CSS selectors target the relevant list based on its relationship with another. Thus the first selector looks for the all `<ul>` elements it finds in the markup, and ensures the text is black, unless a declaration for a nested list says differently

Importantly, the second selector looks for any `<ul>` that is contained by one more above it, using the `ul li ul` descendant selector. In other words, the browser looks and thinks to itself, "Uh, OK. So I ignore the first `<ul>`, and I ignore any `<li>` elements inside it, but when I get to the next `<ul>`, I get to work and make its contents gray" (see Figure 6-18). Of course, browsers don't actually think, which makes your job as web designer that bit harder, but you get the idea of how the browser works its way through the descendant selectors until it finds its target.

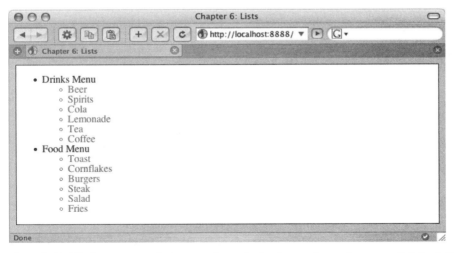

Figure 6-18. *The browser works its way through the descendant selector until it finds its target and turns the secondary list gray.*

Therefore, it becomes easy to define other custom values for each level. Building on our earlier example of assigning custom background images, the CSS can be used to target the second level of list elements specifically.

```
/* Style top-level unordered list and contents */
  ul {
    color:#000;
  }
/* Style second-level unordered list and contents */
  ul li ul {
    list-style-type:none;
    color:#666;
  }
  ul li ul li {
    padding:0 0 0 15px;
    background:transparent url(images/list.gif) no-repeat left center;
  }
```

So now the second-level ul selector (ul li ul) is still ensuring any information within it will be gray, but also turning off bullets for that list only. Also, the extra descendant selector for its list elements (ul li ul li) is tasked with applying a custom background image to those elements only, as you see in Figure 6-19.

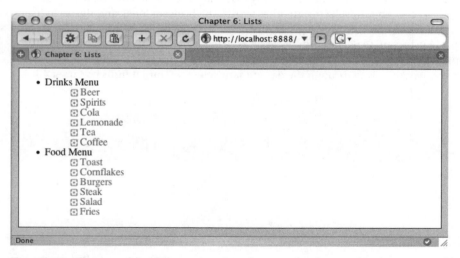

Figure 6-19. *The second-level lists are assigned custom background images using ul li ul li.*

The Possibilities Are Endless

Clearly, this leaves the first ul selector free to have its own custom image declared (using a new selector for its list elements—ul li) alongside its black text color. The possibilities here are endless—literally. For complex site maps and never-ending nested lists, descendant selectors (ul li ul li ul li ul li anyone?) are available for maximum control throughout the hierarchy.

Perhaps a gradually decreasing font size would work for your design, or gradual lightening of color—all done with CSS and no extra markup.

Combine this approach with specific IDs for unordered lists and classes for groups at any level, and you begin to see how complicated yet powerful this approach can be. For now though, we won't go there, but it is something else to keep in your toolbox.

Lists for Navigation

A common feature of web sites built using web standards are navigation menus constructed using an unordered list. Using the `<ul>` element in this sense is semantically correct, with each destination link defined as an individual list item. This approach provides incredible flexibility, allowing the navigation list to be either horizontal or vertical as defined using CSS, and also allows for a seemingly unlimited number of styling approaches.

Already in this chapter you have learned how to take the default vertical list and transform it into a simple horizontal navigation. Now, let's take things a step further and create a good-looking vertical navigation list, where each destination link is styled as though a graphic button.

The Vertical Navigation Bar

A very common feature of many, many web sites is the vertical navigation bar created with simple list markup. The goal here is to turn each list element into a button without using any images whatsoever.

Let's jump back to the concept of the simple list. For this task, a simpler unordered list is useful—just one level of list elements.

```
<ul>
  <li>Beer</li>
  <li>Spirits</li>
  <li>Cola</li>
  <li>Lemonade</li>
  <li>Tea</li>
  <li>Coffee</li>
</ul>
```

Remove All Default Spacing

This brings us back to the very simple display (to refresh your mind, see Figure 6-20). First, the list elements need to be pulled to the top and left edges of the container.

```
ul {
  list-style-type:none;
  margin:0;
  padding:0;
}
li {
  padding:0;
}
```

This ensures you start with a blank canvas. No default spacing is in play. From this point on, all spacing is on your terms, avoiding the confusion that often comes with navigation list styling.

Figure 6-20. *All default spacing is removed from the list.*

Turn List Elements into Buttons

Perfect. Now some styling can be applied to make the list elements look a little more like buttons. The padding can now be adjusted also to provide enough space around the text.

```
ul {
  list-style-type:none;
  margin:0;
  padding:0;
}
li {
  background: #DDD;
  margin: 0;
  padding: 2px 10px;
  border-left: 1px solid #fff;
  border-top: 1px solid #fff;
  border-right: 1px solid #666;
  border-bottom: 1px solid  #aaa;
}
```

In this example, shades of gray and white borders are used to give the buttons a slightly three-dimensional feel. So far, so good, but the buttons are still filling the entire available horizontal space (see Figure 6-21).

Figure 6-21. *A little more like buttons, but a touch too wide!*

Define the Width of the Buttons

It is necessary to define a set width for the buttons, which can be done with the ul selector. Here 160px seems appropriate.

```
ul {
  list-style-type:none;
  margin:0;
  padding:0;
  width:160px;
}
```

Aha! Now the list is looking a bit more like a real navigation menu as you can see in Figure 6-22.

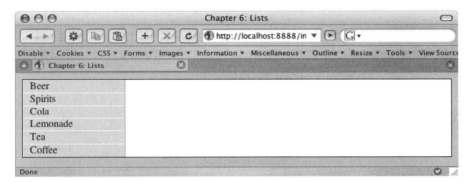

Figure 6-22. *With a set width, the navigation menu is taking shape.*

Final Touches

All that remains is to refine the display a little more. Thus font values are added with a short-hand declaration, and the unordered list is given a border, a margin, and 2 pixels of padding to create whitespace around the buttons.

```
ul {
  list-style-type:none;
  margin:5px;
  padding:2px;
  border:1px solid #333;
  width:160px;
  font: bold 12px 'Lucida Grande',Verdana,sans-serif;
}
li {
  background: #DDD;
  margin: 0;
  padding: 2px 10px;
  border-left: 1px solid #fff;
  border-top: 1px solid #fff;
  border-right: 1px solid #666;
  border-bottom: 1px solid #aaa
}
```

As you can see in Figure 6-23, the finished navigation menu looks pretty good, despite not actually linking to anything yet (you'll learn how to create exciting link buttons in Chapter 7).

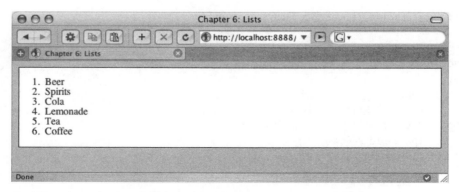

Figure 6-23. *The finished vertical navigation bar*

This might be a good point to take what you have learned about navigation lists thus far and experiment with your own `border`, `background`, and `margin` values to personalize your list and get a feel for this vital element of CSS-based design. In Chapter 7, you will also see how this approach can be applied to vertical navigation bars.

The Ordered List

The ordered list is a convenient way to mark up a list of items with each preceded by a number. (X)HTML makes this possible with the `<ol>` element. As this author's thirst is clearly not yet quenched, let's again take the drinks list and this time place it inside an ordered list.

```
<ol>
  <li>Beer</li>
  <li>Spirits</li>
  <li>Cola</li>
  <li>Lemonade</li>
  <li>Tea</li>
  <li>Coffee</li>
</ol>
```

The beauty of the ordered list is its flexibility. If it were necessary to add another drink to the list at any point, the automatic numbering would compensate appropriately, renumbering all list items that followed. The basic unstyled list can be seen in Figure 6-24.

Figure 6-24. *The ordered list without styling*

Remember that other list-style-type declarations can be made to replace the autogenerated numbers with other characters, such as upper-alpha, lower-alpha, and upper-roman.

Controlling the Ordered List

While the default unordered list works like magic, there may be occasions where you wish to replace the default numerical characters with your own custom numbers. This is relatively simple, but does involve extra markup. The first thing to do is to identify each list item with its own unique class.

```
<ol>
  <li class="one">Beer</li>
  <li class="two">Spirits</li>
  <li class="three">Cola</li>
  <li class="four">Lemonade</li>
  <li class="five">Tea</li>
  <li class="six">Coffee</li>
</ol>
```

It should be noted that by utilizing this method, you are removing the browser's ability to automatically number your list items should you wish to insert another item in the middle. The reason an ordered list is useful here though is that if the style sheet were unavailable, the default numbers would be returned, and the list would still be ordered, keeping things semantically correct. The following approach will of course work for unordered lists, too.

Creating Custom Numbers

The next step is to create the images you will use to replace the default text numbers. For this example, six images were needed, all saved as GIF images (see Figure 6-25). The size is the same as the custom bullets used earlier in the chapter (12×12 pixels).

Figure 6-25. *The six custom images required for the customized ordered list*

Declaring the Numbers Using the Unique Classes

Now for the CSS. Notice that list-style-type:none is declared in the ol selector to turn off the default numbers (remember that this means no numbering will be displayed if the images are not available). Also, left padding is used to allow enough space for the custom number images. The padding needs only to be assigned to the li selector, as it is a value that is shared across all following selectors. Nothing new about that, but what is new is the six new selectors for each class that has been added to each list item.

```
ol {
  list-style:none;
}
li {
  padding:0 0 0 25px;
}
.one {
  background: transparent url(images/ol1.gif) no-repeat left center;
}
.two {
  background: transparent url(images/ol2.gif) no-repeat left center;
}
.three {
  background: transparent url(images/ol3.gif) no-repeat left center;
}
.four {
  background: transparent url(images/ol4.gif) no-repeat left center;
}
.five {
  background: transparent url(images/ol5.gif) no-repeat left center;
}
.six {
  background: transparent url(images/ol6.gif) no-repeat left center;
}
```

So you now have six selectors that correlate with the classes assigned to the ordered list. Mixing all of this together and loading the page in the browser gives the basic customized list you see in Figure 6-26.

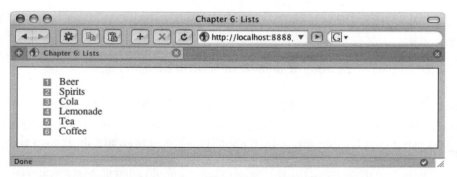

Figure 6-26. *The ordered list now features the smashing custom numbers.*

Dressing Up the Ordered List

With the custom icons working, you are now free to add further styling to the ordered list. Many of the declarations used to create the vertical navigation list earlier are reused here, specifically the background colors and borders.

Note, however, that the unique classes added to each list item overrule any background-color declaration in the li selector, so background-color needs to be declared for each class. The padding is also adjusted to replicate that in the vertical navigation example, allowing the custom numbers and list item text to be spaced appropriately.

```
ol {
  list-style-type:none;
  margin:5px;
  padding:2px;
  border:1px solid #333;
  width:160px;
  font: bold 12px 'Lucida Grande',Verdana,sans-serif;
}
li {
  margin: 0;
  padding: 2px 10px 2px 25px;
  border-left: 1px solid #fff;
  border-top: 1px solid #fff;
  border-right: 1px solid #aaa;
  border-bottom: 1px solid #666
}
.one {
  background:#DDDDDD url(images/ol1.gif) no-repeat 3px center;
}
.two {
  background:#DDDDDD url(images/ol2.gif) no-repeat 3px center;
}
.three {
  background:#DDDDDD url(images/ol3.gif) no-repeat 3px center;
}
.four {
  background:#DDDDDD url(images/ol4.gif) no-repeat 3px center;
}
.five {
  background:#DDDDDD url(images/ol5.gif) no-repeat 3px center;
}
.six {
  background:#DDDDDD url(images/ol6.gif) no-repeat 3px center;
}
```

One further change is made to the shorthand background-position property for each custom number. Instead of left, a value of 3px is specified to pull the custom image away from the left border of the list item. The end result looks very similar to the earlier vertical navigation, except the custom numbers are in place, as shown in Figure 6-27.

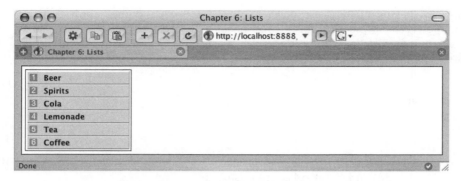

Figure 6-27. *Custom ordered list numbers combined with further styling*

The drawbacks of this technique are obvious, but the benefits are far-reaching. One drawback is that this method works well only for ordered lists that are unlikely to grow or be reordered, as you are now overruling the default browser action of reordering and number adjustment.

A major positive is that you can now see how easy it is to take greater control of any kind of list, as the method of applying unique classes to list elements will of course work for unordered lists also. I've said it before and I'll say it again—the possibilities are literally endless.

To Conclude...

The approaches explained in this chapter are incredibly important for any web designer, as the list is a fundamental ingredient of any build. Get to grips with lists and the many methods of wrestling them into submission, and you're well on your way to professional status.

In the next chapter, the subject of links will come to the fore. In that chapter you will take the vertical navigation list created earlier and turn it into a fully functional navigation bar with dynamic links that hover and reflect the selected page.

Chapter 8 will place emphasis back on lists, looking at something fancy called the definition list, and much of what you have learned so far will also be very useful for table and form styling that follows soon. Your CSS arsenal is growing rapidly, and pretty soon all of these bits and pieces will be pulled together into a more complex page. Things are going great, so refill the teapot and grab some biscuits.

■■■

CHAPTER 7

Links

Rare is the web page that doesn't link to another. Without **links** (a.k.a. **hyperlinks**), nobody would go anywhere. A Google results page would be pointless, web-based advertising wouldn't exist (possibly not such a bad thing), and if somebody managed to reach your home page, they'd be hard pushed to find their way anywhere else.

As somebody pretty familiar with (X)HTML, it is probably fair to assume that you have created a link already, but managing to link to another web page is only the beginning. With CSS, links become magical objects that can be both beautiful and functional. From the humble rollover color to advanced image maps and complex menus, link styling is a vast and ever-evolving area of web design that is essential to master.

A fundamental factor with links is accessibility. Whenever you create a link, you have to consider the end user. Basic concepts such as visited and active links need great care, and any complex link treatment needs to be considered from all possible standpoints. In a nutshell, a link has a very important role to play, and its basic functionality should never be compromised in pursuit of beauty or creativity. That said, there are a million-and-one things to do with links to enhance the user's experience, and many of them are out-and-out fun.

Link Markup

Let's start with an (X)HTML recap. The basic link is a simple beast, whether you are using either text or an image, and it's one of the first bits of code that most of us get to grips with. The basic markup for a text link is as follows:

```
<a href="http://www.google.com">Google</a>
```

Or to use an image as the link, you'd use the following, ensuring that the alt attribute is used to provide relevant link text should the image not be available:

```
<a href="http://www.google.com"><img src="images/google.gif" ➡
alt="Visit Google" /></a>
```

Further to this basic link, other attributes are available, such as title, used to provide a tool tip of additional information when the user hovers over the link:

```
<a href="http://www.google.com" title="Visit the best search engine ➡
in the world">Google</a>
```

This basic markup is often all that is needed to provide the perfect hook for simple CSS rules. Naturally, as links are self-contained elements, they can be combined with parent elements such as lists, or housed in custom containers in order for more specific descendant selectors to take effect and treat links in different ways depending upon where they sit in the page.

Default Link Styling

By default, browsers treat links in a particular way. Anyone who has created a link without applying CSS will be aware that the default browser style sheet will render unvisited links in dark blue, visited links in purple, and so on, and that these links will be underlined. This convention was intended as a staple approach to the Web by its early founders—an easily recognizable method of quickly analyzing which links on a page the user has already visited. A number of web personalities still believe that this convention is too important to dismiss, but the fact is that for a number of years designers have dispensed with this law in favor of link styling more in keeping with their designs. Dark blue is not always the best style for a link, and we'd be foolish to think it is—what if it doesn't suit your site theme?

Simple CSS Rules

The first thing many web designers want to do is change the color of the link text, and have that color change as the visitor places the cursor over that link text. To begin, let's first set up a new template with which to work, and then approach some simple CSS link declarations.

Setup

Create a new template called `links.html` and paste the following markup into it (note that in the examples the following is placed inside the `<body>` element, and also inside a `container` div as in previous chapters):

```
<h2>Introducing the band</h2>
  <p>To find out more about members of <a href="#">The Dead Goods</a>, please ➡
  select the appropriate person for a full profile.</p>
    <ul>
      <li><a href="links.html">Simon Collison</a></li>
      <li><a href="#">John Lennon</a></li>
      <li><a href="#">Jimi Hendrix</a></li>
      <li><a href="#">Jeff Buckley</a></li>
      <li><a href="#">Kurt Cobain</a></li>
      <li><a href="#">Janis Joplin</a></li>
      <li><a href="#">Keith Moon</a></li>
    </ul>
```

If a fictitious rock group featuring mostly dead people isn't your thing, feel free to create your own. Be aware though that when word gets around about *The Dead Goods*, they'll be getting a lot of publicity, and nobody will care about your band.

Notice that the link to myself links to the actual template created. This allows a visited link state to be available at all times—essential for checking the visited link styling to be added shortly. Notice also that one link is placed in the opening paragraph, and the rest are correctly defined as list items. Save the template, load `links.html` in your browser, and it should look something like Figure 7-1.

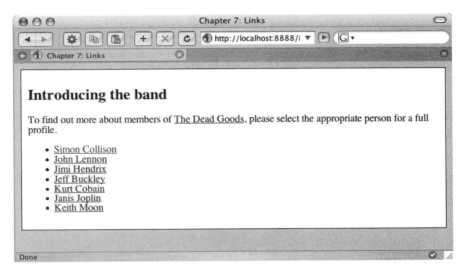

Figure 7-1. *The basic page template with no link or list styling. Sid Vicious failed the audition.*

Notice that all links are the default dark blue, aside for the link to Simon Collison, which of course links to the page in view—that's the visited link, displayed in purple (or slightly lighter in this noncolor book).

Next, link to an external style sheet called `links.css`. (You should know how to do this by now. If not, it's back to Chapter 1 with you!). Add declarations for the body selector, and also for the `container` div if you are using one.

Changing Link Color

Now you can add some simple CSS rules to take control of the links. This is done with the pseudo classes `:link`, `:visited`, `:active`, and `:hover`.

All Links

First, the pseudo class `:link` is combined with the a element selector (from the `<a href`... part of the link markup), creating the selector `a:link`.

```
a:link {
  color:#F00;
  }
```

This very simple selector targets all instances of the `<a>` element and turns all unvisited links to red. Any visited links will still be purple, as thus far you have not created a selector to override the browser's default visited link style.

Visited Links

To show visited links, simply create a selector for the `<a>` element with the `:visited` pseudo class.

```
a:visited {
  color:#999;
  }
```

Now all unvisited links are red, and all visited links will be light gray (see Figure 7-2). It is very important to make visited links appear different from unvisited ones. It is an accepted convention and instantly highlights any links already followed on that machine. The light gray used in this example is perhaps too big a change, but the book is not in color, so I had to use something obvious!

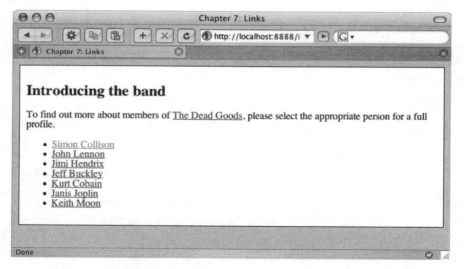

Figure 7-2. *The a:link selector has transformed all unvisited links to red, and the a:visited selector has made the visited link gray.*

A Lot Less Bovver with a:hover

Imagine you have a vast list of links, or a paragraph chock-full of them. Without some form of interaction, the user could easily click the wrong link and be taken to the incorrect destination. The answer to this problem is the powerful `:hover` pseudo class, which aside from being a great usability aid is also rather attractive.

Again, the selector first looks for all instances of the `<a>` element, but will only be performed when the user mouses over the link text.

```
a:hover {
  color:#333;
  }
```

This simple rule will turn any link text dark gray on mouseover without exception, whether the link is visited or unvisited.

Active

The :active pseudo class takes care of the link styles when the mouse button is actually clicked, and is another very useful usability aid.

```
a:active {
  color: #000;
  }
```

With this example, as the user clicks the link, the text will turn black for as long as the current page remains in view, acting as an extra clue to show the user where he or she is about to be taken.

A Note About Order: LoVe HAte

If you have created your pseudo classes in the order shown previously, you will now have the following selectors in the links.css style sheet:

```
a:link {
  color:#F00;
  }
a:visited {
  color:#999;
  }
a:hover {
  color:#333;
  }
a:active {
  color:#000;
  }
```

Notice that the first letter of each pseudo class is in bold, giving us the letters *L V H A*. This order is very important of you wish for the links to behave properly, and can be remembered as **Lo**Ve **HA**te.

For example, if you were to place the a:hover selector above the a:visited selector (giving you the order L H V A), you would have a situation where the a:hover declaration would have no effect upon the visited state, due to how the cascade works. The text would remain light gray even on hover, going against expected behavior. There may be cases where such an approach is required, but this will be rare and is probably best avoided.

Other Useful Link Properties

Now that you understand the basics of CSS link control and can affect any of the four core link states, it is worth considering some other very useful properties designed specifically for links, and some more universal properties that can also be applied.

text-decoration

So far, you may have noticed that all links, regardless of state, are underlined with a color matching the link text. This is a default style that is very easily removed using the text-decoration property. Possible values are none, underline (the default value), overline, line-through, and blink. These values are very self-explanatory, but again be very aware of how usable and intuitive your links are when custom styles are used. For example, some designers argue that placing a line through text looks more like a corrected error than anything else, and a blinking link isn't going to endear you to your visitors at all. Likewise, the overline value conveys a confusing message if used on its own, whereas a combination such as text-decoration: overline underline might make more sense. In most cases, a responsible designer is most likely to simply turn underlines on or off, depending on the situation.

The text-decoration property can be applied to any of the four link states, as in this example for the :hover pseudo class:

```
a:hover {
  color:#333;
  text-decoration:none;
  }
```

This is a fairly sensible approach, as on hover, the link color will change to satisfactorily identify the link, so underlines are not needed. It is generally recommended that all other link states carry an underline to distinguish them from normal inactive text, and it is not a good idea to identify links with color alone—spare a thought for those visitors who are colorblind.

Using Borders with Links

If the text-decoration property just doesn't float your boat, then the good old border property might do what you need. Turning off the default underlines and replacing them with custom bottom borders can create some pretty neat effects.

Here, all basic links will be given a thin dashed underline, which is actually a 1-pixel bottom border:

```
a:link {
  color:#F00;
  text-decoration:none;
  border-bottom:1px dashed #333;
  line-height:150%;
  }
```

Note that unlike the text-decoration property, here the border can be a different color from the link text, so you have red text with dark gray underlines (see Figure 7-3). Also, with a line-height declared, you ensure that the underline doesn't encroach upon any text underneath it.

Chapter 7: Links
http://localhost:8888/i
Chapter 7: Links
Introducing the band
To find out more about members of The Dead Goods, please select the appropriate person for a full profile.
Simon Collison
John Lennon
Jimi Hendrix
Jeff Buckley
Kurt Cobain
Janis Joplin
Keith Moon
Done

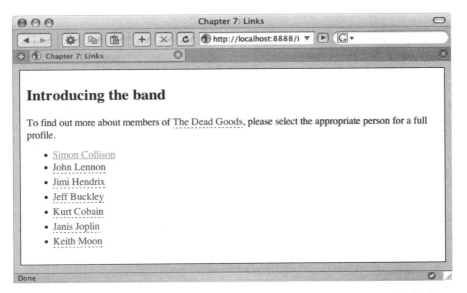

Figure 7-3. *Using a bottom border to create a more interesting underline for links*

This approach will surely get your mind racing. A rather impractical but fun experiment is to take the basic `:link` selector and use it to turn basic links into buttons, using just CSS.

```
a:link {
  color:#F00;
  text-decoration:none;
  border:1px solid #333;
  background:#CCC;
  padding:2px;
  line-height:150%;
  }
```

Thus a border surrounds the entire link text, spaced 2 pixels away from the text thanks to some padding, and all of this happening over a light gray background, as shown in Figure 7-4.

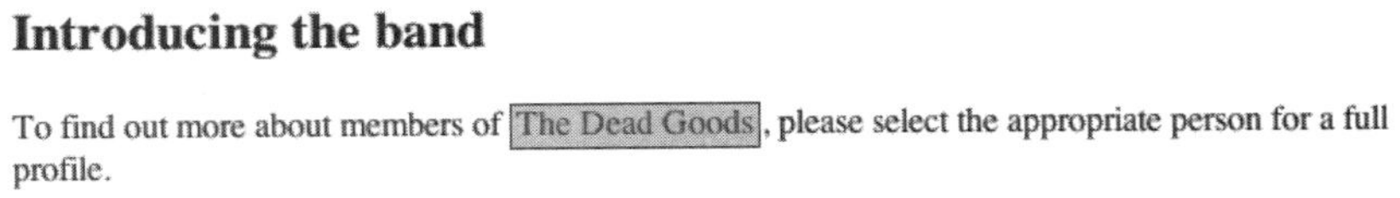

Introducing the band
To find out more about members of The Dead Goods, please select the appropriate person for a full profile.

Figure 7-4. *More complex styling is used to turn a basic unvisited link into a simple button.*

With such an approach, obviously similar treatment for the three other link states would also be necessary.

Adding Symbols with Background Images

In the previous example, the unvisited links were given a specific background color, so it should also be obvious that a background image can also be applied to links. The great thing here is that a different background image can be applied to each of the four link states, further aiding usability by providing a visual indicator alongside the more traditional text variations.

For this example, the goal is to use an arrow symbol to indicate links not yet visited and a checkmark to indicate links already visited. For this you will need two small GIF images similar to those in Figure 7-5, sized approximately 12×12 pixels.

Figure 7-5. *The images arrow.gif and checkmark.gif, magnified 500%*

As each image is 12 pixels in width, it makes sense to provide enough padding to the right of the link text for the image to be placed. Here, 15 pixels are declared for the right padding. Also, the arrow image is assigned to the background property for the :link pseudo class, set to only appear once, at right center. The checkmark image is assigned in an identical way for the :visited pseudo link.

```
a:link {
  color:#F00;
  padding:0 15px 0 0;
  background:url(images/arrow.gif) no-repeat right center;
  }
a:visited {
  color:#999;
  padding:0 15px 0 0;
  background:url(images/checkmark.gif) no-repeat right center;
  }
```

And so all unvisited links appear with a small arrow symbol to their immediate right, and any visited links have a neat checkmark in place of the arrow, as you can see in Figure 7-6.

In this example, only two link states have been affected. As things stand, both the active and hover states will place the arrow symbol to the right of the link text, but there is nothing to stop you defining a custom symbol for those states also. Adding an angled arrow to the hover state, for example, would be particularly effective.

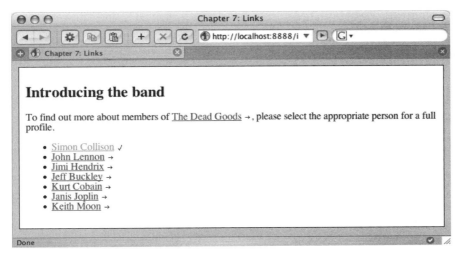

Figure 7-6. *Using background images, all unvisited links have an arrow symbol, whereas visited links are checked.*

Targeting Links with Descendant Selectors

In the previous section, the four pseudo classes were used to apply CSS rules to all links wherever they appear on the page. There will undoubtedly be situations where you need a specific link treatment for a specific section of the page (such as the footer, main navigation, or a sidebar). Thankfully, this is easily achieved with a few more selectors.

In the example template links.html, most of the links are contained in an unordered list, but one is within the first paragraph. As the latter is contained in a separate parent element, it can be targeted with a descendant selector and treated differently.

The four pseudo classes can be individually rewritten for any links inside paragraphs, by again assigning the color for each state, for instance. However, it is likely that some of the default link styles will still be needed, and that all that is really needed is a few new declarations.

In this example, existing color declarations assigned in the existing pseudo classes (red for unvisited, gray for visited, and so on) are to be retained. Here are the defaults that control all links anywhere on the page:

```
a:link {
  color:#F00;
  }
a:visited {
  color:#999;
  }
a:hover {
  color:#333;
  text-decoration:none;
  }
a:active {
  color: #000;
  }
```

These default pseudo classes can be left alone; as all that is needed is a new descendant selector that applies extra declarations to these existing classes.

```
p a:link, p a:visited, p a:hover, p a:active {
  color:#F00;
  padding:2px;
  border:1px dashed #999;
  text-decoration:none;
  }
```

Here, the browser will look first for a paragraph, and then any link elements contained within. If one or more is found, the new declarations will be added to the existing pseudo classes. So, in addition to the color declaration in the :link pseudo class, the new declarations (padding, border, and text-decoration) will be applied also, as shown in Figure 7-7.

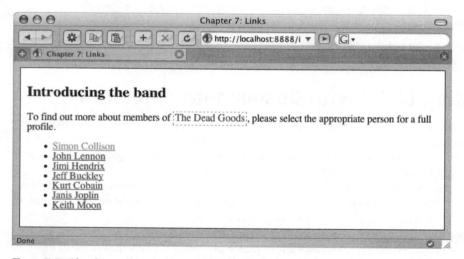

Figure 7-7. *The descendant selector targets only links found within any paragraph elements.*

Therefore, the same treatment can be given to links housed within another element, such as the list of links in the unordered list. To revisit the background images example from earlier in the chapter, the links in the list could be targeted as follows:

```
ul a:link {
  color:#F00;
  padding:0 15px 0 0;
  background:url(images/arrow.gif) no-repeat right center;
  }
ul a:visited {
  color:#999;
  padding:0 15px 0 0;
  background:url(images/checkmark.gif) no-repeat right center;
  }
```

Using this targeted CSS combined with the paragraph pseudo links would ensure that only links inside paragraphs had padding and dashed borders, and only links in the unordered list were combined with arrow and check box symbols. Any links outside of these two elements would simply be styled using the colors defined in the default pseudo classes.

Transforming a Navigation Bar with Links

In the previous chapter, some simple CSS was used to transform a simple unordered list into a vertical navigation bar. Pretty as that was, it was useless in that it didn't actually link anywhere, so as promised back then, it is now time to make that simple list work as a navigation tool.

I assure you that many seasoned web developers still don't understand what is going on with their lists, links, and padding in navigation bars, and very often way too many selectors are used when only a few are needed. Combining the simple walkthrough from Chapter 6 with what follows might actually give you more understanding of what is going on than some of the experts have.

Prepare the Template

This example takes the list styling from Chapter 6 and reworks it for a list of links. Create a new template called `linkslist.html`. Again, note that in the examples the following is placed inside the body element, and also inside a `container` div as in previous chapters. Here, the list markup is the same as in Chapter 6, except that each item is now a hyperlink. The markup and CSS files are of course available with the source code for this book (see the Chapter 7 folder).

```
<ul>
  <li><a href="#">Beer</a></li>
  <li><a href="#">Spirits</a></li>
  <li><a href="#">Cola</a></li>
  <li><a href="#">Lemonade</a></li>
  <li><a href="#">Tea</a></li>
  <li><a href="#">Coffee</a></li>
</ul>
```

Now create the `linkslist.css` file either by copying the `lists.css` file from Chapter 6 or using the version provided in the source code downloads. Remove any existing declarations for `<ul>` and `<li>` elements, and ensure the following declarations are added alongside existing declarations for `<body>` and `container`:

```
ul {
  list-style-type:none;
  margin:5px;
  padding:2px;
  border:1px solid #333;
  width:160px;
  font: bold 12px 'Lucida Grande',Verdana,sans-serif;
  }
li {
  background: #DDDDDD;
```

```
margin: 0;
padding: 2px 10px;
border-left: 1px solid #fff;
border-top: 1px solid #fff;
border-right: 1px solid #aaa;
border-bottom: 1px solid #666
}
```

This will display the unordered list almost exactly as it did in the previous chapter, except that the list items are now links, and as there are no pseudo class declarations in the style sheet, the links display in the default blue and are underlined (see Figure 7-8).

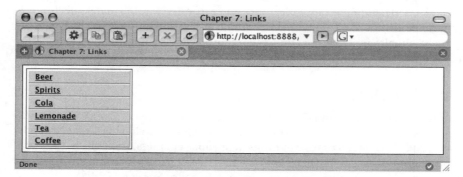

Figure 7-8. *The vertical navigation bar now has links added to the list items, styled blue and underlined by default.*

Define All Shared Link Declarations and Clickable Area

The next step is to define any shared declarations for links within the unordered list. For this example, let's turn off all underlines. If you decide that perhaps you'd like underlines on the hover state, simply remove the `ul a:hover` selector from the grouping.

Very importantly, the `padding` declaration must be removed from the `li` selector and placed instead in the grouped values for the pseudo classes. This is because the whole list element needs to be a clickable link, so by adding that padding in the pseudo classes, the active area is not merely the link text, but is increased to the whole link element.

Finally here, `display:block` is added. This ensures that the active link area is the whole width of the link element. This means that one can follow the link by clicking anywhere in the list element, not just by clicking the link text (see Figure 7-9).

```
ul a:link, ul a:visited, ul a:hover, ul a:active {
  display:block;
  padding:2px 10px;
  text-decoration:none;
  }
```

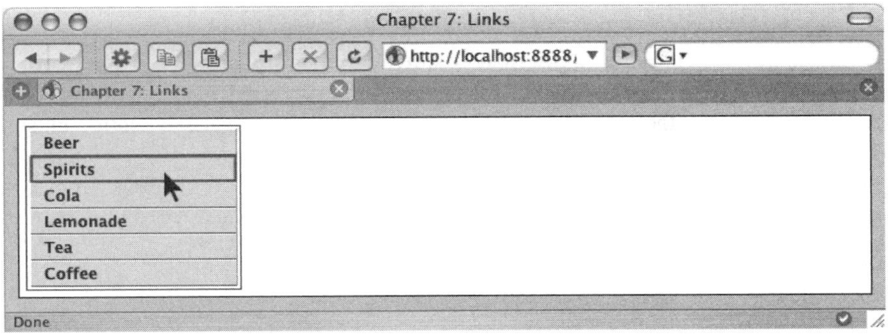

Figure 7-9. *By removing padding from the li selector, and instead placing it in the grouped pseudo classes alongside display:block, the whole list element becomes a clickable link, highlighted here with the outline.*

Next, unique selectors can be added to assign specific declarations for each link state. Note that again the selector descends through ul and a before the pseudo class is stated, ensuring the rules are targeted and will not affect links elsewhere in the page.

```
ul a:link {
  color:#000;
  }
ul a:visited {
  color:#666;
  }
ul a:hover {
  color:#F00;
  }
ul a:active {
  color:#333;
  }
```

Figure 7-10 shows the resulting navigation bar with the "Spirits" link shown in three different states. While it is styled just like the linkless list from Chapter 6, now each item is of course a link, and the links turn red on hover and a midrange gray when visited.

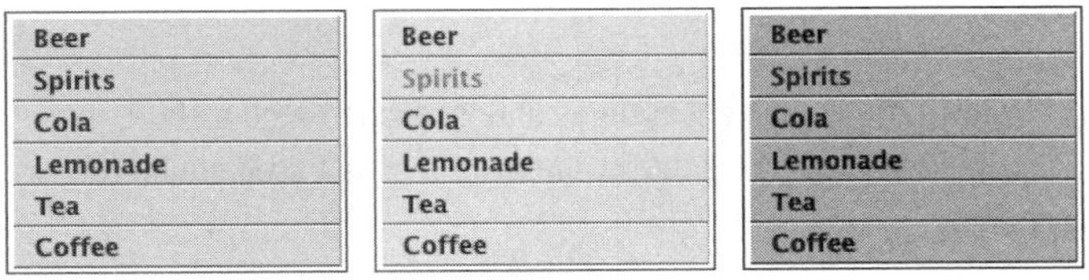

Figure 7-10. *The list items are now links, and the link states from left to right are link, visited, hover.*

Define Background Colors

So far, the link text is changing depending on the link state, which is smashing, but I bet you also want to change the color of the whole link background on hover, right?

This is very simply done by declaring a background color in the appropriate pseudo class. In the following CSS, the hover pseudo class is given a white background:

```
ul a:hover {
  color:#F00;
  background:#FFF;
  }
```

As a result, when the mouse is placed over a link, the text turns red, and the whole background of the list item becomes white, as shown in Figure 7-11.

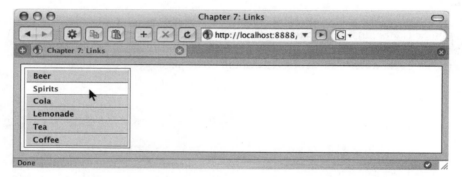

Figure 7-11. *On hover, the whole list element is rendered with a white background and red text.*

Obviously, you could also define a background color for visited links or any pseudo classes. It is a very simple technique when it is boiled down, and one that can transform not just navigation bars, but also any kind of list.

Highlight the Current Page

The final trick is to highlight a link if you are actually viewing that page. For static web pages, this requires a particular link to be identified by adding a unique ID to the parent list element.

■**Note** With dynamic systems such as content management systems and languages such as PHP, the unique ID could be added in a more convenient fashion by testing for the current page based on the URL or other identifier, and placing the ID accordingly.

Let's say that for the Lemonade page, you wish to reflect that the user is actually viewing that page, and therefore make it obvious that clicking that link again would be pointless. All that is needed is for the unique ID to be added to that particular list element.

```
<ul>
  <li><a href="#">Beer</a></li>
  <li><a href="#">Spirits</a></li>
  <li><a href="#">Cola</a></li>
  <li id="current"><a href="#">Lemonade</a></li>
  <li><a href="#">Tea</a></li>
  <li><a href="#">Coffee</a></li>
</ul>
```

A new CSS selector is required to declare the appropriate styles for the current ID. Because the ID is combined with the :link pseudo class, any values declared in this selector will override those specified in the link pseudo classes.

```
#current a:link {
  color:#FFF;
  background:#333;
  }
```

The result can be seen in Figure 7-12. For my money, this is a very neat and simple method of highlighting the current page.

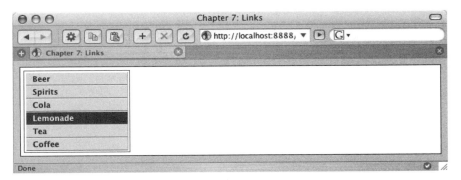

Figure 7-12. *By adding a unique ID to the appropriate list element, the current page is highlighted.*

To Conclude…

This chapter could have been 300 pages long, so rich is the seam of knowledge spanning links and how to manipulate them. It should however be more than enough to set you on the road to link-based fame and fortune. Like most CSS concepts, the foundations are actually very simple once you take the time to analyze them, and every concept is the starting point for unique and very creative ideas.

The key to great link styling is awareness of the end user. Make hyperlinks accessible and intuitive. Don't confuse people by employing some ridiculous color scheme that has no hierarchy and is based entirely on the color of your pajamas. Think carefully about the contrast between color and background, and consider font and font size. Be creative, and by all means be inventive, but above all, be careful. If there is one thing that frustrates a user above all else, it must be badly thought-out navigation and ill-conceived link treatment.

Links will reappear throughout the rest of the book, so worry not if you haven't found what you are looking for in this chapter. In the meantime, refill that teapot and take a breather, because we are moving on to a more frightening concept over the page—that of tables.

■ ■ ■

CHAPTER 8

Tables and Definition Lists

Certain kinds of information need to be displayed in a certain kind of way—of that there is no doubt. A train timetable needs rows and columns, whether on the Web or in a pocket pamphlet. You can try and do it another way, but it is likely that the answer has been staring you in the face all along—tables are the right tools for the job.

The table has gained a very bad reputation over the last few years, specifically since the wider adoption of CSS for layout, and the fact that many designers (a number of whom still wrongly consider themselves to be "cutting edge") insist on using tables for nontabular data. The problem is heightened when web standards aficionados refuse outright to use tables even when they are appropriate or pour scorn on others who make valid use of them. The poor old table gets stuck in the middle, and I for one feel sorry for it.

The fact is, tables are incredibly useful, and you will need them from time to time. The major issue with tables is that many designers still don't know the correct way to mark them up, never mind make them more attractive and easier to understand with CSS. The trick is to use tables only when necessary, and then make them wholly accessible and darned good to look at.

A much less well-known element is the definition list. Similar to a table in that it provides some semblance of columns and rows, it is a much more limited tool structurally, but combined with CSS it can be the ideal job for displaying basic tabular data, and much more besides. For example, you would use a definition list where terms in a left column need corresponding descriptions in a right column. There is no scope for further columns, and less scope to add accessibility markup than with tables, but this should not be seen as a limitation, as you will see. Definition lists are perhaps as misunderstood as tables, and the aim is to make honest semantic use of them when a table would be too excessive.

This chapter invites both the table and the definition list to stay behind after school and explain themselves. It can be argued that the bad wrap isn't their fault at all—they've just been hanging around with the wrong web designers.

Tables

There are something like 4 billion web pages out there, and it seems like 3.9 billion are proffering advice about how to mark up a table. The area is rather involved and there is much contradiction, due mainly to the ongoing desire to understand how best to deliver data to those with accessibility issues.

A Note About Accessibility

Tables are by their very nature complex. The data itself is ordered into rows and columns, and a specific correlation between both is suggested visually. Sighted users can quickly fathom the visual relationship between a table header and the cells that follow, as it is something that is understood from a young age and forms part of our daily lives.

Blind or vision-impaired people can't use a table so easily, and they rely on a device such as a screenreader to verbally relay the information held in a table. This can be a very complicated or even entirely pointless process if the table has not been crafted carefully. It is the web designer's responsibility to provide the appropriate hooks needed by the screenreader to successfully order the data and establish the correlations between headings and data items in a verbal manner. As this book is predominantly about CSS, it can't cover all of the appropriate requirements for super-accessible tables, so it might be a good point to brush up on your table markup before moving on. (*Web Accessibility: Web Standards and Regulatory Compliance*, by Jim Thatcher et al. [friends of ED, 2006] contains some great information about accessible tables.)

What Is a Table For?

A table is for eating at, putting plants on, or incorrectly (I'm told) putting your feet on. On a web page, the table is more likely to be used to assemble data for timetables, calendars, charts, spreadsheets, and so on. In essence, a table is for tabular data, and tabular data only.

Tabular data could not be organized by CSS layout alone, or would make little sense if you tried to do so. Many designers have concocted methods of rendering complex tabular data such as calendars, timetables, and so on with pure CSS layout and positioning. That's great, and certainly an achievement of sorts, but remove the style sheet, and everything falls apart. The beauty of the table is that it presents information semantically, provides numerous elements for CSS styling, and still makes perfect sense should the style sheet be made unavailable. Figure 8-1 shows a table with and without CSS styles applied.

Case study galleries: UK: Royal Air Force

Gallery	Files	Views	Latest
Royal Air Force			
Lum RR	12	28053	19/01/05
Lum RR responses	26	4261	13/02/06
Top V	23	29470	19/01/05
Top V responses	23	1877	08/12/05

Case study galleries: UK: Royal Air Force

Gallery	Files	Views	Latest
Royal Air Force			
Lum RR	12	28053	19/01/05
Lum RR responses	26	4261	13/02/06
Top V	23	29470	19/01/05
Top V responses	23	1877	08/12/05

Figure 8-1. *The benefits of CSS are obvious in this table taken from the Project Facade web site (www.projectfacade.com). The top table is unstyled, and the bottom has CSS applied.*

The Not Very Occasional Table

Anyone who has built a web page without CSS is probably aware of the basic table elements that are a common feature of many web pages. Layout using the elements `<table>`, `<tr>`, `<th>`, and `<td>` should be familiar to you.

The Basic Table

To recap, `<table>` defines the parent element, and then the `<tr>` element denotes a new table row, with numerous `<td>` elements creating cells. The `<th>` element denotes a column or row heading, and is bold by default. Here's a basic table detailing two rival teams and their recent records in the World Cup (that's soccer, by the way). You can grab all the files for this chapter from the download area at www.apress.com. Here I'm using `table.html` and `table.css`.

```
<table>
  <tr>
    <th>Team</th>
    <th>1998</th>
    <th>2002</th>
  </tr>
  <tr>
    <th>England</th>
    <td>Second Round</td>
    <td>Quarter Finals</td>
  </tr>
  <tr>
    <th>France</th>
    <td>Winners</td>
    <td>Group stages</td>
  </tr>
</table>
```

This produces the very basic table in Figure 8-2. By default it is ugly, squashed, and the rows and columns are undefined.

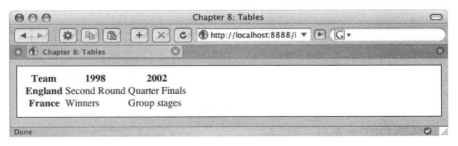

Figure 8-2. *The basic, unstyled table*

How We Used to Style

It is tempting to call on the old faithful attributes `cellpadding` and `cellspacing`, adding them to the opening table tag to produce `<table cellpadding="5" cellspacing="5" border="1">`. Figure 8-3 shows how this additional markup can make the table a little more legible. 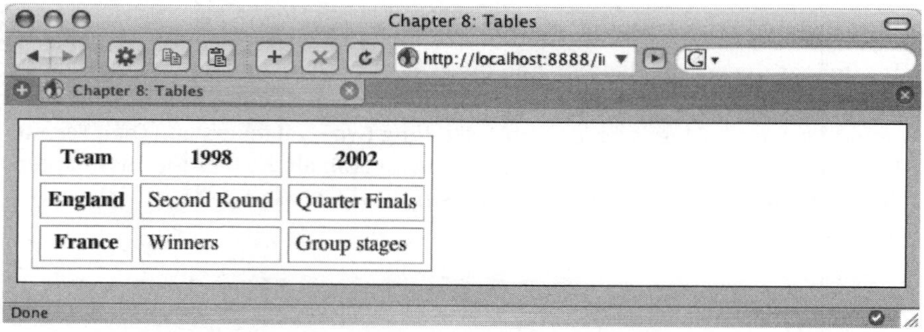

Figure 8-3. *Things improve with some old fashioned presentational markup, but with modern web development this is unnecessary—and verging on the criminal.*

However, these attributes are purely presentational and therefore entirely unnecessary. In theory, no presentational markup should ever be added to the table element. Less clunky and more effective control can be had using a few simple CSS selectors.

CSS to the Rescue

Before you go on, ensure that your table element is free of presentational cruft. Removal of any `cellpadding`, `cellspacing`, or `border` attributes is a must. CSS will take care of all of this, and with considerably more panache and control.

The <table> Element

The first step is to add a selector for the `<table>` element in `table.css`. Here, all that is declared are the `font` properties for the table.

```
table {
  font: normal 12px 'Lucida Grande',Verdana,sans-serif;
  }
```

Already the table is misbehaving. At the time of writing, the latest build of Firefox will create a simple border around the whole table element by default, as shown in Figure 8-4, but this is not the case in Safari or Internet Explorer. The first task is to ensure the display is the same for all browsers, and we'll start by examining the borders of the table and its cells.

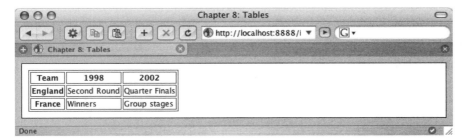

Figure 8-4. *The table selector is defined in the style sheet, and, despite no border declaration, there is a basic border around the table on Firefox only.*

Group Shared Values

So, you now have control of the `<table>` element, which is a good start. The next job is to add some definition to the data contained in the table itself. This calls for a selector to control the individual cells. Later, unique declarations will be made to the `<th>` and `<td>` elements, but there will also be shared values. Here, the two elements are grouped to share the `border` value.

```
th, td {
  border:1px solid #333;
  }
```

Now the individual cells have borders, as you see in Figure 8-5—borders considerably neater and more precise than those available using the `border` attribute in (X)HTML. Importantly, this border declaration will ensure all browsers are showing consistent table styling.

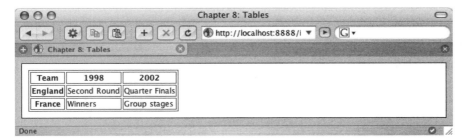

Figure 8-5. *The th and td selectors are used to add very basic 1-pixel borders to each cell.*

Style the Table Headings

The correlation between rows and headers could still be clearer though, despite the default bold text of the `<th>` cells. Also by default, the `<th>` text is centered. Adding a new selector can correct this, and also assign custom `color` and `background` values to the `<th>` element.

```
th {
  text-align:left;
  color:#FFF;
  background-color:#333;
  }
```

The headings and actual data are now clearly differentiated with dark gray background and white text for the <th> cells (see Figure 8-6).

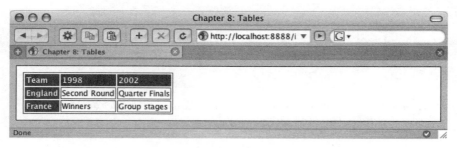

Figure 8-6. *The <th> cells are clearly defined.*

The <td> Element

Now a new selector is required for the data cells. The td selector can be used to style every remaining data cell. A similar treatment to that given to the navigation list items in Chapters 6 and 7 seems an appropriate balance to the dark gray <th> cells.

```
td {
    background-color: #DDDDDD;
    border-style:solid;
    border-width:1px;
    border-color:#FFF #AAA #666 #FFF;
    }
```

Now the table is looking a little more resolved, as you can see in Figure 8-7. There is, however, one glaringly obvious problem so far—that of spacing. Everything is still scrunched together.

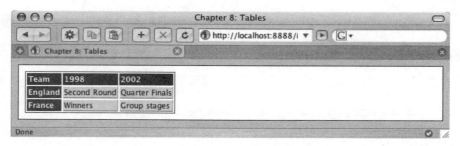

Figure 8-7. *Getting there. Both the <th> and <td> cells are now benefiting from some simple CSS.*

This Section Is Just Padding

Earlier the shared <th> and <td> declarations were grouped using the th, td selector. Now, a padding value that both will share can be added.

```
td, th {
    border:1px solid #333;
    padding:3px;
    }
```

This extra padding does the work of the old cellpadding attribute, but gives you considerably more control. It will also be easier to adjust padding should you wish to later just by adjusting the value in the style sheet, potentially for all tables across your web site, which is much easier than having to trawl through all your (X)HTML templates and adjust all those cellpadding values. Figure 8-8 shows the progress so far.

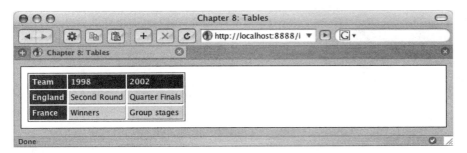

Figure 8-8. *Considerably more stylish, thanks to a little padding*

The Final Touches

The table is nearly finished, and all that remain are a few tweaks to the existing CSS selectors. The <td> cells have a slightly three-dimensional quality owing to the colors of the borders, and it would be good to do something similar for the <th> cells.

Adding tonal gray border declarations for the <th> element and removing the basic border declaration from the grouped th selector leaves the final CSS as follows:

```
table {
  border: 1px solid #333;
  font: normal 12px 'Lucida Grande',Verdana,sans-serif;
  }
td, th {
  padding:3px;
  }
th {
  text-align:left;
  color:#FFF;
  background-color:#333;
  border-style:solid;
  border-width:1px;
  border-color:#CCC #666 #000 #CCC;
  }
td {
  background-color:#DDDDDD;
  border-style:solid;
  border-width:1px;
  border-color:#FFF #AAA #666 #FFF;
  }
```

The final table is looking pretty tidy (see Figure 8-9), and stylistically this is something that could not be achieved with basic (X)HTML markup.

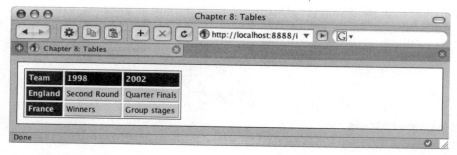

Figure 8-9. *The finished table*

Creating the three-dimensional effect for each cell would not be possible with the outdated (X)HTML border attribute, so CSS has a greater role to play here. The table markup remains completely untouched. No extra markup was required to get from the plain black-and-white and scrunched-up table to the sexy final example in Figure 8-9.

border-collapse

The border-collapse property is a very useful tool used to replace the outdated cellspacing attribute in HTML, which was used to reduce or remove the default space placed between each cell.

You may have noticed that earlier in the chapter, the example table had spacing in between each cell. The CSS used did not add that using margins; it was already there.

Consider the following CSS. The aim is to apply a 1-pixel line at the base of each cell to create a continuous line right across the table from left to right.

```
table {
  border:0;
  font: normal 12px 'Lucida Grande',Verdana,sans-serif;
  }
td, th {
  padding:3px;
  }
th {
  text-align:left;
  border-bottom: 1px solid #000;
  }
td {
  border-bottom: 1px solid #666;
  }
```

In theory, this should work, but the browser will automatically apply a few pixels of whitespace between each cell, as shown in Figure 8-10.

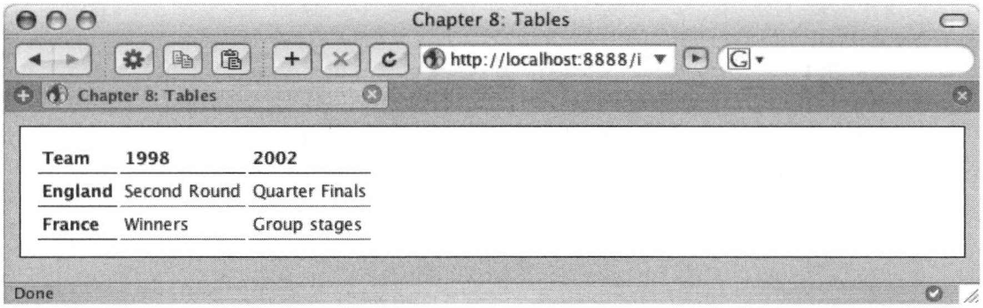

Figure 8-10. *The lines below each row should be continuous, but the browser automatically places whitespace around each.*

This is where the life-saving border-collapse property comes into play. In prehistoric times, designers would declare the attribute cellspacing="0" to collapse this whitespace, but this is no longer acceptable, as this is purely presentational markup. So, a simple addition to the table selector is required.

```
table {
  border:0;
  border-collapse:collapse;
  font: normal 12px 'Lucida Grande',Verdana,sans-serif;
}
```

This simple declaration is all that is needed to remove the default cellspacing in one fell swoop, as shown in Figure 8-11. It's a little-known method, but it sure is effective, and again is proof that the wizards who invented CSS knew what they were doing.

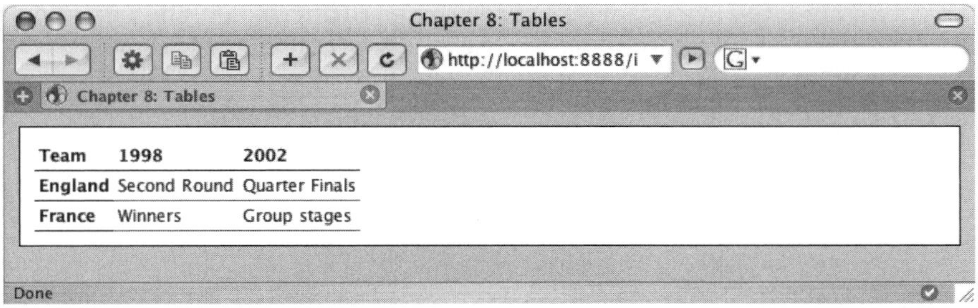

Figure 8-11. *The border-collapse property is used to remove all default whitespace between the cells.*

Further Reading

Several other table-specific CSS properties are available, although these involve much more complex techniques than can be covered in this book. For more information about the various table models and relevant browser support, view the Tables specifications from the W3C (www.w3.org/TR/REC-CSS2/tables.html).

Customizing Elements

As you have seen, many of the properties already discussed through the previous chapters can be used with the table selectors, such as border, padding, background-color, and so on.

One brilliant way of customizing the usually drab table is by deploying carefully crafted background images to add emphasis to heading cells, or even transform the entire table.

Background Images

Taking the example from the border-collapse section of this chapter, the following CSS will produce the table shown previously in Figure 8-11.

```
table {
  border:0;
  border-collapse:collapse;
  font: normal 12px 'Lucida Grande',Verdana,sans-serif;
  }
td, th {
  padding:6px;
  }
th {
  text-align:left;
  border-bottom: 1px solid #000;
  }
td {
  border-bottom: 1px solid #666;
  }
```

This table is a good basis for some heavy customization, but it will be more interesting to add a few more rows and columns. The <th> cells have also been removed from the left, and a <caption> element added to give the table context. The <caption> element is an optional table component that displays a caption/title for the table directly above, below, or to either side of the table.

```
<table>
  <caption> World Cup record: France</caption>
  <tr>
    <th>1986</th>
    <th>1990</th>
    <th>1994</th>
    <th>1998</th>
    <th>2002</th>
  </tr>
  <tr>
    <td>Don't know</td>
    <td>Don't care</td>
    <td>Not bothered</td>
    <td>Winners</td>
    <td>Group stages</td>
  </tr>
</table>
```

That's better—now there is a bit more data to play with (see Figure 8-12). As you can see, this author is just a little bitter about how his team's performance matches up with its Gallic rivals.

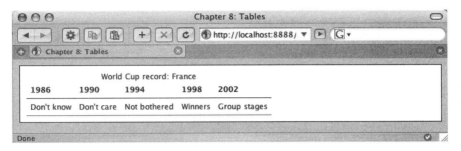

Figure 8-12. *The table is expanded, and a <caption> element is added.*

This table is quite legible as it stands, but there is always room for a little more CSS. For this example, a background image can be used to spread the full length of the table heading. The image in Figure 8-13 is a small GIF tile, 25 pixels square.

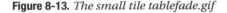

Figure 8-13. *The small tile tablefade.gif*

The background-image declaration will be added to the <th> element (as one of several background properties declared with shorthand). Although there are five separate <th> cells across the top of the table, the use of border-collapse:collapse will ensure that the GIF appears to tile seamlessly across the whole row. Note that a selector has been added for the <caption> element also.

```
table {
  border:0;
  border-collapse:collapse;
  font: normal 12px 'Lucida Grande',Verdana,sans-serif;
  }
caption {
  font-weight:bold;
  font-size:15px;
  padding:10px;
  }
td, th {
  padding:6px;
  }
th {
  text-align:left;
  background:#FFF url(images/tablefade.gif) repeat-x;
  border-bottom: 1px solid #000;
  }
```

```
td {
  border-bottom: 1px solid #666;
  }
```

The `background-repeat` value `repeat-x` is used (as part of the shorthand declaration) to tile the image horizontally, and the result is a neat fade effect that transcends the whole row of `<th>` cells, as shown in Figure 8-14.

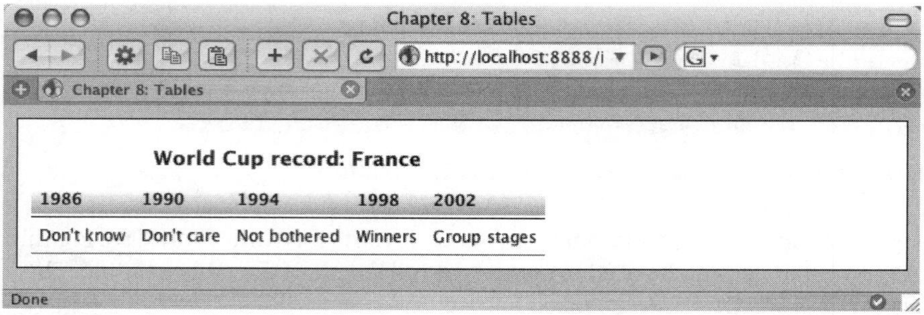

Figure 8-14. *The tablefade.gif image is tiled the length of each <th> cell, and, due to border-collapse, the lack of whitespace between each cell gives the impression of one seamless background image.*

Of course, the use of background images with tables doesn't stop here. A background image can be applied to any table element, be it the whole table, all `<td>` elements, or even individual cells, although you'll need a class for the latter.

Background Images with Classes

In the previous table, you may have noticed that those pesky French actually won the World Cup in 1998 (on home soil, I might add). This is obviously a great achievement, and one worth highlighting.

So far in this chapter, selectors have been used to influence all instances of a particular element, such as making all `<th>` text align to the left or adding a background image to all `<th>` cells.

However, it is easy to single out one instance of an element and overrule any existing CSS applied to it, using our old friend the class. Here, a reusable class called `winners` has been added to the appropriate `<td>` element:

```
<table>
  <caption>World Cup record: France</caption>
  <tr>
    <th>1986</th>
    <th>1990</th>
    <th>1994</th>
    <th>1998</th>
    <th>2002</th>
  </tr>
```

```
<tr>
  <td>Don't know</td>
  <td>Don't care</td>
  <td>Not bothered</td>
  <td class="winners">Winners</td>
  <td>Group stages</td>
</tr>
</table>
```

Now all that is needed is a simple selector for the winners class. Here, the basic declarations for table cells are overruled by specifying bold white text on a red background:

```
.winners {
  font-weight:bold;
  color:#FFF;
  background-color:#F00;
}
```

Reloading the page in the browser shows the table cell with a completely red background and white bold text (which appears shaded in Figure 8-15). All other cells are unaffected.

Figure 8-15. *The appropriate cell is given a class attribute in order to deliver unique styling.*

Naturally, this method can also be used to give the cell a custom background image. In this case, rather than tile an image across the whole cell, it will be more fun to use a custom icon to denote the fact that the team actually won. The custom icon, shown in Figure 8-16, is 25 pixels square.

Figure 8-16. *Custom icon for the "Winners" table cell*

The CSS is relatively simple and builds upon the simple list icons used in Chapter 6. It is important to note that padding equal to the width of the icon is applied to the right of the class.

```
.winners {
  font-weight:bold;
  padding-right:25px;
  background:#FFF url(images/star.gif) right center no-repeat;
}
```

The `<td>` cell with the `winners` class will now compensate for the image by widening the cell by 25 pixels, and then placing the icon in that space by obeying the declared `background-position` values as part of the shorthand background declaration (see Figure 8-17).

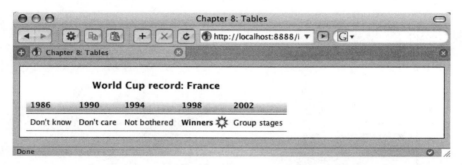

Figure 8-17. *The custom icon is in place to the right of the text in the appropriate cell.*

This little taster should get the light bulbs flashing in your head. The possibilities here are endless, and many a drab table has been spruced up remarkably with the addition of a few symbols and targeted background colors.

Definition Lists

Misunderstood and ignored—that's the definition list. Put simply, it is a list like any other, except that it has two parts, not one. In some senses, it bridges the gap between the basic list and the table, providing an extra method of laying out simple data couplets without the limitations of the unordered list or the complexities of the table.

Definition List Markup

This book is unavoidably about (X)HTML, even though the title is *Beginning CSS Web Development*. It seems appropriate that this section about definition lists begin with a fairly thorough recap of definition list markup and variations, as so few web designers are making use of this concept.

All definition lists consist of two main ingredients: a term and a description. A definition list is built using three essential elements: a container (`<dl>`), a definition term (`<dt>`), and a definition description (`<dd>`).

```
<dl>
  <dt>England</dt>
    <dd>Terrible soccer team</dd>
  <dt>Brazil</dt>
    <dd>Unbelievably good soccer team</dd>
</dl>
```

Figure 8-18 shows the unstyled result in the browser. Each definition term and definition description is separated by a line break and a default left margin. The example also proves that definition lists are often used to also be very blunt with the truth.

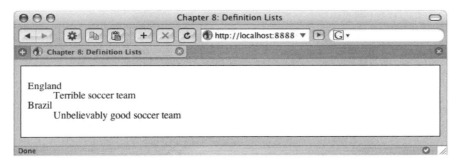

Figure 8-18. *A basic, unstyled definition list*

The inherent flexibility of the definition list means that you can use multiples of <dt> and <dd> within a definition list. In the next example, two descriptions are owned by one definition term.

```
<dl>
  <dt>England</dt>
    <dd>Terrible men's team</dd>
    <dd>Improving women's team</dd>
</dl>
```

As you can see in Figure 8-19, the result shows that items remain grouped as expected. The descriptions are placed again with a default left margin, each on a new line.

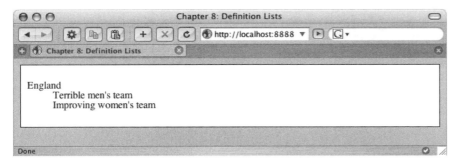

Figure 8-19. *Two definition descriptions for one term*

The next example illustrates how two terms might be needed to inform just one description.

```
<dl>
  <dt>England (men)</dt>
  <dt>England (women)</dt>
    <dd>Two teams with varying degrees of success</dd>
</dl>
```

Figure 8-20 shows the resulting browser display.

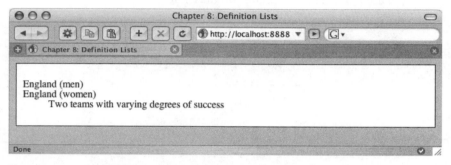

Figure 8-20. *Two terms, one description*

Incorporating Other Elements

Definition lists aren't flexible—they're *very* flexible! You can incorporate block-level elements in the definition description, such as the <p> and <ul> elements. In the following example, the description text is housed inside a paragraph:

```
<dl>
  <dt>England Soccer team</dt>
  <dd><p>Terrible soccer team. Still, won the World Cup in 1966, which is ➥
  something to cling on to.</p></dd>
</dl>
```

Here, only one paragraph is used, as Figure 8-21 illustrates, but there is no limit to how many block-level elements you place within the <dd> element.

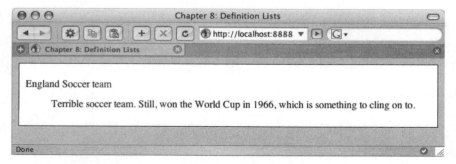

Figure 8-21. *One term, with a paragraph inside the definition*

> ■**Note** While it is brilliant to be able to use block-level elements within the definition description, you sadly cannot use block-level elements inside the definition term element. Watch out for that!

A List Inside a Definition List

Ah, the power of the unordered list, but enhanced by being placed inside a definition list. Here, the team name is placed inside the definition term element, and the players are listed inside the definition description element.

```
<dl>
  <dt>England Soccer Team</dt>
  <dd>
    <ul>
      <li>David Beckham</li>
      <li>Wayne Rooney</li>
      <li>Michael Owen</li>
      <li>Steven Gerrard</li>
    </ul>
  </dd>
</dl>
```

This approach clearly adds clarity to the definition, and a very obvious hierarchy is established (see Figure 8-22).

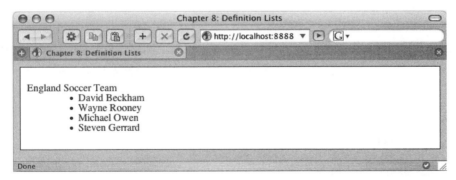

Figure 8-22. *Now a list is used inside the description.*

Sprinkle in a Little CSS

Taking what you learned back in Chapter 6, it should be pretty easy to take control of the unordered list contained inside the definition description element.

Using the exact same CSS used back then to turn a basic unordered list into a navigation-style menu, the same effects can be applied in this instance. Here's the CSS once more:

```
ul {
  list-style-type:none;
  margin:5px;
  padding:2px;
  border:1px solid #333;
  width:160px;
  font: bold 12px 'Lucida Grande',Verdana,sans-serif;
  }
li {
  background-color: #DDDDDD;
  margin: 0;
  border-style:solid;
  border-width:1px;
  border-color:#FFF #AAA #666 #FFF;
  }
```

Figure 8-23 shows the result of this enhancement.

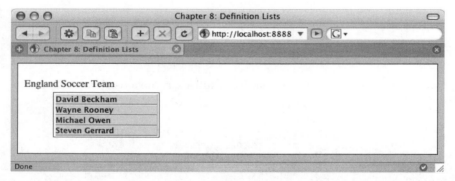

Figure 8-23. *With CSS appplied, the unordered list inside the definition description element is radically transformed.*

The dl Selector

Now the whole definition list can be styled to match using simple selectors. Taking the basic selectors dl, dt, and dd, very similar styles can be applied to bring the whole section together. First, the main <dl> element is declared.

```
dl {
  padding:2px;
  border:1px solid #333;
  font: bold 12px 'Lucida Grande',Verdana,sans-serif;
  }
```

Notice here that up until this point only the unordered list had any declared font values. To apply font values to the whole definition list element and its children, the font declaration is moved from the ul selector to the dl selector.

Also, the default top and bottom margins are removed using margin:0, and border and padding is applied that directly matches the unordered list styling. Figure 8-24 shows the progress so far.

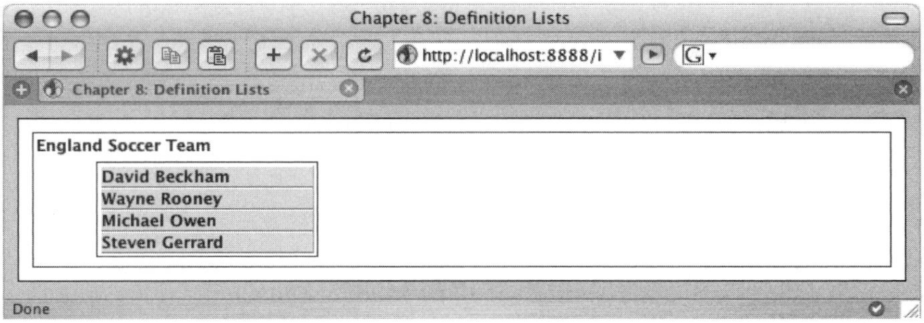

Figure 8-24. *Progress so far, with basic CSS applied to the outer <dl>element*

The dt Selector

Next, the definition term needs to work a bit harder. As block-level elements cannot be used inside the <dt> element, if the term is to look more like a heading, it needs to be done with CSS.

```
dt {
  background-color: #DDDDDD;
  padding:2px;
  border-style:solid;
  border-width:1px;
  border-color:#FFF #AAA #666 #FFF;
}
```

Again, values very similar to those of the unordered list are declared. The padding, background, and borders are identical, and things are looking better, as you see in Figure 8-25.

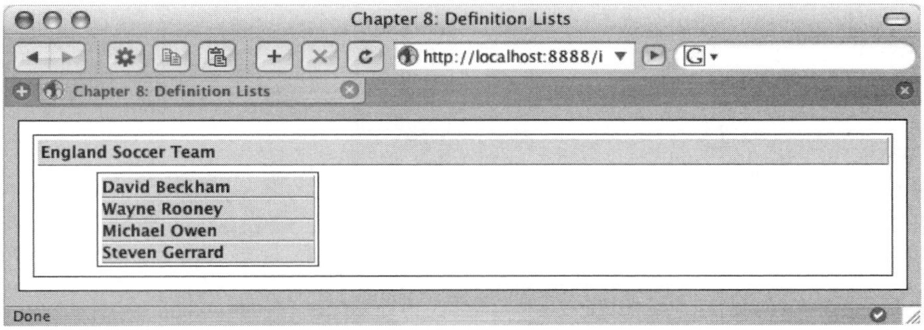

Figure 8-25. *With the rules declared in the dt selector, the <dt> and list within the <dd> are matching, although the <dt> clearly looks like a heading.*

The dd Selector

Next the definition description element is defined. Very simply, all that is needed is to remove the default margin that pushes it away from the left edge of the containing <dl> element.

```
dd {
  margin:0;
  }
```

This ensures everything is aligned to the left, overriding the default margin applied by the browser, and wrestling complete control back your way.

Rework the Unordered List

Now is a good time to rework the unordered list. The padding of 2px is changed to 0 for the ul selector so that the default value is still overridden. If the padding remained, the list would be pushed away from the edges of the <dd> element.

Also, the border is no longer needed to avoid clunkiness, and the set width of 160px is also no longer required.

```
ul {
  list-style-type:none;
  margin:5px 0 5px 0;
  padding:0;
  }
li {
  background-color: #DDDDDD;
  margin: 0;
  padding:2px;
  border-style:solid;
  border-width:1px;
  border-color:#FFF #AAA #666 #FFF;
  }
```

As a result of these tweaks, the various elements are all aligned nicely. The definition term is positioned exactly over the definition description, and the unordered list sits perfectly inside that, as shown in Figure 8-26.

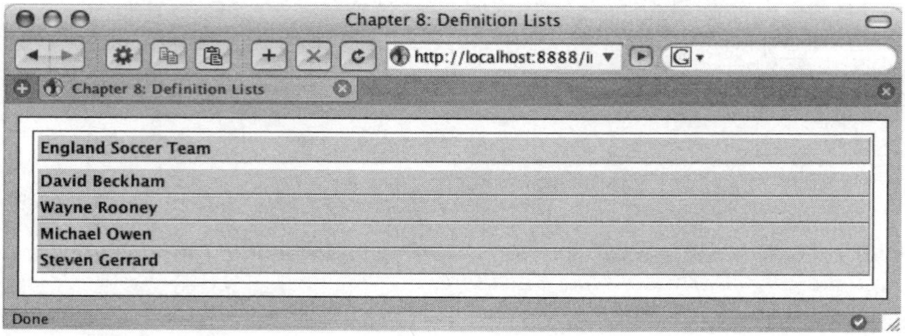

Figure 8-26. *Everything is nicely aligned, thanks to careful tweaking of margin and padding on the ul, li, and dd selectors.*

Final Adjustments

Finally, all that is required is to define a set width for the whole shebang. This can be done using the dl selector, as everything else falls inside of it and will therefore contract to fit.

```
dl {
  width:160px;
  margin:0;
  padding:2px;
  border:1px solid #333;
  font: bold 12px 'Lucida Grande',Verdana,sans-serif;
}
```

It also seems that now everything is aligned, the <dt> element isn't looking so much like a heading anymore, so a simple background and color tweak can be made to compensate.

```
dt {
  color:#FFF;
  background-color: #333;
  padding:2px;
  border-style:solid;
  border-width:1px;
  border-color:#FFF #AAA #666 #FFF;
}
```

This brings us to a finished, hugely transformed definition list, as shown in Figure 8-27. Note that if you applied a width of 100% to the definition list, it would be flexible enough to stretch and fit any container you placed it in, making it an ideal component for sidebar navigation. The beauty of all of this is that no additional markup is required in the (X)HTML—the CSS takes care of everything.

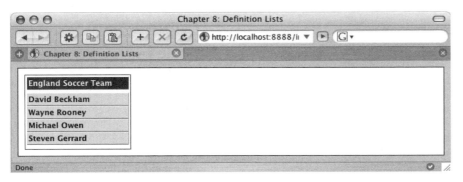

Figure 8-27. *The finished definition list containing a simple unordered list*

Care with Definition Lists

The important thing to note here is the great flexibility of the definition list, and despite its lack of popularity, these methods are excellent for breaking down smaller pockets of data where laziness might normally make one reach for a table.

However, I have seen numerous incidences of definition lists being used to basically emulate complex column layouts akin to misused tables.

It has also been observed that search engines may not index definition list content in the expected manner. Just because you style the `<dt>` element to look like a heading does not mean Google will treat it as such. It should also be noted that key markup used to enhance table markup cannot be applied to definition lists, and if this is of concern in a particular instance, use a table.

Further Reading

A one-stop shop for all things definition lists has to be the excellent article "Definition lists—misused or misunderstood?" (`www.maxdesign.com.au/presentation/definition/`) on the hugely useful Max Design web site. There you will also find many brilliant CSS treatments of definition lists including simple image galleries and more tailored formatting.

To Conclude...

I'm sure you'll agree that was a lot of fun! Maybe. It is important to be prepared for any kind of data formatting, and to know how to display it appropriately. Knowing when to use a table and when to use a definition list is something that will come with experience.

This chapter merely skims the surface of table styling, and certainly hasn't enough room to explore all available table markup. That said, grasping these basic styling concepts should assist you when it comes to more complex tables. Half the battle is in knowing what CSS approaches you can exploit, with the other half being the trial and error involved.

Hopefully, this chapter has also made you aware of how similar CSS approaches can be applicable to different formatting options, such as how the wonderful styles you created for a table can be modified for a definition list. This is something you'll see much more of in the next chapter, with basic chunks of CSS being reused for different approaches. It might be worth sticking the kettle on and spending a moment or two reflecting on how far you've come. You're halfway to being a professional!

■ ■ ■

CHAPTER 9

Forms

Without forms, a web site generally works in only one direction. Pages contain information and images, the user reads this information or looks at the images, and that is that. Forms allow the user to interact with the web site by exchanging data.

Forms are used for a huge number of purposes, from fairly simple functions such as logging in to a web application, leaving comments, and providing contact info, right up to enabling article entry, serving as questionnaires, and allowing résumé uploads, and can exist on one page or be spread across several. Forms are the only sensible method of collecting data from your visitors, and they are something we all have to embrace.

Web designers are often scared of building forms for a number of reasons. The general consensus is that they are difficult to implement successfully, hard to lay out without resorting to tables, and difficult to make accessible for all visitors.

While this chapter doesn't deal with making forms actually work (due to space and scope constraints),[1] it will illustrate that forms are actually quite timid beasts that are very easily tamed with a combination of well-constructed markup and carefully applied CSS. Hopefully, after working through this chapter, your confidence in form building will be stronger, and the variety of possible approaches discussed will buoy you up somewhat.

This chapter covers the following areas:

- Basic form markup refresher

- A brief look at markup intended to make forms more accessible

- How to style common form elements and create a reusable block of CSS

- Three possible approaches to form layout—the table, paragraphs, and finally the definition list

Markup Refresher

The great thing about forms is that a correctly marked-up form provides a large number of elements upon which to hang the CSS. If all the appropriate (X)HTML elements are in place, very little or no extra markup is required to successfully apply the CSS you create. If this isn't an

---

1. Entire books have been written on the programming languages used to process forms on the Web, such as PHP, JavaScript, and ASP.NET, so a discussion here is way out of scope for this book. However, check out the online catalog at www.apress.com for an extensive list of books that do cover these technologies, and much more besides.

incentive to ensure you are using the appropriate elements in your forms, then I don't know what is.

Before we get to the CSS playground, let's first stop off at the markup service station and ensure you are familiar with all of the markup that should be commonplace in all forms.

Form Elements

If you consider yourself a master of form markup, feel free to skip to the CSS stuff later in this chapter, where you'll come to grips with transforming these humble elements into sexy page widgets. However, it might be useful to bookmark this section, as it is important that data collection elements are correctly marked up if the CSS is going to stick. This refresher breezes through the common form elements, looking at the correct syntax and best-practice approaches for each.

Elements for Data Input

First, let's run through the most common elements used to submit data through a form interface. In most cases, the `<input>` element is specified, and the method of form construct is declared with the `type` attribute (such as `type="text"` or `type="checkbox"`). The key exception is the `<textarea>`, as you'll see.

text

Unlike HTML, XHTML requires all `<input>` elements to be self-closed with a forward slash, so watch out for that. For a basic text `<input>`, the `type` attribute is specified as `text`.

```
<input type="text" name="email" id="email" />
```

Note that the element is assigned a unique `name` (used to identify that piece of data wherever it is used) and also a unique ID.

maxlength and size

It is common to assign a set character limit for text `<input>` fields also. The `maxlength` attribute provides a simple method of assigning this limit; ensuring users are prevented from entering more than the specified number of characters.

The `size` attribute can be used to declare the physical width of the `<input>` field, measured in characters. The following example creates a text `<input>` that will be the length of 20 characters, but will allow up to 50 characters to be entered.

```
<input type="text" name="email" id="email" maxlength="50" size="20" />
```

Later in this chapter, you will see that the `size` attribute is not always necessary, as the length of the text `<input>` can be controlled much more accurately with CSS.

checkbox

The `checkbox` `<input>` type is used for optional data, and where more than one answer can be given. The markup is very similar to that of the text `<input>`, except that a value is given that will be passed on through the form if the user checks the check box.

```
<input type="checkbox" name="checkbox" id="checkbox" value="n" />
```

Of course, an unlimited number of check boxes can be used within a form, although each one will require its own unique value.

radio

This `<input>` type is similar to the check box, except that the radio button is used when only one answer can be given. You could have 15 radio buttons in a form, but each would share the same name, and the user could only select one value. Selecting another radio button would result in the previous selection being turned off.

```
<input type="radio" name="radio" id="radio" value="n" />
```

Radio buttons are an awkward `<input>` type to use in forms currently, as their display is so different across the browsers. Specifically, they look awful and ragged in Firefox.

submit

Without this vital `<input>` type, users would be unable to actually send you their data. The submit button should be placed outside of the form `<fieldset>`, and be clearly visible.

```
<input type='submit' value='Send this enquiry' />
```

The `value` attribute is used to place the user-friendly text within the submit button. It is always nice to link this directly to the purpose of the form, so "Request Feedback", "Log In", and "Confirm Payment" are good values here, whereas "Go" and "Submit" can often be too ambiguous.

<textarea>

Still an `<input>` type, but not marked up as such, `<textarea>` is used to create a text `<input>` with much more capacity for data, and no limit on how much can be placed into it. If the user types in more than the visible `<textarea>` displays, a scrollbar will automatically appear, allowing the user to navigate up and down through his or her submitted data.

```
<textarea name="message" id="message" rows='11' cols="30"></textarea>
```

The familiar `name` and `id` attributes are used, as well as `rows` and `columns`, which dictate how wide and how tall the visible area of the `<textarea>` will be, measured in characters. Unlike the other `<input>` types, the `<textarea>` element is not self-closed and requires a closing `</textarea>` tag.

<select>

The `<select>` element (also known as the *drop-down menu*) is a brilliant space-saving option that will be familiar to everyone.

```
<select name="subject" id="subject">
  <option value="">Select</option>
  <option value="Option 1">Option 1</option>
  <option value="Option 2">Option 2</option>
</select>
```

Again, name and id are used to identify the inputted data, although again like <textarea>, the <select> element is closed manually, this time with the corresponding </select> tag. Unlimited option values can be used, so long as each has a unique value. Notice that the first <option> element has an empty value attribute as it is used merely as a label (Select) to encourage the user to choose an option.

Accessibility Aids

Just using the basic <input> elements described earlier would make your form work perfectly well in most cases, but many more useful elements are available, and for good reason.

Any responsible web designer will want his or her forms to be usable by any visitor, including those with visual impairment, or even totally blind users. Let's walk through some very important elements that should be used for any form in any circumstances. The following elements help define the structure of your forms (<fieldset> and <legend>) and can add semantic meaning to the form constructs (<label>), as well as offer alternative methods of navigating through them (<tabindex>).

<fieldset>

The <fieldset> element brings much to proceedings. Its main purpose is to group <input> fields into sections.

Imagine a questionnaire with 20 or so inputs. The first three <input> fields are for personal data such as name, e-mail address, and post code. These three fields could be grouped together inside one <fieldset> element and the remaining questions grouped inside another <fieldset>.

CSS designers like <fieldset> for it also creates a perfect container where an extra <div> might have had to be used.

```
<fieldset>
  form tags go here (form, select, option, etc)
</fieldset>
```

By default, <fieldset> draws a simple border around its contents, defining that section of the form. It goes without saying that <fieldset> ends up shouldering a lot of the styling applied to the form by acting as the main parent element.

<legend>

We are not talking about John Wayne or Marlon Brando here. The descriptive <legend> element is used to describe the contents of its parent <fieldset>, and most browsers will stylishly place the <legend> text over the top of the <fieldset>'s top border with a white background to remove the border directly underneath.

```
<fieldset>
  <legend>Enquiry Form</legend>
    form tags go here (form, select, option, etc)
</fieldset>
```

The <legend> element does a similar job to the <caption> element used to identify a table. Yet again it is another perfect hook upon which some simple CSS can be hung.

<label>

Creating a relationship between the <label> element and the ID of the corresponding <input> is vital if you want those using a screenreader to successfully navigate through your form. This means that even if in some cases a <label> appears below its corresponding <input> field, or to the left, or to the right, or even miles away on the web page, the screenreader can still link the two for the benefit of the user. It keeps the form focused and organized.

```
<label for="email">Email</label><input type="text" name="email" id="email" />
```

The <label> must be linked to the <input> using the for attribute, specifying that <input> field's ID exactly.

tabindex

The tabindex attribute allows users to navigate the focus of the form element using just the keyboard (normally by using the Tab key). The order is typically in numerical order, where each attribute is given a numerical value. This is an excellent way of ensuring mobility-impaired users can successfully use your form.

```
<label for="firstname">First Name</label><input type="text" name="firstname" ➥
id="firstname" tabindex="1" />
<label for="surname">Surname</label><input type="text" name="surname" ➥
id="surname" tabindex="2" />
<label for="email">Email</label><input type="text" name="email"➥
id="email" tabindex="3" />
```

So in this example, pressing the Tab key one time would highlight the firstname <input>, pressing the Tab key two times would highlight the surname <input>, and the email <input> is the third form <input> that a user would navigate to using the keyboard, by pressing the Tab key three times. Note that by default, the browser will assign its own tab order to a form, so using tabindex is your opportunity to specify the order as you want it, overriding the default.

accesskey

Using the accesskey attribute is another excellent method of ensuring that mobility-impaired users can navigate through your form.

```
<label for="email" accesskey="3">Email</label><input type="text" ➥
name="email" id="email" />
```

Here, when the user presses Alt+3, the focus of the form will shift straight to the <input> field that correlates with the <label> for email. Not all browsers recognize the accesskey attribute.

Ready-Made IDs

In the previous section, lots of elements were discussed that can of course have specific CSS applied to them to control the style of the form. You might also have noticed that each <input> field has its own unique ID. These IDs are not mandatory for the (X)HTML to render the form constructs, but they are of course key to processing the submitted data once the form is submitted.

You already know that by giving an element a unique ID you are able to target it specifically, even if many other elements of the same type exist in the same file. Thus, most forms are pre-prepared for targeted styling by singling elements out according to their ID. Here are two examples:

```
<form action="" method="post" id="enquiryform">
```

An ID attached to the `<form>` element ensures that any CSS required only for that form could be declared as a descendant of the enquiryform ID.

```
#enquiryform input {
  width:100%;
  }
```

This selector would ensure that all `<input>` fields belonging to a form identified as enquiryform will stretch to fit their containing element. An additional selector could then be used to make any necessary exceptions to this rule by using the unique ID of a particular form field.

```
<input type="text" name="name" id="name" />
```

In this example, this particular `<input>` field could be styled differently from others by using its ID, name.

```
#name {
  width:200px;
  }
```

Now all `<input>` fields owned by enquiryform would be 100% width, except the one with the name ID, which would be 200px in length.

Browser Rendering of Form Elements

A major issue that it is very important to be aware of is the variation in how different browsers render common form elements such as input fields, select menus, check boxes, and so on. Regrettably, there are huge differences in display, and it is sadly not possible to make form elements look the same on all browsers using CSS or any other method (except maybe Flash).

This can be a big problem, especially in situations where a form or specific form element is designed to fit into a very specific holding element. One can spend all day tweaking the style of an input field, for example, making it look just right in Firefox, only to load up Safari or Opera and see that it looks completely different and is breaking out of its containing element.

Safari on the Mac is undoubtedly a sexy browser, and by default it displays form elements in a very desirable way. Unfortunately, these defaults are pretty much all you'll get from Safari, no matter how many attractive borders or specific sizes you throw at it. While widths, margins, and padding values will have an effect in most cases, the swollen bubble look of submit buttons and select elements will remain (unless you replace buttons with custom images of course), and you'll be hard-pressed to do any nifty border styling for input fields.

Equally awkward is the way Firefox displays check boxes and radio buttons. The latter in particular look awful—all jagged as if they were punched out of the screen with a blunt pencil.

Figure 9-1 shows the sheer variety of outcomes of a select element across the browsers. They not only look different, but also perform differently. Safari, for example, will show the whole menu when you click it, whereas most Windows-based browsers will show only the top few, and a mini-scrollbar is used to view those below.

Figure 9-1. *How browsers display the default select element*

Likewise, look at all the variations of the humble input field in Figure 9-2. A plethora of different borders, fonts, and internal padding are used, and even the greatest CSS designer in the world wouldn't be able to match them all up for every browser.

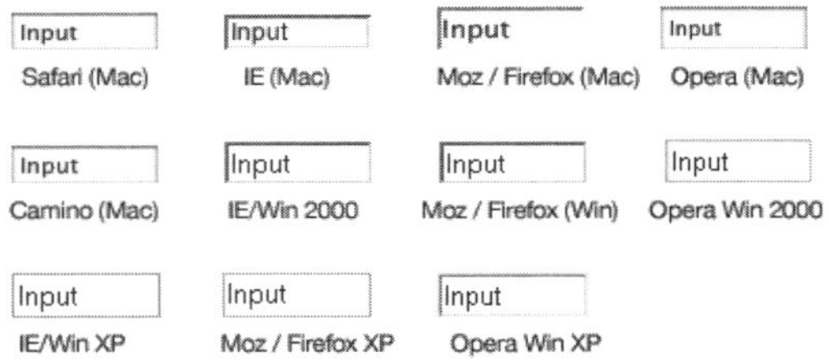

Figure 9-2. *How browsers display the default text input*

The submit button is different in that you could specify an image to replace the default button styling, as follows:

```
<input type="image" src="submit.gif" value="submit" />
```

That said, the variety of button displays across the browsers is exasperatingly varied, as shown in Figure 9-3. The Mac browsers (Safari, Opera Mac, Camino) do create gorgeous bubble buttons, but most (even Firefox on a Mac) resort to flat buttons. The good thing about the latter is that they are at least easily styled with some simple CSS.

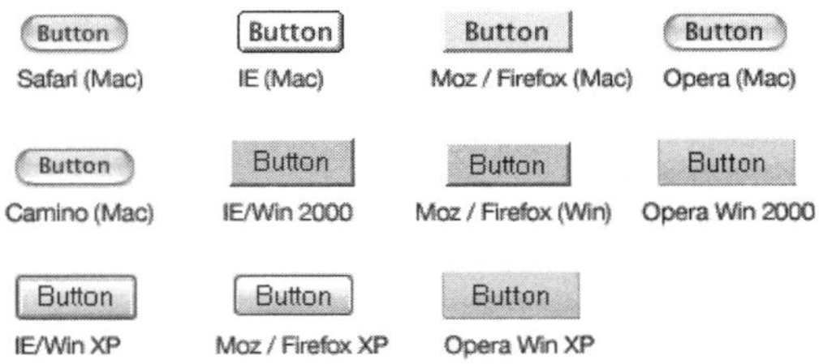

Figure 9-3. *How browsers display the default submit form type*

Caution is always needed when it comes to cross-browser form styling. Do try and get your form to display how you desire in your favorite browser, but be sure to check the display in all available browsers before launching your site, just to make sure nothing goes horribly wrong.

For a more in-depth overview of how browsers render these elements, as well as check boxes, radio buttons, and other form elements, be sure to check out Roger Johansson's excellent article "Styling Form Controls" (`www.456bereastreet.com/archive/200409/styling_form_controls/`).

Basics of Form Styling

Later in this chapter, three sensible methods of laying out a form will be discussed, but for now, let's assume that you have a form laid out using a simple table, as that is the way many of us begin form layout. The main focus at the moment is on the actual form elements within the table.

The goal here is to produce a block of CSS that can be used specifically for common forms—a chunk of CSS that can act as a starting point for any form and be tweaked as necessary depending on the given situation. This base CSS will apply sensible styles to common elements such as `<input>`, `<textarea>`, `<fieldset>`, `<legend>`, and so on, regardless of whether the form is laid out with a table or one of the other methods I'll cover.

Prepare a File and Style Sheet

Create a file called `forms_table.html` and paste the table layout (X)HTML into the `<body>`. In the head of the file, link to a new style sheet called `forms_table.css`. Save the template.

```
<form action="" method="post" id="enquiryform">
  <fieldset>
    <legend>Enquiry Form</legend>
      <table cellpadding="3" cellspacing="3" border="1">
        <tr>
          <td colspan="2">Fields marked * are compulsory.</td>
        </tr>
        <tr>
          <td><label for="subject">Subject *</label></td>
         <td><select name="subject" id="subject" tabindex="1">
           <option value="">Select</option>
           <option value="Option 1">Option 1</option>
           <option value="Option 2">Option 2</option>
         </select></td>
        </tr>
        <tr>
          <td><label for="name">Name *</label></td>
          <td><input type="text" name="name" id="name" tabindex="2" /></td>
        </tr>
        <tr>
          <td><label for="email">Email *</label></td>
          <td><input type="text" name="email" id="email" tabindex="3" /></td>
        </tr>
```

```
        <tr>
          <td colspan="2"><label for="message">Message or enquiry below</label></td>
        </tr>
        <tr>
          <td colspan="2"><textarea name="message" id="message" ➥
           rows="11" cols="30" tabindex="4"></textarea></td>
        </tr>
        <tr>
          <td><label for="updates">I would like to receive updates: </label></td>
          <td><input type="checkbox" name="updates" id="updates" value="n" ➥
          tabindex="5"/></td>
        </tr>
    </table>
  </fieldset>
  <input type='submit' value='Send this enquiry' />
</form>
```

Load forms_table.html in your browser, and it should look something like what appears in Figure 9-4.

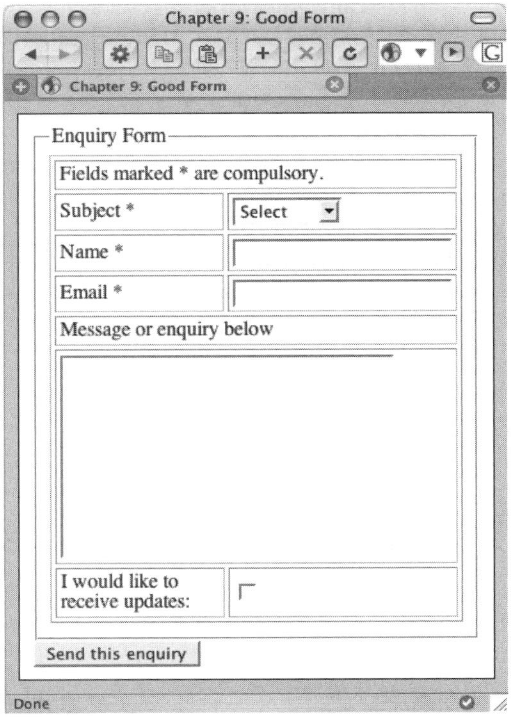

Figure 9-4. *Form layout within a table*

Create the new style sheet called `forms_table.css`, and save the file. You should use this style sheet to examine all the following examples in this section.

Remove Default Form Spacing

You already know that different browsers display form elements in numerous ways. Well, they also apply their own specific `margin` and `padding` values to the `<form>` element.

To get off to a clean start and begin with a blank canvas, it is a good idea to turn off this default spacing by adding a selector for the `<form>` element.

```
form {
  margin:0;
  padding:0;
  }
```

There may be no discernable difference in the browser you are using, but at least you know that there will be consistency in spacing across all browsers before you continue.

Nifty Borders for Text <input> and <textarea>

Some modern browsers will allow you to use a cool value called `double` to draw a double border around `<input>`, `<textarea>`, and `submit` form inputs. Specifically, this works effectively for Firefox, Camino, Opera, and IE Win/Mac. Safari, however, will completely ignore this declaration.

```
input, textarea {
  border: 3px double #333;
  }
```

Figure 9-5 shows how this simple approach draws the neat double border around any input element.

This is a very useful method of further defining the input areas of forms, and can be argued to be a usability enhancement. It looks especially good when a bold color is used for the actual border, and by targeting certain input fields by their IDs, different-colored borders could be assigned to different input fields to suggest correlations between them.

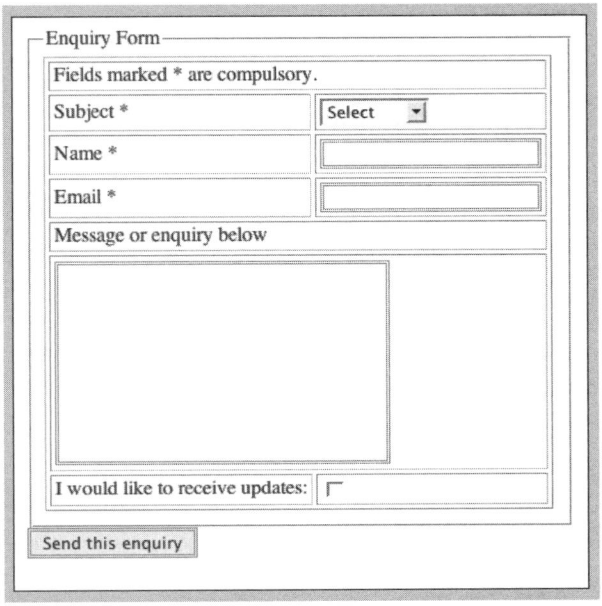

Figure 9-5. *The <input> and <textarea> elements now have a stylish border on most modern browsers (excluding Safari).*

Width of <input> and <textarea>

Nothing makes a form look more uncared for than a jumble of varying length input fields. Even if you specify a value for the size attribute, there will be variation between the lengths of standard text inputs and <textarea> fields. Thankfully, a little targeted CSS is all that is needed.

Specifying a width of 100% would ensure that all input elements (and <textarea> fields in this case) would stretch to fit their containing element (a table cell, for example).

```
input, textarea {
  width:100%;
  border: 3px double #999999;
  }
```

That's great, but look at the example in Figure 9-6. As the submit button is also an <input> element, so it too is stretched the full width of its table cell, which is not desirable.

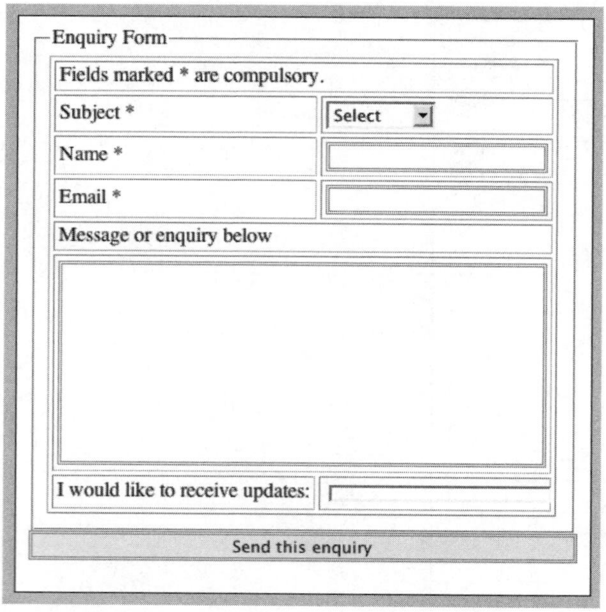

Figure 9-6. *The <input> and <textarea> elements now stretch to fill the available area, but sadly so does the check box and also the submit button.*

A better approach is to target only the input fields that need to be 100% width, and for this the unique ID of each comes in very handy indeed. Rather than declare a blanket rule for all input types, the rule is only applied to the inputs with the appropriate IDs.

```
#name, #email, #message {
  width:100%;
  }
input, textarea {
  border: 3px double #999999;
  }
```

This is preferable as it is much more controlled, and nothing is better in CSS than a nice targeted rule. Figure 9-7 shows that the appropriate elements are still stretched the full width of their table cells, but the submit button is restored to its default length.

The same approach can be applied to the <select> element by finding its unique ID and adding it to the grouping.

```
#name, #email, #message, #subject {
  width:100%;
  }
```

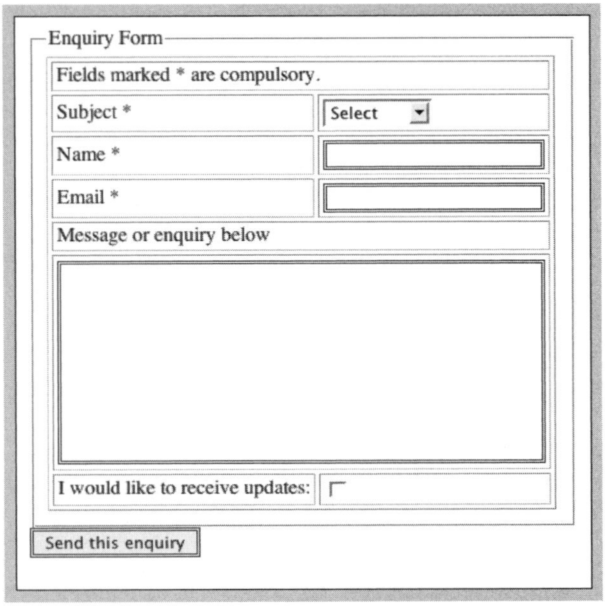

Figure 9-7. *By applying border and width to certain input fields using their IDs, elements that mustn't fill the whole cell are left unaltered.*

As Figure 9-8 shows, the width of the `<select>` element is now also 100%, perfectly inline with the text input below it.

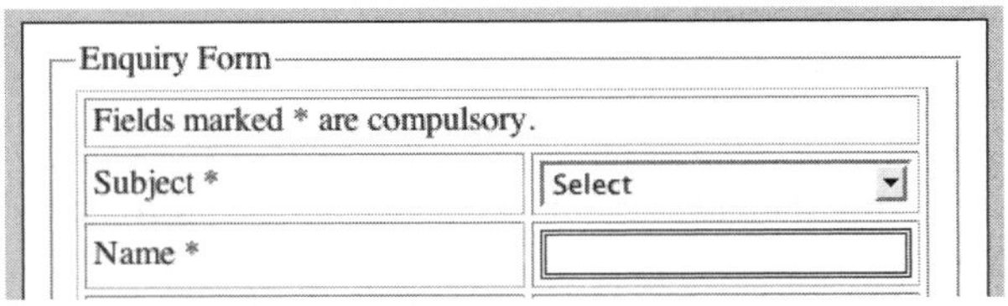

Figure 9-8. *The <select>element is now also stretching the width of the table cell.*

<label>

The great thing about text contained within the `<label>` element is that it can be treated differently from any other text inside the `<fieldset>` or table. Any label text will probably need to be highlighted, perhaps bold?

```
label {
  font-weight:bold;
  }
```

This will produce the clearly defined label text shown in Figure 9-9. Note that all other text within the <fieldset> remains normal weight.

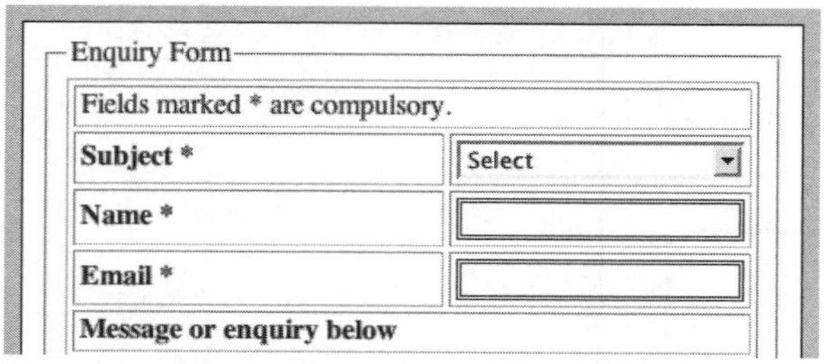

Figure 9-9. *The <label>element is now bold.*

Don't feel that you have to stop there. I have seen some very creative approaches to the <label> element, with clever use of contrasting color and background to apply focus to particular elements at a given time.

<fieldset>

As previously mentioned, the <fieldset> element acts as parent to all form elements grouped within it, and can therefore be a key part of a successfully styled form.

Typically a custom border would be applied to create a visual clue that certain elements belonged together, such as in this example which overrides the default border of the <fieldset>.

```
fieldset {
  margin:0 0 10px 0;
  padding:5px;
  border:1px solid #333;
  }
```

In the example, all form elements are grouped inside one <fieldset>, and the 1-pixel gray border replaces the default border (see Figure 9-10).

If more than one <fieldset> were to be used in one form, it would be important to group any shared values for all <fieldset> elements in the style sheet, or perhaps define unique values to each by attaching a unique ID attribute to each in the (X)HTML.

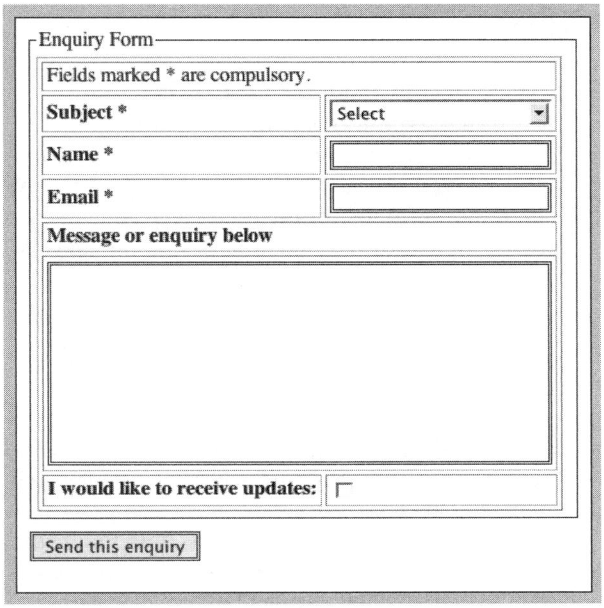

Figure 9-10. *The effect of CSS applied to the <fieldset>element*

<legend>

The default formatting of the <legend> element gets us off to a great start, owing to the way the browser positions it over the top of the <fieldset> border. A few background and border values are all that are needed to transform the <legend> element into something a little more stylish.

```
legend {
  background-color: #DDDDDD;
  margin: 0;
  padding:5px;
  border-style:solid;
  border-width:1px;
  border-color:#FFF #AAA #666 #FFF;
  }
```

Figure 9-11 shows how the preceding CSS creates a three-dimensional affect akin to that applied to lists in Chapter 6 and links in Chapter 7.

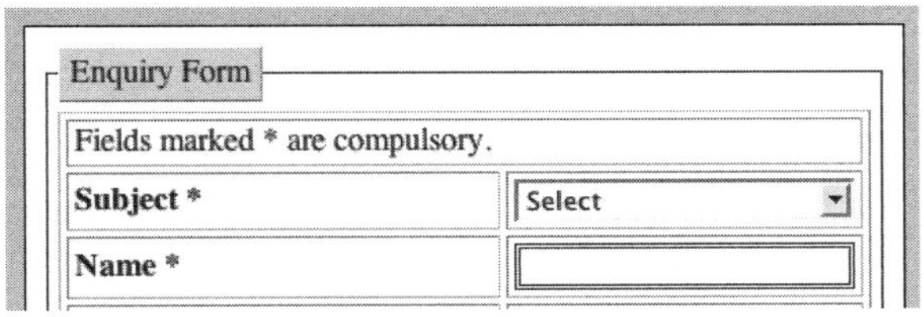

Figure 9-11. *With CSS applied, the <legend> element now looks three-dimensional.*

The Form CSS Block Is Complete

The result of all that careful CSS tweaking is a set of CSS selectors that can be used again and again to quickly get your forms off to a good start. The full list of rules is shown just inside the next section, and is also available to download with the source code for this chapter.

It might be a good idea later to have a fresh go at these rules and define your own reusable set of styles for your forms. Having such devices at your disposal is key to increased productivity and fast prototyping—very few web designers start everything from scratch every time. Always look for blocks of CSS that can be put on one side for a rainy day, essentially building up your own library of jump-starts.

Three Approaches

There are many, many ways of laying out a form within a web page, and it is fun to look at the source code of some well-known sites and see how well or how badly they do it. For my money, there are only three real options, selected specifically because they are accessible, stylish, and provide a great number of ready-made elements to attach CSS to.

The three options are the table, combined paragraph and break elements, and finally the definition list. As you read on, see which you think is the best solution. At the end of the chapter I will impart my thinking on this subject, but rest assured that if any or all of the three were not acceptable, I wouldn't be discussing them. It all boils down to having the right approach for the right form.

About Each Example

Each example first shows you the unstyled version—how it will appear should the style sheet be unavailable or turned off by the user. This is very important for any section of a web page, but especially so where forms are concerned. To have the display compromised when CSS is unavailable could result in dual frustration—for you by losing valuable input (or even a sale if it's cash that ticks your buttons), and for the user by being unable to interact properly or purchase your product.

Also, each example gets off to a fast start by utilizing the *form CSS block* created in the previous section. There is no need to go through the styling of input fields and other elements for each example, as most styles from the form CSS block will fall gracefully into each layout, aside from a few exceptions that will be dealt with accordingly.

Here's the full CSS for the form CSS block once more:

```
form {
  margin:0;
  padding:0;
  }
fieldset {
  margin:0 0 10px 0;
  padding:5px;
  border:1px solid #333;
  }
```

```
legend {
  background-color: #DDDDDD;
  margin: 0;
  padding:5px;
border-style:solid;
  border-width:1px;
  border-color:#FFF #AAA #666 #FFF;
  }
label {
  font-weight:bold;
  }
#name, #email, #message, #subject {
  width:100%;
  }
input, textarea {
  border:3px double #333;
  }
```

Let's get stuck in then, dealing first with the most common method of laying out a form—the good old table.

Table-Based Forms

The traditional approach to laying out a form involves a table. Nobody seems totally sure whether form fields constitute tabular data, but the fact remains that tables are ideally suited to form layout, and for very complex forms there is no workable alternative.

Let's revisit the example form held within a table from the "Basics of Form Styling" section earlier in this chapter.

Prepare

If you haven't already prepared a file and style sheet for a table-based form (as described in the section "Basics of Form Styling"), set these up as follows:

Create a file called forms_table.html and paste the table layout (X)HTML from the "Basics of Form Styling" section into the <body>. In the <head> of the file, link to a new style sheet called forms_table.css. Save the template.

Create the new style sheet called forms_table.css, and paste the form CSS block (from the beginning of this section) into it, and save the file. Load forms_table.html in the browser, and you should see something similar to Figure 9-4.

Take Control of the Table

Taking what you learned about basic table styling in Chapter 8, some simple rules can be declared to bring the default table styling under control.

Here, the main table borders are turned off, and border-collapse is used to remove the default padding from between the table cells. The font properties are also set right away.

```
table {
  border:0;
  border-collapse:collapse;
  font: normal 12px 'Lucida Grande',Verdana,sans-serif;
  }
td, tr {
  padding:6px;
  }
td {
  border-bottom: 1px solid #666;
  }
```

Shared padding is declared for both the <tr> and <td> elements, but a bottom-border is applied only to the <td> cells. Thanks to border-collapse, this will create the effect of a continuous line separating each row of the form (see Figure 9-12).

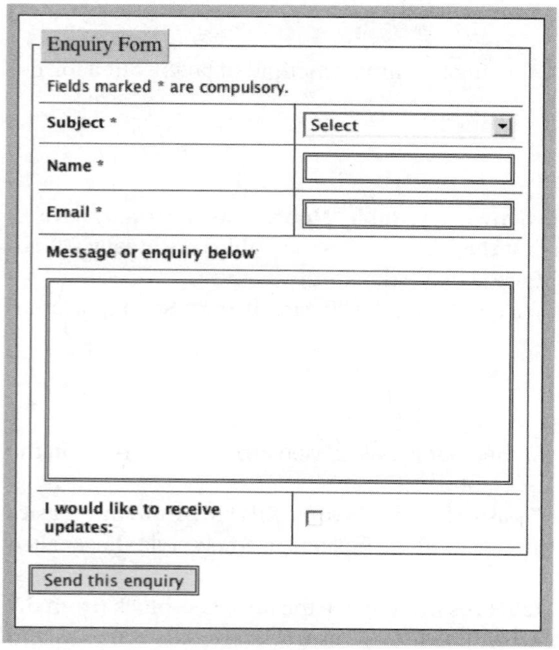

Figure 9-12. *Table with basic styling applied*

Next, a background color is declared for each row. This could also have been declared for the table selector, but this would have resulted in a larger gray area stretching past the <tr> borders.

```
tr {
  background:#DDDDDD;
  }
```

The Final CSS for the Table-Based Form

The full CSS for the table-based form follows. Now might be a good time to experiment with background images and colors to further personalize your form.

```
table {
  border:0;
  border-collapse:collapse;
  font: normal 12px 'Lucida Grande',Verdana,sans-serif;
  }
td, tr {
  padding:6px;
  }
tr {
  background:#DDDDDD;
  }
td {
  border-bottom: 1px solid #666;
  }
form {
  margin:0;
  padding:0;
  }
fieldset {
  margin:0 0 10px 0;
  padding:5px;
  border:1px solid #333;
  }
legend {
  background: #DDDDDD;
  margin: 0;
  padding:5px;
  border-style:solid;
  border-width:1px;
  border-color:#FFF #AAA #666 #FFF;
}
label {
  font-weight:bold;
  }
#name, #email, #message, #subject {
  width:100%;
  }
input, textarea {
  border:3px double #333;
  }
```

Figure 9-13 shows the finished form.

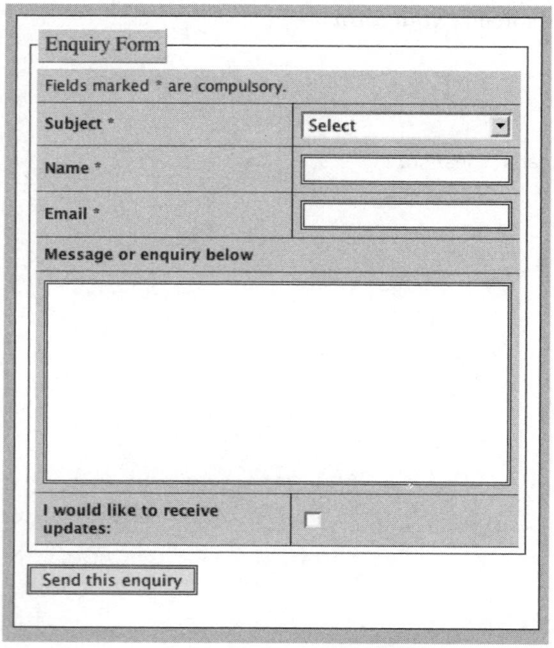

Figure 9-13. *The finished table-based form layout*

Tables certainly assist the building of forms and are good way of ensuring that various form elements stay where you want them to. Most designers favor having the element on the left and the input fields on the right, and therefore use tables exclusively. However, the following two examples are worthy of consideration, and arguably bring a little more panache to the form layout without seeking to compromise any of this functionality.

Paragraph and Break Element Layout

Right, forget tables now, as we move on to something much simpler and arguably much more accessible. With this approach, each label and input field is contained within its own paragraph element, and the break tag is used to provide a little extra control within.

This is a particularly good solution if you care strongly about how your form will look without a style sheet. The use of the break tags will ensure that the structure remains in place, and the default `margin` and `padding` of the paragraphs will ensure that each `<label>` and `<input>` field is still spaced nicely.

Prepare

Create a file called forms_pbr.html and paste the following markup into the <body>. In the <head> of the file, link to a new style sheet called forms_pbr.css.

```
<form action="" method="post" id="enquiryform">
  <fieldset>
    <legend>Enquiry Form</legend>
    <p>Fields marked * are compulsory.</p>
    <p><label for="subject">Subject *</label><br />
      <select name="subject" id="subject" tabindex="1">
        <option value="">Select</option>
        <option value="Option 1">Option 1</option>
        <option value="Option 2">Option 2</option>
      </select></p>
    <p><label for="name">Name *</label><br />
      <input type="text" name="name" id="name" tabindex="2" /></p>
    <p><label for="email">Email *</label><br />
      <input type="text" name="email" id="email" tabindex="3" /></p>
    <p><label for="message">Message or enquiry below</label><br />
      <textarea name="message" id="message" rows="11" cols="30" ➥
      tabindex="4"></textarea></p>
    <p><label for="updates">I would like to receive updates: </label><br />
      <input type="checkbox" name="updates" id="updates" ➥
          value="n" tabindex="5"/></p>
  </fieldset>
  <input type="submit" value="Send this enquiry" tabindex="6" />
</form>
```

Run tables_pbr.html in the browser and the result should be similar to that in Figure 9-14.

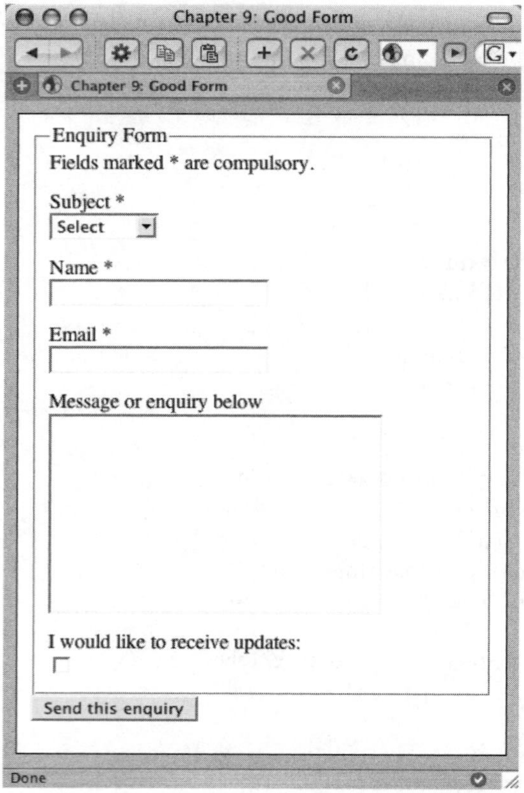

Figure 9-14. *Form layout out using paragraph and break elements*

Why Not Make the <label> Element Block Level?

This is on the face of things a good idea. Rather than add the much-scorned <br> tags after each element, it's true that adding display:block to the label selector would result in the input field wrapping underneath the label, on a new line. This would certainly make the markup cleaner, as in this example:

```
<p><label for="name">Name *</label>
<input type="text" name="name" id="name" tabindex="2" /></p>
```

However, what is going to happen should the style sheet be unavailable? Unfortunately, the <label> would no longer be block level, which is a real bummer. Figure 9-15 shows what would happen in such a situation, where the style sheet is unavailable, and no <br> tags are in use to shunt the input fields onto new lines.

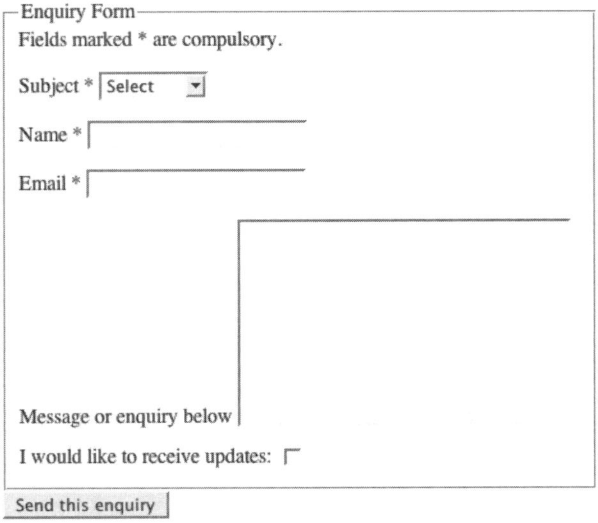

Figure 9-15. *With the style sheet removed, the <label> elements are no longer block level, and, as a result, everything looks squashed.*

There ends the case for block-level <label> elements. Of course, if the powers that be were to turn <label> into a block-level element, this debate wouldn't be necessary; but it is, because they won't, and that's that.

Apply the Form CSS

Create the new style sheet called forms_pbr.css, paste the form CSS block into it, and save the file. Load forms_pbr.html in the browser, and you should see something similar to Figure 9-16.

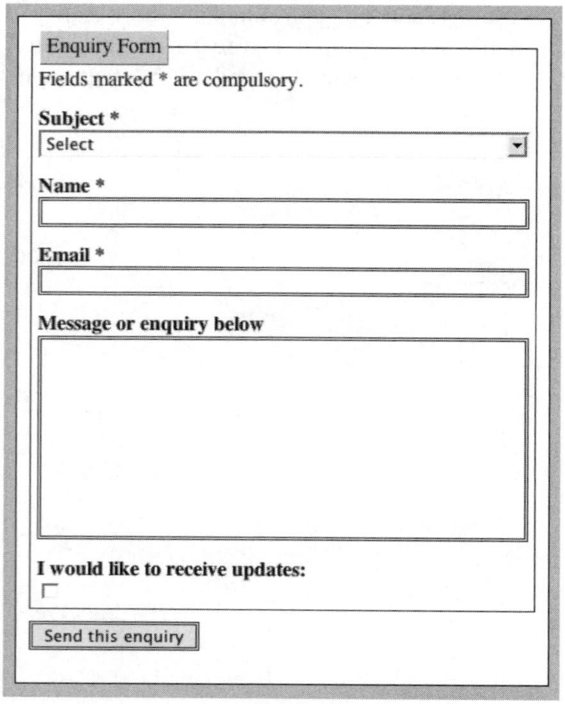

Figure 9-16. *The layout with the form CSS block appplied*

The first thing worth noting is that the `<select>` element is way too long, stretching as it does for the full length of the `<fieldset>`. This is easily remedied by removing the `<select>` element's unique ID (`subject`) from the grouping that controls input widths.

```
#name, #email, #message {
  width:100%;
  }
```

Now the `<select>` element is defaulting to the width of the longest item it contains (see Figure 9-17), which is pretty standard, and should suffice.

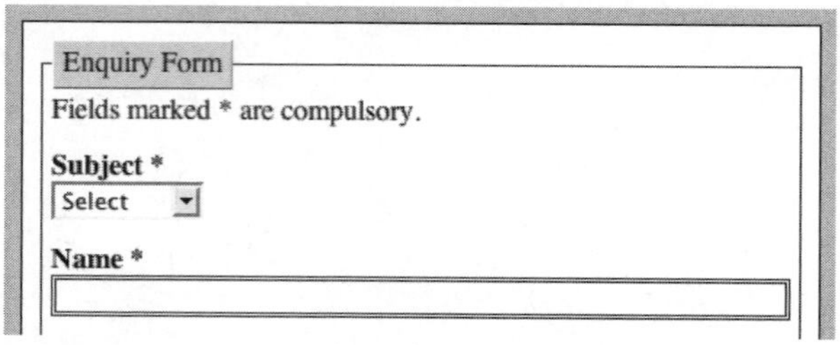

Figure 9-17. *The <select> element is now reduced to its default size.*

If you are not happy with this default width, create a new selector for the `subject` ID and declare a value in pixels or percentage that suits your design.

`<fieldset>` Background

There are now two possible ways to color the background of the form. The first is by declaring a background color for the `<fieldset>` element.

```
fieldset {
  margin:0 0 10px 0;
  padding:5px;
  border:1px solid #333;
  background:#DDDDDD;
  }
```

This is fine if all you need is a block background color (see Figure 9-18). There is, however, a much better approach using the existing paragraph elements.

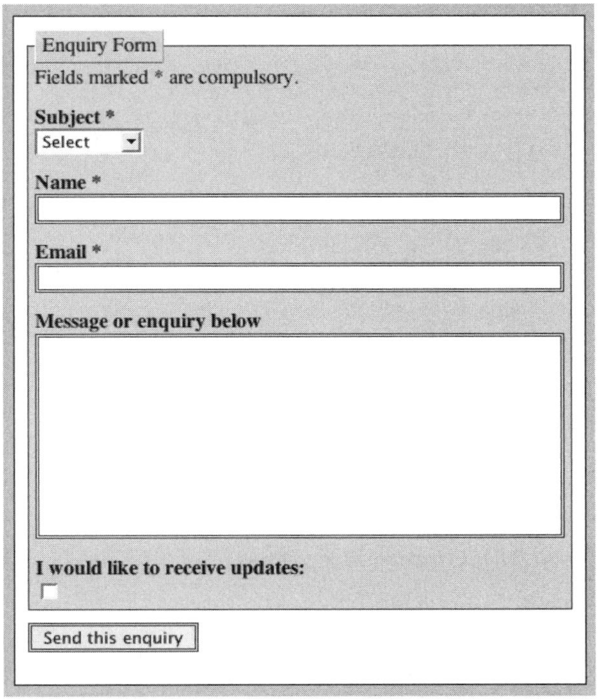

Figure 9-18. *<fieldset> background*

Paragraph Background

So `<fieldset>` is fine if you need a solid block of color behind your form, but many designers like to clearly define each `<label>` and `<input>` field. Luckily, this can be done by making the paragraphs work a little harder.

By declaring values only for paragraphs contained within the `<fieldset>`, the `<label>` and `<input>` fields can be separated easily.

```
fieldset p {
  margin:3px 0 2px 0;
  padding:5px;
  background:#DDDDDD;
  }
```

Figure 9-19 shows that each paragraph has a solid gray background, with whitespace controlled by the margin value in between, clearly defining each `<label>` and `<input>`.

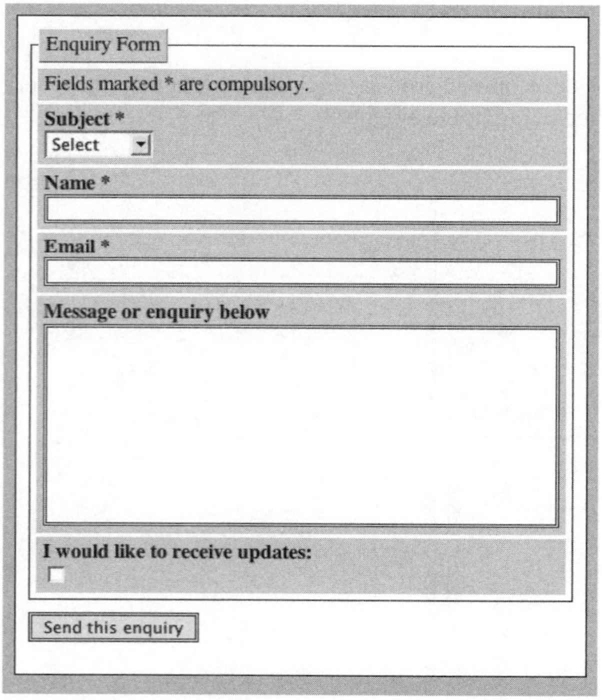

Figure 9-19. *Paragraph backgrounds clearly define the label and input sets.*

Final Adjustments

All that is needed now is to fine-tune the layout. The final CSS follows, with further additions highlighted with bold text. Note that font values are set on the parent element (`<fieldset>`), and minor adjustments to margins in several selectors have been made to further tweak the spacing of the elements.

```
form {
  margin:0;
  padding:0;
  }
fieldset {
  font: normal 12px 'Lucida Grande',Verdana,sans-serif;
  margin:0 0 10px 0;
  padding:5px;
  border:1px solid #333;
  }
fieldset p {
  margin:3px 0 2px 0;
  padding:5px;
  border:1px solid #666;
  background:#DDDDDD;
}
legend {
  background-color: #DDDDDD;
  margin: 0;
  padding:5px;
  border-style:solid;
  border-width:1px;
  border-color:#FFF #AAA #666 #FFF;
  }
label {
  font-weight:bold;
  }
#name, #email, #message {
  width:100%;
  }
input, textarea {
  margin:5px 0 5px 0;
  border:3px double #333;
  }
select {
  margin:5px 0 5px 0;
  }
```

The final result, shown in Figure 9-20, is a very pleasing form, clearly laid out and using considerably less code than the table version.

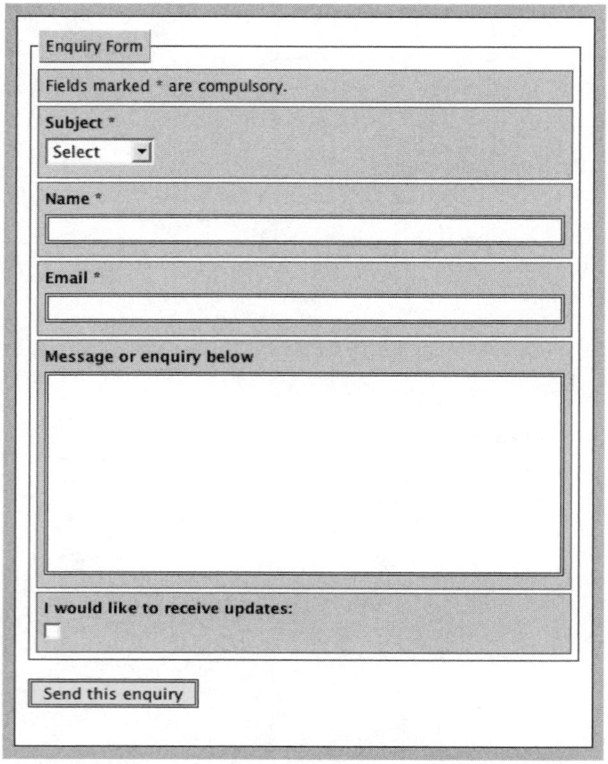

Figure 9-20. *The finished form laid out with paragraphs and break elements*

The only drawback here is that `<label>` and `<input>` fields are not aligned on the same line, as they were with the table layout. If this is something that bothers you, perhaps the next example might be worth your consideration.

Definition List Layout

Back in Chapter 8, you learned the various uses of the often forgotten definition list, all of which were perfectly acceptable, and not likely to cause any kind of consternation.

So can a definition list be used to lay out a form? Well, more and more designers are saying, "Yes," although no official guidelines suggest that this is what a definition list is for. That said, it is a perfect structural tool for the job, as you'll see.

Prepare

Create a file called forms_dl.html and paste the following markup into the body. In the <head> of the file, link to a new style sheet called forms_dl.css.

```
<form action="" method="post" id="enquiryform">
  <fieldset>
    <legend>Enquiry Form</legend>
    <p>Fields marked * are compulsory.</p>
    <dl>
      <dt><label for="subject">Subject *</label></dt>
      <dd><select name="subject" id="subject" tabindex="1">
        <option value="">Select</option>
        <option value="Option 1">Option 1</option>
        <option value="Option 2">Option 2</option>
      </select></dd>
      <dt><label for="name">Name *</label></dt>
      <dd><input type="text" name="name" id="name" tabindex="2" /></dd>
      <dt><label for="email">Email *</label></dt>
      <dd><input type="text" name="email" id="email" tabindex="3" /></dd>
      <dt><label for="message">Message or enquiry below</label></dt>
      <dd><textarea name="message" id="message" rows="11" cols="30"➧
      tabindex="4"></textarea></dd>
      <dt><label for="updates">I would like to receive updates: </label></dt>
      <dd><input type="checkbox" name="updates" id="updates" value="n" ➧
      tabindex="5"/></dd>
    </dl>
  </fieldset>
  <input type="submit" value="Send this enquiry" tabindex="6" />
</form>
```

Save the template, and run it in your browser. The layout is already quite pleasing, with the labels to the left and the input fields shifted below and indented from the left edge of the definition list (see Figure 9-21).

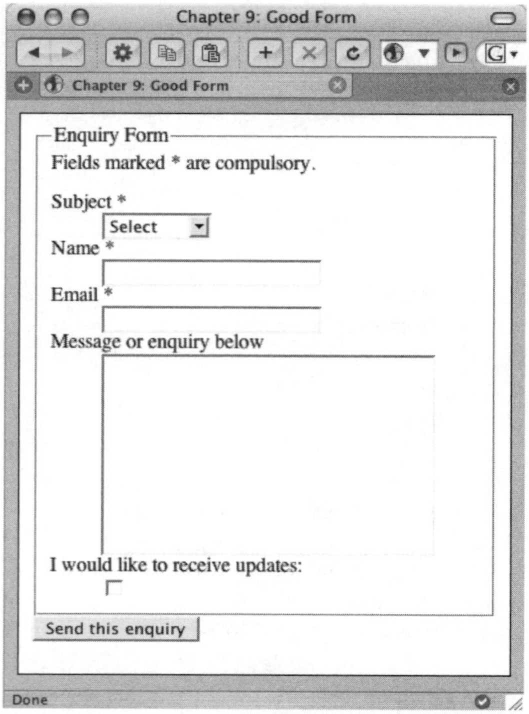

Figure 9-21. *Form layout with a definition list*

It goes without saying, however, that some smashing CSS will make it even more appealing.

Two Stages of CSS

Create a new style sheet called `forms_dl.css`, and save the file. The CSS approach to this definition list is in two parts. First, the definition list needs bringing into line.

Remove Default Indenting

In Chapter 8, you learned all about the default margins of the definition list. The first job here is to again remove the default `margin` by adding the following selector to the `forms_dl.css` file:

```
fieldset dd {
  margin:0;
  }
```

The result of this tweak, shown in Figure 9-22, brings the display to a similar starting point as that of the paragraph and break element layout, with <input> fields wrapping directly under the <label> element. Of course, what is really happening is that the <dd> element is wrapping underneath the <dt> element.

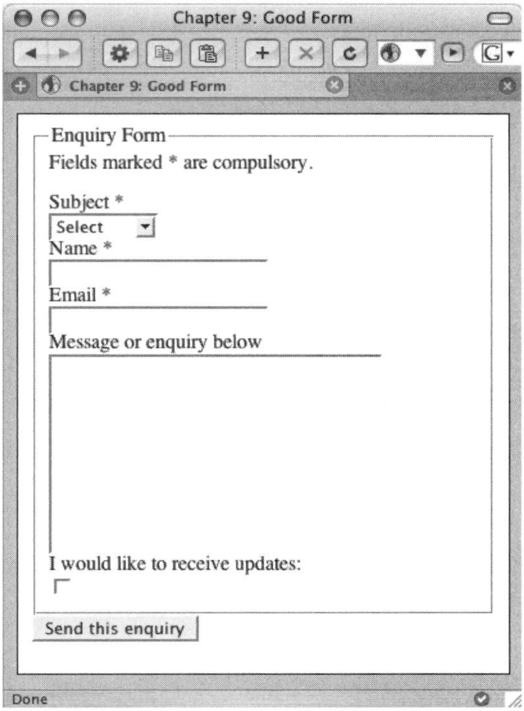

Figure 9-22. *Default indenting removed from the <dd> element*

That's a good start, but the whole point of using a definition list is so that <label> and <input> elements can be placed on the same line, but be spaced evenly. This is where the float property comes in.

Float It

First, bring in a dt selector, a descendant of the <fieldset>. Several major adjustments are made here.

The float property is used to ensure that all <dt> elements float to the left, which results in all <dd> elements appearing directly to the right of these, bringing each onto the same line, as it were. Floats are one of the most commonly used things in the brave new world of CSS layouts, and so will be covered in much more detail in Part 2 of this book.

Note that the <dt> element is given a width of 150px to ensure that each is the same width, regardless of how much text each contains. This neatens up the form and will make sure all input fields to the right are aligned equally.

Notice also that light gray borders are temporarily added so that we can see what's going on in the browser, and that some simple padding is specified to space things out a little.

```
fieldset dt {
  float:left;
  width:150px;
  padding:5px;
  border:1px solid #CCC;
  }
fieldset dd {
  margin:0;
  padding:5px;
  border:1px solid #CCC;
  }
```

Figure 9-23 shows that when this is viewed in the browser, a problem is immediately evident. Basically, if the container or browser window is too narrow to accommodate the <textarea>, it will still wrap underneath its corresponding <dt> element.

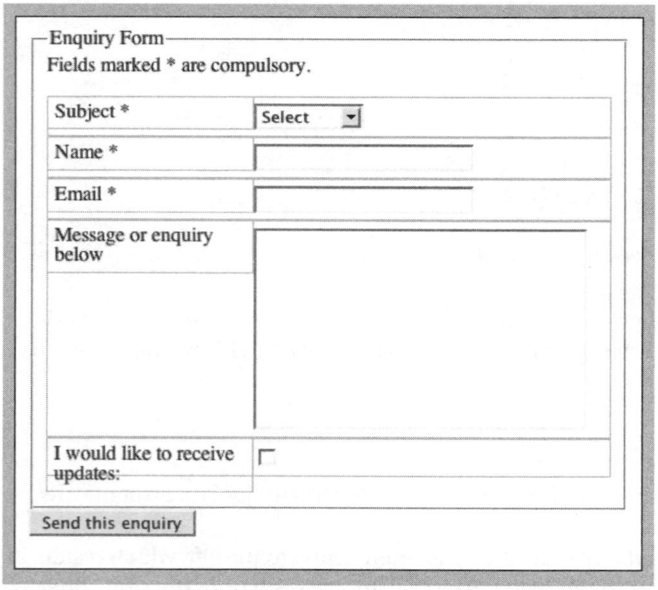

Figure 9-23. *The temporary gray outlines show that without a set width for the <dd> element, the <textarea> wraps under its corresponding <dt> element.*

This is easily fixed by assigning a set width to the <dd> element. Here, 450px is enough to accommodate a <textarea> defined as 30 characters wide with its columns="30" attribute and value. Notice also that the temporary gray borders have been removed from the fieldset dt and fieldset dd selectors.

```
fieldset dd {
  width:450px;
  margin:0;
  padding:5px;
  }
fieldset dt {
  float:left;
  width:150px;
  padding:5px;
  }
fieldset dd {
  margin:0;
  padding:5px;
  }
```

As a result of the new width value for the <dd> element, the form is now looking pretty neat and tidy (see Figure 9-24).

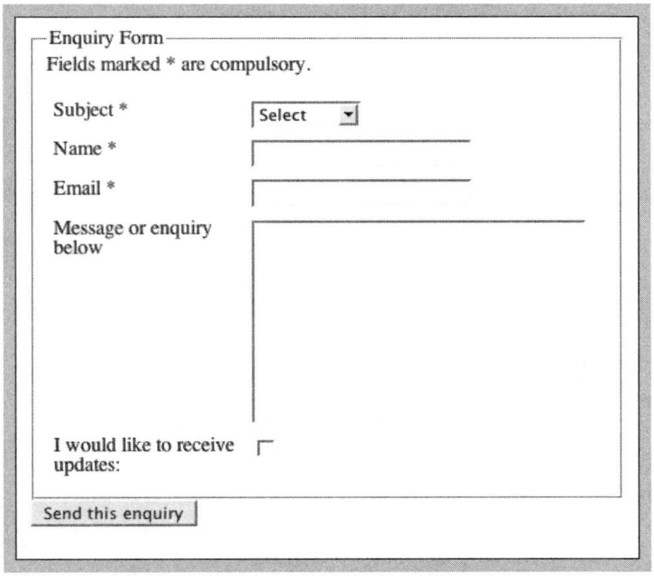

Figure 9-24. *The <dd> elements (containing input elements) are floated next to the <dt> elements (containing <label> elements).*

As it stands, this might even be enough for some basic approaches to form layout, but remember that the pre-prepared form CSS block is sitting there waiting to be thrown into the pot.

Apply the Form CSS Block

Now add the form CSS block you prepared earlier (it should still be hot) into `forms_dl.css` below the CSS you have created for this layout. Load `forms_dl.html` in the browser, and you should see something similar to Figure 9-25.

Figure 9-25. *The input fields are wrapping underneath the <label> elements.*

Straight away there is a problem. Once again, the `<input>` fields are wrapping underneath the `<label>` element. As you can see from the gray lines around the elements, it is actually the width of the input fields (now 100%) causing the `<dd>` elements to shift underneath the `<dt>` elements.

To counter this problem, a new width value is required for the offending `<input>` elements. To do this, find the grouping of unique IDs for those elements and replace the 100% value with one of 280px.

```
#name, #email, #message, #subject {
  width:280px;
  }
```

Why 280px, you ask? Well, the outer container is 450 pixels wide. The <dt> element has already been set to 150px, and we need to compensate for padding applied inside the definition list. Therefore, 280px is small enough to ensure that the <input> fields will slot back into the allotted space for the <dd> element. The result can be seen in Figure 9-26.

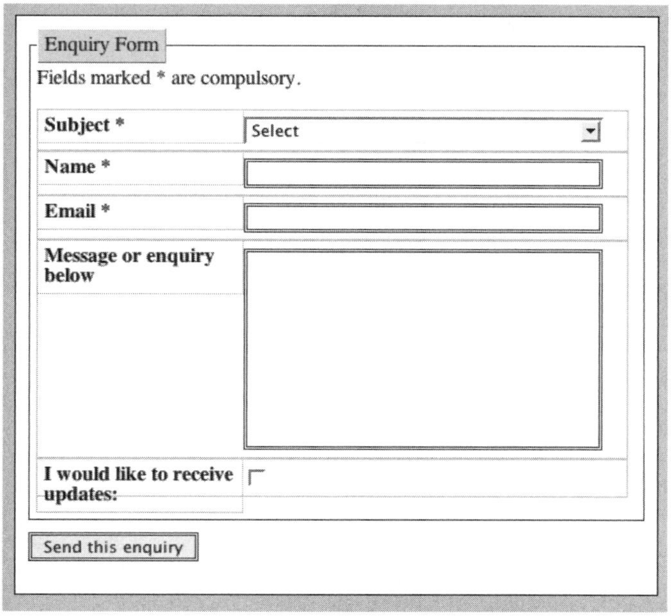

Figure 9-26. *With a simple width adjustment for input fields with specific IDs, everything now aligns correctly.*

Set the Background Color

This time around, there are no paragraphs to apply background-color to, and to apply it to all the individual <dt> and <dd> elements would result in a less-than-perfect box (look at the gray outlines of these elements in Figure 9-26 to see why). Therefore, the job falls to the outer definition list.

```
fieldset dl {
  border:1px solid #666;
  background:#DDDDDD;
  }
```

Almost there, but notice that where the <label> text wraps to two lines (the final <label> of the form) the text breaks out of the definition list element, as shown in Figure 9-27.

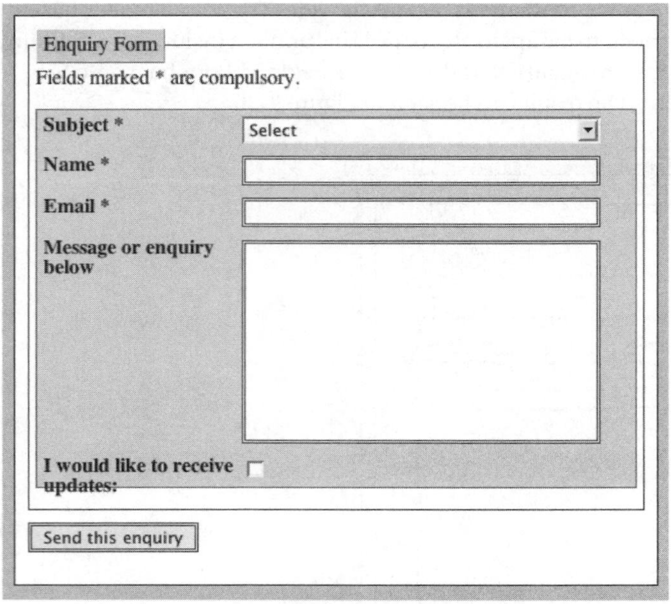

Figure 9-27. *The whole definition list has a gray background, but the last label's text is breaking out of the box.*

This quirk is a result of using the `float` property to align the `<dt>` elements. All floats need to be cleared, in order for following elements to compensate for them, and this will be discussed in much more detail in Part 2 of this book. Thankfully for now, there is a tidy workaround.

Simply assigning 15 pixels of bottom `padding` to the definition list will ensure that the final `<label>` element will have enough space in which to wrap.

```
fieldset dl {
  padding-bottom:15px;
  border:1px solid #666;
  background:#DDDDDD;
  }
```

Figure 9-28 shows that this simple method has ensured that there is enough remaining space inside the definition list for the wrapping `<label>`.

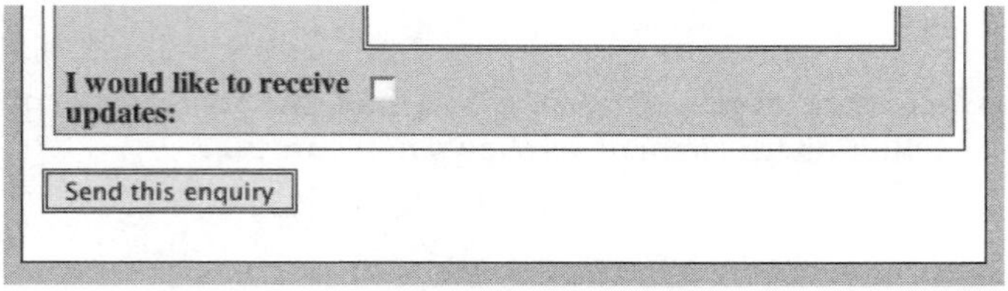

Figure 9-28. *The escaping label text is solved with padding on the definition list.*

A Few Final Touches

All that remains now is to make everything gel together. The final CSS for the definition list and form elements follow. Note that a new selector for the paragraph within the `<fieldset>` is added, used to make the paragraph appear as though in a box to match the definition list, and that font properties have again been set.

```
fieldset dl {
  padding-bottom:15px;
  border:1px solid #666;
  background:#DDDDDD;
  }
fieldset dt {
  float:left;
  width:150px;
  padding:5px;
  }
fieldset dd {
  width:450px;
  margin:0;
  padding:5px;
  }
form {
  margin:0;
  padding:0;
  }
fieldset {
  margin:0 0 10px 0;
  padding:5px;
  border:1px solid #333;
  font: normal 12px 'Lucida Grande',Verdana,sans-serif;
  }
fieldset p {
  padding:5px;
  border:1px solid #666;
  background:#DDDDDD;
  }
legend {
  background: #DDDDDD;
  margin: 0;
  padding:5px;
  border-style:solid;
  border-width:1px;
  border-color:#FFF #AAA #666 #FFF;
  font-weight:bold;
  }
```

```
label {
  font-weight:bold;
  }
#name, #email, #message, #subject {
  width:280px;
  }
input, textarea {
  border:3px double #333;
  }
```

The final layout can be seen in Figure 9-29. Another very neat solution, matching the capabilities of the table, but without all the extra markup it brings with it.

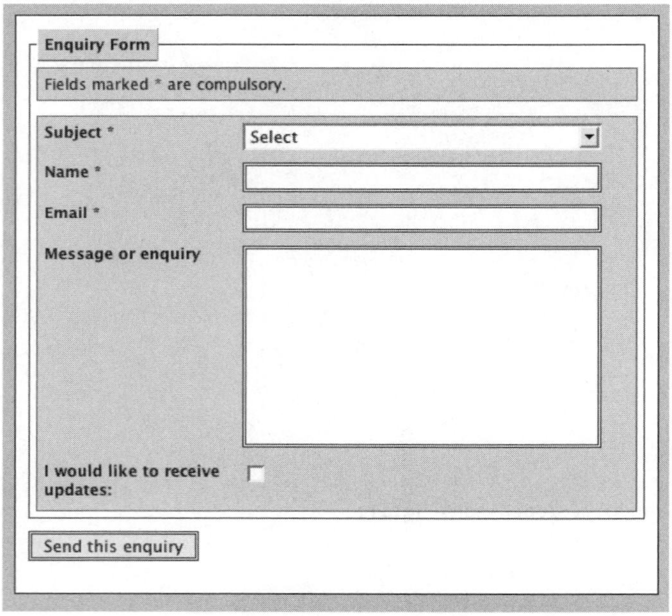

Figure 9-29. *The finished form laid out with a definition list*

So Which Approach Is Best?

You've just worked through three sensible approaches to form layout—tables, paragraphs and break elements, and definition lists. So which one is the best?

Well, it's hard to say. I personally prefer the layout using paragraphs and break elements, as it produces very lean code and is very accessible for any user. However, when it comes to very complex forms, this approach becomes limiting, and the desire to align elements to the right of the label becomes very tempting, especially if working with multiple check boxes, for example.

The table approach requires that you also include many elements left out in this example, such as `<caption>`, `<th>`, and other accessibility aids. Users not only have to navigate a form but also a table, so while you shouldn't be afraid to use a table, think whether a particular form needs one or whether it is simple enough to just use paragraphs.

The definition list approach is gaining popularity, but nobody is sure whether it is legal or not. It's certainly not illegal, and it will still produce valid code, but do consider the alternatives before you plump for the definition list.

The answer is that no method is correct. Each will be applicable in different scenarios, and like most aspects of web design, there is no perfect approach.

To Conclude...

This chapter merely skims the scum floating on the surface of the duck pond, and at this stage this author is delighted that this book is not called *Advanced CSS Web Development*. What's more, interesting things are always happening in the web design industry, and approaches to building accessible forms are like shifting sand. It pays to pay attention to industry web sites and blogs for all the latest information and techniques, but especially where forms are concerned. Also, always be sure to test your forms in a number of situations and get friends (or even usability testing groups) to rip them apart. You might end up rebuilding them from scratch, but you'll be a better web designer as a result.

If the world of styling forms with CSS has tired you out, I strongly suggest you go out and buy the biggest teapot you can find, come back, and fill it with very strong tea, as Part 2 of this book gets serious. It's time to start pulling all the fragments together and begin thinking about layout. Stage 1 of your learning is complete.

PART 2

■■■

Logical Layouts

Part 1 of this book dealt primarily with the common elements of any design and how to transform them with CSS. Taking what you learned in Part 1, you could now make a rather smart-looking web site styled with CSS that has just one drawback—it would be entirely vertical. Part 2 of this book looks at the numerous methods of pulling everything together into custom layouts, and how to think horizontally by placing the content into columns.

Layout concerns the placement of text, images, and other elements within your design. How these elements are arranged, both in relation to each other and in relation to the overall design scheme, affects how the content is viewed and received by the end user, and can immediately convey a specific mood or motive and provoke a specific reaction in return.

Semantic markup combined with CSS provides immense power when it comes to layout, and it is perfectly possible to radically alter the entire layout of a web page with minimum fuss, thanks to the inherent flexibility of CSS. Even better, you can use a few simple CSS rules to alter layout depending purely upon the purpose of particular pages. What if you need three columns for the home page, but just two for article pages? No problem. One simple change to the `<body>` element can call the required CSS and adjust the layout.

Chapter 10, "Layout Basics," deals with the basic fundamentals of CSS layouts—the grounding you need before you can really progress.

Chapter 11, "Classic Layouts," will focus upon the many, many choices to be made when it comes to layout: two, three, or four columns; fixed, liquid, elastic, or variable fixed width; floated or positioned layout? We'll also investigate something called the Box Model, with specific regard to margin and padding, and how to get your columns to behave when viewed with older browsers.

Chapter 12, "Layout Manipulation," will look at smart methods of manipulating layout depending on the purpose of the page, and how the semantic flow of the document can be altered with CSS for display purposes.

Chapter 13, "The Journey from Layout to Template," gets even more pragmatic, looking closely at the most common elements used in typical web layouts, such as mast-heads, logo placement, navigation, and footers, evaluating the best approaches to each and exploring how to overcome common problems that inevitably occur.

Chapter 14, "Usability and Accessibility Enhancements," moves a step further by examining numerous methods for improving access to your content using some clever CSS techniques. Your pages will already be accessible by default, but here the focus shifts to some cool additions you can make to enhance the user experience further.

Chapter 15, "Tips, Tricks, and Troubles," is a selection box of some of the cooler things that can be done with CSS, making clever use of existing CSS properties to control your content. This chapter also dips its toe into the fascinating world of hacks and filters that can be used to help serve varying content to varying browsers, and also looks briefly toward the forthcoming Internet Explorer 7. There are also some top tips for finding out why things aren't going as expected, with a super-useful troubleshooting section.

Chapter 16, "Case Study: *The Dead Goods*," rounds off the book with a juicy sample web site built using many of the techniques detailed in this book. It has columns, clever images, a nifty logo—and dead rock stars!

CHAPTER 10

■■■

Layout Basics

First up in Part 2, this chapter will introduce the fundamental CSS layout tools available to us, such as floats and positioning, by exploring how they can be applied to basic elements. With a core understanding of these key concepts, you'll be armed and ready to face all aspects of CSS layout.

Specifically, this chapter will cover

- Floats and clearing
- Positioning

Floats and Clearing

The concept of floats is key to layout using CSS. Floats allow you to rebel against the linear nature of the flow of elements on a page, as the example in Figure 10-1 demonstrates. Without floats, each element would be placed below the one above, and pages would be very long indeed. There would be no columns and no inline images, and we'd all still be relying on tables for layout.

When you float an element, it becomes a block-level element that can then be shifted to the left or right on the current line. A floated box is laid out according to the normal flow of elements, but it's then taken out of the flow and shifted to the left or right as far as the containing element will allow. Content such as text can flow down the right side of a left-floated box and down the left side of a right-floated box. Floats are a must for placing images in context, creating columns, and generally allowing designers to think horizontally.

Great, right? Well, yes. However, there are quirks. Elements following a floated element will wrap around it. If you do not want this to occur, those following elements need to be "cleared," essentially reverting back to the natural flow of page elements.

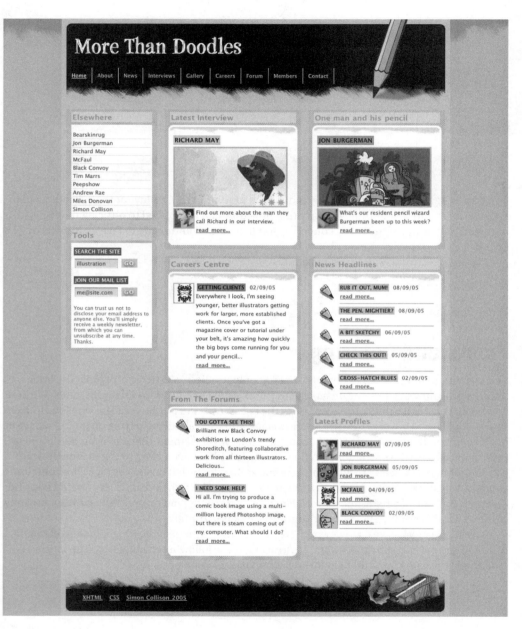

Figure 10-1. *More Than Doodles (http://doodles.cssmastery.com) uses floats for the whole layout. All images and columns are floated to some degree.*

Floats are also required to ensure containing elements do their job and actually contain any floated elements within. Failing to clear those floated elements can result in a container collapsing long before the end of the child elements it contains (see Figure 10-2). Clearing will be covered in more detail later in this chapter and be featured throughout the various examples in this second part of the book.

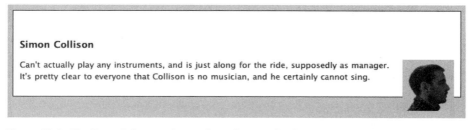

Figure 10-2. *If a floated element is not cleared correctly, the containing element may not recognize it, and it will collapse after nonfloated elements.*

The float Property

If an element needs to be taken out of the natural flow of elements, it can be floated. Three possible values are available for the float property:

```
float:left
float:right
float:none
```

The first two values are pretty obvious, whereas none might not be. We'll look at this later in the chapter. By gaining a core understanding of floats, you will be prepared to go into battle with floated columns for layout, and it is worth working through a few basic examples before moving on. Let's look at a couple of common uses for floats.

Floating Images

The goal here is to align a small image next to a block of corresponding text. This approach is most commonly used to place a thumbnail image inline with basic introduction text for an article.

To follow these examples, it is worth setting up a new (X)HTML file and corresponding external style sheet. Let's jump back to this author's ridiculous aspirations to be in the world's greatest rock 'n' roll band. Place the following (X)HTML in a new file called floats.html:

```
<html>
  <head>
    <title>Chapter 10: Layout Basics</title>
    <link rel='stylesheet' media="screen" type='text/css' href='float.css' />
  </head>
  <body>
    <div id="container">
      <h2>Introducing the band</h2>
    </div>
  </body>
</html>
```

Save the file. Note that an external style sheet called float.css is referenced in the <head> element of the document. Create float.css and paste the following code into it:

```
/* Specify blanket rules for all elements */
body {
  font-size:80%;
  font-family:'Lucida Grande',Verdana,sans-serif;
  margin:10px;
  background-color:#CCC;
  }
/* Container for all page content */
#container {
  padding:10px;
  border:1px solid #000;
  background-color:#FFF;
  }
/* Rules for headings */
h1 {
  font-size:150%;
  }
h2 {
  font-size:140%;
  }
h3 {
  font-size:120%;
  }
p {
  font-size:100%;
  line-height:150%;
  }
```

Save float.css and load the (X)HTML file in your browser. So far it is pretty unremarkable—just a container element and a level 2 heading.

Next, create a small thumbnail image, roughly 80×80 pixels, and place it in your images directory. Now copy and paste the following (X)HTML for a simple biography into the content area of the file, being sure to add the appropriate path to your image.

```
<html>
  <head>
    <title>Chapter 10: Layout Basics</title>
    <link rel='stylesheet' media="screen" type='text/css' href='float.css' />
  </head>
  <body>
    <div id="container">
      <h2>Introducing the band</h2>
      <h3>Simon Collison</h3>
        <img src="/images/collison.gif" alt="Simon Collison's mugshot" />
```

```
      <p>Can't actually play any instruments, and is just along for the ride, ➥
      supposedly as manager. It's pretty clear to everyone that Collison is no ➥
      musician, and he certainly cannot sing.</p>
    </div>
  </body>
</html>
```

Save and load the file. It should look something like Figure 10-3. In itself this is not an ugly layout, but with the image sitting on its own line, it is taking up valuable page real estate.

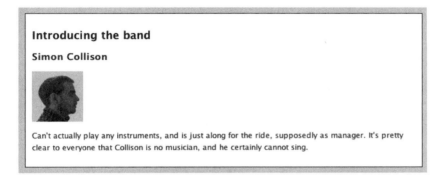

Figure 10-3. *A basic profile featuring a heading, image, and paragraph*

It must be time to float the image. First, define the image element by applying a simple <div> element as its parent.

```
<h3>Simon Collison</h3>
  <div class="image_float"><img src="/images/collison.gif" alt="Simon ➥
Collison's mugshot" /></div>
  <p>Can't actually play any instruments, and is just along for the ride, ➥
  supposedly as manager. It's pretty clear to everyone that Collison is no ➥
  musician, and he certainly cannot sing.</p>
```

With this <div> in place, the image can now be easily manipulated using a simple float. Note that you could also float the image by declaring image_float as a class within the <img> element.

```
<h3>Simon Collison</h3>
  <img src="/images/collison.gif" alt="Simon ➥
Collison's mugshot" class="image_float" />
  <p>Can't actually play any instruments, and is just along for the ride, ➥
  supposedly as manager. It's pretty clear to everyone that Collison is no ➥
  musician, and he certainly cannot sing.</p>
```

The second approach can be considered preferable, as it uses less markup. For this example, we'll use the first method, where the <img> element is wrapped with a <div>, as this provides greater control for us to apply further styling to the <img> element at a later date.

Floating Left

As previously noted, the float property can be given values of left, right, or none (the latter useful to override any blanket floats where an exception is needed). Let's first float the image left.

Add the following chunk of CSS to the float.css style sheet and save the file:

```
.image_float {
  float:left;
  margin:0 5px 5px 0;
  }
```

Here, as well as define the float, right and bottom margins have been declared using short-hand to ensure the text surrounding the image will not sit against its edges. Figure 10-4 shows the result.

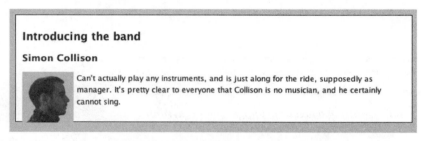

Figure 10-4. *The image is successfully floated left, but why isn't the container stretching vertically to contain it?*

Not bad, but not perfect. The float is working, in that the image is indeed floating to the left, and the paragraph text is flowing around it to the right, spaced away nicely by the declared margin. The problem, however, is that the containing <div> (container) doesn't recognize the float, and as a result it is not expanding vertically to contain the <image_float> element, only the now-less-tall paragraph. It must therefore be a good time to look at clearing floats. Might be worth making a cup of strong tea before you read on.

Clearing Floats

Elements following a floated element will wrap around that floated element. For example, if an image floats left and is followed by paragraph text, that text will wrap around the image and continue directly underneath it if long enough. If you do not wish this to happen, you can apply the clear property to those elements that follow the float.

Four options are available for the clear property:

```
clear:left
clear:right
clear:both
clear:none
```

Usefully, `clear:none` is available should you need to single out an element that is typically cleared, but needs to not be cleared for whatever reason. For example, there may be an occasion where you reuse a cleared element numerous times, but in one instance you'd prefer text to wrap around it rather than have it appear below. In such an instance, a new class could be added to that element where `clear:none` overrules the `clear` property of the parent element. Let's look at the other `clear` values in more detail.

clear:left

By specifying `clear:left`, the element is moved below the bottom outer edge of any left-floated elements.

Consider the following (X)HTML. The wording will change slightly with each example, but essentially it will not change in structure. We'll revisit these techniques a little later to help with the layout of the musician profiles in the *Introducing the Band* examples, but first let's look at each in a more generic sense.

```
<h2>Clearing left</h2>
  <div class="floatbox"></div>
  <p>This paragraph is being cleared left, so it will be moved below the bottom ➥
  outer edge of the floated gray box.</p>
```

Some simple CSS selectors are used first to define paragraph properties and second a simple gray box that will be floated left.

```
p {
  font-size:100%;
  line-height:150%;
  }
.floatbox {
  float:left;
  width:60px;
  height:60px;
  background-color:#999;
  border:1px solid #000;
  }
```

This gives us the layout in Figure 10-5.

Figure 10-5. *Without clearing the paragraph, the text sits right up against the gray box.*

The text is lying, as the text is blatantly still wrapping around the box. So, we need the paragraph to clear the floated gray box. To do this, the clear property is added to the paragraph selector, as follows:

```
p {
  clear:left;
  font-size:100%;
  line-height:150%;
  }
.floatbox {
  float:left;
  width:60px;
  height:60px;
  background-color:#999;
  border:1px solid #000;
  }
```

Notice that the box is still floated left, and that the paragraph is now cleared left. This will force the paragraph to begin on a new line underneath the box (see Figure 10-6).

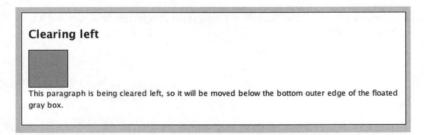

Figure 10-6. *The gray box is floated left, and the paragraph is cleared left.*

clear:right

Specifying clear:right will ensure that the element is moved below the bottom outer edge of any right-floated elements directly above.

Let's examine another example built upon the previous one. In the CSS, all that is needed is to change the instances of left to right.

```
p {
  clear:right;
  font-size:100%;
  line-height:150%;
  }
```

```
.floatbox {
  float:right;
  width:60px;
  height:60px;
  background-color:#999;
  border:1px solid #000;
}
```

Figure 10-7 shows that while the box is now floated to the right, the paragraph retains its position on a new line, as it is cleared right.

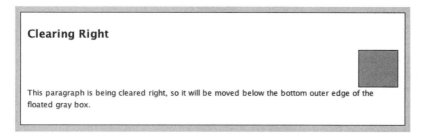

Figure 10-7. *The gray box is floated to the right, and the paragraph is cleared right to ensure it appears on a new line, below the box.*

Failing to change the paragraph's clear value from left to right would result in the paragraph text appearing to the left of the floated box, and on the same line. This can of course be desired in some circumstances.

clear:both

By specifying clear:both, the element is moved below all floating elements, regardless of whether they are floated left or right. In this example, the box is floated left, but the clear property for the paragraph is given the both value.

```
p {
  clear:both;
  font-size:100%;
  line-height:150%;
}
```

In the (X)HTML, a simple level 3 heading is added after the floated box. This heading has no float or clear properties. As Figure 10-8 shows, the heading will wrap around the floated box, whereas the paragraph will clear all elements preceding it.

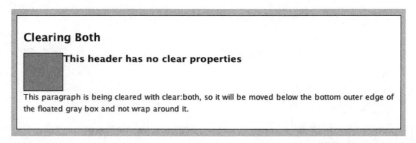

Figure 10-8. *The gray box is again floated left. The second heading has no clear value and so wraps around the box. The paragraph, however, clears both.*

Clearing Your Floated Image

So, back to our floated image problem. Remember that although the image is being floated left, and the text is flowing around it correctly, the containing element is not recognizing the float, and is ending after the paragraph, and not the taller image (as shown earlier in Figure 10-5). Clearing the float can now solve this problem, but the solution is less than perfect, in that it calls for an extraneous element to be applied.

The Extraneous spacer <div>

Were there another element following the paragraph (such as another level 3 heading), the clear property could be defined for that element, removing the need for a special element to do the clearing. We'll do this later, but for now, there is no following element, so the extraneous spacer <div> is needed.

■**Note** One of the bugbears of CSS design is that in some cases, to achieve certain effects, we end up going against the principles we hold most dear. The idea of adding meaningless extra markup to benefit presentation is a horrible one, but if we want the same results across all platforms, it remains a necessary evil in some situations. This is definitely true for clearing floats within containing elements.

Immediately after the `<p>` element, add the spacer `<div>` element as follows:

```
<h3>Simon Collison</h3>
  <div class="image_float"><img src="/images/collison.gif" alt="Simon Collison's ➡
  mugshot" /></div>

  <p>Can't actually play any instruments, and is just along for the ride, ➡
  supposedly as manager. It's pretty clear to everyone that Collison is no ➡
  musician, and he certainly cannot sing.</p>
<div class="spacer"></div>
```

This horrible element is unquestionably presentational, but unavoidably necessary to force the container to stretch vertically to hold the image. The next step is to define CSS rules for the spacer:

```
.spacer {
  clear:left;
  }
```

By giving clear a value of left, the spacer is moved below the bottom outer edge of both the image_float element and the paragraph. Although the spacer is invisible in the final result (see Figure 10-9), it is now forcing the container to expand vertically to contain it.

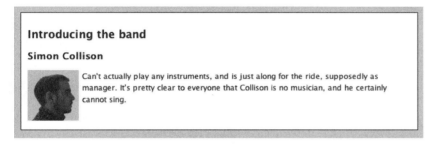

Figure 10-9. *The container is now forced to stretch vertically to accommodate all the elements within.*

Clearing the float is necessary in most similar situations, as it may be unknown as to how much paragraph text is to flow around the floated element. If more paragraph text were added so that it extends beyond the height of the floated image, the spacer would not be necessary, as the container would expand to contain the paragraph (see Figure 10-10). Still, to be on the safe side, it is worth adding the spacer should the text be decreased at a later date.

Figure 10-10. *With or without clearing the float, if the nonfloated element (the paragraph) is "taller" than the floated element, the container will behave properly.*

Handling Multiple Floats

Obviously, there is more than just me in the band, and it is necessary to introduce the other members, like Mr. Hendrix on lead guitar. It makes sense to add more profiles underneath my own, within the main container.

As Figure 10-11 demonstrates, without the use of spacer <div>s, things aren't quite right. Aside from the fact that the container doesn't recognize the float and collapses too early, note also that Mr. Hendrix's profile begins alongside my image. The level 3 heading is correctly wrapping around my floated image. Correct, but ugly.

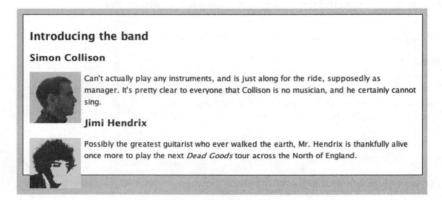

Figure 10-11. *The second profile begins too early, correctly wrapping around the floated image from the previous profile.*

The first approach here might be to add a spacer <div> after each profile, as follows:

```
<h3>Simon Collison</h3>
  <div class="image_float"><img src="/images/collison.gif" alt="Simon ➥
  Collison's    mugshot" /></div>
  <p>Can't actually play any instruments, and is just along for the ride, ➥
  supposedly as manager. It's pretty clear to everyone that Collison is no ➥
  musician, and he certainly cannot sing.</p>
  <div class="spacer"></div>
<h3>Jimi Hendrix</h3>
  <div class="image_float"><img src="/images/hendrix.gif" alt="Jimi Hendrix's ➥
  mugshot" /></div>
  <p>Possibly the greatest guitarist who ever walked the earth, Mr. Hendrix ➥
  is thankfully alive once more to play the next <em>Dead Goods</em> tour ➥
  across the North of England.</p>
  <div class="spacer"></div>
```

That's fine, and it works (see Figure 10-12), but now the layout is using two instances of the extraneous presentational spacer element, adding unnecessary markup bloat. There are seven people in this band, so that means by the end of the profile section, there will be seven instances of the spacer element. I don't know about you, but I'm not very comfortable with that. There has to be a better way.

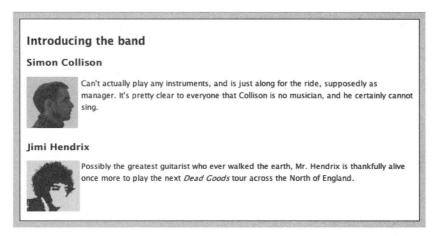

Figure 10-12. *With spacer <div>s, each profile is clearly distinct, but the design now uses two instances of the extraneous presentational markup.*

Clearing with Existing Elements

So how can the number of spacers be reduced? Earlier I mentioned that if there were another element following the paragraph (such as another level 3 heading), the clear property could be defined for that element, avoiding the need for a spacer <div>. Well, as there are now more profiles, there are now other elements following each block of profile information.

Here, a level 3 heading begins each profile, so this will be the element used to clear the float above. Focusing on the markup inside the container, let's add a couple more profiles to the (X)HTML. Note that all but the very last spacer is removed.

```
<h2>Introducing the band</h2>
  <h3>Simon Collison</h3>
    <div class="image_float"><img src="/images/collison.gif" alt="Simon ➥
    Collison's mugshot" /></div>
    <p>Can't actually play any instruments, and is just along for the ride, ➥
    supposedly as manager. It's pretty clear to everyone that Collison is no ➥
    musician, and he certainly cannot sing.</p>
```

```
<h3>Jimi Hendrix</h3>
   <div class="image_float"><img src="/images/hendrix.gif" alt="Jimi Hendrix's ➡
   mugshot" /></div>
   <p>Possibly the greatest guitarist who ever walked the earth, Mr. Hendrix➡
is thankfully alive once more to play the next <em>Dead Goods</em> tour across➡
   the North of England.</p>
   <h3>Janis Joplin</h3>
   <div class="image_float"><img src="/images/joplin.gif" alt="Joplin's ➡
   mugshot" /></div>
   <p>Lorem ipsum dolor sit amet, consectetuer adipiscing elit. Vestibulum in ➡
   lacus. ... Quisque vitae lorem placerat risus posuere congue. ➡
Integer a orci.</p>
   <h3>John Lennon</h3>
   <div class="image_float"><img src="/images/lennon.gif" alt="Lennon's ➡
   mugshot" /></div>
   <p>Lorem ipsum dolor sit amet, consectetuer adipiscing elit. Vestibulum in ➡
   lacus. ... Quisque vitae lorem placerat risus posuere congue. ➡
Integer a orci.</p>
   <div class="spacer"></div>
```

That last spacer will still be required, as the final profile has no elements following it, but still needs to be cleared to force the container to stretch around it.

Now the level 3 heading can be used to clear the floats that precede it. The same clear value used in the spacer is applied to the selector for h3:

```
h3 {
  clear:left;
  padding-top:20px;
  font-size:120%;
  }
```

Note that padding-top is also declared to create more space between each profile and make things a bit prettier. Now, the level 3 heading is doing all the work, clearing the preceding float and ensuring each profile begins on a new line (see Figure 10-13).

Introducing the band

Simon Collison

Can't actually play any instruments, and is just along for the ride, supposedly as manager. It's pretty clear to everyone that Collison is no musician, and he certainly cannot sing.

Jimi Hendrix

Possibly the greatest guitarist who ever walked the earth, Mr. Hendrix is thankfully alive once more to play the next *Dead Goods* tour across the North of England.

Janis Joplin

Lorem ipsum dolor sit amet, consectetuer adipiscing elit. Vestibulum in lacus. ... Quisque vitae lorem placerat risus posuere congue. Integer a orci.

John Lennon

Lorem ipsum dolor sit amet, consectetuer adipiscing elit. Vestibulum in lacus. ... Quisque vitae lorem placerat risus posuere congue. Integer a orci.

Jeff Buckley

Lorem ipsum dolor sit amet, consectetuer adipiscing elit. Vestibulum in lacus. ... Quisque vitae lorem placerat risus posuere congue. Integer a orci.

Kurt Cobain

Lorem ipsum dolor sit amet, consectetuer adipiscing elit. Vestibulum in lacus. ... Quisque vitae lorem placerat risus posuere congue. Integer a orci.

Keith Moon

Lorem ipsum dolor sit amet, consectetuer adipiscing elit. Vestibulum in lacus. ... Quisque vitae lorem placerat risus posuere congue. Integer a orci.

Figure 10-13. *Introducing the entire band. The level 3 headings are now clearing the floats above them, reducing the number of spacer <div>s from seven to just one.*

The major benefit of clearing floats with existing elements should be obvious. The amount of presentational markup is reduced dramatically, with just one final spacer needed instead of seven. Markup is leaner, and complete float control is achieved.

Floating Right

It is just as simple to float images to the right, and some designers prefer to use this approach, as it generally looks neater. The lines of text that wrap unevenly (unless lines of text are given equal length using text-align:justified, which has very unpredictable results) to create a jagged right edge can be neatened up nicely by placing the image to the right.

The first step is to simply adjust the value of the float to right, and to define margins to the left of the image instead of the right.

```
.image_float {
  float:right;
  margin:0 0 5px 5px;
  }
```

The result can be seen in Figure 10-14. Images are floating in the right place, but the clearing is no longer working. The second level 3 heading is wrapping around the first image, and the container is no longer stretching to accommodate everything.

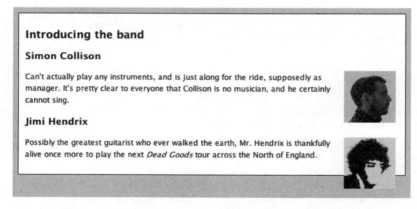

Figure 10-14. *Images are floating right, but without declaring clear:right, the floats are being ignored by following elements.*

Thus, a simple adjustment to the two selectors used to clear floats is required. Where before we were clearing left, we now need to simply clear right.

```
h3 {
  clear:right;
  padding-top:20px;
  font-size:120%;
  }
.spacer {
  clear:right;
  }
```

The level 3 heading is now moved below the bottom outer edge of the right-floating images, and we return to the natural flow of elements (see Figure 10-15).

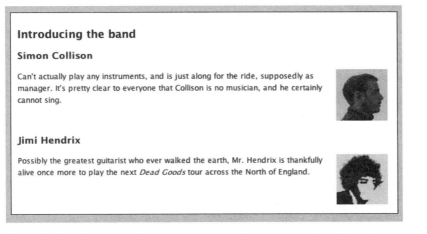

Introducing the band

Simon Collison

Can't actually play any instruments, and is just along for the ride, supposedly as manager. It's pretty clear to everyone that Collison is no musician, and he certainly cannot sing.

Jimi Hendrix

Possibly the greatest guitarist who ever walked the earth, Mr. Hendrix is thankfully alive once more to play the next *Dead Goods* tour across the North of England.

Figure 10-15. *The natural flow of elements following floats is achieved by clearing below the bottom outer edge of the floated images.*

These approaches to floats merely skim the surface of possibilities, and by applying floats to things like dates, icons, and links, some very neat, space-saving effects can be achieved. Importantly, these basics will also form the crux of our approach to column layout in the next chapter.

Positioning

Positioning allows designers to place (X)HTML elements with a greater accuracy using some simple CSS rules. The position property determines the reference point for the positioning of each element box. All boxes start out being positioned in the normal flow of elements in the document. The position property allows us to rebel against this natural placement. Get comfortable and empty your mind before you delve into this section, for CSS positioning is a difficult beast to tame. Before CSS2 came along, building web sites bore little resemblance to traditional page layout principles. Designers are used to being unrestricted when it comes to positioning, layering, and being very specific about where items belong on a page.

Thankfully, the rules can be (to a certain degree) bent and manipulated to break free from the restrictions of table-based design and the idea of the Internet as a basic information tool. With positioning, designers can be truly creative. Regrettably, positioning is a very difficult subject to understand right off the bat.

This section will only scratch the surface of positioning. The examples that follow are designed to introduce you to the basic principles of CSS positioning; hence the results aren't so stunning at this stage.

In the next chapter, these principles will be adopted and expanded upon to create very flexible layouts and unique page elements. As key layout tools, these principles need to be in your mind early, so don't forget what you pick up here, as you'll need it in Chapter 11.

Let's begin by defining the four main types of positioning as quickly and simply as possible, before looking at each in more detail:

- *Static positioning*: The easiest to understand, and closest to what you have already been doing in this book. This term basically describes how elements are placed by default. The browser takes your (X)HTML and parses it into the individual elements, applying CSS to each as directed, and finally collating all of this into the visible web page. The final position an element takes as a result of this is its static position, and as such, it is nothing particularly special.

- *Absolute positioning*: Much cooler; absolute positioning allows you to dictate where the top-left corner, bottom-right corner, or other point of reference of an element will sit in relation to the nearest parent element that has been positioned out of the flow of the document. When the web page is scrolled, the elements retain their position against each other, and all scroll with the page as though glued together.

- *Fixed positioning*: Even cooler! Fixed positioning allows an element to be placed in relation to the actual browser window. Therefore, if the page is scrolled, everything moves with it, except the fixed element, which holds its ground x pixels from the top, left, right, or bottom of the browser window.

- *Relative positioning*: A relatively positioned element is relative to where it would normally be positioned *statically*. That is, relative to where it would sit by default. For example, if applied to a heading, you are defining where it should be relative to where the browser would normally put it.

Basic Position Properties and Values

Opening this can of worms fully, there are many possible properties to be used when positioning elements. For now, concern yourself only with the following properties:

```
position
top
left
bottom
right
```

Other position-related properties will come into play later in the book, especially when you come to learning about layouts. For now, let's look at how position and associated properties affect basic elements.

position

Four values are available for position that reflect the four methods of positioning: static, absolute, fixed, and relative. This declaration is necessary in order for your positioning to be applied the way you desire. The static value is the default, as the browser will position elements statically anyway. The position property will be covered fully when we come to exploring each value shortly.

top, left, bottom, right

Once the position of the element is defined, the top, left, bottom, and/or right properties are used to offset that element by the given values. All values can be defined using length, percentage, or auto.

As stated, the offset is entirely dependent upon the value of the position property, the results of which can be as shown in Table 10-1.

Table 10-1. *Offset Outcomes Based Upon position Value*

position	Offset
static	No effect. Browser will place elements in their default positions.
absolute	The element is placed to the top, right, bottom, left, or combination thereof of the nearest parent element that has been placed out of the document flow.
fixed	The element is placed to the top, right, bottom, and/or left of the browser window.
relative	The element is placed to the top, right, bottom, and/or left of the element's default position.

Examples

By applying CSS to the (X)HTML example, it is easy to see how each position value works with the same top and left values.

Note that for our position examples, the following (X)HTML is used, and the aim will be to control the position of the image (<img>) element.

```
<div id="container">
  <h3>Simon Collison</h3>
    <div class="image_float"><img src="/images/collison.gif" ➡
alt="Simon Collison's mugshot" /></div>
    <p>Can't actually play any instruments, and is just along for the ride, ➡
supposedly as manager. It's pretty clear to everyone that Collison is no ➡
musician, and he certainly cannot sing.</p>
</div>
```

The container div is given specific width and height values so that the browser window can be forced to scroll in order to see the effects of all position values.

```
/* Define the container for positioning examples */
 #container {
    width:400px;
    height:400px;
    margin:10px;
    padding:10px;
    border:1px solid #000;
    background-color: #FFF;
 }
```

```
p {
  font-size:100%;
  line-height:150%;
  }
```

Now you are ready to play with positioning. Perhaps you should grab a stiff drink first.

static With either no position whatsoever or `position:static` declared, the paragraph and image are arranged inside the container in their default (static) positions, as in Figure 10-16.

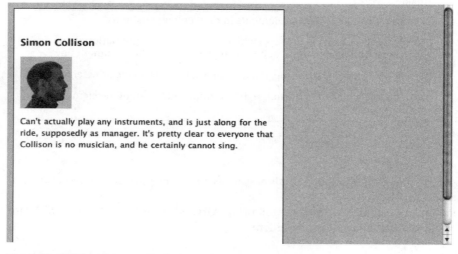

Figure 10-16. *The elements in their static positions*

relative OK, now the `position` value is changed to `relative` to achieve a result based on the static position.

```
/* Define image position */
  img {
    position:relative;
    left:400px;
    }
```

This time, the image appears 60px above its original position (thanks to the negative top value) and 400px from the left of the static position (where it would appear by default), as in Figure 10-17.

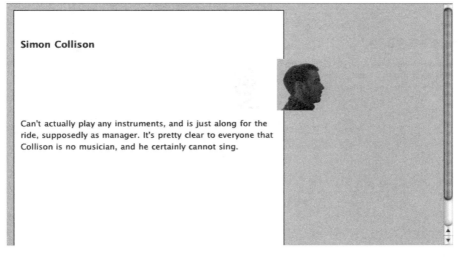

Figure 10-17. *The image appears 400px to the right from its static position, using position:relative.*

This time, the position relates not to any parent element or to the browser window, but specifically to the properties of the element itself. Notice that the gap remains between the heading and the paragraph, where the image would normally sit in its default position.

absolute Let's move the image again. Here, the position is first defined as absolute, and then the coordinates are set using top and right.

```
/* Define image position */
 img {
  position:absolute;
  left:400px;
  }
```

By declaring left as 400px respectively, and combining this with position:absolute, the image is moved appropriately in relation to the viewport, as in Figure 10-18.

Note that the paragraph has shifted up, and that there is no gap where the image would be naturally. Also, while it might appear that the image is positioned in relation to the browser window, it isn't fixed, and if scrolled, the elements all move together as if glued into place. Thus, the image is absolutely positioned.

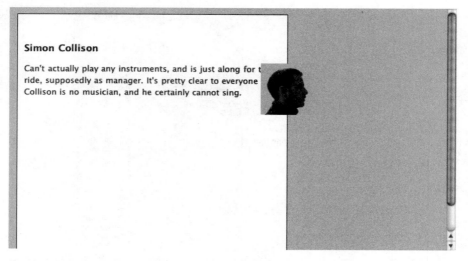

Figure 10-18. *The image is 400px from its static position, now that position:absolute is used.*

Now the cool bit. An absolutely positioned element is designed to take its point of reference from the nearest positioned element. So, let's see what happens when the parent element (the container) is positioned relative to where it would normally sit.

```
/* Container for all page content */
 #container {
    position:relative;
    top:100px;
    width: 400px;
    height: 400px;
    margin: 10px;
    padding:10px;
    border: 1px solid #000;
    background-color:#FFF;
    }
/* Define image position */
  img {
    position:absolute;
    left:400px;
    }
```

Here, the container is moved 100px from where it would normally sit, using position:relative and top:100px. So, because the image inside is absolutely positioned, it will take its starting point not from the viewport, but from its original position within the container. Notice in Figure 10-19 that everything has moved down 100 pixels from where it all appeared in the previous figure.

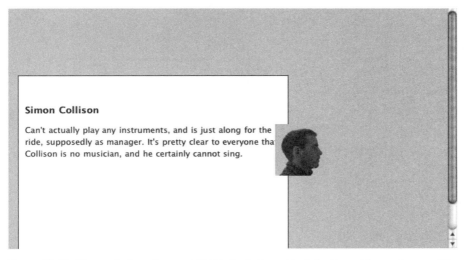

Figure 10-19. *The container is moved 100 pixels from its default position using position:relative. As the image is absolutely positioned, it also moves down 100 pixels, because it takes its point of reference from the nearest positioned element—the container.*

fixed This is cool. Here, the position is defined as fixed, but the coordinates remain the same. Note that the container is reverted back to its default (static) position.

```
/* Container for all page content */
   #container {
   width: 400px;
   height: 400px;
   margin: 10px;
   padding:10px;
   border: 1px solid #000;
   background-color:#FFF;
   }
/* Define image position */
  img {
   position:fixed;
   left:400px;
   }
```

As a result of this change, the image's position will appear to be the same as in the absolutely positioned example. The real surprise comes when you scroll the page (see Figure 10-20).

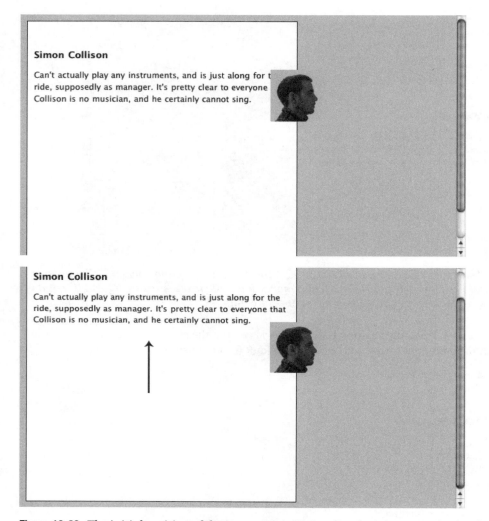

Figure 10-20. *The initial position of the image (top). Notice that the image remains in place despite the page scroll, its position fixed in relation to the viewport.*

Using magic (well, position:fixed) the image remains in view always, fixed 400px from the left of the browser window. This technique has numerous possibilities, and is perfect for navigation elements or forms that need to appear in view no matter how far the user scrolls down the web page. It should be used with caution, however, due to poor support in much older browsers such as Netscape 4.7 and below. Netscape 4.7 and below (along with certain other elderly browsers) suffer from a poor positioning model known affectionately as the "sucks ass" method. This causes perfectly logical, *valid* positioning to fail miserably, and thus also causes users of these browsers to think that the terrible presentation of your completely valid layout is somehow *your* fault. This user behavior completely justifies using any and all techniques at your disposal to hide complex CSS from those browsers.

Position This in Your Mind

As I mentioned earlier, these examples hint only slightly at the power of CSS positioning, and there are many more properties that can be embraced to create some stunning page layouts and content holders that perhaps defy your expectations of the humble browser.

To Conclude...

Good work, soldier. If this chapter was the assault course, the next is the battle. Now that you have passed out of float and positioning college with flying colors, you are now ready to apply what you have learned to more complex CSS layout.

Floats and positioning are only as complex as you make them. Simple procedures such as those covered in this chapter are relatively painless once you get to grips with the quirks. Incredibly adventurous designs can be developed using these techniques, and I urge you to experiment as much as possible with these concepts.

In the next chapter, you'll get to grips with column-based layout, one of the most fundamental steps to becoming a CSS professional. Things are getting a little more exciting.

Classic Layouts

CSS layout is easy—really easy. At least, it might be in ten years' time. Right now, and for the last few years, it's been an area of web design where cross-browser difficulties and other limitations have caused much disagreement and despair. Most importantly, it is an area where decisions are not to be made lightly.

A key factor in choosing a layout is audience. As you will be well aware by now, not every visitor to your web site will have the same browser, and many will not be regularly updating their browsers. They will not share an identical screen resolution, but will definitely have their browser windows at varying widths. Some will be using a PC, some a Mac, and some particularly clever ones might be using homemade machines cobbled together from old washing machine parts and cornflake boxes. The truth is, your wild aspirations will have to take a backseat as you begin to design for the lowest common denominator. It's tough, but you are designing for your audience, and not for yourself.

This chapter will examine some of the most common approaches to CSS layout with particular emphasis on flexibility and cross-browser performance. Deciding which layout is best for your web site is entirely up to you.

We'll also investigate something called the Box Model, with specific regard to margin and padding, and how to get your columns to behave when viewed with older browsers.

Specifically, this chapter will cover

- Types of layout

- Liquid floated two-column layout

- Liquid floated three-column layout

- Liquid positioned two-column layout

- Liquid positioned three-column layout

- The Box Model

- Fixed floated layout

- Fixed positioned layout

Types of Layout

Since the dark ages, one of the major topics of discussion for web designers has been layout, and out of these discussions have come a proliferation of descriptive terms for the various types of layout: *fixed width, liquid, elastic,* and *variable fixed width,* for starters. Then there are other decisions to be made: should there be two, three, or four columns, and should the columns be floated or positioned? As you might expect, this section introduces but a few of the possible options available.

Let's begin by seeking to define the two most common types of layout that will be covered in this book, plus a brief explanation of some other approaches as a stepping-stone for the curious.

Fixed

A **fixed-width** layout has its total width and the widths of its columns defined using static width measurements, typically pixels. A fixed-width layout does not stretch to fill the browser window, and remains its set width whatever you do to it (see Figure 11-1).

Figure 11-1. *The Shoutout web site (www.shoutout.info) is fixed at 720px width, and the width remains unchanged whatever the window width.*

The benefits of a fixed-width layout are obvious. By having a predetermined width for the whole layout and its columns, the designer can be certain that window width and screen resolution will not compromise his or her precious design, specifically with regard to carefully measured internal elements such as banners, images, and carefully positioned text.

On the downside, this means that whatever width you declare for your whole design is served to everyone. A 780-pixel-width design might look great on an 800×600 screen resolution, but it starts to look a bit dwarfed on a spanking new iMac 17" screen with a 1280×1024 screen resolution. Also, anyone viewing your site with a viewport of less than 780 pixels is going to get horizontal scrollbars by default, which nobody really wants.

Liquid

A **liquid** (or **fluid**) layout expands and contracts to fill the browser window; Figure 11-2 shows an example of this type of layout. Typically the columns will have widths declared using percentage measurements, where the browser window (or possibly an all-encompassing containing element) is 100%.

Figure 11-2. *The One Nottingham web site (www.onenottingham.org) expands and contracts to fill the browser window, thanks to columns specified using percentages.*

An advantage of a liquid layout is that it adapts to suit the available viewing space. This is a double-edged sword, however: while this is favorable for window widths from, say, 700 pixels to 1024 pixels, at larger window sizes sentences can become incredibly long and difficult to follow line by line. It is also more difficult to design images and banner elements to fit liquid columns, where graphics may need to acknowledge the stretching or expanding containing element and attempt to fit.

If we lived in an ideal world, all browsers would be as smart as Safari or Firefox for example, where the deliciously useful `max-width` CSS property can be applied to stop the expansion of the layout at a set width. Regrettably, IE6 and below on the PC do not support this, and similar results cannot be achieved without some rather complex jiggery-pokery. However, it appears that this will be fixed with the release of IE7. Hurray.

Elastic

The concept of the **elastic** layout is an interesting one, but it takes you into a world of browser bugs and difficulties. While an elastic layout isn't fixed, it is also stopped from getting too wide, as you can specify a maximum width and a minimum width in pixels, ems, or percentages (see Figure 11-3). The great benefit here is how the whole layout can scale when text is resized.

Figure 11-3. *The BraemoreGemini web site (www.braemoregemini.com) stops expanding at a certain browser size (top) and will only contract to a defined width (bottom).*

The elastic layout is a more advanced layout option beyond the scope of this book, but if you are curious, Patrick Griffith's article "Elastic Design" (www.alistapart.com/articles/elastic/) is a good place to start.

Variable Fixed Width

Seeing the term **variable fixed width**, you're probably thinking, "How can a layout be both variable and fixed?" Certainly this sounds like a contradictory term or oxymoron. The idea is that the layout changes automatically to best accommodate the user's window size. For example, if the browser window is wide enough, the layout may contain three fixed-width columns. If the window width falls below a particular width, one column is seamlessly placed under another, creating a two-column layout with the entire markup still present, just reshuffled, as Figure 11-4 demonstrates.

Figure 11-4. *At Colly Logic (www.collylogic.com), if the window is wider than 1020 pixels, the user sees three columns (top); if it is narrower than 1020 pixels, the third column drops below the second (bottom).*

The most reliable method is to use JavaScript to assess the window width and change the CSS of the web page as a result. Similar results can be achieved using pure CSS, although not without a few cross-browser problems.

Richard Rutter collated some of the best methods in his article "Variable Fixed-Width Layout" (`www.clagnut.com/blog/1663/`), and at the time of writing, this author's blog uses a smidgeon of JavaScript to achieve this affect (`www.collylogic.com/?/comments/redesign-notes-1-width-based-layout/`).

Before You Build

Before moving forward, it's worth preparing a basic (X)HTML file you can use to follow the examples in this chapter.

The first job is to create a new file called `columns.html`, containing the following (X)HTML:

```html
<html>
  <head>
    <title>Chapter 11: Classic Layouts</title>
    <link rel='stylesheet' media="screen" type='text/css' href='columns.css' />
  </head>
  <body
    ...column content goes here...
  </body>
</html>
</body>
```

Save the file. Notice that in the head of the file we are linking to an external style sheet called columns.css. Create columns.css and place the following rules into it:

```css
/* Specify blanket rules for all elements */
  body {
    font-size:80%;
    font-family:'Lucida Grande',Verdana,sans-serif;
    margin:10px;
    }

/* Rules for headings */
  h1 {
    font-size:150%;
    }

h2 {
  font-size:140%;
  }

h3 {
  font-size:120%;
  }

/* Default paragraph styles */
  p {
    font-size:100%;
    line-height:150%;
    }
```

Save columns.css. The style sheet contains nothing special at this stage, just a few simple rules to control the look of the text, and a 10-pixel margin on the body element. With the preparation out of the way, you can now get stuck into some cool layouts. Let's go.

SEMANTICALLY CORRECT NAMING CONVENTIONS

Thinking semantically, it is very important to use sensible, explanatory names for the IDs and classes that you create. Existing (X)HTML elements all have explicitly clear names that never compromise your markup; so neither should your custom elements.

Imagine for a second that you are building a site that has multicolored text. Opening paragraphs might be blue, some headings green, and highlighted text yellow. You'll probably set about creating custom classes that you'll apply as spans around specific areas of text. That's fine.

The trick is to not be too specific with your naming conventions. Defining a class called `green` might make sense at the design stage, but once it has been littered throughout many pages of a web site, and it comes time to redesign, your code is going to be lying when your `green` class is actually now rendering text as pink.

It makes more sense to use descriptive names, such as `highlight` or `intro_paragraph`. If you are using a class to turn heading text red only in your "services" section, call that class `services_heading` or something similar that retains its integrity no matter how many times you redesign and recolor.

Later in this chapter in the section "Column Swapping Using Only CSS," you'll also see good examples of why your columns need to be named sensibly. What are you going to do when your `sidebar_left` is repositioned to the right? You might feel better if you'd called it `sidebar_a` or `secondary_col`.

For more thoughts on the wider interpretation and adoption of shared naming conventions, visit Andy Clarke's article "What's in a Name" (`www.stuffandnonsense.co.uk/archives/whats_in_a_name.html`).

Liquid Floated Two-Column Layout

For the first layout, the goal is to create a simple two-column layout, featuring a main column and a sidebar that stretches to fit the width of the browser window—totally liquid.

Masthead and Footer

All examples in this chapter also involve two other main sections—masthead and footer. These are included in each example as they are almost always required in any layout, especially when first getting to grips with CSS layout.

The masthead stretches the full width of the layout and typically holds a logo and possibly the main navigation, plus any other important tools such as a search box or accessibility links (access key information, style switcher, and so on), and serves to tidy up the top of the layout.

The footer tidies the whole thing up at the base of the layout, again stretching the full width of any columns. The footer is typically used to store important information such as copyright info, links to legal information (accessibility statement, terms and conditions, etc.), and possibly a credit for the mighty web designer. In recent months, many designers have been exploiting the footer as a place to collate the kind of secondary information usually found in a sidebar, perhaps in conjunction with a basic one-column layout.

The graphic in Figure 11-5 shows a wireframe of the basic two-column layout we are aiming to replicate using CSS.

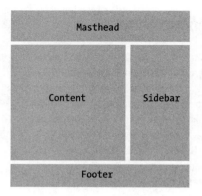

Figure 11-5. *Simple diagram of the two-column layout with masthead and footer*

With the diagram as a guide, we can now think about the structural (X)HTML needed to divide the page into specific sections. Before beginning any layout, it is always worth "wireframing" your intended structure using Photoshop or another trusted application—or maybe even some old fashioned tools called pens and paper.

■**Note** Remember that every time you create a new column `<div>`, you also create a new parent element for any elements it contains. This means that you can be even more specific with your CSS and how you target certain elements using contextual selectors.

The Floated Sidebar

Based upon our wireframe, the structural (X)HTML can now be added to the columns.html file. For this method, it is very important that the sidebar ID appears before the content ID in the markup, to ensure that the top edges of the two columns will line up. This is not entirely semantic in approach, as it is likely that you will want your main content to come first, but this is a necessary evil for this example.

If you are working through this example, be sure to place the following markup inside the `<body>` element of columns.html.

```
<div id="masthead">
  ...masthead content goes here...
</div>
<div id="sidebar">
  ...sidebar content goes here...
</div>
<div id="content">
  ...main content goes here...
</div>
<div id="footer">
  ...footer content goes here...
</div>
```

We're on the way. Save the file and load it in the browser. As you can see in Figure 11-6, at this stage everything is still totally linear. Note that in the screenshot, headings, paragraphs, and list items have been added in each section, and I advise you do something similar to get your example working as though it were a real page. The sample file columns.html contains the markup used for Figure 11-6.

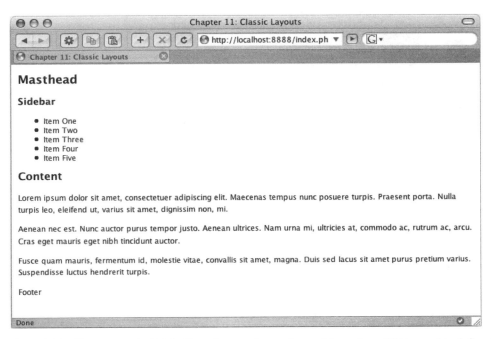

Figure 11-6. *The content is divided into four main sections, although no CSS is used to define these at this stage.*

Styling the Masthead and Footer

Before moving on, let's apply some basic styles to two of our sections—specifically masthead and footer. All we're going to do here is add identical rules for each, defining the section with a black border and gray background, and applying some padding to beef them up a bit.

```
/* Masthead */
  #masthead {
    padding:10px;
    border:1px solid #000;
    background-color:#CCC;
    }
/* Footer */
  #footer {
    padding:10px;
    border:1px solid #000;
    background-color:#CCC;
    }
```

OK. The result, shown in Figure 11-7, doesn't look too bad at this stage. The masthead and the footer are both clearly defined and stretching the full width of the browser window.

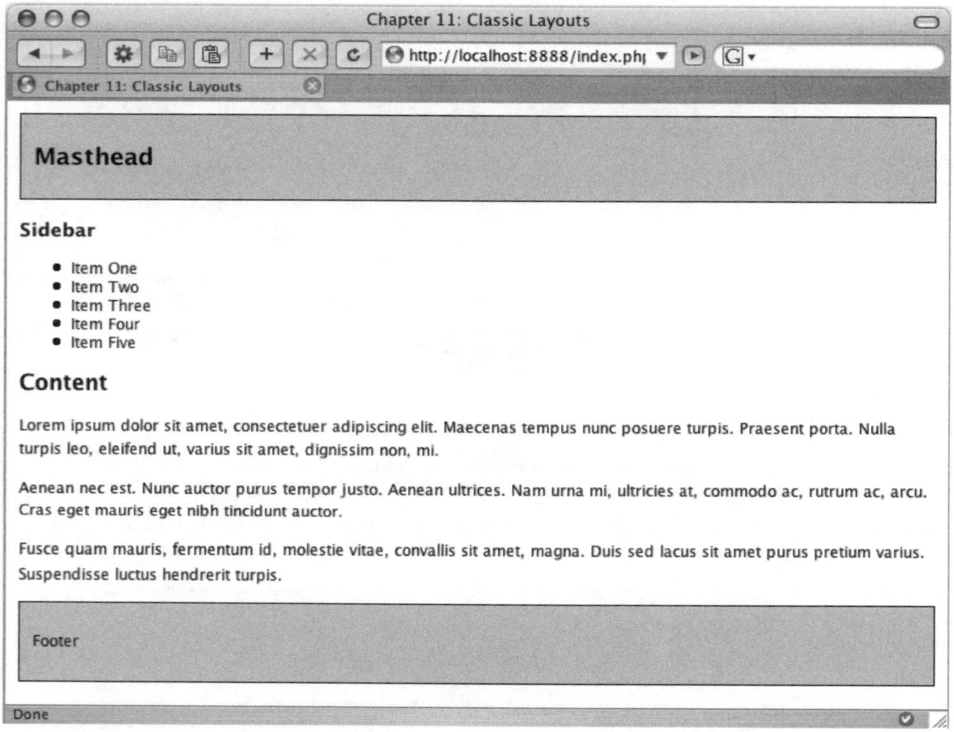

Figure 11-7. *Two of the four main sections (masthead and footer) are clearly defined with simple CSS rules.*

Time to Float the Sidebar

Now it's time to think horizontally. The first step is to create the illusion of two columns by floating the sidebar in much the same way as we floated the images in Chapter 10.

First, the content ID rules are declared, virtually the same as the rules for masthead and footer except that there is no background color.

Identical rules are declared for the sidebar ID, with the crucial addition of float:right, which will force sidebar to sit to the right.

```
/* Masthead */
  #masthead {
    padding:10px;
    border:1px solid #000;
    background-color:#CCC;
    }
```

```
/* Content */
  #content {
    padding:10px;
    border:1px solid #000;
    }

/* Sidebar */
  #sidebar {
    float:right;
    padding:10px;
    border:1px solid #000;
    }

/* Footer */
  #footer {
    padding:10px;
    border:1px solid #000;
    background-color:#CCC;
    }
```

This simple additional CSS creates the suggestion of columns as shown in Figure 11-8. Note that the sidebar is only as wide as its content, and that the text contained in the content ID flows neatly around it.

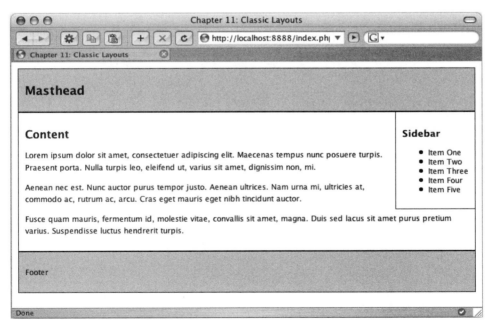

Figure 11-8. *By floating the sidebar to the right, the suggestion of two columns is beginning to form.*

Real Columns

Our "columns" thus far aren't really columns at all. The content ID still stretches the full width of the window, and the sidebar is really just a floated box within it. To achieve real columns, we need width, and we need margin.

Here, the first decision is to decide upon the width ratio for your columns. As this layout is liquid, and we are dealing with a layout that is 100% width of the browser window, our two columns need to be defined using percentages.

First, a percentage width is declared for the sidebar. In this example, I'm going for 36% of the total available.

The next step is to declare a right margin for the content ID that is just a bit larger than the sidebar. If the right margin were the same width as the sidebar, the two sections would budge up against each other, so a slightly larger margin is declared to ensure some space between the two. Here, I've chosen a right margin of 40% of the total available width. Doing this will mean that the main content area will be 60% width by default (100% − 40% margin = 60%), and we need not declare this. The result is a space to the right of the content ID in which the sidebar can comfortably fit, with 4% to spare. This 4% is the gutter between the two columns.

Note as well that a margin value has been declared for masthead, and that bottom margins for content and sidebar have also been added to allow the content and sidebar IDs a little room to breathe, and that clear:both has been added to the footer to ensure that it will always appear below the two columns.

```
/* Masthead */
  #masthead {
    margin:0 0 10px 0;
    padding:10px;
    border:1px solid #000;
    background-color:#CCC;
    }
/* Content */
  #content {
    margin-right:40%;
    margin-bottom:10px;
    padding:10px;
    border:1px solid #000;
    }
/* Sidebar */
  #sidebar {
    float:right;
    width:36%;
    margin-bottom:10px;
    padding:10px;
    border:1px solid #000;
    }
/* Footer */
  #footer {
    clear:both;
```

```
padding:10px;
border:1px solid #000;
background-color:#CCC;
}
```

The result of these simple changes is that the content ID will always have a 40% right margin, whether there is a sidebar or not. This ensures that the text will no longer wrap around the floated sidebar, which still isn't a real column, but it sure as hell looks like one now (see Figure 11-9).

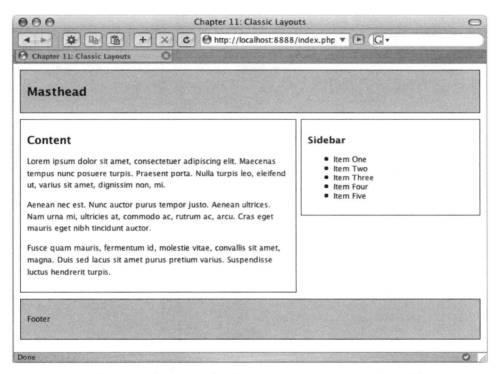

Figure 11-9. *Declaring a right margin for the main content area gives the sidebar more room to breathe, as the two columns have clearly defined boundaries.*

As the columns have a thin border around them, it is clear that they are of an uneven height. Without the borders it wouldn't matter, but with borders or a background color, it's going to look wrong. In Chapter 12, we'll look at a neat little trick called *faux columns*, which makes use of a simple tiled background image to fool us into thinking that columns are of an equal height.

So, that's a basic two-column layout using a floated sidebar. As it stands, it is more than enough to create a typical blog layout or simple web site, and it should be obvious how you could get to work styling up the main sections and child elements using what you have learned from Part 1 of this book to get a basic web site together. There are, however, many more layout options available to you, including alternative methods of creating a liquid two-column layout, which we'll look at next.

WHY MUST EACH COLUMN HAVE A BOTTOM MARGIN?

Good question. In this chapter, each column has a bottom margin of 10 pixels to create a space between them and the `footer`. So, instead of having to add this declaration to every column, can it not just be added to the `footer` using a top `margin`?

Sadly not, is the answer. The CSS2 specifications back up this harsh answer (www.w3.org/TR/CSS2/visuren.html#flow-control). When you clear a float, the top `margin` of the clearing element (the `footer` in this case) is automatically increased so that the top `border` clears the bottom outer edge of the floated elements. Therefore, with no top `margin` on the footer and no bottom margins on the columns, the minimum clearance is done automatically, and in this case, 10 pixels is the same more or less as the automatically added top margin, so there's no difference.

So you *must* use a bottom margin on the floated columns in order to create a visible margin between them and the cleared footer, Good fun this, isn't it?

Liquid Float Left, Float Right

The previous method of floating just the sidebar was good, and works. Still, from a semantic point of view, the main sections were in the wrong order in the markup (sidebar before content). The beauty of the float:left/float:right approach is that we can return to more semantically structured markup.

If you are still working through the examples, first switch the order of the content and sidebar IDs in columns.css, so that the order is as follows:

```
<div id="masthead">
  ...masthead content goes here...
</div>
<div id="content">
  ...main content goes here...
</div>
<div id="sidebar">
  ...sidebar content goes here...
</div>
<div id="footer">
  ...footer content goes here...
</div>
```

For this approach, there are no amendments needed for the masthead or footer, and if you are happy with the width of the sidebar, that too can remain unaltered.

Notice, however, that a couple of changes have been made to the content ID selector. Here, it is being floated left, the margin has been removed, and in its place a percentage width is declared.

```
/* Content */
  #content {
    float:left;
    width:54%;
```

```
    margin-bottom:10px;
    padding:10px;
    border:1px solid #000;
    }
/* Sidebar */
  #sidebar {
    float:right;
    width:36%;
    margin-bottom:10px;
    padding:10px;
    border:1px solid #000;
    }
```

If no padding was set for either ID, the two widths could be larger. You could use, for example, a content ID of 60% width, and a sidebar ID of 36%, which would give a space in between the two of 4%. However, with 10 pixels of padding declared for each (totaling 40 pixels in width), the content ID has a smaller width of 54% to compensate for this.

Figure 11-10 shows that the final layout is virtually identical to the floated sidebar example we worked through in the previous section, but under the hood the markup makes more sense semantically.

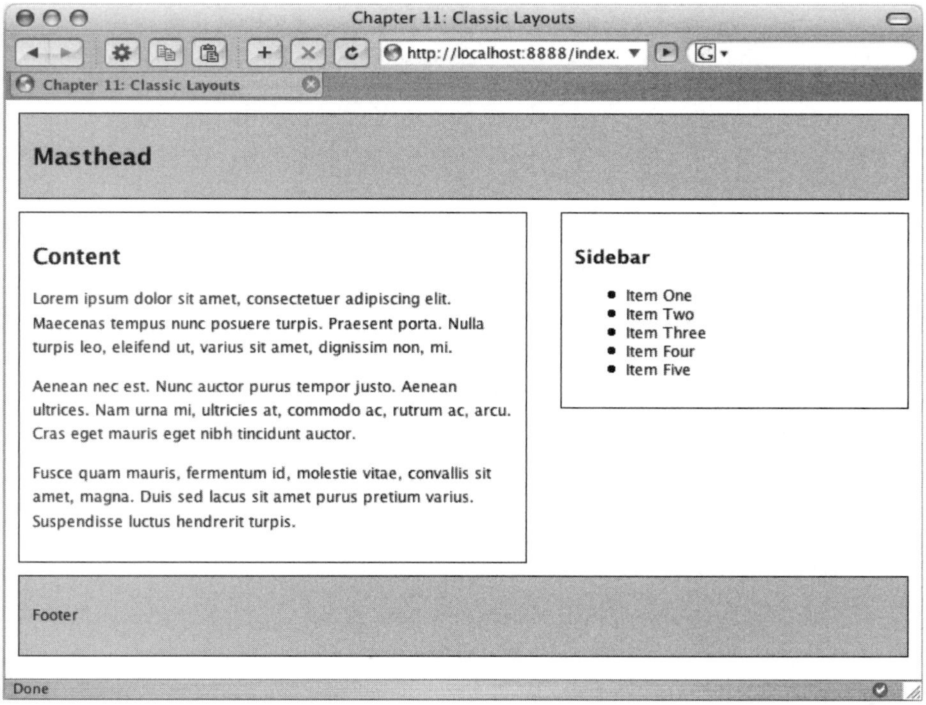

Figure 11-10. *Two-column layout achieved by floating the content ID to the left and the sidebar to the right*

Liquid Floated Three-Column Layout

Let's jump back to the first floated sidebar example, where to succeed the sidebar element needs to be placed before the content element. Here's the (X)HTML again, but notice that the sidebar ID has now been removed, and instead we have two new sidebars, one called sidebar_a, and one called sidebar_b, just above it.

```
<div id="masthead">
  ...masthead content goes here...
</div>
<div id="sidebar_a">
  ...sidebar acontent goes here...
</div>
<div id="sidebar_b">
  ...sidebar b content goes here...
</div>
<div id="content">
  ...main content goes here...
</div>
<div id="footer">
  ...footer content goes here...
</div>
```

Next a couple of simple changes are needed to the CSS used for the floated sidebar method. As there will be an extra column in play pretty soon, it is sensible to decrease the width of the existing sidebar to 25%, and allow less space for it (30%) in the content ID. Importantly, the sidebar ID used earlier has gone, so a new selector has been added called sidebar_b to match one of the new (X)HTML elements.

```
/* Masthead */
  #masthead {
    margin:0 0 10px 0;
    padding:10px;
    border:1px solid #000;
    background-color:#CCC;
    }

/* Content */
  #content {
    margin-right:30%;
    margin-bottom:10px;
    padding:10px;
    border:1px solid #000;
    }

/* Sidebar B */
  #sidebar_b {
    float:right;
```

```
    width:25%;
    margin-bottom:10px;
    padding:10px;
    border:1px solid #000;
    }

/* Footer */
  #footer {
    clear:both;
    padding:10px;
    border:1px solid #000;
    background-color:#CCC;
    }
```

This reworked CSS combined with the additional markup produces the layout in Figure 11-11. Notice that as the `sidebar_a` element appears first in the markup, and as of yet has no matching selector, it floats above the reworked columns.

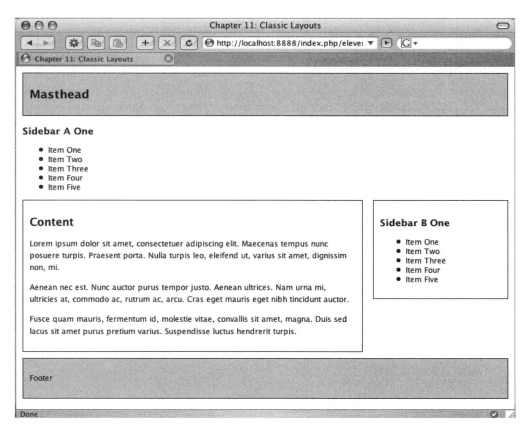

Figure 11-11. *The additional element appears above the columns that are still floated.*

The next stage is to create a space to the left of the content ID in which the new sidebar can be floated. This calls for a left margin declaration for the content selector.

```
/* Content */
  #content {
    margin-left:30%;
    margin-right:30%;
    margin-bottom:10px;
    padding:10px;
    border:1px solid #000;
    }
```

Finally, rules for the new sidebar_a ID are declared. The values are identical to those of the existing sidebar_b, except that in this instance sidebar_a is floated left.

```
/* Sidebar A */
  #sidebar_a {
    float:left;
    width:25%;
    margin-bottom:10px;
    padding:10px;
    border:1px solid #000;
    }
```

Now that one sidebar is being floated left and one floated right, and owing to the adequate left and right margins of the content ID, all three columns are sitting perfectly, and will stretch and contract to fit the browser window without collapsing (see Figure 11-12).

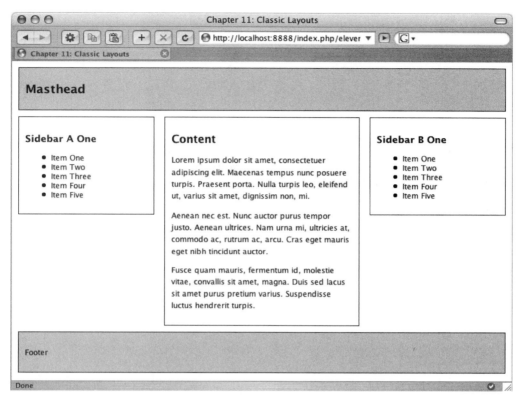

Figure 11-12. *The finished three-column layout*

Column Swapping Using Only CSS

You are about to witness the true power of CSS layout. Notice in Figure 11-12 that in each sidebar, the list headings contain either an *A* or a *B*, depending upon whether they are in sidebar_a or sidebar_b. Remember that the two selectors are as follows:

```
/* Sidebar A */
  #sidebar_a {
    float:left
    width:25%;
    margin-bottom:10px;
    padding:10px;
    border:1px solid #000;
    }
```

```
/* Sidebar B */
  #sidebar_b {
    float:right;
    width:25%;
    margin-bottom:10px;
    padding:10px;
    border:1px solid #000;
    }
```

Notice that the float properties are highlighted. Now here's the clever bit. To switch the position of the columns from left to right and vice versa, just one simple change to each selector is required. Basically, just switch the two rules over.

```
/* Sidebar A */
  #sidebar_a {
    float:right;
    width:25%;
    margin-bottom:10px;
    padding:10px;
    border:1px solid #000;
    }

/* Sidebar B */
  #sidebar_b {
    float:left;
    width:25%;
    margin-bottom:10px;
    padding:10px;
    border:1px solid #000;
    }
```

Simply by swapping the float values over, the columns are moved by magic (well, by good planning and CSS), resulting in the layout captured in Figure 11-13.

This trickery is made possible due to the symmetrical nature of this layout. Both sidebars are the same width and have almost identical properties, and the space allotted to each by the content ID's margins are identical.

This shuffling of columns further brings home the importance of correctly naming IDs. What kind of nonsemantic mess would we be in here if the sidebars had words such as *left* or *right* in their names? This method also demonstrates the unbeatable flexibility of a layout built upon CSS. Can you imagine doing this with a table layout? Thought not.

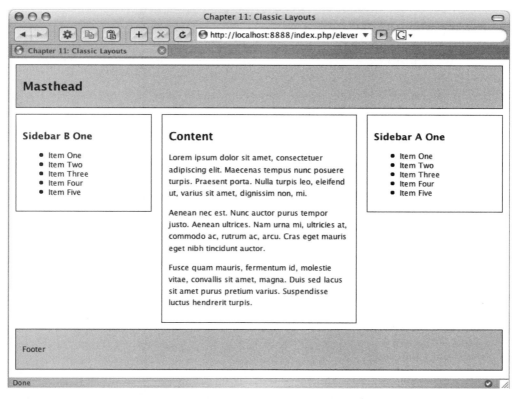

Figure 11-13. *By switching the float values of the two sidebars, the sidebars switch from left to right and vice versa.*

Liquid Positioned Two-Column Layout

For this approach, you can stick with the markup used in the previous floated two-column layout example (where content precedes sidebar). Using positioning for layout can be advantageous as there is no correlation between the order of the sections in the markup and their final positions when styled with CSS positioning. This time, however, there will be changes to the masthead CSS.

Height Is Important

In this example, a set height is required for the masthead, as this will be used as a reference to help us position the sidebar in a little while. This set height would typically be informed by the content of the masthead.

Let's imagine that a company logo is to be placed in the masthead and that it is 60 pixels in height. This measurement informs the first step toward a positioned layout.

```
/* Masthead */
  #masthead {
    height:60px;
    margin:0 0 10px 0;
    border:1px solid #000;
    background-color:#CCC;
    }
/* Apply padding to heading to avoid Box Model woes */
  h1 {
    padding:0 0 0 10px;
    }
```

The padding has also been removed from the masthead at this stage to keep things simple, and instead added to the h1 selector. (To find out why, skip to the section "The Box Model" later in this chapter.) The next step is to declare a right margin for the content ID as we did in the floated sidebar method earlier in the chapter. When the sidebar is positioned later, it will be slotted into the space created by this right margin.

```
/* Content */
  #content {
    margin-right:40%;
    margin-bottom:10px;
    padding:10px;
    border:1px solid #000;
    }
```

Now the cool bit. As mentioned, the sidebar now needs to be positioned into the space to the right of the content ID.

It is very important when using positioning to be mindful of any extra issues that might flaw your positioning. In this example, note that there is 10 pixels of padding around the whole body element, and that there is also a 10-pixel margin directly below the masthead, as illustrated in Figure 11-14. There is also a 1-pixel border around each edge.

We need to add these measurements to the height of the masthead (60 pixels) in order to know exactly how far from the top of the browser window the sidebar needs to be. In this case, it's 10 + 1 + 60 + 1 + 10, equaling 82 pixels from the top of the window.

```
/* Sidebar */
  #sidebar {
    position:absolute;
    top:82px;
    right:10px;
    width:30%;
    margin-bottom:10px;
    padding:10px;
    border:1px solid #000;
    }
```

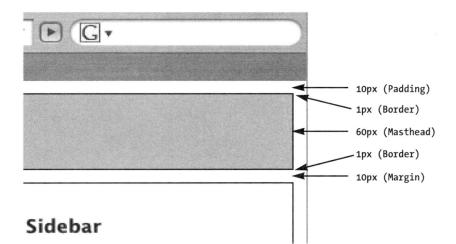

10px (Padding)

1px (Border)

60px (Masthead)

1px (Border)

10px (Margin)

Figure 11-14. *Calculating the distance between the top of the browser window and the top of the sidebar in order to position it perfectly*

Note that `right:10px` is also specified to ensure that the sidebar does not push up against the right edge of the browser window, and therefore honors the 10 pixels of padding around the `<body>` element.

With the sidebar positioned in place, the layout is looking pretty good (see Figure 11-15).

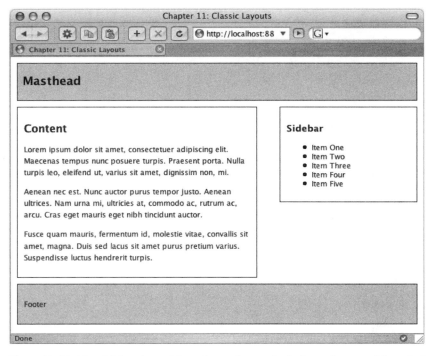

Figure 11-15. *The sidebar is positioned exactly 82 pixels from the top of the window and 10 pixels from the right.*

Footer Woes

This approach has a hidden problem that won't be so hidden once the sidebar contains more elements. Look at Figure 11-16, and notice how the sidebar overlaps the footer now that I've added three more lists.

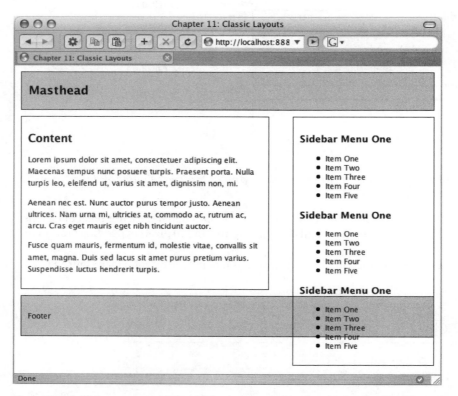

Figure 11-16. *If the contents of the sidebar grow too far, the sidebar itself will overlap the footer.*

Remember that with a floated sidebar, the footer could be cleared to ensure it began after the columns. With positioning, however, the sidebar has been taken out of the normal flow of elements, and the footer can't "see" this.

The best approach here is to make the footer work like the content ID, by giving it a right margin and thus creating space for the sidebar.

```
/* Footer */
  #footer {
    margin-right:40%;
    padding:10px;
    border:1px solid #000;
    background-color:#CCC;
    }
```

This works well, but the footer no longer stretches the full width of the layout (see Figure 11-17). Another problem is that the greater the difference in amount of content between content ID and sidebar ID, the more unbalanced the layout will look. Still, it's an option.

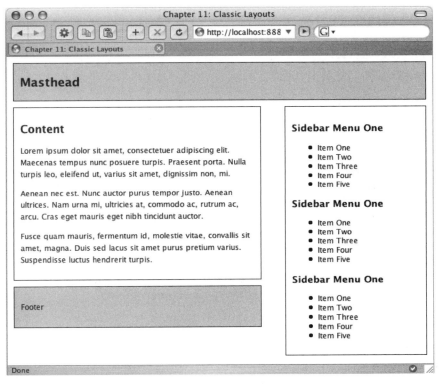

Figure 11-17. *By declaring a right margin for the footer, the sidebar is free to grow vertically without compromising the layout.*

Liquid Positioned Three-Column Layout

This is a bit of a jump forward, but moving from two columns to three using the positioning method isn't too difficult really. Remember how we adjusted the right margin of the main content ID to allow space for a sidebar? Well, all we have to do is something similar with the left margin.

First of all, sidebar is removed, and two new sidebars need to be added to the markup. They can be placed anywhere, seeing as CSS positioning will be used to place them visually. To stay semantic, let's add them after the content ID. Again, these changes can be made to the columns.html file.

```
<div id="masthead">
  ...masthead content goes here...
</div>
<div id="content">
  ...main content goes here...
</div>
<div id="sidebar_a">
  ...main content goes here...
</div>
<div id="sidebar_b">
  ...sidebar content goes here...
</div>
<div id="footer">
  ...footer content goes here...
</div>
```

Notice that the new ID is called sidebar_a and the previous sidebar is now called sidebar_b. It is important to use naming conventions that make sense no matter where the columns are positioned, as using CSS positioning, sidebar_a could be placed on the left or the right, as could sidebar_b, so names such as sidebar_left and sidebar_right would be semantically incorrect. If you are working through this example, be sure to amend the CSS selector if you have changed the name of your sidebar.

First, let's make some space to the left of the content ID by declaring a left margin wide enough to accommodate the new sidebar, plus a little space between the two.

```
/* Content */
  #content {
    margin-left:30%;
    margin-right:30%;
    margin-bottom:10px;
    padding:10px;
    border:1px solid #000;
    }
```

Notice that the space allotted by each margin is decreased slightly, as there will be three columns instead of two, and it therefore makes sense to have slightly narrower sidebars.

Next, a new selector for sidebar_a is required, and sidebar is renamed to sidebar_b.

```
/* Sidebar A */
  #sidebar_a {
    position:absolute;
    top:82px;
    left:10px;
    width:25%;
    margin-bottom:10px;
    padding:10px;
    border:1px solid #000;
    }

/* Sidebar B */
  #sidebar_b {
    position:absolute;
    top:82px;
    right:10px;
    width:25%;
    margin-bottom:10px;
    padding:10px;
    border:1px solid #000;
    }
```

For each sidebar, the widths are a little smaller than in previous examples, as we are of course allowing less space for each sidebar.

Finally, to prevent sidebar_a from overlapping the footer if there is too much content within it, a left margin identical to that of the content ID needs to be declared for the footer.

```
/* Footer */
  #footer {
    margin:0 30% 0 30%;
    padding:10px;
    border:1px solid #000;
    background-color:#CCC;
    }
```

These very simple amendments take just a few seconds, but result in a perfect positioned three-column layout that stretches to fit the width of the browser window (see Figure 11-18).

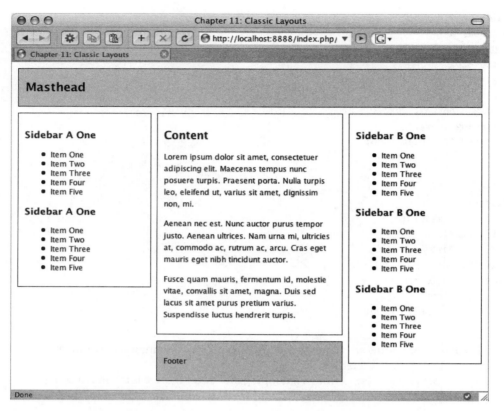

Figure 11-18. *A three-column layout achieved using absolute positioning and a few simple amendments to the previous two-column version*

Swapping the Sidebars

As with the floated three-column layout, it is easy to move the sidebars from left to right and vice versa. Again, notice in Figure 11-18 that in each sidebar, the list headings contain either an *A* or a *B*, depending upon whether they are in sidebar_a or sidebar_b. The two selectors are as follows:

```
/* Sidebar A */
  #sidebar_a {
    position:absolute;
    top:82px;
    left:10px;
    width:25%;
    margin-bottom:10px;
    padding:10px;
    border:1px solid #000;
    }
```

```
/* Sidebar B */
  #sidebar_b {
    position:absolute;
    top:82px;
    right:10px;
    width:25%;
    margin-bottom:10px;
    padding:10px;
    border:1px solid #000;
    }
```

Notice that the left and right properties are highlighted. To switch the position of the columns, just switch the two rules over.

```
/* Sidebar A */
  #sidebar_a {
    position:absolute;
    top:82px;
    right:10px;
    width:25%;
    margin-bottom:10px;
    padding:10px;
    border:1px solid #000;
    }

/* Sidebar B */
  #sidebar_b {
    position:absolute;
    top:82px;
    left:10px;
    width:25%;
    margin-bottom:10px;
    padding:10px;
    border:1px solid #000;
    }
```

This simple amendment sees the sidebars switch position, as shown in Figure 11-19.

As with the floated three-column layout, this is possible due to the symmetrical nature of this layout. Again, both sidebars are the same width, and have equal space in which to sit.

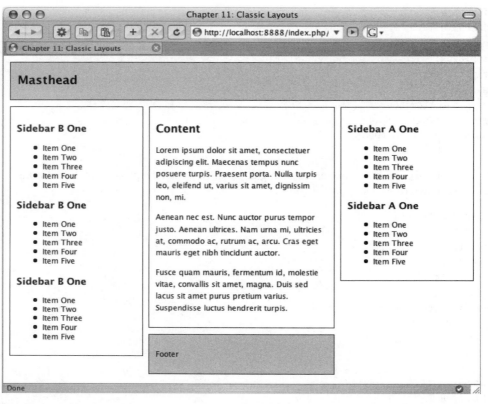

Figure 11-19. *By switching the left and right properties of the two absolutely positioned sidebars, the sidebars switch from left to right and vice versa.*

Fixed-Width Layout

Previous layouts in this chapter have been liquid in their approach, with widths declared using percentage values. It is of course perfectly possible, and very common, to use set widths declared using pixels. This approach can provide greater control and is still favored by many web designers. There is one small problem though—older versions of Internet Explorer are going to take one look at your code and render it somewhat incorrectly if you so much as think of using padding and/or borders. With this most troublesome of browsers in mind, let's look at an absolute fundamental of CSS layout—the **Box Model**.

The Box Model

Before you start using fixed widths for your columns, it is imperative that you get to grips with the Box Model. If you think you might need to apply margins or padding to any of your columns, you need to be aware of the miscalculations these will cause in IE5 and IE5.5 on a PC. Go get some tea, because this is a bit of a tough one.

So What's the Problem?

In any standards-compliant browser, the total width for a containing element and its padding and border is calculated as the combined values of that container's width plus its padding and border. This means that a 300px container is 300px plus values for padding and border. This is how it should be.

However, IE5 and IE5.5 get this wrong by subtracting the widths of the border and padding from the width value. This means that a 300px container ends up being much narrower. If padding is declared as 20px, then the actual width of the container in these browsers will be 300 – 20 – 20, equaling 260 pixels. Ouch. The container shrinks.

Let's examine this in more painful detail, using the following simple declaration as an example:

```
/* Sidebar_a */
  #sidebar_a {
    width:300px;
    padding:10px;
    border:10px solid #000;
    }
```

Although the sidebar itself is 300 pixels in width, the space required to accommodate it needs to be equal or greater than all the widths added together. This will be border-left + padding-left + width + padding-right + border-right, which equates to 10 + 10 + 300 + 10 + 10, giving a total width of 340 pixels. Figure 11-20 shows the Box Model as it is on modern browsers.

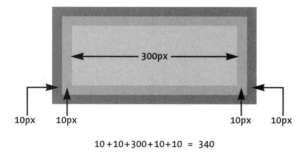

Figure 11-20. *The Box Model as it is intended*

However, on good old IE5 and IE5.5, the result is somewhat different. In this case, the calculation will see the border and padding values subtracted from the width value. Figure 11-21 shows how IE5/Win and IE5.5/Win interpret the Box Model.

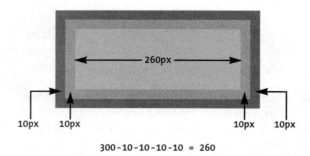

300-10-10-10-10 = 260

Figure 11-21. *The Box Model as IE5/Win and IE 5.5/Win understand it*

Many people are still using IE5 and IE5.5, especially in offices with backward IT departments, or at home on Timmy's old PC rescued out of the garage. This problem might have been fixed in IE6, but it cannot be ignored. Thankfully, there is a solution.

The Box Model Hack

By exploiting a parsing bug found only in IE5 and IE5.5, two different widths can be declared, only one of which will be read by these problematic browsers. Let's take the previous sidebar declarations as an example.

```
/* Sidebar_a */
 #sidebar_a {
   width:300px;
   padding:10px;
   border:10px solid #000;
   }
```

All modern browsers such as Safari, Firefox, and IE6 and above will understand the width declared. That is still only serving one width though, so the Box Model hack is required. Here's the CSS again, but with the extra hack.

```
/* Sidebar_a */
 #sidebar_a {
   padding:10px;
   border:10px solid #000;
   width:340px;
   voice-family:"\"}\"";
   voice-family:inherit;
   width:300px;
   }
```

So what is happening here? Well, the adjusted width for IE5 and IE5.5 comes first. The width in this case is the total of the correct width, plus border and padding values. As worked out in Figure 11-16, that total width is 340 pixels.

Next, voice-family is used, as it is not a visual CSS property and will not affect the final display, plus some jumbled syntax that fools IE5 and IE5.5 into thinking that the declarations are over for this selector.

Finally, the correct width (the actual width of the container) is declared for sensible browsers. And that is the Box Model hack, as invented one dark night in a laboratory by the amazing Tantek Celik (www.tantek.com).

Extra Caution for the Opera Browser

Sadly, the hack isn't perfect, as some CSS2-compliant browsers can choke on the parsing bug and end up delivering the width intended for IE5 and IE 5.5. This is the case for Opera, and if we are going to "be nice to Opera" (as this little amendment is known), a couple of extra lines are required in the declaration.

```
/* Sidebar_a */
  #sidebar_a {
    padding:10px;
    border:10px solid #000;
    width:340px;
    voice-family:"\"}\"";
    voice-family:inherit;
    width:300px;
    }
  html>body #sidebar {
    width:300px;
    }
```

If there were world enough and time, I might seek to explain what is going on there, and you might even want to know. Thankfully, if you are like every other responsible web designer out there, you'll be content simply with the fact that the hack exists and works. Now, let's get back to fixed-width layout before your eyes start to bleed.

Fixed and Floated Three-Column Layout

With the Box Model under your belt, you can fix your widths with confidence. For this example, we'll take the liquid floated three-column layout created earlier. Here's the (X)HTML again:

```
<div id="masthead">
  ...masthead content goes here...
</div>
<div id="sidebar_a">
  ...sidebar content goes here...
</div>
<div id="sidebar_b">
  ...sidebar content goes here...
</div>
<div id="content">
  ...main content goes here...
</div>
<div id="footer">
  ...footer content goes here...
</div>
```

Next the existing CSS from the liquid floated three-column layout can be reworked for our fixed version. The first decision to make is how wide the layout should be.

Declare Total Width in the Body

For this example, I decided that the total width for the layout would be 760 pixels. The first step is to define this width in the body declaration.

```
/* Specify blanket rules for all elements */
  body {
    width:760px;
    margin:10px;
    font-size:80%;
    font-family:'Lucida Grande',Verdana,sans-serif;
    }
```

Doing this will ensure that any element floated right will not seek to stick to the right edge of the browser window.

Fix Masthead and Footer

With the figure of 760 pixels in mind, the properties of both masthead and footer need examining. Paying consideration to the Box Model, if both masthead and footer are to be 760 pixels in width, their specified width needs to be 760 pixels minus border and padding. That gives us $760 - 1 - 10 - 10 - 1 = 738$. Therefore the declared widths will be 738 pixels.

```
/* Masthead */
  #masthead {
    width:738px;
    margin:0 0 10px 0;
    padding:10px;
    border:1px solid #000;
    background-color:#CCC;
    }

/* Footer */
  #footer {
    clear:both;
    width:738px;
    padding:10px;
    border:1px solid #000;
    background-color:#CCC;
    }
```

Column Widths

Now the columns need to have their set widths declared. With a working area of 760 pixels, again the properties of each declaration need to be considered.

Content

Here, the final width value of the content ID is somewhat dictated by the fact that we need to allow for existing border, padding, and margins. Taking values from left to right we have 200 + 1 + 10 + 338 + 10 + 1 + 200, equaling 760 pixels.

```
/* Content */
  #content {
    width:338px;
    margin-left:200px;
    margin-right:200px;
    margin-bottom:10px;
    padding:10px;
    border:1px solid #000;
    }
```

From this, we know that each sidebar has a maximum allowance of 180 pixels. The margins suggest 200 pixels are allowed, but this includes an extra 20 pixels either side of the content ID to space the columns apart.

Sidebars

Here we need to get really mathematical. Each sidebar must be no wider than 180 pixels, including padding and border values. Subtracting the border and padding values from 180 gives us a width value of 158 pixels for each sidebar (180 − 1 − 10 − 1 − 10 = 158).

```
/* Sidebar A */
  #sidebar_a {
    float:left;
    width:158px;
    margin-bottom:10px;
    padding:10px;
    border:1px solid #000;
    }

/* Sidebar B */
  #sidebar_b {
    float:right;
    width:158px;
    margin-bottom:10px;
    padding:10px;
    border:1px solid #000;
    }
```

Safe in the knowledge that the combined widths of both sidebars and main content do not exceed 760 pixels, we can be sure that the layout will look as it does in Figure 11-22 on modern browsers.

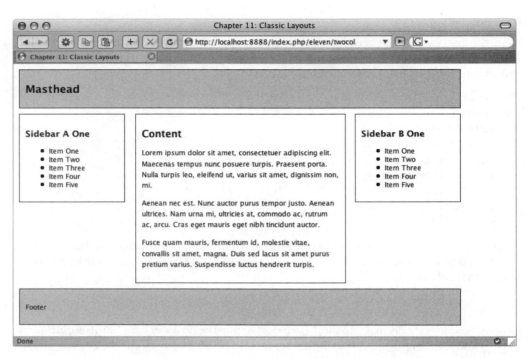

Figure 11-22. *The fixed and floated three-column layout as it appears using Firefox. Everything is in its right place.*

Hacking the Box Model for IE5

Knowing what you know about the Box Model as it is interpreted on IE5 and IE5.5, you'll be aware that things won't look so perfect on those browsers. Time to hack.

For each declaration, the Box Model hack is added, owing to the fact that each makes use of padding and border values.

```
/* Masthead */
  #masthead {
    margin:0 0 10px 0;
    padding:10px;
    border:1px solid #000;
    background-color:#CCC;
    width:760px;
    voice-family:"\"}\"";
    voice-family:inherit;
    width:738px;
    }
  html>body #masthead {
    width:738px;
    }
```

```
/* Content */
  #content {
    margin-left:200px;
    margin-right:200px;
    margin-bottom:10px;
    padding:10px;
    border:1px solid #000;
    width:360px;
    voice-family:"\"}\"";
    voice-family:inherit;
    width:338px;
    }
  html>body #content {
    width:338px;
    }

/* Sidebar A */
  #sidebar_a {
    float:left;
    margin-bottom:10px;
    padding:10px;
    border:1px solid #000;
    width:180px;
    voice-family:"\"}\"";
    voice-family:inherit;
    width:158px;
    }
  html>body #sidebar_a {
    width:158px;
    }

/* Sidebar B */
  #sidebar_b {
    float:right;
    margin-bottom:10px;
    padding:10px;
    border:1px solid #000;
    width:180px;
    voice-family:"\"}\"";
    voice-family:inherit;
    width:158px;
    }
  html>body #sidebar_b {
    width:158px;
    }

/* Footer */
```

```
#footer {
  clear:both;
  padding:10px;
  border:1px solid #000;
  background-color:#CCC;
  width:760px;
  voice-family:"\"}\"";
  voice-family:inherit;
  width:738px;
  }
html>body #footer {
  width:738px;
  }
```

Adding these hacks ensures maximum compatibility across all browsers. It is good to know that what looks great on your up-to-date copy of Safari or Firefox will also look pretty good on old versions of Internet Explorer. The final result as viewed using IE5.5 can be seen in Figure 11-23.

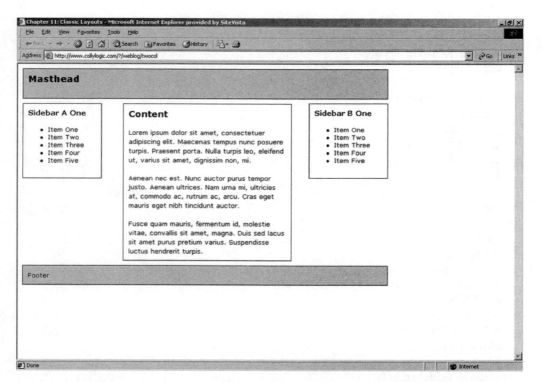

Figure 11-23. *Thanks to the Box Model hack, the floated three-column layout behaves correctly on IE5.5/Win.*

To Conclude...

I think you'll agree that this has been a marathon chapter. Getting under the skin of CSS layout and the inevitable quirks is a major step in becoming a CSS professional. Many designers know enough to use CSS layout for modern browsers, but not so many bother to get to grips with the Box Model and its subtle nuances so they can support older browsers. Just as many might be comfortable with floats, but feel inadequate when it comes to positioned layouts. Some, dare I say it, make a living blatantly copying carefully crafted layouts from other web sites, but you're already way ahead of them.

As ever, keep experimenting. Having the knowledge is one thing, but regularly building layouts from scratch is the only way to become fully comfortable with all the methodologies. This chapter has barely scratched the surface of CSS layout, and you'll doubtless be aware of other useful approaches, whether hinted at in this book, or from your time surfing the Internet.

With basic layouts under your belt, the fun begins in earnest. The next chapter deals with manipulating your layouts for even greater flexibility, and following that we examine the multitudinous methods of bringing core elements such as logos, navigation bars, and images into your layouts.

CHAPTER 12

■■■

Layout Manipulation

How does your layout perform on the big stage, under the glare of the lights? Importantly, how easy is it for you—the web designer—to manipulate the layout to suit changing content?

This shorter chapter details two extremely useful concepts that professional web designers make use of on a regular basis. First, we'll look at switching layouts using an ID to trigger specific CSS selectors for a specific situation. This is a simple concept that makes templating much easier and helps you get the most out of your style sheets.

Later in this chapter, you'll learn how to overcome a common problem where you'll want your columns to be the same height, but can't specify equal heights in the style sheet without backing yourself into a corner. Specifically, you'll see how a background image can be used to create faux columns, where each column appears to be the same height, regardless of content (when in reality the heights still differ), allowing the columns to expand to hold any amount of content.

Let's dive straight in and get to grips with these super-useful layout methods. There are just a couple of examples of each approach, but it should be clear how the inherent flexibility of each can bolster the way you approach layout and save you an immeasurable amount of work.

Switching Layout with Contextual Selectors

Depending on what you want each page of your web site to do, you have the option of changing the values of CSS rules accordingly using contextual selectors.

By adjusting the ID attribute applied to the `<body>` element of your (X)HTML file, you can change the behavior of any child elements—that's any elements within the whole `<body>` element.

Remember that a selector such as h2 {color: #333} would render all level 2 headings in a document dark gray. So let's say you have an `<h2>` in your sidebar, which you'd prefer to render in red. Simply create an h2 selector that is contextual of your sidebar, for example, `#sidebar h3` {color: #FF0000}. Thus you have two selectors separated by a combinator—in this case a single whitespace character, tailored to target a particular instance of an element in your (X)HTML document. That's a **contextual selector**.

So why not use this method for the opening `<body>` tag of each page? After all, assigning IDs and classes to the body is the easiest way to control a number of selectors in your CSS, for everything in your `<body>` section will be open to its influence if you so desire.

Setup

Let's jump straight to the three-column floated layout created in Chapter 11. First, create a new file called switch.html, or grab the switch.html file from the download area. Either way, you'll need the (X)HTML for the floated three-column layout detailed in Chapter 11. Notice that we are referencing an external style sheet called switch.css.

```
<html>
  <head>
    <title>Chapter 12: Layout Manipulation</title>
    <link rel='stylesheet' media="screen" type='text/css' href='switch.css' />
  </head>
  <body>
    <div id="masthead">
      <h1>Masthead</h1>
    </div>
    <div id="sidebar_a">
      <h3>Sidebar A One</h3>
        <ul>
          <li>Item One</li>
          <li>Item Two</li>
          <li>Item Three</li>
          <li>Item Four</li>
          <li>Item Five</li>
        </ul>
    </div>
    <div id="sidebar_b">
      <h3>Sidebar B One</h3>
        <ul>
          <li>Item One</li>
          <li>Item Two</li>
          <li>Item Three</li>
          <li>Item Four</li>
          <li>Item Five</li>
        </ul>
    </div>
    <div id="content">
      <h2>Content</h2>
        <p>Lorem ipsum dolor sit amet, consectetuer adipiscing elit.➡
           Maecenas tempus nunc posuere turpis. Praesent porta. Nulla➡
           turpis leo, eleifendut, varius sit amet, dignissim non, mi.</p>
        <p>Aenean nec est. Nunc auctor purus tempor justo. Aenean➡
           ultrices. Nam urnami, ultricies at, commodo ac, rutrum ac,➡
           arcu. Cras eget mauris eget nibh tincidunt auctor.</p>
        <p>Fusce quam mauris, fermentum id, molestie vitae, convallis➡
           sit amet, magna. Duis sed lacus sit amet purus pretium➡
           varius. Suspendisse luctus hendrerit turpis.</p>
    </div>
```

```html
    <div id="footer">
      <p>Footer</p>
    </div>
  </body>
</html>
```

Next, prepare switch.css, either by creating a new file with the following declarations or by grabbing the switch.css file from the download area.

```css
/* Specify blanket rules for all elements */
  body {
    width:760px;
    font-size:80%;
    font-family:'Lucida Grande',Verdana,sans-serif;
    margin:10px;
    }

/* Rules for headings */
  h1 {
    font-size:150%;
    }
  h2 {
    font-size:140%;
    }
  h3 {
    font-size:120%;
    }

  p {
    font-size:100%;
    line-height:150%;
    }

/* Masthead */
  #masthead {
    margin:0 0 10px 0;
    padding:10px;
    border:1px solid #000;
    background-color:#CCC;
    width:760px;
    voice-family:"\"}\"";
    voice-family:inherit;
    width:738px;
    }
  html>body #masthead {
    width:738px;
    }
```

```
/* Content */
  #content {
    margin-left:200px;
    margin-right:200px;
    padding:10px;
    border:1px solid #000;
    width:360px;
    voice-family:"\"}\"";
    voice-family:inherit;
    width:338px;
    }
  html>body #content {
    width:338px;
    }

/* Sidebar A */
  #sidebar_a {
    float:left;
    padding:10px;
    border:1px solid #000;
    width:180px;
    voice-family:"\"}\"";
    voice-family:inherit;
    width:158px;
    }
  html>body #sidebar_a {
    width:158px;
    }

/* Sidebar B */
  #sidebar_b {
    float:right;
    padding:10px;
    border:1px solid #000;
    width:180px;
    voice-family:"\"}\"";
    voice-family:inherit;
    width:158px;
    }
  html>body #sidebar_b {
    width:158px;
    }

/* Footer */
  #footer {
    clear:both;
    margin:10px 0 0 0;
```

```
    padding:10px;
    border:1px solid #000;
    background-color:#CCC;
    width:760px;
    voice-family:"\"}\"";
    voice-family:inherit;
    width:738px;
    }
html>body #footer {
    width:738px;
    }
```

The CSS is at this stage identical to that used in Chapter 11 to create the fixed-width floated three-column layout, so much of it should be familiar to you. If you have not yet read Chapter 11, I advise you do so in order to understand all the complicated width declarations. Loading switch.html in your browser should result in the layout in Figure 12-1.

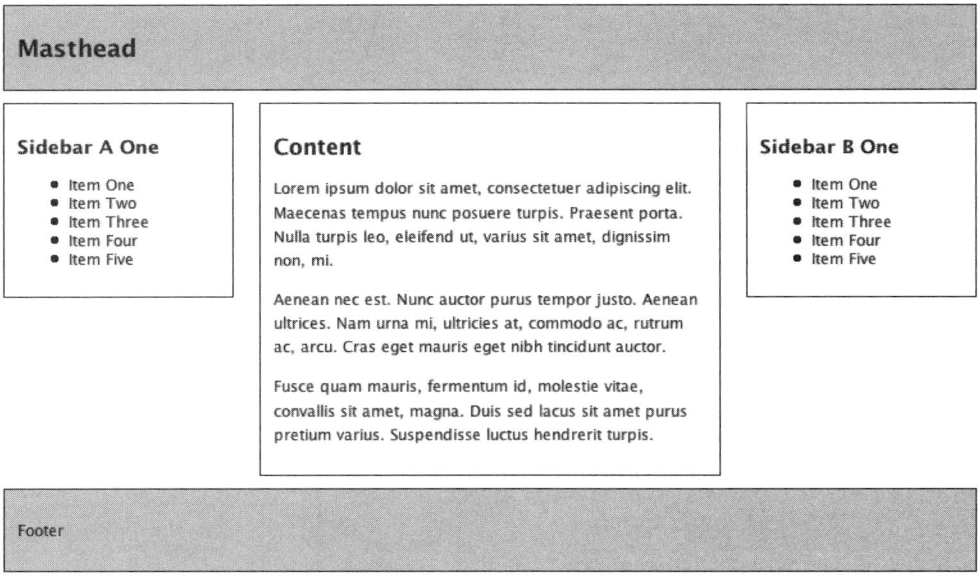

Masthead

Sidebar A One

- Item One
- Item Two
- Item Three
- Item Four
- Item Five

Content

Lorem ipsum dolor sit amet, consectetuer adipiscing elit. Maecenas tempus nunc posuere turpis. Praesent porta. Nulla turpis leo, eleifend ut, varius sit amet, dignissim non, mi.

Aenean nec est. Nunc auctor purus tempor justo. Aenean ultrices. Nam urna mi, ultricies at, commodo ac, rutrum ac, arcu. Cras eget mauris eget nibh tincidunt auctor.

Fusce quam mauris, fermentum id, molestie vitae, convallis sit amet, magna. Duis sed lacus sit amet purus pretium varius. Suspendisse luctus hendrerit turpis.

Sidebar B One

- Item One
- Item Two
- Item Three
- Item Four
- Item Five

Footer

Figure 12-1. *The three-column layout originally created in Chapter 11*

The Body

Over the next few sections you will see how adjusting the attribute applied to the <body> element can trigger specific contextual selectors to radically adjust the layout.

Switching Columns

Let's begin with a relatively simple change that reflects the way the sidebars were swapped over in the previous chapter. The difference here is that instead of adjusting the existing declarations for `sidebar_a` and `sidebar_b` to float them left or right, you'll create two alternative versions of those selectors that will be triggered by the ID attribute declared for the `<body>` element (see the next section) and in turn override the basic declarations.

Prepare the `<body>` Element

The first task is to apply an ID attribute to the `<body>` element in the (X)HTML file. For the purpose of this walkthrough let's call it `switch`, although in the real world the ID might reflect the purpose of that file, so you might use `home`, `about`, `article`, or similar.

```
<body id="switch">
```

This now gives us an ID that can be used to put other elements into context. In other words, our sidebars (and every other element) are now contained within the `switch` ID, and can therefore be controlled with more contextualized CSS.

Add New Contextual Selectors

The existing selectors for `sidebar_a` and `sidebar_b` will remain as they are, as these ensure that in normal circumstances `sidebar_a` is floated to the left and `sidebar_b` to the right. These are the default states. To make the switch, new contextual selectors are required to adjust specific values.

```
/* Sidebar A */
  #sidebar_a {
    float:left;
    padding:10px;
    border:1px solid #000;
    width:180px;
    voice-family:"\"}\"";
    voice-family:inherit;
    width:158px;
    }
  html>body #sidebar_a {
    width:158px;
    }

/* Adjust sidebar_a in switch context */
  #switch #sidebar_a {
    float:right;
    }

/* Sidebar B */
  #sidebar_b {
    float:right;
    padding:10px;
    border:1px solid #000;
    width:180px;
    voice-family:"\"}\"";
```

```
    voice-family:inherit;
    width:158px;
    }
  html>body #sidebar_b {
    width:158px;
    }

/* Adjust sidebar_b in switch context */
  #switch #sidebar_b {
    float:left;
    }
```

Notice that each new sidebar selector is preceded with the switch ID, placing it into context. All that is then required is to declare values specific to that situation. So, in this example, the float values are switched (see Figure 12-2).

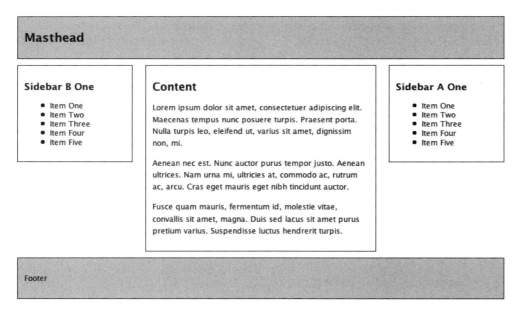

Figure 12-2. *The switch ID applied to the <body> element triggers alternative selectors for the columns and switches them from left to right and vice versa.*

How good is that? Simply by adjusting the ID applied to the body element, major changes can be made on a per-template basis. Let's take this one step further.

From Three to Two Columns

A common approach to layout is to use a three-column layout for a home page or other heavy content page, and to revert to a two-column layout for article pages where more focus is required for the actual information and less extraneous information is required.

In this example, the right column will be removed and the main column will be extended to fill the gap it leaves, giving us a simpler two-column layout. Note that by replacing the switch ID in the <body> element, the sidebars will revert back to their correct positions.

A New <body> ID

The first job is to replace the switch ID with another. This time around, let's use an ID called twoCol.

```
<body id="twoCol">
```

If the CSS stayed the same, this would make little effect, as there is no selector for twoCol at present. The layout would be as it was when we started, with the sidebars in their original positions.

Add New Selectors in the Style Sheet

The approach here is similar to that in the previous example, where the new selectors are placed into context by the preceding twoCol ID. First, the #twoCol #content selector is declared, and any properties requiring new values are declared—only widths in this example.

```
/* Content */
  #content {
    margin-left:200px;
    margin-right:200px;
    padding:10px;
    border:1px solid #000;
    width:360px;
    voice-family:"\"}\"";
    voice-family:inherit;
    width:338px;
    }
  html>body #content {
    width:338px;
    }

/* Adjust content in twoCol context */
  #twoCol #content {
    margin-right:0;
    width:540px;
    voice-family:"\"}\"";
    voice-family:inherit;
    width:536px;
    }
  html>body #twoCol #content {
    width:536px;
    }
```

The next step is to hide `sidebar_b` when a descendant of `twoCol`. Here, `display:none` is used to hide the entire sidebar.

```
/* Sidebar B */
  #sidebar_b {
    float:right;
    padding:10px;
    border:1px solid #000;
    width:180px;
    voice-family:"\"}\"";
    voice-family:inherit;
    width:158px;
    }
  html>body #sidebar_b {
    width:158px;
    }
/* Adjust sidebar_b in switch context */
  #switch #sidebar_b {
    float:left;
    }
/* Adjust sidebar_b in twoCol context */
  #twoCol #sidebar_b {
    display:none;
    }
```

These simple changes transform the layout into a two-column version with just one switch of the `<body>` ID. The result can be seen in Figure 12-3.

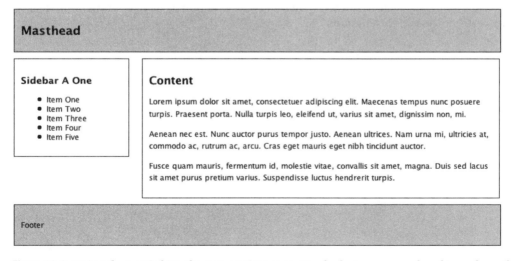

Figure 12-3. *Using the twoCol ID, the appropriate contextual selectors are used and transform the layout accordingly, with the second sidebar hidden completely.*

These examples work well as suggestions of how the <body> ID combined with contextual selectors can create incredible flexibility in your layouts. There is also no reason why you couldn't take the same approach with IDs applied to other elements, such as a contextual selector based upon the ID of one of your columns, where a particular ID was specified to control child elements within that column. The possibilities are endless.

Note that these examples reuse the same (X)HTML file to get the point across, and we simply change the <body> ID each time. In practice, you would typically make these ID decisions with each new template you create. Therefore, when first creating your article pages, there would be no third column in the markup anyway, so there would be no need to hide that column.

■**Caution** Remember, use `display: none` wisely. Leaving unwanted markup in a page only serves to up the bloat quota. There is also a school of thought that suggests it's a search engine optimization no-no. Google may wonder why you are hiding content from the user and may assume you're up to no good.

Faux Columns

A major problem that CSS gives us is how to make columns an equal height. Elements only stretch as far as they need to, and a sidebar with only a small amount of information will not magically expand to match the height of a main column featuring the entire works of Charles Dickens. In rare situations where the amount of information held in columns is known and is unlikely to change, fixed heights can be declared for all columns, but in the real world this is inappropriate, as articles are of indeterminable length in most situations.

This brings us to a neat little trick that gives the impression of equal-height columns even if in reality their heights are different—**faux columns** (the term was actually coined by Dan Cederholm). The effect, shown in Figure 12-4, is achieved by using a background image tiling vertically behind the columns.

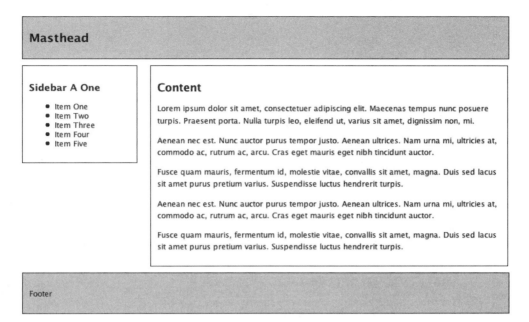

Figure 12-4. *With borders around each column, it is clear that each expands only to contain its content, and that both have very different heights.*

Get Set Up

For this example, you'll need the faux.html and faux.css files, available from the download area. These files are simplified versions of the final two-column layout you arrived at through the previous section, with no <body> ID attribute, and no mention of the third column in the CSS—a clean start.

Let's remove the borders around the columns and instead apply background color to each. Knowing what you now know about the Box Model from Chapter 11, you'll not be surprised that the widths have been adjusted by 2px to account for the width of the removed borders.

```
/* Content */
  #content {
    margin-left:200px;
    margin-right:0;
    padding:10px;
    background-color:#CCC;
    width:560px;
    voice-family:"\"}\"";
    voice-family:inherit;
    width:560px;
    }
  html>body #content {
    width:560px;
    }
```

```
/* Sidebar A */
  #sidebar_a {
    float:left;
    padding:10px;
    background-color:#999;
    width:180px;
    voice-family:"\"}\"";
    voice-family:inherit;
    width:160px;
    }
  html>body #sidebar_a {
    width:160px;
    }
```

With `background-color` specified for each column, it is clear that the left column is somewhat shorter than the main column, and that color alone cannot help here (see Figure 12-5).

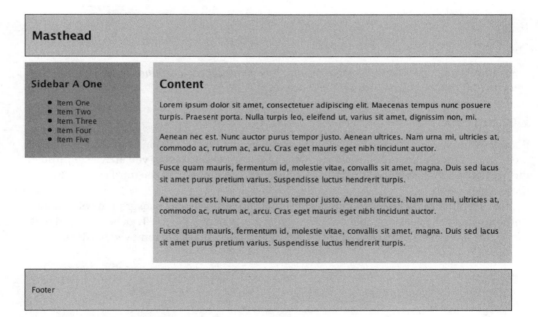

Figure 12-5. *Now background color is used to define the column heights, but still the columns expand only as much as they need to in order to contain the child elements.*

Define the Column Area

It must be time for faux columns! First, you will need to add the `container` div that will surround the two columns and become the area where the tiled background image will do its stuff. If there were no `masthead` or `footer`, this container would not be necessary, as the tiled image could be applied to the `<body>` element. For this example, the effect needs to be limited to a defined area only.

```
<div id="container">
  <div id="sidebar_a">
    <h3>Sidebar A One</h3>
      ...sidebar content goes here...
  </div>
  <div id="content">
    <h2>Content</h2>
      ...main content goes here...
  </div>
</div>
```

You now have a defined area in which the magic can happen.

Create the Background Image

Before declaring the CSS for the container div, the faux column tile needs to be created. This image needs to accurately reflect the widths of the two columns. Therefore, the given width values are used for each gray box. The left, darker, column is 180 pixels in width, and the right, wider, column is 560 pixels in width, as shown in Figure 12-6. The image can be any height, as it will tile accordingly, although the shorter the better for decreased file size.

Figure 12-6. *The background image that will be tiled vertically*

Add the Container Selector

Next, declare values for the container selector. All that is needed here is to declare values for the background property. This places the faux column tile and ensures it repeats vertically, thanks to repeat-y.

```
/* Container that holds all columns */
  #container {
    background:url(/images/faux.gif) repeat-y;
    }
```

It is also a good idea to remove the background-color declarations for the column selectors.

```
/* Content */
  #content {
    margin-left:200px;
    margin-right:0;
    padding:10px;
    width:560px;
    voice-family:"\"}\"";
    voice-family:inherit;
    width:560px;
    }
```

```
html>body #content {
  width:560px;
  }

/* Sidebar A */
  #sidebar_a {
    float:left;
    padding:10px;
    width:180px;
    voice-family:"\"}\"";
    voice-family:inherit;
    width:160px;
    }
  html>body #sidebar_a {
    width:160px;
    }
```

Save the faux.css file and reload faux.html in your browser. If all has gone to plan, both columns should now appear to be the same height, as in Figure 12-7.

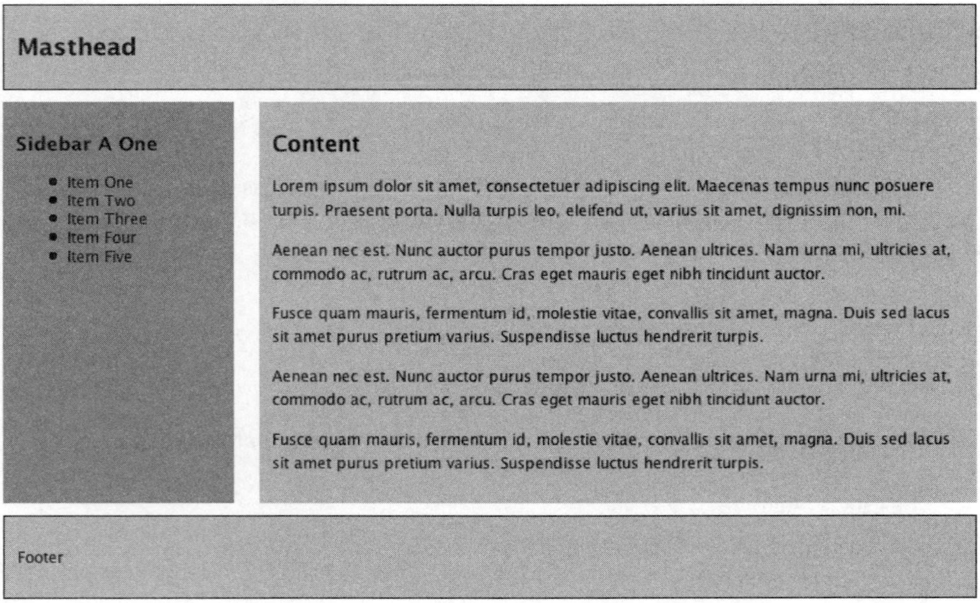

Figure 12-7. *Thanks to the tiled background image, both columns appear to be the same height.*

What About the Box Model?

That is a very good question. Extra marks for reminding me about that. Previously, the background image created is based on the preferred widths, and not the widths declared as part of the Box Model hack. Therefore the widths of 180 pixels and 560 pixels are inaccurate for IE6.

Even so, the faux column method will still work, as the columns have no borders to suggest their actual placement horizontally. In other words, they are defined visually only by the background image. This means that even though the columns are narrower on IE6, everything will still look right, so long as there is enough padding around the content of each column.

Note Your best bet is to try and avoid use of padding and borders with columns if possible, as this ensures equal results across browsers. No borders and padding means that the Box Model hack is not necessary. With the previous faux columns example, it would be better to apply any required padding to the child elements inside each column, such as the headings and paragraphs.

Fluid Faux Columns

The faux columns method is not so applicable to a fluid layout, where columns have no set width and vary based upon the width of the browser window. There are ways to apply faux columns to fluid layout, however, but it's a rather complex affair beyond the scope of this book. If it is something you want to experiment with, it's worth reading the excellent article "Creating Liquid Faux Columns" by Zoe Gillenwater (www.communitymx.com/content/article.cfm?cid=AFC58).

To Conclude...

I hope the two approaches we've walked through in this chapter get you thinking. In particular, the idea of switching layouts by triggering specific contextual selectors based on an ID declaration is key to a whole world of possibilities with CSS, and certainly something to bear in mind when embarking upon a new project. It will just make your life so much easier to adjust selectors for certain layouts, and of course you needn't stop with the <body> ID, as this method is useful for redefining any element.

The faux columns trick you will likely need less often, but it's still a good one for the old toolbox. You might find it useful to combine ID-based layout switching with faux column images to create a super-flexible layout that suits any kind of layout. Just remember to be mindful of how your layouts work cross-browser, especially when it comes to IE6.

In the next chapter, we'll begin to look at the nuts and bolts of your designs, dealing with typical page divisions such as mastheads, footers, and navigation, and how to get the most out of each and also how to approach complex out-of-the-box examples. Buckle in.

■ ■ ■

CHAPTER 13

The Journey from Layout to Template

It's now time for a fun chapter. You have worked so hard to get this far, that it seems appropriate to pull a few of your newfound skills together and walk through some common features of most web sites to produce a working template. Templates are starting points, where you begin to think about carving up the content and making it fit into set areas of the web site. This is the second step toward a completed design, where common page elements are incorporated into the column layout. These common elements will appear in many of your future designs, and they are flexible enough to become starting points for any job.

Specifically, we'll look at four common parts of the template—the masthead, headings (<h1>, <h2>, etc.), simple navigation, and footer. By the end of the chapter, these four parts—combined with the basic two-column layout you have already mastered—will form a basic yet reasonably attractive design. These methods form the basics of most similar approaches, and they should get the cogs in your head whirring round as you begin to see the potential for each in your forthcoming designs.

In the final chapter of this book, you can get to grips with the amazing *Dead Goods* case study, where some of these approaches will be revisited through more complex applications, and many more of the skills you have used so far will be incorporated. For now, let's walk together through several basic approaches to a page design and skirt a few common problems as we go.

■**Note** You can grab the completed files for this chapter from www.apress.com. The initial files (masthead.html and masthead.css) contain only the base (X)HTML and CSS for the two-column layout, and it is these files you will need to work through the examples. There are also two completed versions, with bubble_footer.html and bubble_footer.css featuring the first footer example, and action_footer.html and action_footer.css featuring the more complex footer example.

Masthead

The masthead is typically that part of the page that identifies the author or owner of the web site through name, logo, and possibly strapline. Most often, all the impact is created using graphics such as a logo, or a photographic image with logo or site title placed over the top.

There are a million and one ways to approach the masthead, but to get the ball rolling, let's look at a simple approach that is still implemented incorrectly by many.

Basic Masthead

Open `masthead.html` and you'll find the following basic markup for the plain masthead. This simply defines the section of the page and places the name of the site inside a level 1 heading.

```
<div id="masthead">
  <h1>Masthead</h1>
</div>
```

Styling Your Masthead

The simplest way to give your web page an attractive masthead is by applying one big, fat background image to the `masthead` div. Note that the white logo text (rendered in the lovely Sharktooth typeface) is part of the image. The image to be applied here is the full width of the page (760 pixels) and 150 pixels in height, and therefore the height of the `masthead` is declared as 150 pixels, and the background image is declared.

```
/* Masthead */
  #masthead {
    margin:0 0 10px 0;
    width:760px;
    height:150px;
    background:url(/images/masthead1.gif) no-repeat;
    }
```

The result can be seen in Figure 13-1. This looks OK, although the `<h1>` element is on show, top left of the embedded white logo text.

Figure 13-1. *The masthead image is in place, but the logo is not clickable, and the <h1> element is still visible.*

This is not the only problem. As well as the <h1> spoiling things, the logo itself is not a clickable link. Typically, designers will want the logo to be a link back to the home page of the web site—good practice as visitors will expect this. As the logo text here is part of the background image, it cannot be made clickable without some complex advanced CSS using coordinates and other dark magic.

The Smarter Masthead

Let's start again. The first job here might be to hide the <h1> element, using a simple selector as follows.

```
#masthead h1 {
  display:none;
  }
```

Using display:none ensures that the <h1> element is hidden. This will do for now, but we'll soon revisit this heading.

Now the graphics need to be reworked to make the logo clickable. For this two images are required. The first is a tile that can be repeated horizontally to fill the masthead div. This has been made by taking a thin slice of the original masthead background image (see Figure 13-2).

Figure 13-2. *Tile for masthead*

The next step is to rework the masthead selector to make that tile fill the given width.

```
/* Masthead */
  #masthead {
    margin:0 0 10px 0;
    width:760px;
    height:150px;
    background:url(/images/mastheadback.gif) repeat-x;
    }
```

This simple amendment gives us the masthead shown in Figure 13-3.

The final step is to crop the logo from the original masthead image, losing nothing from the top or left edges to ensure the logo gradient matches that of the tiled masthead background (see Figure 13-4).

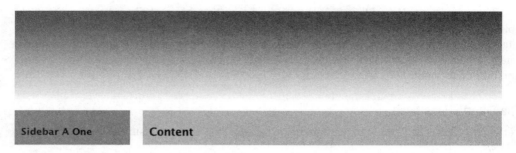

Figure 13-3. *The tiled image gives us just a masthead gradient at this stage.*

Figure 13-4. *The logo image is cut from the original full masthead image.*

It will now be apparent that hiding the <h1> element was premature, as it will now be used to contain the logo image. Notice that the alt attribute for the image reflects the text of the image itself. If the image were unavailable, the site would still be put into some context thanks to this alternative text.

```
<div id="masthead">
  <h1><a href=""><img src="/images/logo1.gif" alt="Masthead" /></a></h1>
</div>
```

Now revisit that h1 selector, and remove the display:none rule. You need to ensure that there is no default or inherited margin or padding. If there were, this could cause the logo to sit a few pixels away from the top-left corner, resulting in the two gradient backgrounds jarring against each other.

```
#masthead h1 {
  margin:0;
  padding:0;
  }
img {
  border:0;
  }
```

It is important to be aware that by default, any images acting as links will be given a thin blue line by the default browser style sheet, unless you override this value. Therefore, all borders for images are given a value of 0.

This reworking of the masthead, shown in Figure 13-5, provides a much more useful approach, with a clickable logo and two images with a smaller combined file size than the original one image.

Figure 13-5. *The logo is now clickable.*

Floated Right Content (Search Tool)

The reworked masthead looks good, and should be a flexible-enough approach for most simple mastheads. Still, there is a big gaping space to the right of the logo just begging for some useful addition. Personally, I think this looks like the ideal place for a search box.

Markup First

Within the masthead, the logo markup is untouched, and the search <form> element is placed inside a new container called searchbox.

```
<div id="masthead">
  <h1><a href=""><img src="/images/logo1.gif" alt="Masthead" /></a></h1>
  <div class="searchbox">
    <form>
      <fieldset>
        <legend>Search the site</legend>
        <input type="text" name="keywords" size="15" /> <input type="submit" ➥
        value="Go" />
      </fieldset>
    </form>
  </div>
</div>
```

And a Little More CSS

The trick here is to float the <h1> element to the left, and float searchbox to the right. In previous chapters, it was often necessary to clear floated elements with ugly extra markup such as a spacer div, but there is no call for that here, as the masthead has a fixed height and will therefore not collapse.

Note that the h1 selector now ensures that the element is floated to the left, and that the new container searchbox is floated right. Inside this new container, basic <form> elements (covered in Chapter 9) are placed.

```
/* Masthead */
  #masthead {
    margin:0 0 10px 0;
    width:760px;
    height:150px;
    background:url(/images/mastheadback.gif) repeat-x;
    }

  #masthead h1 {
    float:left;
    margin:0;
    padding:0;
    }

/* Search box holding the search form */
  .searchbox {
    float:right;
    width:220px;
    margin:15px;
    }

/* form items only inside searchbox */
  .searchbox legend {
    border:1px solid #666;
    padding:3px;
    background-color:#CCC;
    }

  .searchbox input {
    border:3px double #666;
    }

/* Turn off any default image borders */
  img {
    border:0;
    }
```

Notice also that the <form> element selectors are contextualized by prefixing the searchbox selector, so as to avoid any future conflict with <form> elements that might appear elsewhere on the web site.

The result can be seen in Figure 13-6, with the logo retaining its position to the left of the masthead container, and the new search tools fitting snugly to the right.

This is a very useful approach, as many designers like to fill that big gap in the masthead with something or other, whether that be search tools, mailing list sign-up tools, user options, or even one of those zingy starburst splats announcing that the site is "New!" or in "Beta" or "For Sale!". Whatever the reason, knowing how to split your masthead in half is a useful method that you'll almost certainly use at some point or other. What's more, it's the kind of approach that suits fluid layouts just as well, as left is left and right is right whether you are fluid, fixed, or otherwise.

Figure 13-6. *Search tools added to the space at the right of the masthead*

Headings

Earlier in the "Masthead" section of this chapter, the logo image was placed within the `<h1>` element, which is perfectly acceptable so long as alternative text is available. To not place image-based headings in this way would remove the underlying hierarchy that `<hn>` elements provide, making your content less attractive to search engine robots, and more importantly less easy to understand for visitors with images unavailable or turned off.

Very often, you will want (or be forced) to use a typeface for headings that is not web safe (see Chapter 4 for an overview of web-safe fonts), and often this will require an image. Naturally, what's good for the `<h1>` is good for any other `<hn>` element, just so long as the `alt` attribute is used sensibly.

Figure 13-7 shows an image featuring the same typeface (*Sharktooth*—I love it) as the logo image, effectively keeping the design "on brand," as fancy designers like to say. In other words, it will match the logo, but will be much smaller, roughly echoing the default scale through the (X)HTML headings.

Sidebar

Figure 13-7. *Sidebar heading image*

As with the masthead logo, the image element is placed within the level 3 heading element, with the matching `alt` attribute value.

```
<div id="sidebar_a">
  <h3><img src="/images/sidebar.gif" alt="Sidebar" /></h3>
    <ul>
      <li>Item One</li>
      <li>Item Two</li>
      <li>Item Three</li>
      <li>Item Four</li>
      <li>Item Five</li>
    </ul>
</div>
```

The same process is used to place the image for the level 2 heading ("Content"), except that the image text is roughly midway in scale between the `<h1>` and `<h3>` images to ensure that a visual hierarchy is obvious. As Figure 13-8 shows, the logo (`<h1>`) is clearly largest in scale, with the "Content" heading (`<h2>`) a little smaller, but still quite bold, and finally the "Sidebar" heading (`<h3>`) the smallest.

Figure 13-8. *Custom headings still suggest a hierarchy of information, mirroring the headings structure of the (X)HTML.*

Free from the restraints of real text, it is easy to get carried away and misuse images in such situations. Nobody should tell you that images within such important structural elements are a no-no, but that doesn't mean they aren't open to abuse. Remember to retain a sense of hierarchy when using images within heading elements, and only use them if you are determined to use a specific typeface or visual effect that cannot be had with real text or CSS treatment.

Navigation

As you work your way through this book, you'll probably be noticing lots of short, sharp snippets of code that you'll want to shunt into your layouts as you begin to experiment. This seems like a good point to liberate a simple list from Chapter 6, as this will fulfill a common page requirement (navigation) and help pull this template together quickly.

All of the files available for this chapter will feature a simple unordered list (<ul>) in the sidebar column. By applying the following CSS, any <ul> elements found in the sidebar will be rendered with three-dimensional list items as detailed in Chapter 6.

```
#sidebar_a ul {
  width:160px;
  padding:0;
  list-style-type:none;
  font:bold 12px 'Lucida Grande',Verdana,sans-serif;
  }

#sidebar_a li {
  background-color:#DDD;
  margin:0;
  padding:2px 10px;
  border-width:1px;
  border-style:solid;
  border-color:#fff #666 #aaa #fff;
  }
```

Figure 13-9 shows the result thus far. This super-quick approach is already transforming this simple template into a respectable design—albeit rather gray.

Figure 13-9. *Now that the unordered list in the sidebar has been styled, the page design is beginning to look a little more professional.*

Now all that is needed is a stylish footer to round off the design. The next section doesn't have one though—it has *two*. Grab a quick cup of tea, and we'll move on.

Cool Footers

So far, the layouts in this book have featured a section designated as a *footer*. Typically, the footer will run the full length of the layout, and it is usually used to display information at the bottom of the content hierarchy, such as copyright information, accessibility or validation information, and possibly contact details or company legal information.

However, 2006 has seen the birth of the *action-packed* footer. An action-packed footer does a bit more than just display the "less important stuff." It will be bigger, bolder, and uncut, acting as an extra smorgasbord of navigation items such as links to archived articles, music or book recommendations, or even an author or company profile. Gone are the days when a footer merely ended the page. Now it is just as likely to be an all-encompassing launchpad to other areas of the web site. Of course, nothing is really that new, and big feet have been around for a long time, but at the time of writing, action-packed footers are cool, and it is worth knowing how to create one.

First, we'll look at a quirky footer, where a simple background image is used to create an amusing page finale. After that, we'll detail the ins and outs of an action-packed version.

Quirky Footer

For the quirky footer, the aim is to use a large background image that blurs the boundary between column area and footer, by acknowledging the background color of the page and having it influence the footer. In this case, the white background of the page becomes the bubble coming out of my mouth.

Let's go through this idea step by step, but consider how you could use an equally inventive image to make your footers that bit quirkier. Armed with a correctly sized image and some well-styled text, the dull footer can be consigned to history.

Prepare the Footer Markup

The first task is to add the information that you want to show in the footer. At this stage, you should not be thinking about the presentation, only the important stuff—the content. Here, it is important to show copyright information and other site acknowledgments, so these go into the markup inside paragraphs.

```
<div id="footer">
  <p>Copyright Simon Collison 2006</p>
  <p>Made with the finest <a href="">XHTML</a> and <a href="">CSS</a>.</p>
  <p>Content protected with a <a href="">Creative Commons</a> license. Some➥
  rights reserved.</p>
</div>
```

The idea is that whatever madness you use to make the footer seem all wacky and zany, the actual markup is never compromised. Basically, I know I'm going to place the information in a comedy bubble, but at no point should I limit the amount of information because I fear it might not fit the graphic. Content is always more important than presentation—but you already know that.

Apply the Background Image

The aim here is to make it look as if I'm speaking the information, so a speech bubble graphic is created. This graphic is exactly the same width as the layout (760 pixels), and has ended up being 128 pixels in height. As you'll see in Figure 13-10, the author needs a shave.

Figure 13-10. *Customized background image for the footer. Simon says . . .*

Now the CSS. The first task is to ensure that there is no internal padding for the footer, or left or right margins. This ensures that the image will sit perfectly, and that any element to be placed within can be positioned using its own CSS rules to avoid confusion.

Next, the background image is declared and set to no-repeat. Sure, it's the same size as the container, but it is worth ensuring there will be no hint of tiling. Finally, the height of the footer is adjusted to match the height of the image.

```
/* Footer */
  #footer {
    clear:both;
```

```
  margin:10px 0 0 0;
  background:url(/images/bubble_footer.jpg) no-repeat;
  height:128px;
  width:760px;
  }
```

Figure 13-11 shows the result in the browser. Note that the juxtaposition of image and text is OK, but not quite right. Longer paragraphs extend beyond the boundary of the speech bubble.

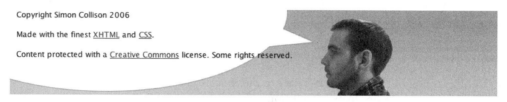

Copyright Simon Collison 2006

Made with the finest XHTML and CSS.

Content protected with a Creative Commons license. Some rights reserved.

Figure 13-11. *The paragraphs are too long, extending outside of the bubble.*

Fine-Tune the Paragraphs

This exact placement of the paragraphs can be controlled by first using 15 pixels of padding at the top of the footer to shunt the first paragraph down further into the bubble, and then by defining properties for all paragraphs that appear inside the footer. The key values are for the paragraph margins, and these can be tweaked until the exact effect is achieved.

Most importantly, the paragraphs are given a width, which is just a bit shorter than the average distance between the left side of the footer and the curve of the bubble. This width declaration will force the text to wrap way before it reaches the curve.

```
/* Footer */
  #footer {
    clear:both;
    margin:10px 0 0 0;
    padding-top:15px;
    background:url(/images/bubble_footer.jpg) no-repeat;
    height:128px;
    width:760px;
    }
  #footer p {
    margin:0 0 6px 35px;
    padding:0;
    width:330px;
    font:13px/120% normal Verdana,Arial,sans-serif;
    }
```

The final result is shown in Figure 13-12, as it would appear in the base of the browser window. It is possible that if more text were used, the paragraph margins and width might need adjusting as the curve sharpens, but it is fine for this example, and the quirky footer is achieved with minimal effort.

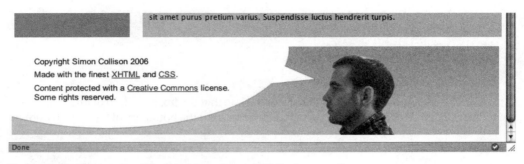

Figure 13-12. *Simon says, "Touch this code, and I'll find you . . ."*

The Action-Packed Footer

With a quirky footer out of the way, it is time to put that to one side and explore the action-packed footer. One of the first to make a big impact with this approach in 2006 was Derek Powazek (www.powazek.com), who uses the action-packed footer to detail who he is, what he's written recently, and what books he is currently recommending (see Figure 13-13).

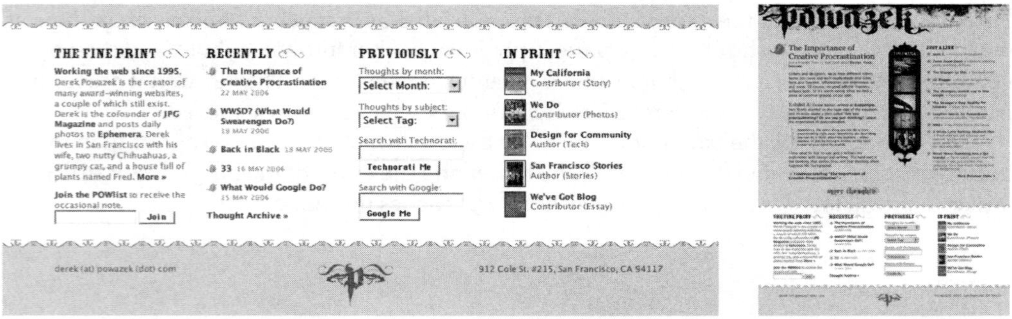

Figure 13-13. *Derek Powazek's action-packed footer, over at www.powazek.com*

It is this kind of super-useful footer that is gaining favor at the time of writing, and it can certainly be a reward for those who manage to make it to the bottom of a long web page. Let's take Derek's example and attempt something similar.

More Action Means More Markup

Yes, it goes without saying that a footer like this cannot be achieved without an increase in markup. For this example, we first think top-to-bottom, and not left-to-right, so although the footer will need four "columns," again content comes first. Therefore, the (X)HTML elements go in first, long before any thought for divisions, columns or otherwise.

Notice that level 4 headings (`<h4>`) are used, as for this layout this is a logical transition of hierarchy from the level 3 heading used in the sidebar earlier.

```
<div id="footer">
  <h4>Small print</h4>
    <p>Copyright Simon Collison 2006</p>
    <p>Made with the finest <a href="">XHTML</a> and➥
      <a href="">CSS</a>.</p>
    <p>Content protected with a <a href="">Creative Commons</a>➥
      license. Some rights reserved.</p>
  <h4>Recent articles</h4>
    <ul>
      <li><a href="">Interesting waffle</a></li>
      <li><a href="">Some amazing news</a></li>
      <li><a href="">Bad news everyone...</a></li>
      <li><a href="">I've won the lottery!</a></li>
      <li><a href="">New website launched</a></li>
    </ul>
  <h4>Archives</h4>
    <form action="#">
      <fieldset>
        <select name="select1">
          <option selected value="/">Select Month:</option>
        </select>
      </fieldset>
    </form>
    <form action="#">
      <fieldset>
        <select name="select2">
          <option selected value="/">Select Year:</option>
        </select>
      </fieldset>
    </form>
    <form action="#">
      <fieldset>
        <select name="select3">
          <option selected value="/">Select category:</option>
        </select>
      </fieldset>
    </form>
  <h4>Recently launched</h4>
    <img src="/images/dpt.jpg" alt="Dirty Pretty Things" />
    <p><a href="">Dirty Pretty Things</a></p>
    <img src="/images/lib.jpg" alt="The Libertines" />
    <p><a href="">The Libertines</a></p>
    <img src="/images/jb.jpg" alt="Jon Burgerman" />
    <p><a href="">Jon Burgerman</a></p>
    <img src="/images/pop.jpg" alt="Poptones" />
    <p><a href="">Poptones</a></p>
</div>
```

This gives us the unstyled, lengthy footer shown in Figure 13-14. Still, all the information is legible without CSS, so at least we know that all will be well should the CSS be unavailable later.

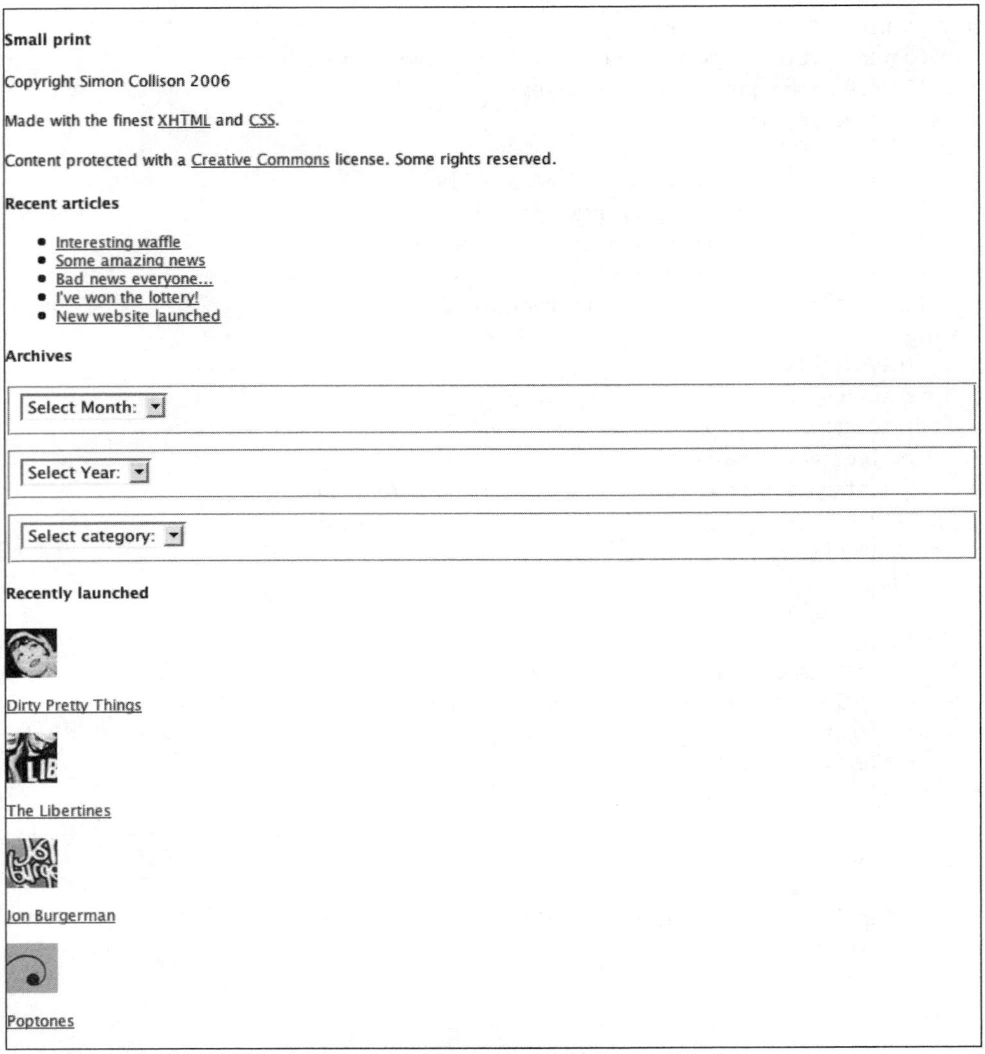

Small print

Copyright Simon Collison 2006

Made with the finest XHTML and CSS.

Content protected with a Creative Commons license. Some rights reserved.

Recent articles

- Interesting waffle
- Some amazing news
- Bad news everyone...
- I've won the lottery!
- New website launched

Archives

Select Month:

Select Year:

Select category:

Recently launched

Dirty Pretty Things

The Libertines

Jon Burgerman

Poptones

Figure 13-14. *The content is held within the footer, but as yet untickled by CSS.*

Divide the Footer into Sections

Before moving on to the style sheet, the footer content needs to be divided into sections so that the "column" effect can be created later. Here, it seems logical that each section will be the same width, so a class seems appropriate, as it can be reused. In this example, the class is called footerCol, and it defines each block of content we wish to separate.

```
<div id="footer">
  <div class="footerCol">
    <h4>Small print</h4>
      <p>Copyright Simon Collison 2006</p>
      <p>Made with the finest <a href="">XHTML</a> and➡
        <a href="">CSS</a>.</p>
      <p>Content protected with a <a href="">Creative Commons</a>➡
        license. Some rights reserved.</p>
  </div>
  <div class="footerCol">
    <h4>Recent articles</h4>
      <ul>
        <li><a href="">Interesting waffle</a></li>
        <li><a href="">Some amazing news</a></li>
        <li><a href="">Bad news everyone...</a></li>
        <li><a href="">I've won the lottery!</a></li>
        <li><a href="">New website launched</a></li>
      </ul>
  </div>
  <div class="footerCol">
    <h4>Archives</h4>
      <form action="#">
        <fieldset>
          <select name="select1">
            <option selected value="/">Select Month:</option>
          </select>
        </fieldset>
      </form>
      <form action="#">
        <fieldset>
          <select name="select2">
            <option selected value="/">Select Year:</option>
          </select>
        </fieldset>
      </form>
      <form action="#">
        <fieldset>
          <select name="select3">
            <option selected value="/">Select category:</option>
          </select>
        </fieldset>
      </form>
  </div>
  <div class="footerCol">
    <h4>Recently launched</h4>
      <img src="/images/dpt.jpg" alt="Dirty Pretty Things" />
      <p><a href="">Dirty Pretty Things</a></p>
```

```
        <img src="/images/lib.jpg" alt="The Libertines" />
        <p><a href="">The Libertines</a></p>
        <img src="/images/jb.jpg" alt="Jon Burgerman" />
        <p><a href="">Jon Burgerman</a></p>
        <img src="/images/pop.jpg" alt="Poptones" />
        <p><a href="">Poptones</a></p>
    </div>
    <div class="spacer"></div>
</div>
```

Note that just before the existing </div> that closes the footer, a meaningless spacer div is added. As the footer will be of an unknown height (dictated by its variable content), and we'll be floating the footerCol sections, this is necessary to clear the floats and ensure the footer does not collapse (see Chapter 10 for a refresher about clearing floats).

Float the Sections with CSS

Ah, the good bit. Just below the existing footer selector, the rules for the reusable footerCol class are declared. The footer is 760 pixels in width, so each section needs to be a little less than a quarter of that width, as the content does not need to fill the footer exactly. Here, 170 pixels seems to work well, as it allows a little room for 15-pixel margins in between each section.

For now, a thin gray border is added so that it is easy to see how the sections are placed. This border will be removed later. Oh, and of course, the sections are floated so that they line up left to right.

```
/* Footer */
  #footer {
    clear:both;
    margin:10px 0 0 0;
    width:760px;
    border:1px solid #000;
    }
/* Reusable class for columns in the footer */
  .footerCol {
    float:left;
    width:170px;
    margin-left:15px;
    border:1px solid #999;
    }
/* Spacer div to follow multiple floated items */
  .spacer {
    clear:both;
    }
```

You will also notice that the spacer div is set to clear:both, ensuring that the footer recognizes when the action is over, and doesn't therefore collapse prematurely. Adding this CSS gives us the neater layout in Figure 13-15.

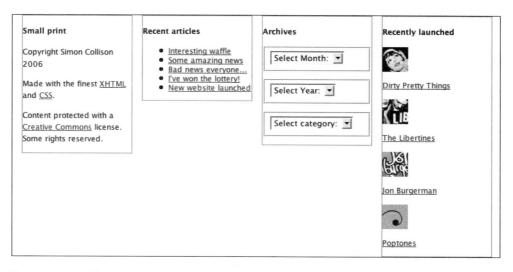

Figure 13-15. *With a reusable class, the footer is split into four floated sections.*

Take Control of the Content

With the sections neatly floated, the focus can now shift to the content within each. The first section is easy to style, as it is nothing more than paragraphs and links. By now, you should be comfortable with targeting these paragraphs using either your default paragraph rules or a contextual selector to target only paragraphs found in the footer.

The second section, containing an unordered list, can also be targeted with a contextual selector. Here, the CSS targets only lists found within the footer, so as to avoid conflict with any other lists in the layout. This CSS is pulled directly from Chapter 6, where `list-style-image` was first used to place a custom bullet alongside each list item.

```
#footer ul {
  margin:0;padding:0 0 0 25px;
  list-style-image:url(/images/list.gif);
  line-height:150%;
  }
#footer fieldset {
  margin:0;
  border:0;
  padding:0;
  }
```

Notice also that all default or inherited `margin`, `border`, and `padding` values are turned off for the `<fieldset>` elements in the third section. This ensures that each `<select>` element is aligned with the heading above. Figure 13-16 shows the progress thus far.

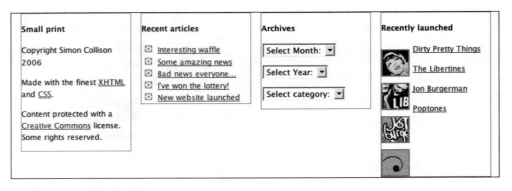

Figure 13-16. *Paragraphs, lists, and fieldsets are all sorted out with CSS.*

The fourth column is a little more difficult, as the goal is to align the images with the corresponding paragraph element. By default, this simply doesn't work. Therefore, the best option is to revisit the markup and add the spacer div underneath each pairing to force separation between each, as we did back in Chapter 10.

```
<div class="footerCol">
  <h4>Recently launched</h4>
    <img src="/images/dpt.jpg" alt="Dirty Pretty Things" />
    <p><a href="">Dirty Pretty Things</a></p>
  <div class="spacer"></div>
    <img src="/images/lib.jpg" alt="The Libertines" />
    <p><a href="">The Libertines</a></p>
  <div class="spacer"></div>
    <img src="/images/jb.jpg" alt="Jon Burgerman" />
    <p><a href="">Jon Burgerman</a></p>
  <div class="spacer"></div>
    <img src="/images/pop.jpg" alt="Poptones" />
    <p><a href="">Poptones</a></p>
  <div class="spacer"></div>
</div>
```

There are advanced methods of achieving the same separation without all this excessive markup, but these are beyond the scope of this book. If you want to try my favorite example, look at "How To Clear Floats Without Structural Markup" (http://positioniseverything.net/easyclearing.html) by Big John and Holly Bergevin.

Now the images can be floated left and given a simple margin to ensure the paragraph text has room to breathe. Also, a thin gray border is added around these images. Note again that the rules only apply to images within the footer.

```
.footerCol img {
  float:left;
  border:2px solid #999;
  margin:0 5px 10px 0;
  }
```

The story so far, with all four sections of the action-packed footer treated with CSS, can be seen in Figure 13-17.

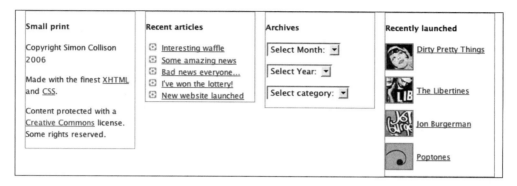

Figure 13-17. *All footer content is tidied with CSS.*

Time for the Fun Bit

Now that all the preparation is out of the way, we can think about how to make a visual distinction between the footer and all of the content above it. For this, a long background image will be used to give the impression of a cut-out-and-keep footer.

First, remove the gray borders added earlier to footerCol (which were used to see how elements were aligning). Also, we increase padding at the top of the footer, creating a space in which to drop the divider image.

```
/* Footer */
  #footer {
    clear:both;
    margin:30px 0 0 0;
    padding:40px 0 15px 0;
    width:760px;
    }

/* Reusable class for columns in the footer */
  .footerCol {
    float:left;
    width:170px;
    margin-left:15px;
    }
```

These adjustments result in the plainer footer shown in Figure 13-18.

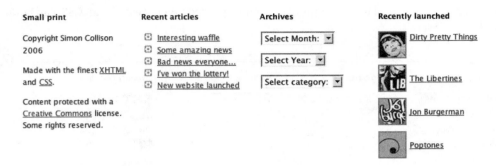

Figure 13-18. *The gray guide borders have been removed, and the footer is in need of a dividing image.*

So, at the top of the footer, before the four sections, there is now a space 40-pixels high, created by increasing the padding on the footer. Into this space, the image shown in Figure 13-19 will be placed.

Figure 13-19. *The dividing image (cutout.gif) will separate the footer from the rest of the content.*

This is achieved simply by declaring the image as the value of the background-image property for the footer, again using background-repeat:no-repeat to avoid tiling the image. Note that these two properties are declared using background shorthand.

```
/* Footer */
  #footer {
    clear:both;
    margin:30px 0 0 0;
    padding:40px 0 15px 0;
    width:760px;
    background:#FFF url(/images/cutout.gif) no-repeat;
    }
```

It has taken a fair few steps, but finally the all-conquering action-packed footer is completed (see Figure 13-20). Hopefully, you will see that the method used is flexible enough to be tweaked to accommodate your own images and number of sections.

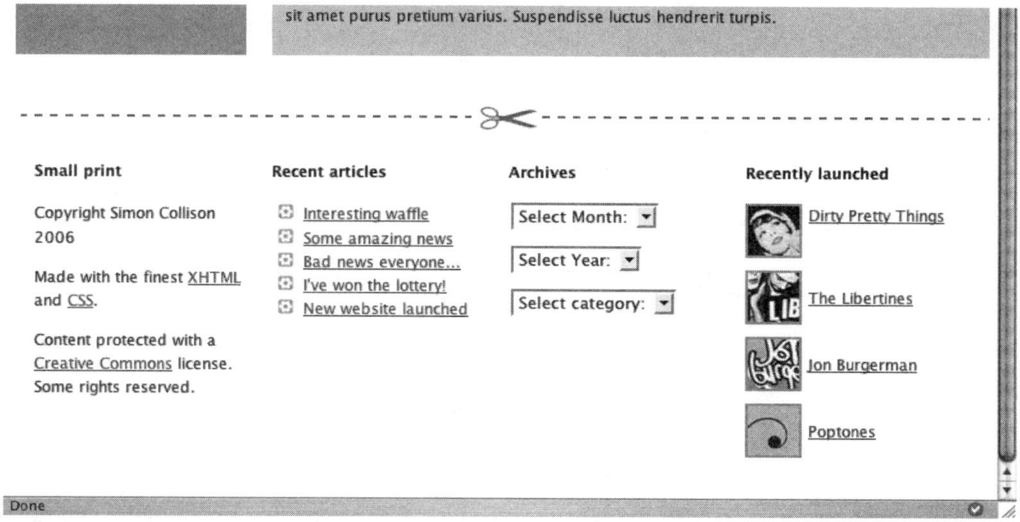

Figure 13-20. *The finished, action-packed footer. They'll come from miles around to scroll to the bottom of your pages.*

Footer-Note

Remember that by adding more and more action to your footer, you increase the amount of work that your file needs to do every time it is viewed. Some seasoned professionals argue that this is a backward step, placing important content out of reach of the casual visitor, and that it plays havoc with the expected hierarchy of a web page.

I disagree, as do many, and find the action-packed footer to be a great reward for scrollers like myself. To not need to return to the top of the page to find another destination is a positive step, so long as the markup remains lean, the information is well presented, and the temptation to overload the footer is avoided.

To Conclude...

Over the course of just a few pages, and with focus on just four key sections of a web page, a simple template has been created. Depending upon which footer you used, and whether or not you got all excited and ended up experimenting with your own graphics and colors, you could have a page that looks a little like the one in Figure 13-21.

Figure 13-21. *This template adds masthead, headings, and footer styling on top of a basic floated two-column layout.*

The whole point here is that you have worked through several basic template elements that you will reuse again and again. This is a real strength, and it is very useful to build a small library of reusable chunks of code that can get future web sites off to a quick start. Templates save you time and money.

At this stage, it is important to acknowledge how far you have come. To be able to take control of lean and mean (X)HTML and transform it—section by section—into a living, breathing design is no small achievement. Well done, you! Have a cookie.

Over the remaining chapters, you will learn how to make your markup accessible and use CSS to provide further tools to aid usability, such as print style sheets and better skip links. You will also pick up a barrow-full of tips and recommendations for better CSS, before moving on to the finale—the *Dead Goods* case study. Wipe those cookie crumbs from your keyboard, and get set for the home straight.

■■■

CHAPTER 14

Usability and Accessibility Enhancements

Let's begin with a law. Anyone and everyone should be able to read your content and use your web site, regardless of ability or platform used. Simple. With regard to the Web, the term **usability** denotes not only the elegance and clarity with which the user interface of a computer program or a web site is designed, but also how easy it is for the target audience to accomplish the appropriate tasks. For example, errors need to be minimized and dealt with, and the user's intended speed and approach should not be compromised. A web site's usability is now considered just as important as performance and robustness.

This in turn brings us to **accessibility**, which, broadly defined in this context, means a web site should be usable by as many people as possible without further modification or parallel versions. It has come to mean the practice of making web pages accessible to people using a wide range of devices, and not just browsers. This is especially important for people with disabilities who require such devices to access the Web.

This book does not discuss all the accessibility requirements of (X)HTML, since our focus here is on CSS. You should, for example, already be dividing large blocks of content into more manageable groups; using heading tags to mark up headings; clearly identifying the target of each link; providing metadata to add semantic information to pages and sites; providing information about the general layout of your site (such as a site map or table of contents); and navigation mechanisms should be used in a consistent manner. For more of these guidelines, be sure to visit the W3C's checklist (`www.w3.org/TR/WCAG10/full-checklist.html`). In this chapter, we'll look purely at how the application of simple CSS can enhance usability and accessibility, with barely any additional markup.

The fact is, working through this book, you have already had your finger on the accessibility pulse, so a big "well done" for that. You now know all about form labeling, scalable content, visible hierarchy, link treatment, and the use of small file sizes using CSS. You feel good.

This chapter doesn't get too advanced, merely skimming the surface of the accessibility pudding. There are a million methods to enhance accessibility, and these are the edited highlights.

Guidelines and Legalities

The Internet has grown at an incredible pace. The original vision that its content should be accessible to all became overlooked as more and more exciting design approaches became possible. Web design became (for the most part) about how good something looked, and not how well it functioned. Thankfully, over recent years the focus has shifted back toward accessibility, and responsible designers and clients realize that in reality, a balance between good looks and functionality is a perfectly viable way forward.

It's all about users being able to access your content and services, regardless of any disabilities they may have. This is yet another reason why the separation of content, behavior, and style is a good thing—if readers can't use CSS or JavaScript, they should still be able to read the actual content.

The law is woolly though, and designers are bombarded with guidelines that often contradict one another, and it is difficult to make informed decisions about the law here. The Internet is a global tool, with a site's users coming from numerous countries. With this in mind, who is to say that USA guidelines are more important than those from the UK, Germany, or Iceland?

The Disability Rights Commission (DRC) estimates that there are around 6.8 million disabled people in the UK alone (that's 19% of the population)—a huge number of which might want to access your web site. If it is not accessible to them, they are going to either be turned off by it immediately or persevere, become frustrated, and then be turned off.

To explain the ins and outs of the guidelines and legalities regarding web design would require a whole book, and probably a book that can rewrite itself monthly. Still, it is important to be aware of the legislation in your country. Following these guidelines will undoubtedly make your web site more accessible, and rarely will this compromise your intentions. For further information, be sure to visit the Accessify web site (www.accessify.com) or pick up a copy of *Web Accessibility: Web Standards and Regulatory Compliance* by Michael R. Burks et al. (friends of ED, 2006, ISBN: 1-59059-638-2).

Without wishing to scare you away from this subject, there is enough space to discuss a couple of high-profile guidelines that garner much debate among responsible folks who work with web sites.

Web Content Accessibility Guidelines

In 1999, the Web Accessibility Initiative (WAI) published the Web Content Accessibility Guidelines (WCAG) 1.0. These are generally accepted as the definitive guidelines for creating accessible web sites. Over the last few years, the WAI has been working on the second edition of these guidelines: the WCAG 2.0, currently at the draft stage, but gaining much interest in the web community, not least for the indecipherable and impenetrable details across 700 pages.

In a nutshell, the WCAG 2.0 draft encourages web developers, media departments, public bodies, companies, and so on to establish their own baseline for progression. This is achieved by first wading through the latest WCAG draft, and then deciding what is applicable to each web project to form one's own baseline (supported technologies, for example), before finally implementing the appropriate technology according to that baseline. It can be a bit daunting at first, but one day it may well be law. For more information (and I mean *lots* of information), visit www.w3.org/TR/WCAG20/. Good luck with that.

Section 508

Section 508 (an amendment to the 1973 Rehabilitation Act in the US) requires that electronic information such as that found on the Web be accessible to absolutely anyone with disabilities, and that they have equal use of such technologies as federal employees and members of the public who do not have disabilities. Initially intended for the US, Section 508 has become an adopted standard around the world, not always enforceable, but a recognized benchmark nonetheless.

Where Section 508 differs from WCAG is that Section 508 is law—under Section 508, covered parties alleging discrimination may institute civil suits based on alleged damages and, if successful, receive monetary awards. In other words, disregard this law, and you may end up in court. For more information, visit `http://en.wikipedia.org/wiki/Section_508`.

User Style Sheets

Just to prove that CSS is not only a great tool for web designers, it also allows web users a broad degree of control over how they see your designs. This is particularly important for users who, for example, have trouble reading your chosen fonts or need to up the color contrasts a little. By specifying his or her own CSS, a user can transform the way web pages are presented. Note that if a user style sheet is employed, it will become the top of the cascade.

For example, a visually impaired user might look to increase the page's contrast by defining bold colors in his or her own style sheet.

```
body {
  color: orange;
  background: black;
  }
```

By specifying orange text on a black background from the outset, the user ensures that text for the web page is more legible for him or her individually. This simple introduction to user style sheets is an idea that doesn't always work. This is CSS, and therefore there are conflicts.

!important

To avoid conflict between the author and user style sheets, users can add a bit more power to their own by utilizing the !important operator. If a user's style sheet uses !important, it takes precedence over any similar author rule. Here, for example, the following rule will ensure that all paragraph text will be very large indeed.

```
p {
  font-size:40pt !important;
    }
```

You can also use !important in your own style sheets, but it will always be overridden by a user style sheet (except in IE, in which case the user must override this by also using !important). Some web designers have been known to use !important alongside other declarations to send different values to Internet Explorer, but a hack such as this is not what !important was intended for. This author has certainly never committed such a heinous crime. Ahem. In Chapter 15, you will learn more about hacks, and why they are best avoided. Don't be slack—avoid the hack.

Inherit

By using inherit with !important styles, the user's style sheet gains greater precedence, making all such declarations applicable to any elements that inherit the values. Consider the following syntax:

```
body {
  color: black ! important ;
  background: white ! important ;
    }

* {
  color: inherit ! important ;
  background: inherit ! important ;
    }
```

Here, the first rule sets the colors of the <body>, and the second rule uses the * selector to target all elements on the page and the inherit property to inherit the colors from the <body>.

For more information about user style sheets, read the comprehensive "User Stylesheets in CSS" (http://dbaron.org/css/user/), or get more familiar with the user side of things by trying one of several provided by the W3C site (www.w3.org/StyleSheets/Core/).

Being Helpful

As a designer, you long to create beautiful, functional things. The thrill of making something that looks good, and works, is what you do. In a world where time is short and clients can be very demanding, there is a tendency for many designers to brush over many of the hidden enhancements, as the visible web site won't really benefit from all that extra work. The client is happy, so that is all that matters, right?

This is where designers let people down. A user with blindness or low vision, deafness or hearing loss, learning difficulties, cognitive limitations, limited movement, speech difficulties, or photosensitivity will be praying that your very important site has all sorts of useful hooks to enable them to navigate quickly and simply, and perhaps using their keyboard alone (that is, without a mouse). Failing to think about these users compromises your otherwise good work, and decreases audience. Think of it this way: an Aston Martin looks good, but isn't it crap unless it has a good engine in it? As usual, the responsibility lies with you.

Styling Abbreviations and Acronyms

Any abbreviations, acronyms, and initials that appear in your (X)HTML should always be contained within the <abbr> element, although some still use the <acronym> element, which does a similar job.

Most browsers render text enclosed within an <abbr> element with a dotted border below or surrounding it. Also, when the mouse hovers over the element, the description is displayed as a tooltip. The exception is, unsurprisingly, IE6 and below, although these browsers will display the tooltip using the outdated <acronym> element. Small wonder people get confused.

Note also that most screenreaders support the <abbr> element and can be set to speak the title attribute when these elements are encountered.

Figure 14-1 shows the typical use of the <abbr> element, as used on the Regional Action West Midlands (RAWM) web site (www.rawm.net).

Notice that the abbreviation is underlined with a dotted line, and on hover, a tooltip appears expanding the abbreviation. As stated, this is a default for all but IE6 and below. It is therefore necessary to add CSS to ensure cross-browser results.

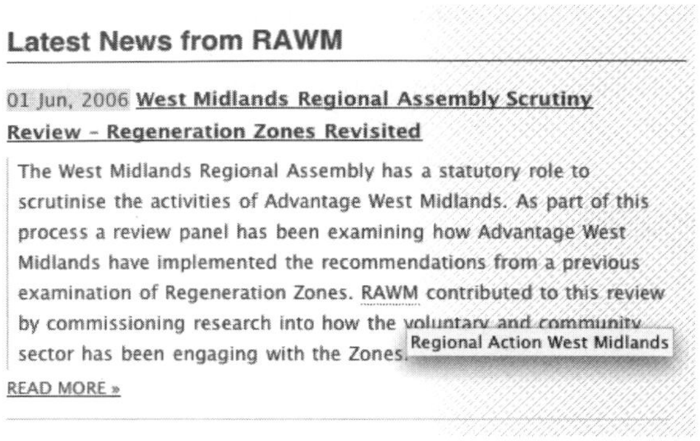

Latest News from RAWM

01 Jun, 2006 <u>West Midlands Regional Assembly Scrutiny</u>
<u>Review - Regeneration Zones Revisited</u>

The West Midlands Regional Assembly has a statutory role to
scrutinise the activities of Advantage West Midlands. As part of this
process a review panel has been examining how Advantage West
Midlands have implemented the recommendations from a previous
examination of Regeneration Zones. RAWM contributed to this review
by commissioning research into how the voluntary and community
sector has been engaging with the Zones. | Regional Action West Midlands |

READ MORE »

Figure 14-1. *The RAWM web site uses numerous abbreviations, all of which can be expanded
thanks to the <abbr> element.*

The (X)HTML

For all instances of the abbreviation, the text needs to be enclosed within the `<abbr>` element,
with the full description added using the `title` attribute. The sample file `abbr.html` is available
from the downloads pages of `www.apress.com`.

```
<abbr title="Regional Action West Midlands">RAWM</abbr>
```

This simple element can now be targeted using a corresponding CSS rule.

The CSS

If the title attribute has been used within the `<abbr>` element, the following CSS can be used to
suggest its existence by applying styling to the browser display. Here, both `abbr` and `acronym` are
used for the selector, just in case any old `<acronym>` elements are used or added by an adminis-
trator. First, a gray dotted `border-bottom` is declared to underline the element. Note also that
the `cursor` property is used to transform the cursor into a question mark on hover. The CSS file
`abbr.css` is also available from `www.apress.com`.

```
/* Style acronymns and abbreviations and change cursor */
  abbr, acronym {
    border-bottom:1px dotted #666;
    cursor:help;
    }
```

This simple rule ensures that IE6 and below will also underline any abbreviations and acronyms.
Naturally, by adding a selector for the `<abbr>` element, you have the freedom to move away
from the default display and get really creative, so long as the user perception of the element
isn't compromised.

Abbreviated Table Headings

Don't forget to provide descriptions for any abbreviations used in your tables also. For the
Dirty Pretty Things web site (`www.dirtyprettythingsband.com`), lots of information is pulled

into the Discography table (see Figure 14-2). There is not enough space to fully label each column, and therefore a simple key is provided using the `<caption>` element.

This key alone should not be considered as enough explanation, and the corresponding letters in the `<th>` cells have been enclosed within `<abbr>` elements.

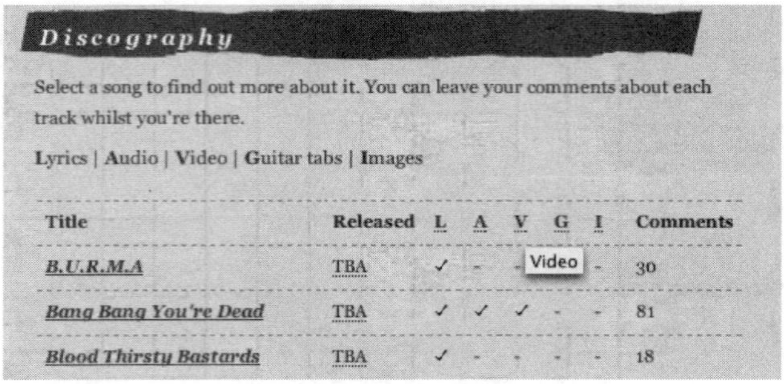

Figure 14-2. *The Dirty Pretty Things discography uses abbreviations to save space within the Discography table.*

Sighted users can obviously use the key or the `<abbr>` explanations. Importantly, for users navigating with screenreaders, each column can now be understood, and the column information has proper context. These additions take just a few minutes to code, but make a world of difference for users with disabilities.

Specialized Style Sheets

In the "Importing and Combining Styles" section of Chapter 1, we looked at sensible management of multiple style sheets and how to serve specific style sheets for specific viewing platforms. A key accessibility method, this approach ensures the most appropriate display of your pages within the confines of the end device. Now it is time to look at the best usage of CSS for these style sheets, and the best approaches for controlling the display and functionality for printing and handheld devices.

Note that no changes to the markup within the whole `<body>` element will be required for either print or handheld style sheets. How's that for CSS power?

Print Style Sheets

How many times have you found an article on the Internet that you wish to print, only to find that when you click Print, it takes half a day to print owing to all the advertising banners, useless sidebars full of links, and the jet black background that is sapping your expensive ink cartridge? Often, I imagine.

Take a look at the article from the Science City web site (`www.science-city.co.uk`) in Figure 14-3. The design has been approached to ensure that the black-with-white-text approach to the overall brand has been carried over to the web site. This is great for the screen, but that black background is going to kill the printer. Also, does anyone really need to print the login tools or unrelated image? And what about the links in the article? They'll be pretty useless on a piece of paper, right?

Figure 14-3. *The Science City web site features a jet black background, which is not ideal for printing.*

All of these questions can be answered with a custom print style sheet. For the Science City example, users can click a "Print version" link to view the print version in their browser using a stripped down (X)HTML file, with much of the extraneous markup removed, and only the print style sheet referenced. This approach isn't necessary if you wish users only to witness the effects of the print style sheet when they grab the paper from the printer. The following steps simply tell the printer to use the print style sheet, ensuring it reworks the design without the need for a new (X)HTML file or any changes to the existing markup.

Prepare the (X)HTML File

Although we covered this in Chapter 1, let's ensure that a print style sheet is specified in the <head> of the (X)HTML file, using the media attribute to describe the role of each style sheet.

```
<link rel="stylesheet" media="screen" type="text/css" href="screen.css" />
<link rel="stylesheet" media="print" type="text/css" href="print.css" />
```

The next step of course is to create the print.css file you have referenced in the <link> element. It is this style sheet where all the work will happen. Some designers copy all of their existing CSS from the screen style sheet into the new print style sheet and edit this down for the simpler print design. However, so long as you use the CSS from the next few steps, you will ensure that the printed version of your page is sleek, simple, and printable.

Think "Headed Paper"

Never lose sight of the fact that your beautifully designed web page will end up on a sheet of office paper. With this in mind, it pays to imagine the end result looking like an office memo or letter—simple margins, black text on headed paper.

First, ensure the background is white by declaring so in the body selector. Also set text to black here, and remove margins.

```
body {
  background-color:#fff;
  color:#000;
  margin:0;
  padding:40px;
  font: normal 14pt/160% verdana,arial,sans-serif;
}
```

Note also that the font-size is turned up to 14pt (always use point sizes for more accurate printing). Often, what seems like a large font-size on screen will be printed much smaller, so aim for a large font-size, and test the results with your own printer.

Serve an Appropriate Logo

Keeping the headed paper example in mind, if your site's logo is white text on a black background or might look a bit odd sat on a white background, you might want to invert or amend this using image-editing software. Ideally, dark text on a white background will suit the print layout and keep ink use down to a minimum, as you will see shortly in Figure 14-4.

Hide Unwanted Page Areas

Typically, the only part of the page you wish to print is the main column holding the article. Any other columns or elements you do not wish to print can be grouped in one selector and set to display:none.

```
/* Hide the following items */
  #sidebar_a, #sidebar_b, #footer  {
    display:none;
    }
```

Normally, it is not advisable to use display:none to hide whole areas of a page, as search engines might see this as suspicious behavior, and these areas will not be hidden if your style sheet is unavailable or removed. However, you can think of the printer as a dumb animal that sits in the corner, seeing as it is not used for viewing web pages, only printing them. Use display:none with confidence for print style sheets.

Change Headings

The next step is to tweak any headings used. Again, it is likely that these will work better with black text. Also, remember that you have increased the default font-size to 14pt; so heading font sizes will need to be increased accordingly, again using point sizes.

```
h2, h3, h4 {
  font-family:Arial,Verdana,sans-serif;
  font-weight:normal;
  line-height:135%;
  color:#000;
  }
h2 {
  font-size:22pt;
  }
h3 {
  font-size:18pt;
  }
h4 {
  font-size:16pt;
  }
h4 a:link, h4 a:visited {
  color:#000;
  text-decoration:none;
  }
```

Note that any headings containing links will also use black text as the :link and :visited pseudo elements are also given black text. There is no need to distinguish links from normal text on a printout, as it is hardly likely that anyone will want to click them!

Links Black

As with links within headings, all other links may as well be black too. Again, the :link and :visited pseudo elements are set to black, and underlines are removed.

```
/* Links black */
  a:link, a:visited, a:active {
    color:#000;
    text-decoration:none;
        }
```

Show URLs

While links need not be shown with color, a user is going to be pretty frustrated if a web site is mentioned in a printed article, but there is no clue given of how to find that site on the Web. It is therefore useful to actually print the URLs alongside mentioned web sites in certain sections of the page.

Earlier we looked at how CSS can generate content before and after an element using CSS pseudo elements (except for IE6 and below, and not initially in IE7). Here, the :after pseudo element is used to perform a specific function after each hyperlink.

The CSS here might look a little alien at first, but it is actually quite simple. Looking at the selector, notice first that we are targeting the main column, ensuring links outside of this column are not printed. Next, the selector seeks any links in this column as the <a> element is declared. Finally, the :after pseudo element is declared, informing the browser that any links within the main column are where this action should happen.

```
/* Show URLs only inside the article container */
  #main a:after {
  content: " (" attr(href) ")";
   font-size:11pt;
   }
```

The value declared for the content property is a little more complex, but it basically tells the browser to perform the action immediately after the content, which is the attribute href, and to place the generated content within brackets (which have to be surrounded with quotes).

Finally, a smaller font-size is set for the URLs using point size so that they do not detract too much from the main text on the printed page.

The Resulting Printed Page

These simple steps ensure that the printed version of the web page is quick and affordable to print, as well as being focused and stripped of anything unrelated. Figure 14-4 shows how these rules transform the Science City article originally shown in Figure 14-3. The difference is huge, and it's a small triumph for accessibility.

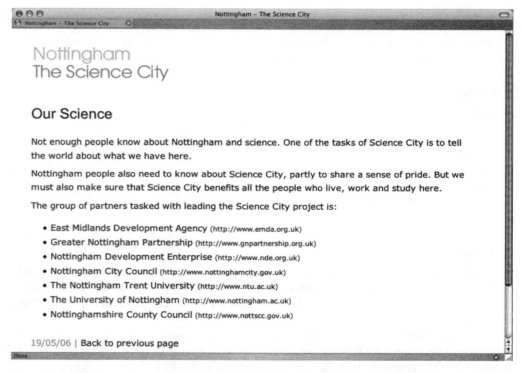

Figure 14-4. *Thanks to the print style sheet, the Science City web site is simplified and much easier to print.*

Mobile/Handheld Style Sheets

Also mentioned first in Chapter 1 were handheld style sheets. Although not supported by all mobile devices, the handheld media type is still in common use as browsers will ignore its content, allowing many cell phone or PDA users to access a stripped-down version of your styling depending upon support.

Delivering web content to handheld media devices is becoming more and more important, as browser-enabled cell phones become popular, and more of us want to stay updated while on the move.

Before we start, note that the technology is not standardized, and what works for one device may not work for another.

Prepare the (X)HTML File

The phone's browser will try its best to make use of your main style sheet. If you specify a handheld style sheet, it should use this instead. Use the `<link>` element since some handhelds don't recognize @import or @media. Some current handheld devices apply screen styles as well as handheld styles, while others ignore both.

```
<link rel="stylesheet" media="screen" type="text/css" href="screen.css" />
<link rel="stylesheet" media="print" type="text/css" href="print.css" />
<link rel="stylesheet" media="handheld" type="text/css" href="mobile.css" />
```

Remove Margin and Padding

Widths and margins can be detrimental to good handheld display. If a screen is only 176 pixels wide, you don't need a 10-pixel margin around your content. Set margin and padding to 0 straight away.

```
/* Remove all default margins and padding */
  div {
    margin:0;
    padding:0;
    }
```

Also, remove all width references from the CSS. Let content wrap the way it wants to. That way your site is better prepared to make sense on PDAs, large phone browsers, and so on.

Serve Up a Header Graphic

Take a look at the BBC site (www.bbc.co.uk) on your cell phone, and see how perfect the header is. This is the only graphic embellishment I'm suggesting, as it makes a great welcome for the user, and doesn't seem to affect download time or compromise page space. My header (see Figure 14-5) is 176 pixels in width by 20 pixels in height, and features my favicon and the name of the site. Simple. Note that the image looks smaller on the mobile device.

Figure 14-5. *Simple header image to be served for those browsing with a handheld device*

Serving this image requires no extra markup. The header selector in the screen style sheet might be used to create a large masthead with all sorts of child elements contained. For the handheld style sheet, however, the same selector simply serves up the mobile image.

```
#header {
  width:100%;
  height:20px;
  background:transparent url(/images/mobile.jpg) no-repeat;
  }
```

As a result, this image will only come into play when the site is viewed using a handheld device with support for the handheld media type.

Add Skip Links

Honestly, even if you don't usually use them (and you should, you know), "skip to content" and "back to top" anchor links are vital when using a mobile device, as scrolling can be a laborious process, and life is too short. Give users the opportunity to jump directly to your main content by linking to the ID of that element, bypassing the navigation menu.

```
<li><a href="#content" title="Skip to article">Skip to content</a></li>
```

And here, the same process is used, except that this link would target an ID nearer the top of the page, such as the main navigation.

```
<li><a href="#navigation" title="Jump to top of page">Back to top</a></li>
```

Remove Extraneous Styling Information

Less is definitely more here. Go through all of your normal styles (which you may have copied into your handheld style sheet) and remove anything hazardous. For example, you could remove all font properties, all background images, all link styling, and many embellishments such as borders and floats (you aren't going to be floating your columns on a 176-pixel-wide screen, are you?). Also, get rid of any navigation list styling. A bulleted unordered list is exactly what the user wants to see on a mobile device.

Make Decisions About Your Images

Don't ban images outright. Instead use CSS to decide which sections should have images removed. Most blogs have 300- to 400-pixel images in entries, which will download on a phone, but you'll only see the left side of them (although some mobile browsers such as Opera Mini will shrink images to fit the window). Images can be removed from certain sections using display:none.

```
#main img {
  display:none;
  }
```

Thus, you can decide in which IDs or classes you want to show images. I guess it's a matter of context. If you are discussing an image in an article, it makes sense to show it, even if it's only part of it. Apply a bit of common sense here, and do what's best for you.

display:none Is Your Friend

Finally, decide whether or not to hide more content from mobile users. Using `display:none` in your `sidebar` selector might be useful. Think about how much scrolling is required once your sidebar is sitting under your main content, and how navigation can become laborious. You could keep the sidebar and use anchors to help the users jump to it and back easily. This will obviously mean amendments to markup, so why not just get rid of the sidebar entirely?

```
/* Remove unwanted columns */
  #sidebar {
    display:none;
    }
```

Test with Opera

The Opera browser has a very useful feature—the **Small Screen** view. By enabling Small Screen, the browser will attempt to display your web site as it would appear when the `handheld` style sheet is used.

This can be an easier and more affordable way of testing your `handheld` style sheet. In Figure 14-6, the window has been narrowed to suggest the approximate width of the average cell phone. Notice that with the `handheld` style sheet in play, the header graphic appears first, and navigating is going to be a more difficult process owing to the increased height of the page. This is the time when "skip" links really come into their own.

Figure 14-6. *Using the Opera browser's Small Screen mode to simulate how Colly Logic looks on a handheld machine*

The Opera browser people have made a strong commitment to browsing the Web with small screens. While the main Opera browser still has a tiny share of the market, the Opera Mini browser (www.opera.com/products/mobile/operamini/), which can be downloaded to cell phones and other handheld devices, is growing in popularity. Always better than whatever default browser your device has, Opera Mini makes browsing the Internet while on the move a much more enjoyable process, and gives us all cause to be optimistic for the future of mobile browsing. There is also a simulation of this browsing experience you can check out (www.opera.com/products/mobile/operamini/demo.dml).

Handheld Compromises

Serving content for handheld devices is all about compromise. Until connections are faster, all users have the same browsers and screen size, and there is better support for CSS and other markup, we'll have to make sacrifices.

Look at your web pages as they appear on a computer. Think about which sections are important to you, and identify the parts you are most likely to want to access while on a train, in the pub, or skiing. Chances are another user's views would correlate with yours. Be ruthless, and chuck out the extraneous stuff. Serve up latest posts, comments, an archives list, and basic background information. The ability to check your comments on the move is liberating.

To Conclude...

As mentioned at the beginning, this chapter could have been enormous. It is worth remembering that without any CSS whatsoever, you can create a perfectly accessible web site. In fact, the misuse of CSS is often the ingredient that causes a site to be inaccessible. For example, the text might have been black on a white background, but you had to go and make it purple on pink.

With every move you make, stop to think. Is what you are about to introduce going to compromise accessibility? Will everything still make sense without images, CSS, or JavaScript? Just because your young eyes enjoy reading 9-pixel Copperplate text, will your grandmother agree as she accesses your site using her Blueberry?

Still, CSS can be employed to enhance the accessibility of every element of a web site, whether it be a form, an image, navigation—anything. Never feel discouraged from experimenting and keep pushing those boundaries. So long as you remember that you are one of 6 billion people, and that no two people are the same, you'll be fine.

■■■

CHAPTER 15

Tips, Tricks, and Troubles

Were there world enough and time, this chapter—like the others that preceded it—would remain focused around a particular topic. Unfortunately, there are 3.73 million topics related to CSS tips and tricks, and covering them all would demand a rather large and expensive book.

Therefore, this chapter is a bit of a smorgasbord, aiming to draw together the most common tips, tricks, and troubles. Over the next few pages, you'll find ideas for maximizing page space by manipulating overflowing content and learn to create incredibly simple CSS rollover images. Later, you'll enter the crazy world of hacks and filters, finding out how to serve separate style sheets to different browsers, before a final delve into common problems and quirks that you need to be aware of.

This chapter will cover

- Rollover images

- Overflow trickery

- Hacks and filters

- Troubleshooting

Rollover Images

A rollover image adds a simple bit of interaction for the user. Place the cursor over a rollover image, and another replaces it. For years, web designers preloaded on-state (i.e., on mouseover—when the mouse is rolled over the image) images to assist the browser in its rollover presentation. Preloading increases the weight of the initial download, but adds to usability by decreasing the wait time for an on-state image to appear. Basically, the browser would only start downloading the on-state image upon rollover, which was why preloading was so important.

In the Old Days

Before widespread adoption of CSS to achieve rollover images, this technique was done the hard way. Following is a typical example of the markup that was required for each and every rollover image. Please note that this chunk is *not* available as a code download!

```
<A HREF="target.html" onMouseOver="rollover('home')" onMouseOut="rollout('home')">
<IMG SRC="/images/home.gif" NAME="home" ALT="Home Page" BORDER="0" ➥
HEIGHT=130 WIDTH=115 ></A>
<SCRIPT TYPE="text/javascript">
<!--
setrollover("/images/home_over.gif");
//-->
</SCRIPT>
```

And this would be linked to a mammoth JavaScript file needed to perform the actual rollover function. Laborious and painful, there is thankfully a much better and easier way using CSS.

The (X)HTML

How is this for reduced markup? All that is required in the (X)HTML is the addition of a class to the <a> element.

```
<a href="target.html" class="rollover">Big Lee Hickman</a>
```

This unobtrusive additional markup allows you to take control of this particular link in any way you see fit using your style sheet.

The Image

Yes, image, not images. Just one image is required for this technique. To get around the preloading problem, both image states are combined as one image. This means that when the user rolls over the image, the on-state image is already available. The trick is to place the two versions side by side as one image, making very sure that each half is of an identical size (see Figure 15-1).

210 Pixels

157 Pixels

420 Pixels

Figure 15-1. *The rollover image is a combination of the two image states. Only one half will be visible at any time.*

With this dual-purpose image prepared, we can now think about the CSS that will be used to slide the image backward and forward depending on the link state.

The CSS

First, the `rollover` class is declared. All that is required is to assign the `width` and `height` of the visible area of the dual image and set the `display` to `block` (to ensure the dimensions are respected). Note that the dimensions match the measurements in Figure 15-1. Also, the image itself is added using the `background` property, set to `no-repeat`.

```
/* Rollover class */
  .rollover {
    display:block;
    width:210px;
    height:157px;
    background:url(/images/rollover.jpg) no-repeat;
    text-indent:-9999px;
      }
```

Note also that the text is indented using a huge negative value (`text-indent:-9999px`). This ensures that the link text does not show, unless the style sheet is turned off or unavailable. In that situation, the user would not see the image, but would still have a clickable text link.

One gotcha to be aware of is that Firefox will currently outline links when they are clicked, placing a thin line around them. While not usually a problem for standard links, if a link has a huge negative value, this is going to look rather ugly, especially with links appearing to the right of your layout. Thankfully, there is a very useful bit of CSS that can be employed to turn such outlines off for all link states, by utilizing the `outline` property as follows:

```
/* Turn off all browser link outlines */
  a {
    outline:none;
    }
```

The next step is to make the magic happen. Remember that in Chapter 7 you learned about the various pseudo link states? Well, these will now be used to create the rollover effect. The three states `:link`, `:visited`, and `:active` are grouped, as they share the same values. For each of these states, the first half of the dual image will be visible.

```
a.rollover:link, a.rollover:visited, a.rollover:active {
  background:url(/images/rollover.jpg) no-repeat;
  }
```

The most important step is to use the `:hover` state to reposition the dual image so that the second half (the rollover state) is in view. To do this, the image is repositioned 210 pixels to the left using a negative position value.

```
a.rollover:hover {
  background-position:-210px 0;
  }
```

This simple method slides the first half of the dual image out of view, bringing the second half into the available space. This happens instantly upon rollover, creating a seamless, simple rollover effect (see Figure 15-2).

Figure 15-2. *On rollover, the second half of the dual image appears automatically.*

It should go without saying that this technique is invaluable for all kinds of interactive images, especially buttons and navigation items. Just make sure that the link still makes sense should the dual image be unavailable.

The Overflow Property

The overflow property defines the way that a child element is displayed when it exceeds its containing element. In other words, if there is too much content, the overflow value will dictate how or whether it should be displayed.

Overflow Values

There are four possible values for the overflow property, as detailed in Table 15-1.

Table 15-1. *Overflow Values*

Value	Description
visible	The content is not clipped. It renders outside the element.
hidden	The content is clipped, but the browser does not display a scrollbar to see the rest of the content.
scroll	The browser displays a scrollbar even if there is enough room to display the entire content.
auto	If there is too much content, the browser will display a scrollbar to see the remainder.

Let's look at two values in particular: auto and hidden.

overflow:auto

I love overflow:auto trickery (whereby specifying the height of a <div> and applying overflow:auto creates a mock <iframe> without all the accessibility headaches of <iframe>s). Take a look at the Style Company web site in Figure 15-3. For this job, all pages needed to be the same height all the way across, regardless of how much content was used.

Figure 15-3. *The Style Company web site (www.stylecompany.co.uk) uses overflow management to ensure all pages are the same height, regardless of content.*

This was achieved by using a container with overflow: auto applied and a set height, ensuring that no matter how much information appears in the container, the total height of the page does not increase. Let's look at creating our own example—a simple news stream using CSS.

The (X)HTML

There is nothing special about the markup. All that is needed is a simple container. Here, it is given a class of stream to denote that it carries all the streamed news items.

```
<div class="stream">
  <p>All the stuff you wanna scroll goes in here.</p>
</div>
```

Note that for this example, you will need to paste plenty of content into this container to see the effect of the overflow, such as masses of Lorem Ipsum text. With that taken care of, we can move on to the nifty styling.

The CSS

Now define the stream selector. First, the size of the box is declared (here it is a square 300×300 pixels), and some padding is declared to ensure the content does not touch the border. Most importantly, the overflow property is given the auto value.

```
.stream {
  width:300px;
  height:300px;
  padding:10px;
  border:1px solid #999;
  background-color:#FFF;
  overflow:auto;
}
```

By giving the box a set height, you ensure that it does not expand or contract based on the content it holds. If there is more content than the box can hold, the scrollbar will automatically appear, allowing you to scroll through the whole text, as you see in Figure 15-4. Brilliant.

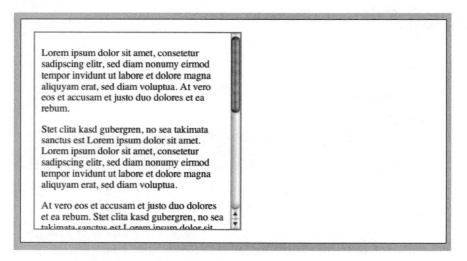

Figure 15-4. *Using overflow:auto to have a scrollbar appear when there is more content than the box can show*

The possibilities here are endless, but be wary of using multiple overflow boxes on your pages. A web page that features umpteen scrollbars can confuse users and look horrible! Still, this is a superb technique that shows great foresight from the creators of CSS.

overflow:hidden

There are occasions when you don't want the overflowing content to show, or you only wish it to appear in certain circumstances. This is where overflow:hidden comes in handy.

For example, you might have a beautiful photograph of some mountains that you wish to use as a banner image. This image is 796 pixels wide, and you know that if you add it to the page, it will always force the site to be at least that wide, and would force horizontal scrollbars if the window was decreased below that width. This is where overflow:hidden can come to your rescue. Let's do it!

The (X)HTML

For this example, I have an image that is 796 pixels in width by 320 pixels in height. The image needs to be placed into the (X)HTML page as follows:

```
<div id="masthead"><a href="#"><img src="images/mountains.jpg" ➥
alt="Mountain banner" width="796" height="320" /></a></div>
```

Note that the width and height of the image is declared to prevent the browser from waiting until after the image loads to render the rest of the layout (it will know how much space to use for the image and get on with implementing the CSS). This is of course totally optional.

The CSS

Here, the container div is also shown, so that you can see the context into which the banner will be placed. Following that, the CSS for the masthead ID is shown. Note that the width is a percentage value (100%) ensuring the masthead always fills the available space. The height is equal to that of the image it will hold. Finally, overflow:hidden is specified.

```
/* Container for all page content */
  #container {
    border:1px solid #000;
    padding:20px;
    background-color:#FFF;
    }
/* Masthead */
  #masthead {
    width:100%;
    height:320px;
    border:2px solid #999;
    background:#CCC;
    overflow:hidden;
    }
```

That is all you need to do. Figure 15-5 shows how the browser deals with the image at three different widths. Under normal circumstances, the thinnest window would force a horizontal scrollbar due to the larger width of the image. Thanks to hiding the overflow, this is skillfully avoided.

Figure 15-5. *Thanks to overflow:hidden, the containing element only reveals as much of the image as the window dictates.*

Combining Classes

It is possible to combine classes. This functionality provides real power when it comes to reusing elements. For example, you can use a containing element as often as you want, but you may not always want the elements it contains to be displayed in the same way. So, you could make several versions of the containing element and set the unique properties for each, but why would you want to repeat the margin, padding, and background styles for each and end up with more class names to worry about? This is where combined classes are really useful, as used on the Poptones web site (see Figure 15-6).

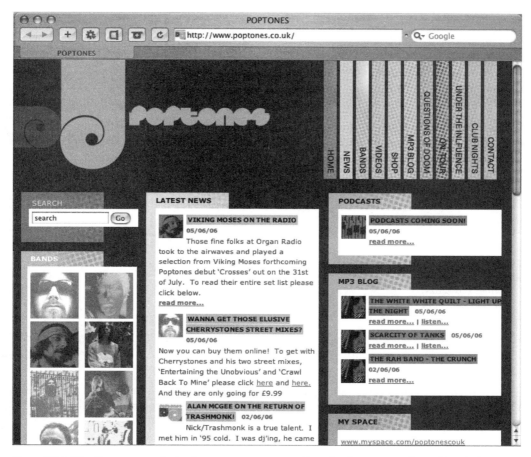

Figure 15-6. *The Poptones web site (www.poptones.co.uk) makes heavy use of combined classes to apply heading background colors that are in line with those of their containing boxes.*

Now, if you wanted an `<h3>` inside a particular `container` to have a red background, you might create the following styles:

```
h3 {
  font-size:110%;
  margin:10px 5px 10px 5px;
  padding:5px;
  }
.custom_background {
  background-color:#F00;
  }
```

You might then call that as follows:

```
<div class="container">
  <h2>Latest News</h2>
  <h3 class="custom_background">Man found in vase</h3>
    content
</div>
```

No! This is extra markup—forced to use a class attribute with each heading to define its color. Instead, create unique selectors for each section, keeping the existing <h3> declaration, and then creating a set of background styles with semantically meaningful names:

```
.news h3{
  background:#F00;
  }
.entertainment h3{
  background:#666;
  }
.sport h3{
  font-size:110%;
  background:#CCC;
  }
.music h3{
  background:#999;
  }
```

Then, all you need to decide is the purpose for each container. Let's say you add a container to house articles about sport. Add the sport attribute to the existing container class, separating the two class names with a whitespace character:

```
<div class="container sport">
  <h2>Sports News</h2>
  <h3>England win 26-0</h3>
    content
</div>
```

Suddenly, all instances of a <h3> heading inside this container take on the light gray background color. Exchange the word "sport" for "music" and now all headings in that container have a darker gray background. Remove the heading rule entirely, and headings have no background color at all.

Hacks and Filters

Hacks and filters are always lumped together it seems. Few talk of one without mentioning the other. However, the two are distinctly different.

Hacks use invalid CSS or parsing bugs—that is, methods of having the CSS work even though the syntax used is not correct (not opening and closing with a curly brace, for example). **Filters** on the other hand use valid CSS that the targeted browser just doesn't support.

CSS hacks and filters can help you selectively apply CSS (or not apply it as the case may be) to various elements. Always remember, though, that instead of using them any time you hit a snag, try finding a more standard cross-browser way to achieve the effect you're after first before resorting to them.

Let's look at hacks in more detail. You have already worked through a hack—The Box Model hack (Chapter 11). You now know that hacks use either naughty CSS or incorrect syntax to make their mark. Hacks exploit the broken bits of browsers—the bits that prevent a browser from being considered "modern" or "standards-compliant," for example. It is very important to consider that these browser manufacturers may or will eventually fix these errors, which might not only render your hacks useless, but also mean your style sheet malfunctions totally.

Safe Hacks

There are some hacks that can be considered as *safe*. Netscape 4 and IE5/Mac are not being developed any more. What we have now are, for better or (usually) worse, the definitive, final versions of these browsers. There will never be a next version that could make a mess of your pages, and therefore it could be considered OK to let these hacks live in your CSS for all time. Let's look at a couple of example hacks.

@import

Early browsers are notorious for malfunctioning when presented with CSS rules they don't understand (Netscape 4 will crash at the sight of certain rules). The @import hack allows you to hide entire style sheets from Netscape 4 and older browsers because they don't understand it— as you learned way back in Chapter 1, the @import rule links to an external style sheet from within another style sheet (be it external or in a <style> element within the <head> of the (X)HTML document). Interestingly, early browsers do not understand this approach and simply ignore it and therefore also the style sheet it refers to.

Using @import

Here is a simple guide to using the @import hack. First, you will begin with two style sheets:

- basic.css (only simple rules for early browsers)

- modern.css (advanced CSS2, rules to override rules in basic.css)

Next, create a third style sheet called import.css that contains only the following:

```
@import "modern.css";
```

Then, link the basic.css and import.css in the <head> of the (X)HTML document.

```
<link rel="stylesheet" type="text/css" href="basic.css" />
<link rel="stylesheet" type="text/css" href="import.css" />
```

Note that the basic.css style sheet must be linked first.

The Effect

Here's what happens. All older browsers (compliant with the original CSS1 specification) will load `basic.css` and `import.css`. However, only modern browsers will understand the `@import` rule and therefore only they will see `modern.css`. As `modern.css` is linked after `basic.css`, its rules will override those in the latter style sheet.

Caio Hack

The Caio hack is named after a bloke called Caio Chassot who invented it. This hack is used to hide certain rules from Netscape 4 (rather than the whole style sheet as with the `@import` hack).

How Do We Say "Caio"?

This hack makes use of a comment like this to begin hiding from Netscape 4:

```
/*/*/
```

This is almost identical to a correct comment, the same as those discussed in Chapter 1; however, there is a forward slash inserted where spaces and words would normally be placed. The poor old browser thinks the comment didn't close, and will therefore ignore all following CSS. To stop the ignorance, just add another standard comment, and Netscape 4 will jump back to life and start reading your CSS again.

Example Caio

Take a look at the following CSS. Note the use of traditional comments within the list of rules, and the single use of the Caio hack (comments highlighted in bold).

```
body {
  color:#000;
  background:#FFF;
 }

/* Netscape 4 is looking the other way */
/*/*/
  body {
    background-image:url(images/we_hate_netscape_banner.jpg);
    }

/* Bring Netscape 4 back into the room */
  ...remaining CSS follows
```

With this example, all browsers (including Netscape 4) will see the first body selector and render black text on a white background. After the hack, however, a background image is specified that shouts "We Hate Netscape!" As this comes after the Caio hack and before the comment that brings Netscape's focus back, this offensive image will not show on that browser. As Netscape 4 is not being developed further, you can use this hack safe in the knowledge that no sudden updates will expose your hatred.

Hide Style Sheets from All but IE/Mac

This super-useful hack is a method of serving style sheets to IE5/Mac only. It validates, and also appears to work for, IE 4.5/Mac, although that version is now extremely rare.

The IE/Mac sheet is linked as follows.

```
<style type="text/css">
  @import("ie-mac.css");
</style>
```

Be very careful not to leave a space between @import and (", otherwise the hack will not work as intended. IE/Mac was once the most standards-compliant browser in existence, but soon its shortcomings with CSS became obvious as better browsers came into being. By serving IE5/Mac-specific styles, dealing with this browser can be a little less problematic. Also, the fact that Microsoft will never, ever upgrade it means that this hack is perfectly safe. Ideally, all Mac users would be browsing with Safari, Camino, or Firefox, but we can't take this for granted (yet).

IE7 Is Coming

Looming over the horizon, like a potentially troubling but nonetheless welcome new friend, is Internet Explorer 7, expected to ship—annoyingly—around about the same time as this book. As such, this author hasn't explored it fully, but so far so good, in that many of IE6's failings have been corrected, and a number of those trusty old hacks will no longer be necessary. As the public beta shows, most of the really annoying CSS bugs from IE6 are now fixed. What's more, there is finally support for a range of CSS2 (and even CSS3) selectors. Let's have a street party! Well, after we've updated all our web sites to make sure they still work in IE7, given that the IE hacks we've used now break our sites in IE7!

The IE7 team have dropped support for the Star HTML hack, which targets problems in IE5 and IE6 that are pretty much removed from IE7. I heartily recommend you read Dave Shea's article "Stop Hacking, Or Be Stopped" (www.thinkvitamin.com/features/css/stop-css-hacking) if you demand more enquiry into IE7 and what it means for CSS hacks.

There are one or two hacks and filters that may be worth readying for IE7, however, especially during the initial evaluation period. Let's look at a couple.

Conditional Commenting

Your old hacks won't work—mostly. The IE team has publicly moaned about hacks—kind of like kids who made a cool exhibit at the science fair, only to have some bullies come along and tell them that while it's great that they invented a money machine, it's too bad that it's held together with duct tape. The IE boys are in favor of an IE-proprietary method known as **conditional comments**. Let's look at what this means.

Out with the Star HTML Hack

Since IE5/Win, web designers have used code like this to filter a rule to IE/Win:

```
* html #selector {
  width:100px;
  }
```

This is known as the Star HTML hack, again exploiting a parsing bug to send different values only to IE5 and upwards. As it is a hack, the best thing to do is avoid it.

The New Way

We should instead be using valid conditional comment syntax to serve up a link to an external CSS file that will contain the IE-specific CSS. Here's an example of the conditional comment that would be placed in the (X)HTML document's <head>, above or below the link to the main style sheet used for other browsers.

```
<!--[if IE]>
  <link rel="stylesheet" href="ie-specific.css" />
<![endif]-->
```

And then in the IE-specific CSS file, the rule that was once the essence of the hack can now be placed neatly in the style sheet.

```
#selector {
  width:100px;
  }
```

This is much better. Conditional comments are authorized, and the IE team won't ever send the FBI to your house for using them. They validate, and even though they're proprietary, when used with discretion, they allow us to accomplish exactly the same thing as CSS hacks.

A Hack Specifically for IE7? If You Must...

At the time of writing, IE7-specific hacks are materializing, such as the Triple-X hack. A targeted CSS filter for IE7, this hack applies or excludes CSS specifically from the newcomer. I'm not one to condone hacks, but then again I never use a ratchet, yet I have one in the tool shed just in case. If you need to know more, go forth to Brothercake's site (www.brothercake.com/site/resources/reference/xxx/) for further instruction.

Troubleshooting

Here is a section that could easily have spanned 426 pages. Every day, vocal CSS users publish more and more findings about quirks, problems, and bugs. Likewise, each designer has his or her own recommendations for more productive CSS.

This is a list of perhaps the most common problems those new to CSS might encounter. If these tips don't help you, don't be downhearted. The CSS community is big, sharing, and search-engine optimized, so get with the Google for a quick answer to your problem if it isn't covered here.

Common Problems

I recommend reading through these problems even if you are currently content. It pays to be aware of the kind of issues that may well crop up, some of which apply to more general CSS use too. Let's begin with a fairly detailed overview of one of the most annoying issues—margin collapsing.

Margin Collapsing

If we're on the subject of mysterious quirks, it makes sense to start with margin collapsing, which will hurt you at some point. The problem can manifest itself in one of two ways when two elements meet: either extra whitespace appears that just can't be removed or you suddenly are unable to add whitespace using margin values. Believe it or not, this is actually supposed to happen!

Example One

In the example shown in Figure 15-7, both paragraph elements have been given a 20-pixel margin. However, because the bottom margin of the first paragraph touches the top margin of the second paragraph, the margins collapse, making the space between both paragraphs 20 pixels instead of 40.

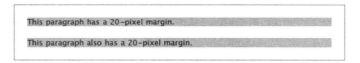

Figure 15-7. *Margin collapse sees only one of the 20-pixel margins having effect.*

Example Two

This doesn't just happen when one block-level element follows another; it also happens when the second element (the light gray paragraph) is the child of the first (the darker gray container) as in Figure 15-8. The top and bottom margins of the paragraph collapse into the margins of the div, leaving just a 20-pixel vertical margin around both elements. Crumbs.

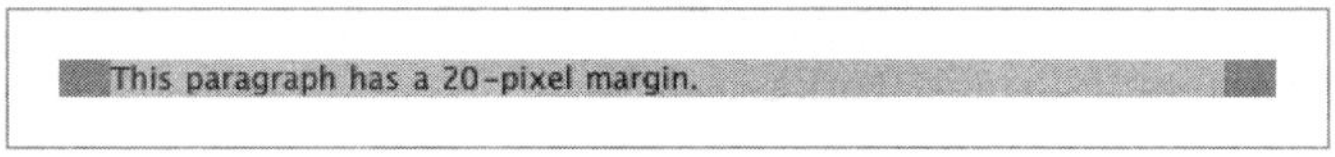

Figure 15-8. *Even with child elements, one of the specified margins has no effect.*

The Solution

There are a number of ways to get around margin collapsing. The easiest is to add a border or 1px of padding around the elements so that the margins no longer touch and therefore no longer collapse (see Figure 15-9).

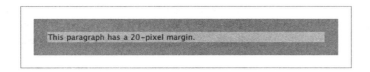

Figure 15-9. *Adding a border or padding value separates the margins and prevents the collapse.*

If relevant, you can also stop margins collapsing by changing the `position` property of the element. Margins of absolutely and relatively positioned boxes don't collapse. Also, if you `float` an element, its margins should no longer collapse. This may or may not be possible, of course.

Perfect Percentage Values Still Break Your Layout

As if life weren't difficult enough as it is, sometimes 50% + 50% does not add up to 100%—not with browsers anyway. The actual value could be 100.1%, which will force some layouts to break in some browsers. To find out if this is happening to you, try changing 50% to 49%, and then retest your layout. Always worth a try.

Flash of Unstyled Content

If for some reason you rely on `@import` alone to import your style sheet(s), you may notice that Internet Explorer will show unformatted (X)HTML for a second or two before applying the CSS. This can be avoided by adding just one `<link>` element or `<script>` element inside the document's `<head>`. For further investigation, take a look at "Flash of Unstyled Content (FOUC)" over at the Blue Robot site (`www.bluerobot.com/web/css/fouc.asp`).

The Selector Has a Matching Element, but Nothing Happens

This is all down to case sensitivity. To cut a short story shorter, if you have a CSS selector called `leftColumn` (note the uppercase C), the value in the (X)HTML must also use identical case. This problem typically occurs with Mozilla-based browsers.

The Background Image Will Not Display

The image is on the server, but it will not show as a background image. You load it via its direct URL in the browser, and there it is, so why not via CSS? Chances are that you have specified the image with quotation marks (`background:url("image.gif");`), which is wrong, but oh so easy to do. Remove the quotations, and the image should appear. The main culprit here is IE5/Mac, as most other browsers will spot your stupidity and work around it.

Recommendations

Here follows several of this author's own favorite tips for fitter, happier, more productive CSS management. None of these are rules or regulations, but they have certainly helped me.

Use a Modern, Standards-Compliant Browser

This will ensure your (X)HTML and CSS will be more on the button from the start, and you won't have to hack as much to support other browsers. Ideally, you should use a Mozilla browser (such as Firefox), Safari, or Opera—and not IE. Working within an outdated browser can have you relying on its inaccurate rendering. Always start with what you know is right and then amend if necessary for elderly browsers. This will also ensure that the whole experience is infinitely more pleasurable.

Avoid Reliance on the Box Model Hack

Earlier in this chapter you learned of the care needed when using hacks of any kind. Remember that as current browsers are updated and bugs are fixed, your hacks might come back to haunt you. You can avoid reliance on the Box Model hack (see Chapter 11 for a recap) by applying padding to the parent element instead of the child that has a fixed width specified.

Track Down Errors by Commenting Out Areas of the Style Sheet

This is a top, top tip, especially useful when your familiarity with a style sheet has waned, or you are working with one created by another person. Often you will find an error in the rendered design, or need to track down a particular problem. The best initial approach is to comment out half of the style sheet and reload the page. If the problem persists, remove the commenting and apply it to the other half. Once you know which half the problem lives in, you can use similar mass commenting to delve in further until you find the culprit. This method is particularly helpful when trying to understand a particular inheritance woe.

Avoid Aggressive Style Sheet Caching During Development

If (like this author's ISP) your Internet service provider caches your style sheets on site, you are going to have a hard time seeing all those little tweaks and changes—until probably Thursday, when they flush it out.

To get around this problem, forget external style sheets while developing. Embed your CSS in the <head> of your test page, forcing it to reload each time you view the page. When it is time to launch, or create further pages, then you can move the CSS from the document into its own external style sheet. This approach isn't always possible, but that is why recommendations are not laws.

Stopped Using a Style? Remove It

I do it. My grandmother does it, and so will you. During development, you will try out styles, use them for a while, and then move on, doing things another way. That is fine, but you end up with lots of unused styles littering your style sheet.

This isn't a major problem, although any unwanted code adds to overall page weight. The main issue is how these unwanted styles might affect those in use. Knowing what you learned about inheritance and the cascade in Chapter 2, you'll be aware that these harmless extraneous styles might be influencing others, causing the oddities on your rendered page. Play safe and either comment them out or remove them altogether.

Validate Your Code

Your CSS looks right. You know it's right, so why isn't it doing what you think it should? Obviously there could be several negative factors, but often it is nothing more than badly formed (X)HTML.

Validated code isn't necessarily accessible code, but it's at least well formed. Run your (X)HTML through the validator to find any unclosed elements or other oversights. Think of your CSS as being like a really expensive Prada coat. It looks much better on Kate Moss than on a bicycle.

To Conclude...

This chapter has hopefully . . . hey, hang on! This is the penultimate chapter. Quickly, put the kettle on and break out the Christmas biscuits—you are a CSS professional!

Over the last 15 chapters, you've blossomed from a mere seed planted in slightly damp cotton wool into a glorious tree full of early springtime flowers. Sure, you have plenty more growing to do, but already people are impressed by your development. Is that a squirrel on your shoulder?

The final chapter of this book is the glorious *Dead Goods* case study—just over the page. This case study will tie together much of what we have been through, drawing examples from each chapter to produce a living, breathing, CSS-based web site. The proof of the pudding is in its standards compliance, as they say.

■ ■ ■

CHAPTER 16

Case Study: *The Dead Goods*

Yes, it's true. On the morning of 12 May 2006, six supposedly dead rock stars walked into the offices of Colly Logic Records and announced their intentions to bring their music to the world once more. The six—Jimi Hendrix, John Lennon, Kurt Cobain, Jeff Buckley, Janis Joplin, and Keith Moon—have actually been on a small island called Flatey just off the coast of Iceland all along, piecing together the songs for their comeback album *Six Feet Over*. Regrettably, founder member Elvis Presley backed out at the eleventh hour, citing ongoing commitments with his cod farm as the reason for his withdrawal.

Anyway, the world awaits, and *The Dead Goods* are going to blow every mind on the planet. In the '60s, '70s, '80s, and '90s, these guys spread the word with peace, love, and good will—but this is 2006, and the band needs a web site. Get the kettle on, kid—you got the job!

The Case Study

The Dead Goods case study errs on the side of complex, but never strays past what you have learned in this book. Basically, it shows you what you can achieve using simple CSS, a large pot of tea, and a sprinkling of ambition.

The layout is reusable in that it is robust enough to cope with most things you can throw at it. The use of images will hopefully get your brain ticking and allow you to think outside of the box by suggesting methods for combining background images that join up to break the boxy nature of much CSS-based design.

The techniques used are *bulletproof* in that they are simple enough not to break no matter how users scale or manipulate your layout as they browse. All in all, it's a contradiction of seriousness and playfulness, and I think you'll enjoy it.

The Process

This case study loosely attempts to emulate the role of the humble CSS designer and his or her position as part of a production line. For example, a design agency might have one person producing mock-ups, another creating the (X)HTML content, and then poor old you at the end tasked with fighting browser inconsistencies, cascades, inheritance, and the limits of CSS as a design tool in comparison with Photoshop's ability to make dreams come true. No worries though—you'll show 'em!

Let's look at three key stages of a typical web build: design, content, and presentation.

Design

Figure 16-1 shows the Photoshop template as it might be delivered from the Photoshop kid. This is what we have to transform into a working CSS design.

Figure 16-1. The Dead Goods *design as mocked up using Photoshop. No code at this stage.*

The mock-up is the result of numerous attempts to emulate the imaginary album artwork and branding supplied by the imaginary record company. During this part of the process, the Photoshop kid may have little or no consideration for the limitations of CSS, although occasionally the CSS designer might provide an underlying grid and a few ground rules. The benefit of this approach is freedom from thinking about boxes and the limits of the web, hence such mock-ups often have images that stretch beyond containers, weird layering, and awkward transparencies among other idealistic treatments.

Guides and Layers

Typically, a mock-up created in Photoshop might use guides (thin horizontal and vertical markers you can drag) to emphasize the underlying grid and also make it easier for the CSS designer to carve up the images (see Figure 16-2).

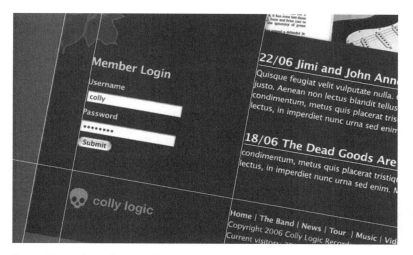

Figure 16-2. *Photoshop guides are used to define the grid and ensure items are aligned.*

Layers (often grouped into folders such as Text, Link States, or similar) allow the designer to hide or reveal areas of the mock-up either individually or many at a time, making the CSS designer's job easier by removing text and images to reveal backgrounds, for example.

Using guides and layers smooths the transition from Photoshopper to coder and can help each side understand a little more about the other's role and approach.

■**Note** *The Dead Goods* mock-up is available to download as a layered Photoshop (PSD) file with guides and further information at www.csswebdevelopment.com/casestudy. The PSD file is also available at www.apress.com.

Content

The content is pure (X)HTML, possibly with a little JavaScript, PHP, or other technology thrown in. Basically, it has no CSS—at all. The only nod toward CSS might be the dividing of the content into page regions, such as `<div>` elements that the CSS designer can utilize for layout. The beauty of getting the content done first is that you know it is separate from presentation. It will make sense without CSS (see Figure 16-3), and apart from additional markup added at the CSS designer's discretion for more intricate styling, the content should remain uncompromised and clean.

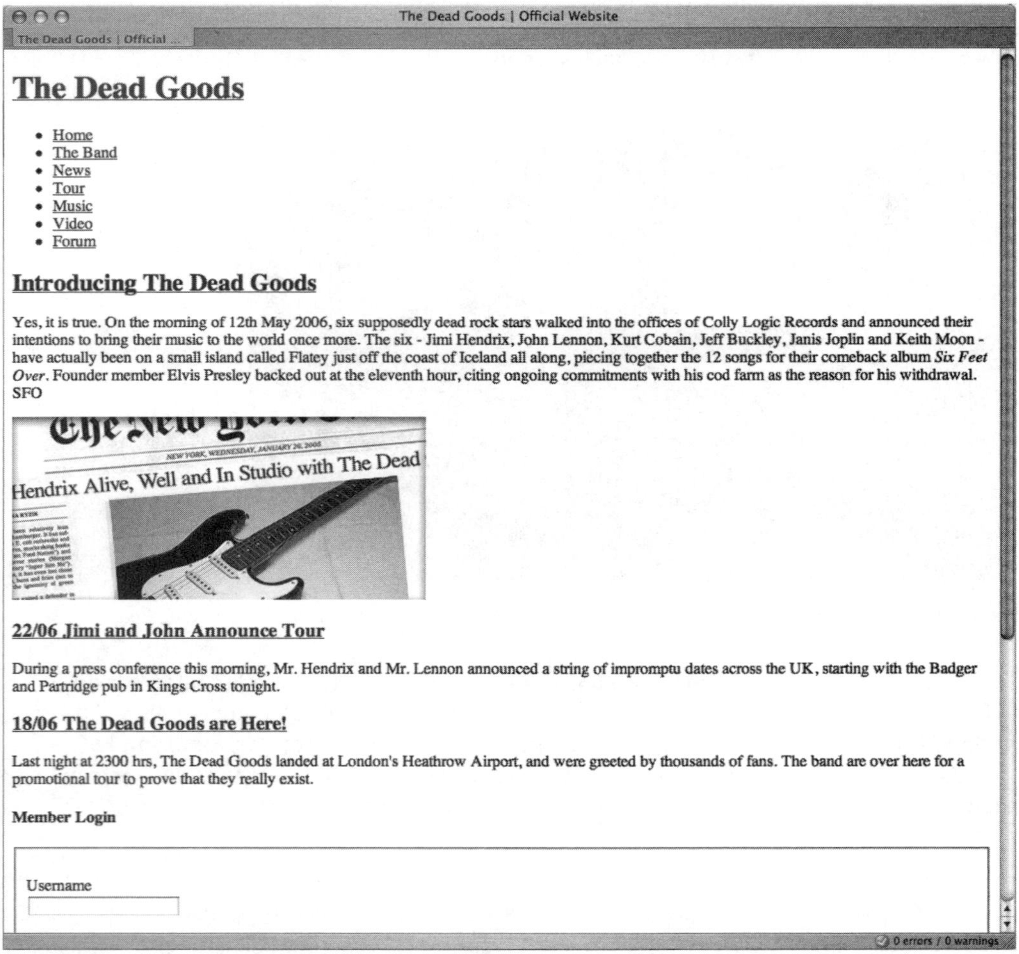

Figure 16-3. *Pure (X)HTML content created with little thought for CSS at this stage*

Presentation

The final part of the process lies with the CSS wizard. With a visual mock-up loaded in Photoshop and a working (X)HTML template loaded in the browser, the CSS work can begin in earnest. It is at this stage that the CSS designer has to make crucial decisions about how to approach the styling, with heavy choices about layout, background images, and usability making it less than easy to jump in with both feet.

Setting Up

As well as the PSD files mentioned earlier, two other files are available to download at www.csswebdevelopment.com/casestudy, plus a zip file of the images used. The deadgoods.html and deadgoods.css files are complete, and feature all of the examples in this case study. It is up to you to choose whether you follow this chapter and use these files as reference or empty the style sheet and rebuild it as you go along.

All images (including background images) are placed in a directory called images, one step up from the root directory.

Wireframing the Layout

OK, let's get started. Back in Chapter 3 you learned about applying borders to divs and other elements to create wireframes, which help you understand how one element relates to another, and also identify problems with alignment and juxtaposition. This case study, being based upon a mock-up that uses Photoshop guides, can be easier to relate to the intentions of the mock-up by applying wireframes.

In deadgoods.css, wireframes are created by applying a 1px border to all <div> elements. In the style sheet the border for the div selector is set to 0. To see the red wireframes, just change this to 1px.

```
/* Wireframing - place borders around all div elements during development */
  div {
    margin:0;
    padding:0;
    border:1px solid #F00;
    }
```

Note If you decide to use wireframes, you will need to set the sidebar to 306px rather than 310px to compensate for the four vertical borders of the two main columns. God bless the Box Model.

A useful alternative for wireframing is the outline property. Outlines do not affect the width of an element in the same way that borders do, but are only supported in Firefox and Safari.

```
/* Wireframing - place borders around all div elements during development */
  div {
    margin:0;
    padding:0;
    outline:1px solid red;
    }
```

Bodywork

The main action is going to be centered in the browser window. Looking back at the cross-browser method covered in Chapter 3, let's make use of the text-align property in the <body> to center the container element. By doing this, all child elements within container will inherit that value and center all their content, so we need to use text-align:left for the columns and footer later.

```
/* Declare body first of all */
  body {
    text-align:center
    }
```

Container

The container, although the parent of every other element in the layout, isn't actually essential. The width value that defines the total width of the content could have been added to the body selector, as could the margin values.

The reason for using container is the background color. Later on, two columns of uneven length will be used. As you will remember from Chapter 12, we often need to use *faux columns* to suggest columns of equal height. As the two columns in this case will both be the same color, we can just use a flat color, sampled from the mock-up. As all other elements will be placed on top of the container, it will fill in any gaps left by uneven columns, preventing the page background from showing through the gaps.

```
/* Container */
  #container {
    width:760px;
    margin:20px auto;
    background:#211E0E;
    }
```

With the container centered in the browser window, it is now time to start carving up the content area into typical regions, similar to those used in Chapter 11.

Masthead

The masthead is very simple at this stage. By grabbing the dimensions of the masthead image from the mock-up, we can see that it is the full width of the container by a height of 263 pixels. As the masthead is block level by default, it will stretch to fit the container horizontally, so we only need to define the height.

```
/* Masthead and descendants */
  #masthead {
    height:263px;
    }
```

Columns

Here we hit the first big decision of the build. How are we going to create the two columns? In this case, from looking at the (X)HTML content, it is clear that although the main content comes before the less important Member Login form, it will need to appear on the right of the Member Login form in the design.

The easiest method is to use floats here. If we float the main column (mainCol) to the right, we can then float the second column (sidebar) right also. As the main content comes first in the (X)HTML, the document flow will place this farthest right, with the next chunk (sidebar) floated just before it.

The Main Column

So, we first define styles for mainCol, and float it to the right. Note that a set width of 450 pixels is declared (exactly the same as the mock-up), and due to the text-align:center declaration in the container, we must also set the content to align left.

```
/* The main column and descendants */
  #mainCol {
    float:right;
    width:450px;
    text-align:left;
    }
```

The Sidebar

The total width of the container is 760 pixels. The main column is 450 pixels wide, which means the sidebar needs to be 310 pixels. The column is floated to the right, and again we must override the text-align value of the container.

```
/* The left column and descendants */
  #sidebar {
    float:right;
    width:310px;
    text-align:left;
    }
```

Footer

The final main division is the footer. In Chapter 10, you looked at methods for clearing floated elements, and this is something we need to do here. If the floats are not cleared, the footer won't acknowledge the end of both columns, only the shortest. As the footer contains child elements, it too needs to override the center alignment it inherits from container.

```
/* The footer and descendants */
  #footer {
    clear:both;
    text-align:left;
    }
```

Organized Layout

With the `container`, `masthead`, both columns, and the `footer` mapped out, what was previously a linear (X)HTML template is now an organized layout, as you see in Figure 16-4.

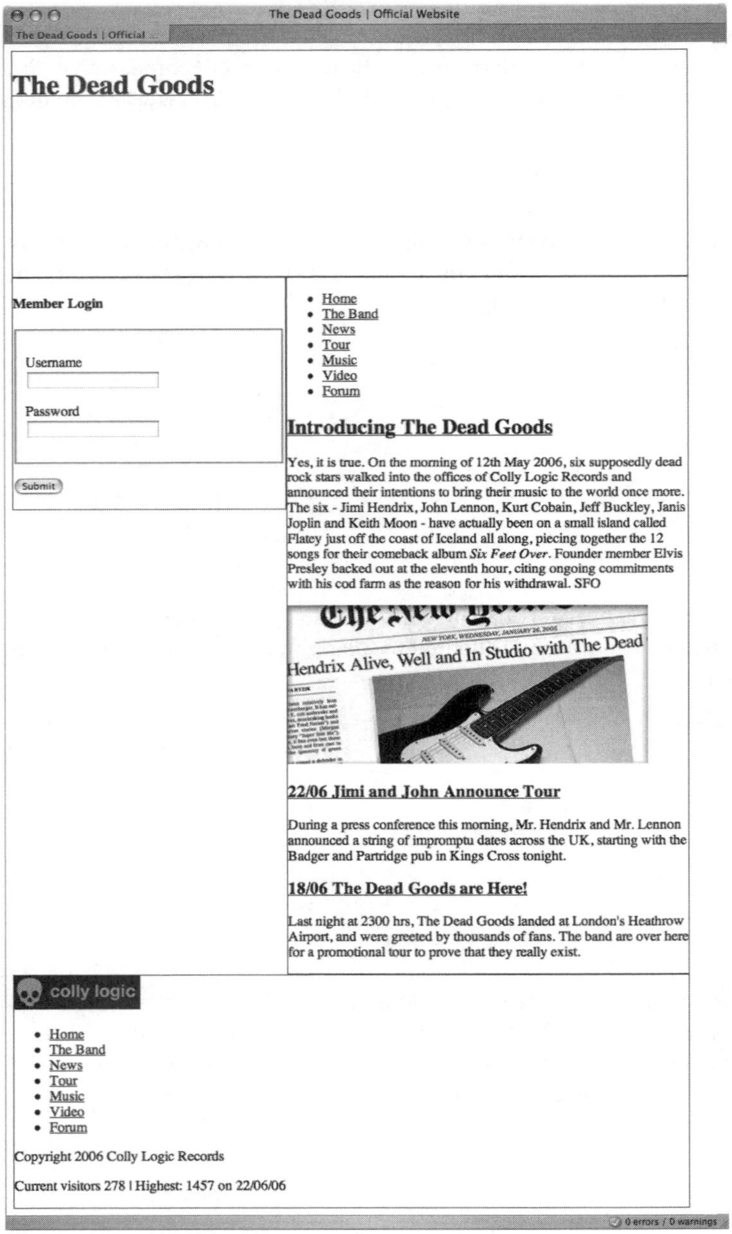

Figure 16-4. *The styling begins. Wireframed div elements are used to organize the content and define a basic layout.*

■ **Note** Figure 16-4 shows the layout with the `background` color removed from `container` and wireframe borders added to describe the divisions more clearly.

Background Work

The next stage involves some coloring-in using background images cut from the mock-up, and the work done at this stage pulls the design together very quickly. Although the design includes several large background images, each uses as much flat color as possible, making them ideal to be saved as GIFs, creating smaller file sizes than more complex images. Let's look at the four main page regions and the background images for each in turn.

Masthead Background

The masthead background image fills the region exactly. The `masthead.gif` image, which you see in Figure 16-5, is 760×263 pixels, saved with 32 colors, and (according to Photoshop) will take approximately 5 seconds to download on a 56K modem.

Figure 16-5. *The masthead.gif image*

Returning to the `masthead` selector in `deadgoods.css`, the image is declared using the background shortcut property. Note that the `background-repeat` value `no-repeat` is used. This is not necessary, but is good practice should the dimensions of the `masthead` area be altered slightly.

```
/* Masthead and descendants */
  #masthead {
    height:263px;
    background:url(masthead.gif) no-repeat;
    }
```

Sidebar Background

For the sidebar (`leftCol`), the leaf motif is used as a strong feature. For this, an image called `back_leftcol.gif` (see Figure 16-6) is used, again saved with 32 colors, and takes approximately

4 seconds to download on an old modem. Note that the first part of the black curve appears in this image. This curve will need to meet with the curve in the main column image later on.

Figure 16-6. *The back_leftcol.gif image*

The trick here is to combine this image with a matching background color (Hex 211E0E) sampled using Photoshop's eyedropper tool. This color is declared alongside the image path as part of the background shorthand property. Notably, this image is also set to show only once using no-repeat.

```
/* The left column and descendants */
  #sidebar {
    float:right;
    width:310px;
    background:#211E0E url(back_leftcol.gif) no-repeat;
    text-align:left;
    }
```

Main Column Background

For the main column (mainCol), the image back_rightcol.gif, shown in Figure 16-7, is used. The main role of this image is to extend the curve started in the sidebar's background image.

Figure 16-7. *The back_rightcol.gif image*

Again, this image will only show once and is also combined with a matching background color.

```
/* The main column and descendants */
  #mainCol {
    float:right;
    width:450px;
    background:#211E0E url(back_rightcol.gif) no-repeat;
    text-align:left;
    }
```

Remember that these columns are children of the container element. As container uses the same background color as the columns, one can always be shorter than the other without the main page background showing through.

Footer Background

Finally, the leaf motif is again used at the far right of the footer. The image is back_footer.gif (see Figure 16-8), saved in the same way as the previous background images.

Figure 16-8. *The back_footer.gif image*

The same background color and background-repeat values are used, but this time around background-position values are used to position the image at the far right bottom of the footer region.

```
/* The footer and descendants */
  #footer {
    clear:both;
    background:#211E0E url(back_footer.gif) right bottom no-repeat;
    text-align:left;
    }
```

Before we move on to child elements of the main page regions, there is just one more background job to be done.

Page Background

As the container is 760 pixels wide and centered in the browser window, the default white page background shows almost all the time. Therefore, we return to the body selector and declare a mid-gray sampled from the mock-up.

```
/* Declare body first of all */
  body {
    background-color:#666;
    text-align:center;
    }
```

Background Work Completed

With these four key background images in place, the template is beginning to resemble the mock-up, as shown in Figure 16-9. Obviously, no consideration has been placed on any of the text as yet, but that'll come next.

Figure 16-9. *Background images and background color applied to the page regions*

Text Treatment

With the bulk of the layout and coloring-in completed, it is time to think about content—specifically the text. When dealing with existing content, it is actually quite fun to get to the text-tweaking stage. This is where all that knowledge of line-height, text sizes, and color can allow you to experiment and find a sensible balance for the template.

Back to Body

The first job here is to take control of the text by declaring some defaults. Way back in Chapter 2 you learned about basing em sizes upon an initial percentage declaration, where all em values can be related to an actual pixel size. This method uses the default value of the font size in the browser style sheet, which cascades into deadgoods.css as a starting point.

As with Chapter 2's example, we'll use a percentage value of 62.5% of the default font size. Also rolled into the font shorthand is the preferred typeface and secondary choices.

```
/* Declare body first of all */
  body {
    background:#666;
    font:normal 62.5% 'Lucida Grande',Verdana,sans-serif;
    text-align:center;
    }
```

This will make an instant difference to the look of the template, but there is more to be done.

Headings

The next task is to wrestle back some control of the headings used in the template. Where values are the same for two or more headings, the declarations are grouped, as with the color values for h2 and h3 selectors. Otherwise, declarations vary, so font sizes based upon the initial percentage value in the body selector and unique margins are declared with individual selectors.

The margin values (used to space headlines away from elements above them) are not given as shorthand, so that we only overrule a specific margin, inheriting the default browser style sheet values for the others. The h4 (used for the Member Login heading) is given an orange color sampled from the orange rays of the masthead image.

```
/* All headings and versions of */
  h2, h3 {
    color:#FFF;
    }
  h2 {
    margin-top:40px;
    font-size:1.6em;
    }
  h3 {
    margin-top:30px;
    font-size:1.5em;
    }
```

```
h4 {
  font-size:1.3em;
  color:#FFE86C;
  }
```

The (X)HTML content uses <h2> and <h3> elements for article headlines, and these act as links to the full articles. Unless overridden, these links will be the default blue as specified by the browser style sheet. Therefore, the link states within <h2> and <h3> elements are targeted using the following grouped selectors:

```
h2 a:link, h2 a:visited, h3 a:link, h3 a:visited {
  color:#FFF;
  }
h2 a:hover, h3 a:hover {
  color:#FFE86C;
  }
```

Column Text

Next the actual article text needs to be considered, by adding declarations to the mainCol selector. Again, the font-size value is based upon the original percentage value in the body, and the color is declared as light gray (CCC)—much easier to read than pure white on dark backgrounds. Note also that line-height is used (as if I wouldn't!) to allow the lines some breathing space and make things more legible.

```
/* The main column and descendants */
  #mainCol {
    float:right;
    width:450px;
    font-size:1.1em;
    line-height:150%;
    color:#CCC;
    background:#211E0E url(back_rightcol.gif) no-repeat;
    text-align:left;
    }
```

Similar declarations are also added to the footer selector, albeit a smaller font-size (0.9em) and a different color (the orange used earlier).

Paragraphs

This layout does not use padding for major page regions, specifically to avoid Box Model woes. This is great, but it does mean that some elements don't know when to stop, such as paragraphs in the main column.

There are several ways to create space between the paragraph text and the right edge of the column. You could use a right margin or padding, for example. For this template, I decided to specify a width for the text. Using a contextual selector, I ensure that this declaration only affects paragraphs within mainCol.

```
#mainCol p {
  width:400px;
  }
```

The Final Touches

This is the home stretch now. At this point in the process, it's time to deal with a few rounding off details. By working through the final key areas of the design, everything will suddenly seem to gel together, and pride will come flowing through your veins. Let's get down and dirty with the main logo, navigation, login form, and footer content, with a couple of cool tricks thrown in for free. This is the pretty icing on the finely crafted cake.

Logo As Home Link

The logo, supposedly an attempt to emulate the hip and swing of the '60s and '70s, uses a typeface called *Groovy Happening JNL* from the Jeff Levine Font Family, available from www.myfonts.com. Note that an Outer Glow layer treatment has been added using Photoshop.

   For the web site, the logo needs to be a clickable link back to the home page (as you looked at in Chapter 13). For this reason, it couldn't be embedded into the masthead background image.

   So, the logo needs to be placed on top of the masthead image. The problem is, the masthead image is not flat—it uses alternating tones of orange. This suggests the logo be cut out and pasted onto a transparent background. Figure 16-10 shows the cut-out logo with a matte edging (as described in Chapter 5), sampled to make a near match for the alternating masthead colors.

The Dead Goods

Figure 16-10. *Logo saved as a transparency with brown matte around edges*

   This requires the <img> element to be added to the (X)HTML document, inside the masthead's <h1> element.

```
<div id="masthead">
  <h1><a href="deadgoods.html"><img src="dg_logo.gif" ~CCC
  alt="The Dead Goods" /></a></h1>
</div>
```

   Now we can get back to the CSS. The img forms part of a contextual selector, ensuring this rule only applies to images found within the masthead. The only key point here is that the left margin is given a value of 310px to align the left edge of the image with the left edge of the main column.

```
/* Main Dead Goods logo */
  #masthead img {
    margin:0 0 0 310px;
    }
```

Turn Off Image Borders

On the subject of images, it is worth noting that many browsers (Internet Explorer, Camino, Firefox, etc.) look at image links a little differently from Safari, for example. Specifically, those browsers will place a blue border around the image to denote its link status. This is great for usability, but pretty awful for your design. A small chunk of CSS is all that is needed to remove these default borders, where the border value is simply set to 0.

```
/* Turn off borders on image links */
  img {
    border:0;
    }
```

In order to preserve usability, it is worth ensuring that alternative obvious links or descriptive text accompanies images that might not be assumed to be a link. For this template, a prominent "Home" link is always visible in the main navigation bar.

Main Navigation

The main navigation is a simple unordered list (see Chapter 6 for a recap on list treatment). Here, we emulate the approach used for inline lists, with a few adjustments to margin, padding, and font-size as required. The key factor here is that the list must wrap to a new line if text size is increased. If this were not so, the list items would be laid over each other, or shunted outside of the container.

The key to a wrapping inline list is to specify a large line-height (200% worked here) for the li selector, and to avoid the temptation to set the height of the unordered list. A set height would allow no room for the list items to wrap under each other.

```
#mainCol ul {
  list-style:none;
  margin:10px 0 10px 0;
  padding:0;
  }

#mainCol li {
  display:inline;
  margin:0 10px 0 0;
  padding:0;
  line-height:200%;
  }

#mainCol li a:link, #mainCol li a:visited {
  text-decoration:none;
  font-size:1.3em;
  font-weight:bold;
  color:#FFE86C;
  }
```

```
#mainCol li a:hover {
  color:#FFF;
  }
```

Highlighting the Current Page

Another list trick is to use CSS to highlight the active page in the navigation list. In Chapter 12, you looked at the control gained by specifying a unique ID attribute to the <body> element. This technique, although quite complex to "get" at first glance, is very easy to employ.

For this template, the <body> element is given the ID home. This means that all other elements are children of this ID. If you look at the (X)HTML for the navigation list, you'll see that each list item has a unique class. The "Home" link has a home class, for example.

The contextual selector looks for any instances where this home class is a child of the home ID. If a match is found, the CSS is applied. In this case, it results in the "Home" link being given a thick orange bottom border.

```
/* Highlighting the current page */
  #home #mainCol a.home {
    border-bottom:3px solid #FFE86C;
    }
```

In theory, all other pages will have IDs such as band, news, tour, and so on added to the <body> element, so they will not be underlined unless you are on that page. These IDs will then be paired with the other class names for the other list items. The preceding CSS only shows the contextual selector for the home page, so other contextual selectors for the remaining sections of the site will need to be grouped with it at a later stage.

Bulletproof Navigation

Figure 16-11 shows the results of all the work done with the navigation list. Note that however much the text size is increased, the links are still perfectly clear, even if they wrap to a new line. Also, the home link is underlined with a thick orange bottom border.

Figure 16-11. *The text size can be resized without compromising usability, and the current page is highlighted.*

Login Form

Based on your comprehensive knowledge of styling forms (Chapter 9), this section should be a breeze. The first task is to take control of the <h4> element. By specifying a top margin value of 550px, you ensure that the login content is placed just below the leaf motif of the sidebar's background image. A 56-pixel left margin ensures that the heading is indented the same distance from the left edge as defined in the mock-up.

```
h4 {
  margin:550px 0 10px 56px;
  font-size:1.3em;
  color:#FFE86C;
  }
```

The actual form elements are fairly straightforward. Default margins, padding, and borders are tweaked or turned off, and the <fieldset> is spaced 56 pixels away from the left edge of the sidebar using a left margin value. Note also that the submit button is spaced 56 pixels from the left edge in the same manner, made possible thanks to the submit class given to the <input> element in the (X)HTML and the matching selector (input.submit).

```
form {
  margin:0;
  padding:0;
  }

fieldset {
  border:0;
  margin:10px 0 10px 56px;
  padding:0;
  }

label {
  font-weight:bold;
  color:#FFE86C;
  }

input.submit {
  margin:0 0 30px 56px;
  }
```

Figure 16-12 shows the resulting Member Login form content. Note that it appears just below the last part of the leaf motif, thanks to that top margin.

Figure 16-12. *The Member Login form styled using CSS to emulate the mock-up*

Footer Content

It is tempting to divide the footer into two columns, seeing as we have two halves of content—a logo on the left and some text on the right. There is a better way though.

Left-Side Logo

The Colly Logic Records logo (see Figure 16-13) has already been placed in the (X)HTML, as it is an image link.

Figure 16-13. *Colly Logic Records—the collyrecords.gif image*

The aim is to emulate a left column by floating the logo and applying enough margin on all sides to prevent the text on the other side from being too close and wrapping under the image. To do this, alongside the float, left and right margin values combined with the width of the image give us 310 pixels—the width of the sidebar. Also, a large bottom margin is declared (60px) to ensure the image element fills the left side of the footer, keeping the text well to the right.

```
#footer img {
  float:left;
  margin:10px 112px 60px 56px;
  }
```

Right-Side Nav and Paragraphs

And so to the right. Things are simpler here, as all we do is copy the CSS for the main navigation, place it in the context of the footer, and tweak it until it mirrors the text on the mock-up. Specifically, the font-size and line-height is reduced.

```
#footer ul {
  list-style:none;
  margin:10px 0 0 0;
  padding:0;
  }
#footer li {
```

```
  display:inline;
  margin:0 10px 0 0;
  padding:0;
  line-height:160%;
  }
#footer li a:link, #footer li a:visited {
  text-decoration:none;
  font-weight:bold;
  color:#FFE86C;
  font-size:1em;
  }
#footer li a:hover {
  color:#FFF;
  }
```

Finally, the paragraphs in the footer have their default margins reduced to decrease the distance between themselves and also the navigation just above.

```
#footer p {
  margin:0 0 3px 0;
  }
```

A Clear Problem

There is a small problem however. As the total height of the navigation and paragraphs is less than that of the logo on the left, the footer collapses too early (see Figure 16-14). Unless there is enough text on the right, the bottom margin under the logo will not be recognized.

Figure 16-14. *Despite best intentions, the footer collapses and the logo pushes beyond the boundary.*

The fix is simple, but not bulletproof. Defining a height for the footer will provide space underneath the content, allowing the logo's bottom margin to come into play and still prevent the paragraphs from wrapping under it.

```
/* The footer and descendants */
  #footer {
    clear:both;
    height:10em;
    min-height:110px;
    font-size:0.9em;
    line-height:150%;
    color:#FFE86C;
    background:#211E0E url(back_footer.gif) right bottom no-repeat;
    }
```

Figure 16-15 shows the improved `footer`. Note that by specifying `height` in ems, and also declaring a `min-height` value, the `footer` can expand if text is resized or more content is added, preventing the contents from bursting out of the boundary.

Figure 16-15. *With a set height for the footer, both left and right elements behave themselves.*

Finished!

Congratulations! Mr. Hendrix himself has called to say that he is incredibly impressed with what "you cats did." Loading the site in his browser, Jimi sees the result shown in Figure 16-16. Yes, Jimi Hendrix uses a Mac. What did you expect? He types with his teeth you know.

Figure 16-16. *Final screenshot of the finished* Dead Goods *web site. It rocks!*

Like Jimi, you too can view the full web site with further sections completed by following the link at www.csswebdevelopment.com/casestudy.

It's the End of the Book!

Our journey has concluded. Sometimes a journey can take you to places not found on any maps, and I hope this has been one of those self-discovery, finding one's self kind of things. I hope this book has been your Marrakech, your Tibet, or your Glastonbury. If you are unlucky, it may have been your reason to give up web design and become a fisherman. If it is the latter, then you are wrong! Read it again!

Thank you for picking up this book and for being responsible enough to bring web standards into your life. You did the right thing. Now then, stuff the tea—let's go get a beer!

CSS Reference

The following tables detail the majority of CSS 2.1 properties, many (but not all) of which have been covered in the preceding chapters. The tables are intended to provide a quick reference, specifically designed to help you avoid misspelling properties and values.

At the time of writing (July 2006), browser support notes are correct, although a final list of supported properties for IE7 is not yet confirmed.

This appendix ends with an overview of CSS shorthand methods and alternative approaches, aimed at making style sheets more manageable and condensed.

Background

Property	Description	Values
background	A shorthand property for setting all background properties in one declaration	background-color background-image background-repeat background-attachment background-position
background-attachment	Sets whether a background image is fixed or scrolls with the rest of the page	scroll fixed
background-color	Sets the background color of an element	color-rgb color-hex color-name transparent
background-image	Sets an image as the background	url none

Property	Description	Values
background-position	Sets the starting position of a background image	top left top center top right center left center center center right bottom left bottom center bottom right x-% y-% x-pos y-pos
background-repeat	Sets if/how a background image will be repeated	repeat repeat-x repeat-y no-repeat

Border

Property	Description	Values
border	A shorthand property for setting all of the properties for the four borders in one declaration	border-width border-style border-color
border-bottom	A shorthand property for setting all of the properties for the bottom border in one declaration	border-bottom-width border-style border-color
border-bottom-color	Sets the color of the bottom border	border-color
border-bottom-style	Sets the style of the bottom border	border-style
border-bottom-width	Sets the width of the bottom border	border-width
border-color	Sets the color of the four borders—can have one to four colors	color
border-left	A shorthand property for setting all of the properties for the left border in one declaration	border-left-width border-style border-color
border-left-color	Sets the color of the left border	border-color
border-left-style	Sets the style of the left border	border-style
border-left-width	Sets the width of the left border	border-width
border-right	A shorthand property for setting all of the properties for the right border in one declaration	border-right-width border-style border-color
border-right-color	Sets the color of the right border	border-color
border-right-style	Sets the style of the right border	border-style
border-right-width	Sets the width of the right border	border-width

Property	Description	Values
border-style	Sets the style of the four borders—can have one to four styles	none hidden dotted dashed solid double groove ridge inset outset
border-top	A shorthand property for setting all of the properties for the top border in one declaration	border-top-width border-style border-color
border-top-color	Sets the color of the top border	border-color
border-top-style	Sets the style of the top border	border-style
border-top-width	Sets the width of the top border	border-width
border-width	A shorthand property for setting the width of the four borders in one declaration—can have from one to four values	thin medium thick length

Margin

Property	Description	Values
margin	A shorthand property for setting the margin properties in one declaration	margin-top margin-right margin-bottom margin-left
margin-bottom	Sets the bottom margin of an element	auto length %
margin-left	Sets the left margin of an element	auto length %
margin-right	Sets the right margin of an element	auto length %
margin-top	Sets the top margin of an element	auto length %

Padding

Property	Description	Values
padding	A shorthand property for setting the padding properties in one declaration	padding-top padding-right padding-bottom padding-left
padding-bottom	Sets the bottom padding of an element	length %
padding-left	Sets the left padding of an element	length %
padding-right	Sets the right padding of an element	length %
padding-top	Sets the top padding of an element	length %

Dimension

The max-height, max-width, min-height, and min-width properties are not currently supported by IE, although full support will arrive with IE7.

Property	Description	Values
height	Sets the height of an element	auto length %
line-height	Sets the distance between lines	normal number length %
max-height	Sets the maximum height of an element	none length %
max-width	Sets the maximum width of an element	none length %
min-height	Sets the minimum height of an element	length %
min-width	Sets the minimum width of an element	length %
width	Sets the width of an element	auto length %

Text

Property	Description	Values
color	Sets the color of text	color
direction	Sets the text direction	ltr rtl
letter-spacing	Increases or decreases the space between characters	normal length
text-align	Aligns the text in an element	left right center justify
text-decoration	Adds decoration to text	none underline overline line-through blink
text-indent	Indents the first line of text in an element	length %
text-shadow	Applies a drop shadow to normal text	none color length
text-transform	Controls the case in an element	none capitalize uppercase lowercase
white-space	Sets how whitespace inside an element is handled	normal pre nowrap
word-spacing	Increases or decreases the space between words	normal length

Font

The font-size-adjust and font-stretch properties are not currently supported by IE, Netscape, or Firefox.

Property	Description	Values
font	A shorthand property for setting all of the properties for a font in one declaration	font-style font-variant font-weight font-size/line-height font-family caption icon menu message-box small-caption status bar
font-family	A prioritized list of font family names and/or generic family names for an element	family-name generic-family
font-size	Sets the size of a font	xx-small x-small small medium large x-large xx-large smaller larger length %
font-size-adjust	Specifies an aspect value for an element that will preserve the x-height of the first-choice font	none number
font-stretch	Condenses or expands the current font family	normal wider narrower ultra-condensed extra-condensed condensed semi-condensed semi-expanded expanded extra-expanded ultra-expanded
font-style	Sets the style of the font	normal italic oblique
font-variant	Displays text in a small-caps font or a normal font	normal small-caps

Property	Description	Values
font-weight	Sets the weight of a font	normal bold bolder lighter 100 200 300 400 500 600 700 800 900

List and Marker

The marker-offset property is not currently supported by IE.

Property	Description	Values
list-style	A shorthand property for setting the properties for a list in one declaration	list-style-type list-style-position list-style-image
list-style-image	Sets an image as the list item marker	none url
list-style-position	Sets where the list item marker is placed in the list	inside outside
list-style-type	Sets the type of the list item marker	none disc circle square decimal decimal-leading-zero lower-roman upper-roman lower-alpha upper-alpha lower-greek lower-latin upper-latin hebrew armenian georgian cjk-ideographoc hiragana katakana hiragana-iroha katakana-iroha
marker-offset	Offsets the list marker	auto length

Positioning

Property	Description	Values
bottom	Sets how far the bottom edge of an element is above/below the bottom edge of the parent element.	auto length %
clip	Sets the shape of an element. The element is clipped into this shape and displayed.	shape auto
left	Sets how far the left edge of an element is to the right/left of the left edge of the parent element.	auto length %
overflow	Sets what happens if the content of an element overflows its area.	visible hidden scroll auto
position	Places an element in a static, relative, absolute, or fixed position.	static relative absolute fixed
right	Sets how far the right edge of an element is to the left/right of the right edge of the parent element.	auto length %
top	Sets how far the top edge of an element is above/below the top edge of the parent element.	auto length %
vertical-align	Sets the vertical alignment of an element.	baseline sub super top text-top middle bottom text-bottom length %
z-index	Sets the stack order of an element.	auto number

Classification

Property	Description	Values
clear	Sets the sides of an element where other floating elements are not allowed	left right both none
cursor	Specifies the type of cursor to be displayed	url auto crosshair default pointer move e-resize ne-resize nw-resize n-resize se-resize sw-resize s-resize w-resize text wait help
display	Sets how/if an element is displayed	none inline block list-item run-in compact marker table inline-table table-row-group table-header-group table-footer-group table-row table-column-group table-column table-cell table-caption
float	Sets where a child element, image, or text will appear in another element	left right none
visibility	Sets whether an element should be visible or invisible	visible hidden collapse

Table

The border-spacing, caption-side, and empty-cells properties are not currently supported by IE.

Property	Description	Values
border-collapse	Sets the border model of a table	collapse separate
border-spacing	Sets the distance between the borders of adjacent cells (only for the "separated borders" model)	length length
caption-side	Sets the position of the caption according to the table	top bottom left right
empty-cells	Sets whether cells with no visible content should have borders or not (only for the "separated borders" model)	show hide
table-layout	Sets the algorithm used to lay out the table	auto fixed

Pseudo Classes

The :focus, :first-child, and :lang properties are not currently supported by IE. Also, IE6 and below only support :hover when used with <a> tags (this will be fixed in IE7). The :focus property is not currently supported in Firefox or Netscape.

Property	Description
:active	Adds style to an activated element, such as a link
:focus	Adds style to an element while the element has focus
:hover	Adds style to an element when you mouse over it
:link	Adds style to an unvisited link
:visited	Adds style to a visited link
:first-child	Adds style to an element that is the first child of a parent element
:lang	Allows the author to specify a language to use in a specified element

Pseudo Elements

The :before and :after properties are not currently supported by IE or Netscape, but they are supported in Firefox 1.5 and above.

Property	Description
:first-letter	Adds style to the first letter of the text
:first-line	Adds style to the first line of text
:before	Inserts content before an element
:after	Inserts content after an element

Outline

None of these properties are currently supported by IE or Netscape, but they are supported in Firefox 1.5 and above.

Property	Description	Values
outline	A shorthand property for setting all the outline properties in one declaration	outline-color outline-style outline-width
outline-color	Sets the color of the outline around an element	color invert
outline-style	Sets the style of the outline around an element	none dotted dashed solid double groove ridge inset outset
outline-width	Sets the width of the outline around an element	thin medium thick length

Shorthand

The following CSS shorthand properties can be used to reduce the size of your style sheet dramatically.

Font Shorthand

Long version, with each property and value listed separately:

```
font-size:1em;
line-height:160%;
font-weight:bold;
font-style:italic;
font-family:Verdana,Arial,sans-serif;
```

Shorthand:

```
font:1em/160% bold italic Verdana,Arial,sans-serif
```

Note This only works if you specify both the `font-size` and the `font-family`—omit either and the rule will be ignored. Also, if you don't specify the `font-weight`, `font-style`, or `font-variant`, then these values will default to a value of `normal`.

Background Shorthand

Long version, with each property and value listed separately:

```
background-color:#CCC;
background-image:url(image.gif);
background-repeat:no-repeat;
background-position:top left;
```

Shorthand:

```
background:#CCC url(image.gif) no-repeat top left
```

Note Omit any of the values from the `background` shorthand, and the browser will use the default values. If you leave out the `background-repeat` value, then any background image will be repeated both horizontally and vertically.

List Shorthand

Long version, with each property and value listed separately:

```
list-style-type:disc;
list-style-position:inside;
list-style-image:url(image.gif)
```

Shorthand:

```
list-style:disc inside url(image.gif)
```

■**Note** Leave out any of the CSS values from the shorthand rule, and the browser will use the default values for each, which are `disc`, `outside`, and `none`, respectively.

Margin and Padding Shorthand

There are four different CSS shorthand commands for `margin` and `padding`, depending on how many `margin` or `padding` values are equal.

Four Different Values

Long version, with each property and value listed separately:

```
margin-top:1px;
margin-right:2px;
margin-bottom:3px;
margin-left:4px;
```

Shorthand:

```
margin: 1px 2px 3px 4px;
```

Three Different Values

Long version, with each property and value listed separately:

```
margin-top:5px;
margin-right:10px;
margin-bottom:3px;
margin-left:10px;
```

Shorthand:

```
margin:5px 10px 3px;
```

Two Different Values

Long version, with each property and value listed separately:

```
margin-top:5px;
margin-right:10px;
margin-bottom:5px;
margin-left:10px;
```

Shorthand:

```
margin:5px 10px;
```

One Value

Long version, with each property and value listed separately:

```
margin-top:10px;
margin-right:10px;
margin-bottom:10px;
margin-left:10px;
```

Shorthand:

```
margin:10px;
```

Note The four shorthand methods can also be applied to padding and border.

Border Shorthand

Long version, with each property and value listed separately:

```
border-width:1px;
border-color:#CCC;
border-style:dashed;
```

Shorthand:

```
border:1px #CCC dashed;
```

Long version, with each property and value listed separately:

```
border-right-width:1px;
border-right-color:#CCC;
border-right-style:dashed;
```

Shorthand:

```
border-right:1px #CCC dashed;
```

■Note You can substitute `right` in the preceding examples with `top`, `bottom`, or `left`.

Two Approaches, Same Result

Example of combining border values to achieve the same result:

```
border:10px solid #CCC;
border-left:5px solid #666;
border-top:5px solid #666;
```

Equivalent version:

```
border:10px solid #CCC;
border-width:5px 10px 10px 5px;
border-color:#666 #CCC #CCC #666;
```

Index

Find it faster at http://superindex.apress.com

Find it faster at http://superindex.apress.com

Find it faster at http://superindex.apress.com

You Need the Companion eBook

Your purchase of this book entitles you to its companion eBook for only $10.

We believe this Apress title will prove so indispensable that you'll want to carry it with you everywhere, which is why we are offering the companion eBook for $10 to customers who purchase this book now. Convenient and fully searchable, the eBook version of any content-rich, page-heavy Apress book makes a valuable addition to your programming library. You can easily find, copy, and apply code—and then perform examples by quickly toggling between instructions and the application. Even simultaneously tackling a donut, diet soda, and complex code becomes simplified with hands-free eBooks!

Once you purchase this book, getting the $10 companion eBook is simple:

❶ Visit **www.apress.com/promo/tendollars/**.

❷ Complete a basic registration form to receive a randomly generated question about this title.

❸ Answer the question correctly in 60 seconds and you will receive a promotional code to redeem for the $10 eBook.

2560 Ninth Street • Suite 219 • Berkeley, CA 94710

eBookshop

ASP **Today**

Apress®
THE EXPERT'S VOICE™

Offer valid through 2/28/07.

FIND IT FAST
with the Apress *SuperIndex*™

Quickly Find Out What the Experts Know

Leading by innovation, Apress now offers you its *SuperIndex*™, a turbocharged companion to the fine index in this book. The Apress *SuperIndex*™ is a keyword and phrase-enabled search tool that lets you search through the entire Apress library. Powered by dtSearch™, it delivers results instantly.

Instead of paging through a book or a PDF, you can electronically access the topic of your choice from a vast array of Apress titles. The Apress *SuperIndex*™ is the perfect tool to find critical snippets of code or an obscure reference. The Apress *SuperIndex*™ enables all users to harness essential information and data from the best minds in technology.

No registration is required, and the Apress *SuperIndex*™ is free to use.

- ❶ Thorough and comprehensive searches of over 300 titles
- ❷ No registration required
- ❸ Instantaneous results
- ❹ A single destination to find what you need
- ❺ Engineered for speed and accuracy
- ❻ Will spare your time, application, and anxiety level

Search now: *http://superindex.apress.com*